POWER AND SOCIETY
IN CONTEMPORARY PERU

other books by the author

Éléments pour une sociologie de l'action: essais de T. Parsons traduits et commentés, Paris, 1955

Esquisse d'une théorie de l'autorité, Paris, 1961

Changements à Puno, Institut d'Amérique latine, Université de Paris, 1962

Peru: physical and administrative

Scale 1": 200 miles

POWER AND SOCIETY
IN CONTEMPORARY PERU

FRANÇOIS BOURRICAUD

translated by

PAUL STEVENSON

PRAEGER PUBLISHERS
New York · Washington

BOOKS THAT MATTER

Published in the United States of America in 1970
by Praeger Publishers, Inc.
111 Fourth Avenue, New York, N.Y. 10003

Originally published by
Librairie Armand Colin, Paris,
in Cahiers de la Fondation
Nationale des Sciences Politiques,
as
*Pouvoir et Société dans
le Pérou contemporain*

© 1967 by Librairie Armand Colin, Paris, France
English translation © 1970 by
Faber and Faber Ltd., London, England

Library of Congress Catalog Card Number: 77–93450

Printed in Great Britain

TO ALL MY PERUVIAN FRIENDS

By dedicating this work to all my Peruvian friends, I wish to express something more than my gratitude and affection towards individuals, and to convey my feeling for a country to which I am attached by sympathetic ties as well as by the bonds of study.

The collection of my material took place between 1959 and 1963. The last chapter was written in 1964; but the work was planned and in large measure written during the winter of 1963–4.

These details are of some importance. To begin with, much has changed in Peru since the end of the 1950s, and the rate of change has increased since 1963. As a result, both Peruvian and foreign observers have in the last few years made exceptional progress in analysing the state of the country. I therefore offer this work with some apprehension, while hoping that it may be of use to those who are interested in relating the problems of political analysis to those of social evolution.

English Publisher's Note

Since the French edition of the book appeared in 1967, events in Peru have taken a dramatic turn with the overthrow of the Belaúnde government by a military group in October 1968 and the subsequent expropriation of the U.S.-owned International Petroleum Company. These developments have merely served to increase the importance of M. Bourricaud's analysis of past conflicts between the country's political and military leaders and of the complicated background to the dispute with the I.P.C.

Contents

Contents

Maps

INTRODUCTION

An Oligarchy Faced with the
Problems of Social Mobilisation

It is over ten years since I first began to be interested in Peruvian affairs. In 1952 and 1953 I collected material relating to social and cultural changes in the department of Puno–one of the most backward or, if the term be preferred, traditional regions of Peru. 'Community studies' were then much in fashion. I soon realised, however, that this perspective was somewhat narrow, and that 'changes in Puno'[1] could only be understood in the light of the transformation affecting the whole of Peruvian society.

In any case, from the outset of my stay in Peru native curiosity led me to take a lively interest in the country's politics. A military leader, General Odría, had been President since October 1948. The Aprista party, active since the late 1920s and still the only mass organisation in the country, was proscribed, and its leader, Haya de la Torre, was a prisoner in the Colombian embassy at Lima, where he had taken sanctuary. Cotton and sugar exporters were doing well and–in the capital at all events–there were pickings for engineers, technicians and administrators. Thanks to public expenditure, a building boom was providing employment for unskilled labour. But the Indian peasants continued to live or die without anyone paying heed to their destitution.

As a young European in the early 1950s, embarking upon the study of a distant Pacific country, I found nothing surprising in this state of affairs. The wretchedness of the illiterate masses, the greed of the oligarchy, the military in the service of the rich, the friends of progress in prison or exile–all this was precisely what I had expected. But I

[1] This was the title of a small work of mine published in 1962 by the Latin American Institute of the University of Paris.

13

realised before long that the picture was over-simplified in at least two respects. In the first place, General Odría's increasing difficulties towards the end of his term of office–under the constitution, the president cannot be immediately re-elected–and his ever-sharper tussles with the oligarchy, including those of its members who had helped or incited him to seize power, made me think that relations between the military and the moneyed classes must be more subtle than I had imagined. Second, the disapproval and resistance provoked in political circles by the General's suspected intention of remaining in power for a second term, despite the constitutional ban, were a sign that the military was not all-powerful and that its sway was restricted by certain rules, both written and unwritten.

I thus came to realise that Peruvian political life possessed a certain order and reflected, more or less clearly, an underlying principle of legitimacy. To be sure, Peru was not a constitutional republic as we understand the term in Europe and North America. The Indian masses were disfranchised since the constitution limits the right of voting to those who can read and write. Political leaders achieved power either by force or as the result of obscure machinations, and the electorate was called upon after the event to ratify, often by questionable procedures, the decisions of a very small group.[1] Thus the governmental machine operated as an instrument of repression on behalf of selfish interests rather than for the advancement of society as a whole.

I was in little danger of error in judging the Peruvian regime to be an oligarchy. Decisions were in fact taken by the few and–more important–for the few. Not only did the masses take no active part in politics, but there was also a case for wondering whether they felt in any way concerned by the disputes and decisions of the handful of men in power. On closer examination, however, the term 'oligarchy' appears inadequate. For example, do the ruling few consist of individuals, families or firms? Are they a homogeneous group, and do they regard one another as partners or rivals? Is their power based on birth, wealth or more objective grounds of ability? As we come to examine the matter, we shall find that the oligarchy's power is a function not only of its composition but of its standing *vis à vis* other groups, which in turn depends on two factors. First, its ability to harness for its own benefit, or at any rate to control, the productive forces of the nation; and second, its success in justifying

[1] For the presidential election of 1956, cf. Part III, chapter 1.

or legitimising this process, in other words causing it to be accepted as beneficial or, at any rate, natural.

The 1950s were on the whole a good period for the Peruvian economy, if we understand by that term the monetary and modernised sector and do not look too closely at the condition of Indian society. Cotton and sugar fetched good prices, bringing in handsome profits to the owners of the large coastal estates on which these export products are grown. The mining industry, which was largely in the hands of U.S. capital (the chief producer of lead and zinc being the Cerro de Pasco Corporation) was also flourishing, its setbacks of 1957 and 1958 having been at least partially retrieved by the exploitation of the Toquepala copper mines from 1959 onwards. Fishmeal began to be exported on a large scale at the end of the decade. Industrial production, three-quarters of which is concentrated in the Lima-Callao area, grew rapidly after 1960. Peru was less affected than most Latin American countries by inflation in the 1950s. Retail prices in Lima did not rise by more than 60 per cent between 1950 and 1964; and the national currency, the sol, which stood at 16 to the dollar in 1950, was worth 27 to the dollar in the latter year.

But there was another side to the picture. The spread of shanty-towns (*barriadas*), the break-up of the old agrarian society as shown by the meagre and almost certainly diminishing yields of the Andean region, and the rapid migration, not to say flight, of population to Lima from certain sierra departments such as Ayacucho–all these appeared to be advance signals of an inevitable catastrophe. Moreover, large sections of the urban population, even among the comparatively well off, such as skilled workers and public and private employees, suffered from rising food prices and housing difficulties. The growth in average real income, borne out by statistics, did not prevent widespread discontent, particularly among the urban middle classes.

The expansion of the modern sector, the decline of the traditional economy, and urban discontents are interrelated aspects of a process which, following Karl Deutsch, we may call 'social mobilisation'.[1] This term, as explained by Deutsch, denotes a world-wide process which affects large sections of the population in 'countries which are moving from traditional to modern ways of life'. He offers several

[1] Karl Deutsch, 'Social Mobilisation and Political Development', *American Political Science Review*, Sept. 1961.

criteria for what he calls this *levée en masse*: (i) the percentage of the population exposed to 'significant aspects of modern life'; (ii) that affected by the mass media of press, radio and television; (iii) the percentage of migrants; (iv) the percentage of the population living in towns; (v) the percentage of those employed in non-agricultural occupations; (vi) the percentage of literates; and (vii) the average income *per capita*. In Peru during the 1950s, the phenomena of migration and urbanisation, which had already made themselves felt in the late twenties, were present on a large scale.[1] The expansion of Lima and the volume of migration from the sierra were plain to all observers and became a staple theme of political discussion.

In the nineteenth and early twentieth centuries, a small group of families took all essential decisions for the country without paying much attention to the opinions or desires of the masses. Of course matters were not quite so clear-cut as this: the civilian oligarchy had to reckon both with the military and with more or less erratic currents of feeling among the populace of Lima, Arequipa or Trujillo. But the mob remained politically unorganised. Although it made itself violently felt in the mass riots that punctuated the first eighty years of the Peruvian republic's history, it did so spontaneously, in favour of, or in opposition to, this or that demagogue or *caudillo*. But the position was different when a more or less identifiable middle class began to press demands with growing insistence, or when, a little later, the workers of the Lima area and the miners of the central region started to form trade unions; or again when rural unrest broke out in parts of the country. Could the oligarchy now cope with the process of social mobilisation which may be roughly considered to have set in around 1925?

We may agree with Deutsch that once this process attains a certain critical level, as it did in Peru in the course of the 1930s, it presents the regime with serious difficulties. According to him, the *levée en masse* has a dual effect.[2] First, it 'brings with it an expansion of the politically relevant strata of the population'. Second, it brings about a change in the quality or style of politics. 'As people are uprooted from their physical and intellectual isolation . . . they . . . come to need provisions for housing, schools and hospitals . . . They need, in short, a wide range and large amounts of new government services.'

[1] On the first results of the 1960 census, cf. François Bourricaud and Olivier Dollfus, 'La population péruvienne en 1961', *Cahiers d'outre-mer*, 1963, pp. 184–200.
[2] Deutsch, art. cit.

16

Introduction

Are we to conclude with Deutsch that 'these needs ordinarily cannot be met by traditional types of government'?

I see little use in speculating on the imminence of revolution or the oligarchy's chances of survival. I prefer to inquire how it has survived up to now, during the first phases of the mobilisation process. Those who predict catastrophe–that is, by and large, Peruvian ideologists and politicians of the extreme left and most foreign observers–resort, when asked to develop their views, to one or both of two metaphors: the dynamic concept of an 'explosion' or the mechanical one of break-up and disintegration. These comparisons emphasise the degree of tension in Peruvian society and also the interrelation of its parts. When I first arrived, I accepted without demur the predictions of catastrophe which I heard around me. The oligarchy was doomed: it was incapable of solving the 'agrarian problem' and the 'Indian problem'; moreover, by opposing industrialisation it was hastening the inevitable explosion. And yet, as the years passed, on each of my successive visits I felt less convinced by these views, though they had meanwhile been sanctioned by most Peruvian and foreign experts.

The first theory which sets out to explain the political consequences of the mobilisation process lays stress on the tensions caused in an oligarchic system by the more or less clearly formulated demands of the newly mobilised masses. From this point of view, the inadequacy of the Peruvian system is manifested. An oligarchy, that is to say a small group encysted in society, is bound to use its power in a limiting and repressive fashion. In its eyes, the function of the state is to ensure order and keep at bay any forces that may threaten its own power. But can it exclude from politics for all time the mass of the population, which is becoming more and more numerous and vociferous and better organised? If we look closer, we shall see that this oligarchy, ill-prepared as it may be for the problems with which mobilisation confronts it, is not lacking in political skill and ingenuity. We shall see, moreover, that in regard to a problem which touches it most closely, that of land reform, it has succeeded in displaying both flexibility and imagination.

It seems to me, therefore, that what I have called the mechanical or dynamic theory, which lays stress on tensions and bids us look out for explosions, is open to two objections, one theoretical and the other practical. In the first place, it ignores the self-regulating capacity of political systems. These, like all forms of human organisation, possess their own autonomy and a real though limited power of self-adjustment. They are not obliged to conform immediately to each and every 'demand' that comes from outside: they may foresee such demands and anticipate or delay their own response. Above all, they are not saddled with objectives which they have no option but to pursue and put into effect. They can define their own purposes in the light of a given set of circumstances and of their own successive positions in regard to those circumstances. The guided missile of which Deutsch writes elsewhere[1] is not trained on a stationary target but enjoys sufficient power of decision to adjust to the successive positions of a moving one. If it does not hit the target at a given moment, it may well do so later even if the object has shifted in the meantime.

If we think of government in terms of cybernetic control, that is to say a system of differentiated organs capable of distinguishing, evaluating and choosing between the more or less urgent 'demands' presented to it, it must be recognised that Peru is not governed or even, perhaps, governable: what is called government there is much more a matter of *imperium*, of pure command, than of control. Peruvian society is still very close to primitive dualism: the masses on the one hand, the élite groups on the other. The differences that exist are both too sharp and too few. Is such a society capable of evolving a consensus whereby opinions and interests are adjusted, to fit in with one another, by a multiplicity of small touches? Is there no way for the have-nots to make their voice heard except by violence, and no way for the oligarchy to maintain itself except by repression?

This brings us back to the mechanical and dynamic imagery which sees power as a confrontation between blind forces. To resolve the dilemma, we must consider the nature of the link between the demands of society and the responses of the political system. This link is essentially a symbolic one, for two reasons. In the first place, there is no term-for-term correspondence between each element of the former complex and each one of the latter. The adjustment is an overall one: individuals or groups whose demands are not satisfied may obtain something else quite different, which suffices to maintain their confidence in the system or to prevent them from rebelling against it. But the adjustment is symbolic, in this sense, not only

[1] Karl Deutsch, *The Nerves of Government*, p. 81.

18

because it consists in compromise but by reason of the manner in which that compromise is effected. Here the theory of information is of value. In a wireless system, for example, the transmitter and receiver are not homogeneous, but, for information to be conveyed, they must be homologous. The subject-matter of the communication is a form or structure which the receiver apprehends directly or after decoding. When we analyse Peruvian political life between 1956 and 1965, we are struck by the fact that highly explosive events such as agrarian violence and police repression did not act as detonators in the way expected and hoped for by our radical friends. Why did these happenings, which, on the mechanical and dynamic view, should have been the immediate forerunners of an explosion, have such feeble and transitory consequences? Following the cybernetic theory, three possibilities suggest themselves. Either a communications system was lacking which would have brought the knowledge of these events to other interested parties; or else this or that event competed with others which excluded it from the circuit and deprived it of actuality; or, finally, the system was insufficiently selective and the news of the event was drowned by 'interference'.

My second objection is to the diagnosis implied by the 'catastrophic' theory. The explosion, or crack-up, or whatever one chooses to call it, is declared to be inevitable because two and only two forces confront each other with growing insistence and violence. But Peruvian society is in fact no longer dualistic. This term, as generally understood, implies not only the coexistence of a modern and a traditional sector (the least disputable aspect as far as Peru is concerned, but also the least important), but also, and principally, the arbitrary domination by a minority group whose orders to the resigned and impotent masses are based on its own interests and backed by naked force. The great defect of this picture is that it ignores the mobilisation process. It may still have been valid for nineteenth-century Peru; but I hope that anyone who reads the first part of this book will agree that it is completely inapplicable to the reality of today.

The dualistic theory, besides opposing an all-powerful oligarchy to the impotent masses, assumes that the oligarchy exercises direct command and that the political regime is only a façade, a handy convention which serves to throw a flimsy veil over oligarchical cynicism. I do not think this view will hold water: the regime is in fact sensitive in some degree to problems of social development. And,

Introduction

in the particular case of land reform, I shall try to show that it is by no means wholly deaf, blind or paralysed.

What is the correct perspective in which to view the Peruvian crisis? As regards dates, I have chosen the period from 1956 to 1964, which includes the presidency of Manuel Prado, the elections of 1962 and 1963 and the first year of Fernando Belaúnde's term of office, and illustrates clearly the merits and limitations of all the rival methods of grappling with Peru's political problem. The sources on which I have drawn are for the most part written ones. In the first part of the book I have made use of the polls recently conducted in Peru on university education and on the *barriadas*. I have also made much use of the press, regarding which some explanation is in order. In the first place, the Peruvian newspapers supplied me with valuable information on the behaviour of the masses and their inclination to violence. In addition, the same sources provided me with essential data concerning political leaders. 'All the news that's fit to print' would not, it is true, be an appropriate motto for *El Comercio*, *La Prensa* or even *Expreso*. The main Lima newspapers are politically committed and sharply polemical in tone. However, their commitment is not on party lines, except for *La Tribuna*, the Aprista organ, whose circulation probably does not exceed 20,000.[1] These papers are in the hands of particular families, such as the Miró Quesadas who own *El Comercio*, or individuals heading a chosen team, such as Pedro Beltrán, the editor of *La Prensa*; and the control of such a newspaper may be a decisive factor in the political game. In Paris, we should not expect M. Pierre Brisson or M. Beuve-Méry to be invited to form a government because the *Figaro* or the *Monde* had succeeded in making things too hot for the existing parliamentary majority. But for more than three years under President Prado, the Peruvian government was headed by a journalist, Pedro Beltrán, the editor and, I believe, the principal shareholder of *La Prensa*. And, in the delicate negotiations with the International Petroleum Company which controls the Talara deposits in the north, President Belaúnde was at great pains to avoid offending the sensitive nationalism of Don Luis Miró Quesada, the editor of *El Comercio*.

The two main Peruvian papers do not fit neatly into any category of the contemporary press. On the one hand, neither *La Prensa* nor *El Comercio* is a money-making concern pure and simple, out to

[1] Whereas that of *El Comercio* and *La Prensa* is about 100,000.

exploit the sensations of the day. An evening tabloid, *Ultima Hora*, which is more or less connected with *La Prensa*, caters for plebeian devotees of murders and love-stories. But, while *El Comercio* wears the sober air of a prestige paper and describes itself as the 'doyen of the national press', it is not the equivalent of the *New York Times* or even *Le Monde*. In its columns, news and comment are not distinguished; fact and value judgments are inextricably confused. However, an essential role is played in politics by both the main newspapers. 'Independent' only in the sense of being non-party, they are allied with certain private interests – e.g. there is a clear link between *La Prensa* and the Sociedad Nacional Agraria – while at the same time defending specific economic theses: *La Prensa* is the outspoken champion of *laissez-faire*, while *El Comercio*'s traditionally nationalist viewpoint has led it to adopt almost 'progressive' attitudes on the social front and especially in matters of foreign trade. We shall see how the former, being committed to the defence of an economic doctrine or policy, sets its face against 'dangerous' solutions, while the latter, dominated by its own obsessions and despite its traditionalist slant, has become the sponsor of a kind of modernism. This conflict of attitudes may be interpreted in terms of personality – Don Pedro against Don Luis – or of the rivalry between two clans; but it is probably more instructive to examine its effect on the possibilities of national renewal or transformation, and to enquire whether or not it conduces to a solution of the principal problems with which the present state of their society confronts the rulers of Peru.

As well as drawing heavily on the press, I also admit to making free use of fictional sources. Some parts of the book must indeed read like works of literary analysis; and I must confess that some of my main hypotheses are based on this type of evidence. My account of the *cholo* and the passivity of the middle classes owes much to my reading of novels. Can this be regarded as a 'scientific' procedure? I would reply that Peruvian literature, and especially the 'indigenist' novel, is a gold mine for the sociologist. It shows us how intellectuals, who mostly belong to the minor provincial bourgeoisie, view their own society. This is all the more valuable since the novel does not merely describe static types but depicts the changes which have taken place in Peruvian society since about 1920. It cannot, of course, be assumed that Indian society is accurately described in the novels which treat of its problems. Ciro Alegría, in *El mundo es ancho y ajeno*, presents the lives of *comuneros* in a way which owes more to picturesque imagination than to experience. But his description of half-caste society, particularly in *Los perros hambrientos*, is based on observation at close quarters and, as it were, from the inside. The tales and memories which formed Alegría's sources are of fairly distant date, going back as they do for thirty or forty years. Arguedas, to whom we owe a great deal, uses more recent material. But even though the general picture which literature offers us of the native scene is open to challenge and now partially out of date, its many episodes and characters throw light on conditions which evolve slowly: patterns of power and domination, and the adjustment of the weak and oppressed to the way of life forced upon them by their masters.

I do not, I repeat, suggest that novels are an exact picture of life. Not all landowners are as cruel as Alegría's characters. But the study of novels enables us to form certain hypotheses which help towards a solution of our problems. For example, the observer of the political behaviour of the Peruvian middle classes is struck by a double phenomenon. They display simultaneously, and one would think contradictorily, an intense verbal aggressiveness towards the power-holding élite, together with a strong fidelity to the creole (*criollo*) tradition, which is not exactly revolutionary. The forms which this aggression takes, the circumstances in which it breaks out, its choice of object and the ways in which it is repressed or diverted – all these are matters on which it would be absurd to neglect the testimony offered us by the indigenist novel. To say that the *cholo*[1] is aggressive does not in itself tell us much. One way to give this statement significance is to put it in comparative form, and another is to define the type of aggression in question. It is here that novels can be of the greatest use to us. If, for example, I notice that the *cholo* is depicted as afraid of his own aggressiveness and seeking to exercise violence by proxy, I am better able to understand, in the political context, how a single individual can display radical impulses and conservative caution. Can this in fact be accounted for by the transference of aggressiveness in the *cholo*? If I put forward a purely personal view on this subject, the reader is not bound to regard it as proven, whereas he would do so if I could present it as based on a statistical enquiry. In point of fact, my position lies between the two: as will be seen, it

[1] This name is given, with a shade of contempt or condescension, to those persons whose origins place them in the indigenous class but who possess some social and cultural attributes which enable them to 'better themselves' and attain higher status.

is based on a careful and by no means arbitrary study of texts. My theory is scarcely even my own: it has been furnished to me by the Peruvian novelists.

It may be objected that we should be wary of cultural stereotypes and literary conventions; but these terms do not apply to the image of diverted aggressiveness in the *cholo* character. So little is this a romantic convention that the novelists in whose work it appears did not see it there and were surprised when I pointed it out to them. It is one thing to depict the creole complacently as combining such qualities as grace, liveliness, cunning and sensuality. But the image of a man who longs to kill but, knowing himself too weak to do so, seeks to use another as the instrument of his murderous passion is hardly a stereotype in which any individual or group would willingly be recognised.

While, then, the hypothesis of diverted or displaced aggressiveness is not proved, it cannot be regarded as a mere stereotype, especially as its application does not seem to be confined to specific social categories. And, whether proved or not, it has its value as an instrument of enquiry. On the one hand it makes possible comparison with other situations where aggression is repressed in its external manifestations, and on the other it enables us to understand the political behaviour of the rebellious yet circumspect middle classes, who grumble fiercely, yet submit.

The scope of this book is limited by the aims I set myself and the material at my disposal. The reader will find in it many hypotheses: these, I believe, could all be verified, but I have only been able to do so in some cases. The first chapter of Part I, for instance, is based on sufficiently ample material for my conclusions to appear well-founded. Chapters 2 and 3 may seem less convincing, since here I was obliged to eke out first-hand observation by means of literary sources. How, indeed, could I have done otherwise? Nothing, it is true, prevented me from instituting a major enquiry into the motivations of the under-privileged classes or the resentments of the bourgeoisie– nothing, that is, except considerations of time and money.

PART ONE

MOBILISATION IN A DUALISTIC SOCIETY

1

The Nature and Forms of Oligarchic Control

The more complex and differentiated a society is, the more difficult it is to identify its governing class. There is no complete agreement as to which groups compose the governing class of an industrial society, though it will be generally admitted that 'capitalists' are among them. Opinions differ as to the respective powers of shareholders, technicians, managers and executives. Do trade union leaders, as well as statesmen, belong to the élite of our society? Such questions can only be answered if we are prepared to discard the prejudices of rival ideologies. The sociologist, on his part, must abandon the attempt to draw up an *a priori* list of groups composing the élite and must consult the man in the street to find out how he visualises the stratification of his own society. Then, having formed a theory of 'prestige' and its distribution in our societies, he must evolve a practical working notion of what constitutes the power of the élite. As Talcott Parsons has well observed,[1] it is not sufficient to say who holds power: we must also be clear about what power is. If Wright Mills, instead of inveighing against the 'clique' which, according to him, monopolises the levers of command, had drawn up a list of the issues on which conflicting interests were opposed, and had also listed the winners and losers in a typical series of games, his book would have been less brilliant but perhaps more authoritative. The power which an individual or group exercises in a community consists, first and foremost, in the ability to make that community adopt the solutions which it or he prefers. If I can be shown that in most cases in which important decisions have been taken, they have

[1] Talcott Parsons, *Structure and Process in Modern Society*, p. 107.

27

been prepared, advocated and finally imposed by the same group or coalition of forces, I will accept that that coalition holds effective power. What is lacking in Wright Mills' book is a demonstration that in major issues of finance, tariffs and credit, the 'corporate rich', as a group, make the law or on the other hand prevent legislation being made against them. It is not hard to understand the omission: he may have refrained from writing the history of these decisions, and thus enabling the student to 'test' the power which he ascribes so lavishly to the élite, simply because this would have brought out too clearly the confusion of interests and uncertainty of outcome; in short the statistical and impersonal character of social decisions which Mills seeks to present as the *fiat* of a few sovereign wills.

Instead of societies characterised by infinitely varied activities and affected by minute, multifarious and continual changes, where the hierarchy of prestige and power is incessantly called in question, let us postulate a society in which progress is very gradual and productivity extremely low. Let us then imagine that by right of conquest or birth, the population is divided into two classes: masters and slaves. Let us suppose that the slaves are the only productive workers, while the masters consume the fruits of their labour. Let us suppose, finally, that this situation is regarded as legitimate by the dominated as well as the dominating class. Such is the case envisaged by Talcott Parsons when he describes under-developed countries as characterised by 'polarisation'. To complete the picture, it suffices to imagine that the ruling class's monopoly of power is based on colonial conquest which has led to the permanent subjection of the vanquished. The present-day rulers, as heirs of the conquerors, appear as an oligarchy in the strictest sense of the term.

Such, more or less, is the usual image of the Peruvian oligarchy—a concise, pregnant formula reflecting a very real situation. What I wish to show in this chapter, however, is that it ignores the most original aspects of that reality and fails to do justice to existing conditions and foreseeable lines of evolution.

'Patrones' and 'gamonales'

It is not without significance that the ruling class in Peru is generally designated as an oligarchy: a term which combines the two ideas of absolute power and power exercised by a small group. It might be added that the members of this all-powerful group are thought of as belonging to 'clans' or 'tribes'. The Apristas have, ever since their party was founded, denounced the *civilistas*, that is to say the great Lima families who, they assert, treat Peru as a conquered country. And a person as level-headed as the ex-president José Luis Bustamante, describing the more conservative section of the ruling class to which he found himself opposed during his unhappy term of office, automatically labelled them as a 'clan . . . a satisfied and self-absorbed (*ensimismado*) group of men, a collection of families (*linajes*) which cannot always boast of ancient titles or even genuinely Peruvian origin'.[1] These words illustrate the widely-held view that the ruling class is a caste or family group. The difficulty begins when we seek to define more closely the internal and external relations of this small coterie. The image most generally accepted is that the Peruvian upper class consists of the absentee landlords of huge estates. Novelists such as Ciro Alegría offer a picture of the *hacendado* or *gamonal* which enables the sociologist to form an exact and detailed picture of this landowner type. We shall now endeavour to fill in some details of this picture and to clarify others.

The action of *El mundo es ancho y ajeno*[2] takes place in the Cajamarca region of northern Peru. But the conditions it describes are not all peculiar to this region, and the author no doubt meant it to be valid as a general picture. The old Indian, Rosendo Maqui, embodies all the virtues and wisdom of his race, and the characters include a variety of equally typical *hacendados*. One of these, to whom the author gives his own surname, is Don Teodoro Alegría, the 'good master' of the valiant bandit Vásquez (*el fiero Vásquez*); another is the cruel and avaricious land-grabber, Don Alvaro Amenábar y Roldán, 'lord of Umay, master of lives and lands for twenty leagues around',[3] and despoiler of the village of Rumi whose chief is the sage Rosendo Maqui himself. The significant feature in the portrait of Don Alvaro is the contrast between his spontaneous outbursts of violence and his concern to save face (*la debida compostura*).[4] The history of the Amenábar family is briefly described. 'Don Alvaro was the son of Don Gonzalo, a determined person, who got hold of Umay, nobody knows exactly how, through a lawsuit with a convent.' The estate which he took over consisted of a vast

---

[1] *Tres años de lucha por la democracia en el Perú*, p. 75.
[2] Ciro Alegría, *El Mundo es ancho y ajeno*, translated as *Broad and Alien is the World*, London, 1942. References are to this edition.
[3] Op. cit., p. 161.   [4] Ibid.

area of flat country and the surrounding mountains. A prudent marriage with Paquita Roldán increased his fortunes. After telling us further that he was clever, hard-working and unscrupulous, the author adds a detail which brings into focus the contrast, already mentioned, between self-control and violent spontaneity: 'He was as likely to open his fist and scatter coins as to clench it on the butt of a gun.' The Umay estate grew: Don Gonzalo began to cast about him and engaged in boundary disputes. But he struck an obstacle when his empire, swollen by ranches, villages and communities of all sizes, came in contact with that of the Córdova family.

'When Don Gonzalo rode up with his men, the judge, the sub-prefect and a group of mounted police, to take possession, they were greeted with a volley of shots. The struggle lasted, off and on, for two years. The subprefect, powerless to intervene or even admonish the big landowners, asked the prefect of the department for orders and reinforcements. The prefect was afraid to undertake to bring two such powerful men to heel on his own authority, and asked Lima for instructions. And Lima, where both the litigants had great influence among the ministers, senators and congressmen, answered never a word. So in the hills between Umay and Morasbamba the fighting and killing went on. The Córdovas imported a first-class shot from Spain, a native of the Pyrenees, and they built a stone fort where they stationed men under his command. Don Gonzalo, who was stubborn but nevertheless level-headed, yielded for the time being' . . .

Baulked from extending southward by the Córdovas, Gonzalo 'began to spread out towards the north. But death carried him off, and Don Alvaro inherited, to the last jot and tittle, his ambition, his plans for power, and his rivalry with the Córdovas . . . Until finally his land extended as far as Rumi, which lay in his path, a defenceless, unsuspecting quarry.'[1]

In these few sentences we perceive the outline of a social type, the *gamonal*, who is traditionally identified with the oligarchy. The *gamonal* is, first and foremost, an accumulator of land. If Ciro Alegría's account were to be taken literally, we should be inclined to suppose that the great estates are a recent creation: for the main action of *El mundo es ancho y ajeno* takes place in the first twenty years of this century. The *gamonal*, moreover, resorts to both cunning and violence to achieve his land-grabbing ends. Don Gonzalo's fortune was based on an obscure lawsuit with a religious order. After

---

[1] Op. cit., p. 163.

this auspicious beginning, he 'suffocated' the country, in Alegría's phrase, under an avalanche of stamped paper. But when legal forms no longer serve his turn, he does not shrink from resort to force. For this purpose he assures himself of every possible ally, and here we notice a third characteristic of the *gamonal*: he is a boss who, when it suits him, enlists the authority of the state to support his designs. The *gamonal* is above the law, which he brushes aside whenever it becomes a hindrance. Compared with him, subprefects and magistrates are of little account, and representatives of the central power know better than to get in his way. If anything can stop him, it is not the strong arm of the law but that of his fellow-*gamonales*. Confronted with the Córdovas, Don Gonzalo backs down because they are stronger than he or because he does not care for the risk of a long and expensive tussle with them. In any case–and this is usually emphasised–the *gamonal*'s empire is built and enlarged at the expense of the native communities. Spoliation of the Indians is the mainspring of his power.

El mundo es ancho y ajeno is an epic tale of the villagers of Rumi, who are first swindled and enmeshed in legal traps by a dishonest lawyer, and finally driven from their lands by gunshot. To illustrate the *gamonal*'s technique of conquest I shall quote from another novelist, less well known and a less skilled narrator than Alegría, but a more poignant master of pathos. In *Yawar Fiesta*, José María Arguedas describes the spoliation of the Indians of Puquio, capital of a province in the department of Ayacucho. 'In olden times', he begins, 'the *puna*[1] belonged to the common folk'. And he goes on: 'In those days, there was not much cattle in Lucanas province. The *mistis*[2] were not interested in the best slopes. The *puna* belonged to everyone.' To what period does 'olden times' refer? This is explained earlier on,[3] where Arguedas, speaking as an Indian narrator, tells us that 'Puquio was a new village for the *mistis*. They came here three hundred years ago, more or less, from other places where they had been working in mines . . . but the mines gave out and they became farmers. They swarmed into Puquio because it was a big village with plenty of native labour.' Thus began the first expropriation, in which the communities (*ayllus*) lost their fields of maize, oats and wheat,[4] and the despoiled Indians were forced to migrate into the highlands

---

[1] The mountain plateau, about 13,000 feet above sea level.
[2] The white men: here in opposition to the *comuneros* or villagers.
[3] José María Arguedas, *Yawar Fiesta*, Festival del Libro peruano, p. 14.
[4] Op. cit., p. 15.

of the *puna*. Then, two or three centuries later, shortly before the time at which the story begins, a second expropriation took place. 'All of a sudden the coastal area, and especially Lima, began to demand cattle-raising on a large scale; and so the *mistis* started taking away the Indians' wheatfields and planting them with lucern.'[1] Thus an almost autarchic and purely regional subsistence economy was disrupted by the growing demand for livestock-breeding from the expanding urban centre of Lima. The *misti*, eager to turn the *puna* into pasturage for the cattle which he could sell for its weight in gold on the Lima market, resorted to every legal device to dislodge the Indian and seize his land. 'Year in, year out, the *mistis* went on digging up papers and documents of all sorts to prove that they were the owners of this or that slope or spring or pasture-ground . . . and with them always came the magistrate, the subprefect, and the captain of gendarmes with a few of his men. The magistrate would talk to the Indians in Quecha and tell them that Señor So-and-so was the lawful owner of the pasture.' Nor was the parish priest absent. 'The *cura* slipped a broad silken stole over his shoulder, gazed into the distance, first in one direction and then in another, after which he murmured a short prayer.' Not to be outdone by the magistrate, he then addressed a brief homily to the Indians which concluded as follows: 'Don Santos (Señor So-and-so) has proved in law that these fields are his. Your respects are now due to him as the master of the Indians who live there. God in His heaven respects the law which is common to all men. Come, *comuneros*, and kiss Don Santos's hand!'[2]

This depicts very well the process of spoliation, though not of course its extent. I need not dwell further on the combination of pettifogging trickery and the use of force, which Arguedas describes on much the same lines as Alegría. What is new in the former's account is the role played by the priest. The reference to God in His heaven may well cause us to take thought, for the God in whose name the priest speaks is not the only one whom the Indians know and fear. For the present, however, let us merely observe that the personal link between the master and 'his' Indians is confused with the relationship between an owner and his property, and this confusion is sanctioned in the name of the Christian God. The lessons which emerge from the passage quoted are three. Firstly, by becoming the owner of the pasture-lands, Don Santos also becomes the master of the Indians who dwell there. Secondly, respect is due to him on this

[1] Op. cit., p. 21.   [2] Op. cit., p. 25.

double account. And thirdly, this order of things which the law of man bids us respect is respected also by God in His heaven.

The *gamonal* is above all a master, a *patrón*. What is the exact meaning of this term? To put it negatively, a *patrón* is someone who does not work–as we see in the following quotation from Arguedas: ' "Does a *misti* know how to irrigate a field or enclose a meadow? Does he know how to clean a wheatfield or mend a road? Can he make tiles or adobe bricks, or even so much as kill a sheep?" '[1] We need not go on: a *misti* or a *patrón* doesn't know how to work, or at all events he doesn't do any. On the positive side, the *patrón*'s distinctive ability is to set others to work, and to see to it that they work for him. Here is Don Alvaro discussing with his lawyer how to enlarge his estate of Umay at the expense of a native community. 'It's a sacred debt I owe my father's memory. Besides, Peru needs men of enterprise who will make people work. What's the good of all this cheap humanitarianism? It's work and more work, and so that there will be work there must be men who will make the masses work.'[2] The *gamonal* thus illustrates after his fashion the Marxist theory of the exploitation of the working man by the capitalist. In exchange for the right to grow, on a few acres of land, the meagre crops necessary for his subsistence, the Indian provides the *gamonal* with virtually unpaid labour. Such is the servitude (*servidumbre*) which, though condemned by law, is far from having completely died out.

But while the *gamonal* is an exploiter, he is also a protector: and it is the combination of these attributes that makes him a *patrón*. In *Yawar Fiesta* we may discover three types of *patrón*, different yet comparable. First of all, the *patrón* who is also a *misti*. As we saw, he does nothing himself, but it is he who provides work. When the dispossessed Indians come down from the *puna* highlands to settle in Puquio, they are reduced to the condition of day-labourers (*jornaleros*). The *patrón* hires them to work in his own fields or on one of the large cotton-growing estates on the coast, which we shall describe later. Thus the Indian comes into contact at Puquio with a second type of *patrón*, the native-born headman whose task is to mobilise the community as an organic unit. It is this native *patrón*, the *alcalde* or *varayok*,[3] who will summon the *ayllu* (the inhabitants of a particular quarter) to help build a house for the new arrival. Finally there is a

[1] Op. cit., p. 17.   [2] Alegría, op. cit., p. 165.
[3] A mixture of Spanish and Quechua: the man with the stick (*vara*).

third type of *patrón*, a half-caste (*cholo*), whose role is that of an intermediary between the Indians and the *mistis*, speaking on the former's behalf and interceding for them. He is thus the embryo of a character we shall meet again, the *tinterillo* or pettifogger.

The three relationships just described illustrate the *patrón*'s protective and mediatory role. He may, in fact, assume either a paternal or an unjust and tyrannical character. An example of the former is Don Teodoro Alegría in *El mundo es ancho y ajeno*. We see him through the eyes of his protégé, Fiero Vásquez, who, wounded and hunted by the gendarmes, takes refuge in Don Teodoro's house. The latter 'was known far and wide as a proud man, beloved and honourable. When he passed through a village, people would take their hats off and he would greet them with "*Adiós compadre! Adiós comadre!*" ' Don Teodoro is not only jovial, courteous and affable: he is also omnipotent, or so Vásquez must have felt when he entered his service. 'He held them all in the hollow of his hand . . . When any of the authorities of Cajabamba–mayor or judge–did wrong, the people would come to Don Teodoro in demand of justice. Then he, at the head of the people, would go after the wrongdoer, make him get on a donkey, and ride him out of town with a band and fire-crackers. The person expelled like this never returned. Don Teodoro explained: "If we complain to the capital, they will pay no attention to us. In Lima they laugh at the provinces and dump their scoundrels on us. So we have our laugh at them too." '[1]

Don Teodoro is the type of the good *patrón* who uses his power in the people's interest: he is not only omnipotent, but kind as well. This is how the link of personal dependence was forged between him and Vásquez. The latter took up his quarters in Don Teodoro's house during the *patrón*'s absence, and Don Teodoro, learning from his wife that she had harboured him, was perturbed at having to take a decision involving a man's life. So, half joking, half serious (*entre serio y campechano*), like a good *criollo*[2] who knows how to get on with people, he started to 'try out' (*pulsear*) the redoubtable Vásquez. The latter, for his part, was not disconcerted–for, as we are told, he 'knew how to say the right thing at the right time'[3]–and introduced himself to Don Teodoro with the words 'Here I am, master . . .

---

[1] Op. cit., p. 112.
[2] The term *criollo* (creole) has in Peru a variety of senses which I shall try to define below: cf. Part I, chapter 2.
[3] Op. cit., p. 108.

through the kindness of my little mother'. Vásquez thus places himself under a double protection: he invokes his 'little mother', Don Teodoro's wife, and disarms the latter by emphasising his own forlornness. 'Here I am, living on your charity; but you're the master.' Each time he addresses Don Teodoro, he repeats the word 'master', thus expressly making the other his protector. The nature of this protection is illustrated by his remark of which the overt sense is to beg for pity and indulgence, but which is also by implication a plea for patronage: 'Master, have you a mother?' By using these words he begs Don Teodoro to protect him as his own mother was unable to do. And indeed, Don Teodoro from that time on feeds and shelters him, helps him to fight his evil inclinations and becomes in a sense his good angel. The bond which comes to exist between the master and Vásquez is a subtle but strong one. As long as Don Teodoro lives on his estates, Vásquez follows him in all his travels about the sierra, and enjoys the *patrón*'s reflected glory. 'It was a pleasure to accompany a man who was such a rider and so popular.'[1] Vásquez becomes still more closely attached to his master (*pegado*, 'stuck', as the author has it) after events lead to his saving Don Teodoro's life. But the bond is breakable, and after Don Teodoro becomes a senator and goes to live in Lima, his long-range protection no longer suffices to preserve Vásquez, the tender-hearted brigand, from the evil courses that lead to his ruin.

After the good master we meet the bad, or at all events the harsh one. Ciro Alegría presents us with a character whom we have already met, Don Alvaro; but I propose to cite the fuller description of Don Julián Aranguena in Arguedas' *Yawar Fiesta*.[2] Here is Don Julián's account of himself. He boasts of his own toughness: 'Yes, I've thrashed the Indians, and they must curse me in their hearts. But I treat them like dogs, neither better nor worse.'[3] This frankness is based on an unshakeably clear conscience. 'That's the way it is. God sent me to Puquio to put up with them.' We may note here the unconscious inversion of a situation in which Don Julián projects on to the Indians the guilt of the suffering which he himself inflicts upon them. On the conscious level, his attitude is a sort of 'denial of reciprocity', to use T. Parsons' term: 'I have no obligations towards the Indians, I may treat them as I please, and I expect nothing from them'. Therefore Don Julián does not expect his Indians to come to

---

[1] Op. cit., p. 111.
[3] Op. cit., p. 175.
[2] *Yawar Fiesta*, chap. 5, et seq.

Mobilisation in a Dualistic Society

his rescue when he is in prison. Why should they? 'They hate me, and they're damned well right.'

Are we to take at face value this emphatic denial of reciprocity, this claim to be above the law? There is in fact a discrepancy between Don Julián's self-portrait and his conduct as Arguedas describes it. How does he behave towards his inferiors? Here we must distinguish: with the *varayok* he is standoffish, but on the whole he treats them decently. One day they come to his house to ask him to make them a present of a bull, Misitu, so that the bravest of the Indians may fight it to the death in the arena on the 28th of July, the national holiday. But the *varayok* are not directly admitted to Don Julián's presence: they have to be announced by the master's servants, who are basking in the sunshine.[1] 'Don Julián, wearing a short waistcoat and carrying a newspaper, came into the patio where the *varayok* were waiting.' A conversation ensues: 'his' Indians, having politely recalled to their master that his lucern fields are part of the land belonging to their *ayllu*, put forward their request for the famous bull. Don Julián replies favourably. He listens to the *varayok*'s civilities, accepts a glass of cane-brandy and courteously brings the interview to a close. But with his servants (*allegados, concertados, cholos*), Don Julián behaves with the utmost violence: he insults them, accuses them of cowardice, reminds them that they are nothing but Indians and threatens to kill them.[2] The 'respect' to which, according to the parish priest, the master is entitled means, first and foremost, that his inferiors must keep their distance, and must endure his outbursts with patience and submissiveness.

In addition to the 'denial of reciprocity', the link between the *patrón* and his dependants is characterised by the fact that it refuses to become institutionalised. Hence the importance which attaches to the master's plighted word. Don Julián expects nothing of his own people; but they can at least expect that he will keep his promises, if he has made them publicly and solemnly. To this extent he is bound *vis à vis* his people, or rather *vis à vis* the public and above all his peers, the other *patrones*, with whom he does not wish to lose face. The principle of honour is thus the sole guarantee of reciprocity in a society whose code seems to deny that its great ones can be bound by anything except their own will. But what is the real significance of the social and physical power which they enjoy–a power which might almost be called 'virile', in view of the sexual connotation of the word

[1] Op. cit., p. 39. [2] Op. cit., p. 106.

36

macho (male) which the rulers of this society like to hear used of themselves. Is the *patrón* what is called elsewhere a cacique? This latter term is seldom used in Peru except by journalists and politicians, and not often by them: it is a foreign expression which does not seem to have taken root. However, it serves to denote a situation in which political and administrative favours are monopolised by an individual, or a very small group whose mouthpiece is a single leader or boss. This man appoints, dismisses and transfers officials at his own good pleasure: benefiting from the delegation or rather disintegration of authority, he takes unfettered decisions in his own interest as regards the building of roads and bridges, hospitals and schools. All this is a recognisable feature of the Peruvian scene; but the monopoly situation is, on the whole, exceptional. I have already quoted Alegría's description of the ruthless struggle between the two landowners of Cajamarca. The *mistis* of Puquio to whom Arguedas introduces us are certainly of less calibre than Don Alvaro Amenábar, but, like him, they live in a divided universe. The reader of *Yawar Fiesta* might at first suppose that Don Julián is the undisputed king of that little world; but in fact his power is subject to attack by the other *mistis*, probably less rich than he, but more artful and more refined—the *alimeñados* (from *limeño*, Liman), whose eyes are fixed on the capital and its representatives. And his Olympus is also exposed to invasion by such characters as the newly-rich merchant, Pancho Jiménez.

Moreover, the small-town *patrón* must reckon with the power which the central government's representatives can bring to bear against him. The subprefect's role is treated somewhat cavalierly in the 'indigenist' novel, for instance in the passage I have quoted from Ciro Alegría, where that official takes good care not to interfere in the quarrel between Don Gonzalo and the Córdova family. We saw, too, how the good *patrón*, Don Teodoro, dealt with corrupt officials by seating them on a donkey and driving them out of the village to the accompaniment of hoots and jeers. But the subprefect, contemptible though he may be, has command over the forces of law and order; and if he can get one of the clans on his side, given boldness and luck he may succeed in overthrowing the highest and most powerful lords. Thus it is that Don Julián Arangüena eventually finds himself in prison along with the *cholo*, Pancho Jiménez.

The oligarchy and the economy

Such is the world of the up-country *patrones* with which indigenist Peruvian literature has made us familiar. But we should not mistake this class of sierra landowners for the oligarchy. In the first place, the sierra itself must be seen in relation to the rest of the country. The *patrones* and *gamonales*, it is true, are masters of huge estates: in Cuzco and Puno in the south, haciendas of over 50,000 acres–the so-called *latifundios*–are by no means uncommon. But the greater part of these vast areas is deserted and under stubble, while much of the remainder lies fallow. The crops, exposed to the rigours of an arid and icy winter, are meagre. The herds which feed on these pasture-lands give meat and wool of poor quality. Thus most of the great estates yield a net revenue which is disappointingly small in relation to the capital invested. The exploitation of unproductive labour, cruel and inhuman as it often is, does not suffice to turn the *gamonal* into a Crœsus. While little has been done to improve agriculture, some progress has been made in stock-rearing. One or two haciendas in Puno and Cuzco, and especially some huge estates in the central departments of Junín and Pasco, have achieved a very respectable level of wool and meat production. But how has this progress been attained? To begin with, pasture-lands have to be enclosed to separate them from those of the native herdsmen; and the *patrón* has to contract debts in order to buy, generally from abroad, good-quality stock with which to develop his sown pastures. Then he tells his Indians that in future their herds are to be kept separate to prevent cross-breeding with his expensively reared stock, and this frequently leads to conflict. As a result, with the exception of a few very large and well-to-do estates, and of some at high altitudes where the native population was sparse, men and nature have combined to resist progress (*tecnificación*), and the up-country *latifundios*, especially in the south, have remained at a very low level of productivity.

By contrast with the sierra, agriculture in the coastal valleys is prosperous and well managed. The yield of the great sugar and cotton plantations places Peru among the world's leading producers of these crops. Coastal agriculture is mechanised and amply equipped, consuming large quantities of fertiliser and anti-cryptogamic products. It employs wage-earning labourers, some of whom come down from the sierra at harvest-time, while others are former *serranos* who now live on the coast, where they are acquiring a new culture and way of life. These labourers have their unions, they make use of the strike weapon and obtain steadily higher wages: they already form part of the monetary sector of the economy. Moreover, coastal agriculture is geared to the export market. Over 60 per cent of the sugar is sold abroad, and about half the cotton crop is available for export after the demand of the home textile industry has been met. Not only does the coast export a large part of its agricultural production but, taking Peruvian exports as a whole, cotton and sugar accounted in 1962 for about 30 per cent of the total, while meat and wool from the sierra probably represented under 5 per cent.

Compared with the outdated and largely unproductive *latifundios* of the sierra, coastal agriculture appears as a highly dynamic sector of the economy. As Alex Zarak noted with satisfaction in *La Prensa*'s special number of 23 September 1963, 'the country has become aware of the importance of export agriculture in the general development of its economy. Irresponsible propaganda against agriculture, especially that part of it which produces for export, is a thing of the past.' In the same number of *La Prensa*, the economist Rómulo Ferrero declared that exports, particularly of cotton and sugar, had played a decisive role in the growth of the Peruvian economy over the past twenty-five years.[1] This being so, it is tempting to discern, in the individuals and families who control the great coastal plantations, the chief if not the sole element of the oligarchy. Can this oligarchy, in fact, simply be equated with the group of sugar and cotton magnates?

Before answering this, we should look at some more figures. While sugar and cotton represent nearly 30 per cent of Peruvian exports and just over 15 per cent of the gross national product, mineral production accounts for between 10 per cent and 15 per cent of the gross national product and 37 per cent of exports. The main feature of the mining industry is not only that it produces for export but also

[1] This view is confirmed by the first results of the 1961 census, which show much more rapid demographic and economic progress on the coast than in the sierra. 'The sierra population has risen by only 35 per cent since 1940. This apparently small increase is due to the cumulative effect of a lower birthrate, a higher deathrate (especially still births) and migration to the lowlands. . . . The relative stagnation of the sierra contrasts with the demographic and economic development of the coastal area, where in 1958 per capita income was three times as high as in the Andes.' François Bourricaud and Olivier Dollfus, op. cit., pp. 184, 200.

that it is, in the main, controlled by foreign capital. In lead and zinc production, the position of the Cerro de Pasco Corporation is the stronger in that it owns the sole factory in which the raw ore is worked. The Marcona iron deposits in the Ica department are operated by an American firm. A national mining industry does exist, but it is plainly dependent on large foreign, especially U.S., interests. To quote the engineer Samamé Boggio (whom we shall meet again when describing the presidential election of 1963), 'Peruvian mining is still at the colonial stage ... It has not yet achieved the final result of producing refined metals which can themselves be used to make machinery for processing purposes.'[1] The dependent state of small-scale mining (*pequeña minería*) is evident in three main respects. First, the ore has to be refined by the Cerro de Pasco Corporation; then American freighters must be paid to transport it to the U.S.; and finally, Washington imposes an import duty on Peruvian metal to protect the mining interests of the American west. However, thanks to the intermediary of the Corporation, Peruvian-owned mines enjoy a quota on the U.S. market.

The oligarchy has more than one string to its bow: not only export agriculture and mining, but also banking and speculation in real estate. It is to be found ensconced at such vantage-points of the economy as the credit distribution system. It is not only an oligarchy of landowners, urban and rural, but also of bankers, businessmen and even industrialists. In short, it is present wherever there is money to be made. It does not produce chiefly for the home market, but sells its goods in New York, London and Hamburg. It makes an effort to find foreign outlets for its crops: the cotton trade is not wholly in its hands, but for the most part it controls the marketing of sugar. An oligarchy of exporters, therefore; but, since it controls the bulk of credit resources, it is also in a position to finance imports. These in turn are chiefly geared to its own needs: farm machinery, fertilisers, anti-cryptogamic products and mining equipment. Apart from thus satisfying the needs of coastal agriculture and mining, imports include general types of machinery and semi-durable consumer goods such as cars and electrical and household equipment.

Let us now consider the boards of directors of some of the main companies. What first strikes us is the recurrence of particular names; but there are distinctions to be noticed here. Let us take the case of the managing director (*gerente general*) of one of the principal

[1] *Informaciones comerciales*, No. 102, June 1958, p. 11.

banks, the third largest in terms of the total value of deposits. This man, the relative of a former President of the Republic, is also the chairman of an insurance company and a building society; he owns theatres and cinemas and the principal cement factory.[1] If we turn now to the chairman of the largest bank in terms of deposits (whose brother is chairman of the bank which ranks second in the same order), it transpires that he is also the chairman of an insurance company, a director of a building society and the first president of the chief electrical concern. Membership of a board of directors is not, of course, synonymous with control of a business. Too many studies of power problems have been vitiated by confusion between shareholding, ownership and control. I may possess a large block of shares without controlling the firm in question, or I may control an enterprise while possessing only a small fraction of its capital; or again, I may enjoy a more or less fictitious degree of control as a figurehead or observer. The 'I' in such cases may be an individual capitalist, a firm or a financial group. In the case of the two gentlemen I have mentioned, their association with the top management of the enterprises in question is combined with ownership of a large proportion of the capital. The number of shareholders in the major Peruvian concerns is generally small, as witness the extremely limited activity of the Lima stock exchange. Generally speaking, the directors of a business are also its owners. Who are the shareholders? In the countries best known to us, they may be individuals, companies or groups. In Peru, I should be inclined to say that the typical shareholder is a family or *gens*.

A Peruvian magnate does not speak or decide for himself alone, but on behalf of his sons, nephews and cousins, whose wealth he administers. Each *gens* has its paterfamilias–or *patrón*, to use a term already familiar to us. Every such family will of course have its poor relations. It may also happen that the younger son of an illustrious *gens*, having enjoyed high position, is reduced, if not to penury, at any rate to dependence on the good graces of a brother-in-law, cousin or nephew who keeps him on short commons. It is often difficult for the paterfamilias to know how to exercise his authority. Either he may behave like a genuine patriarch, thinking only of the

[1] Based on the list of the most important and well-established concerns as given in the *Vademecum del Inversionista* published by the Banco de Crédito, 1962–3. The list is not complete, for some of the firms with which the person in question is connected do not figure in the *Vademecum*, though they may be among those which yield the largest rates of profit.

aggrandisement of the clan, and using the differing aptitudes of each of its members to capture the largest possible number of strategic positions; or he may think first, if not of himself, of his own immediate family in ascending or descending line. In the latter case, each brother will enjoy a fairly large degree of autonomy within his private domain. Nevertheless, the relations between elder and younger brothers may be regulated for the benefit of the *gens* as a whole. For example, if the elder is felt to be too powerful or enterprising, a particular field of activity may be reserved for his junior who arouses less misgiving. While using the terms 'elder' and 'younger', it should be borne in mind that the head of the family is not always chosen by right of primogeniture. He may, for instance, be a brother-in-law who happens to be the ablest and most energetic member of the group or to enjoy the best advantages, through his wife's connections or those of his other relatives.

The concentration of power is not always due to kinship but may also have personal causes. Let us imagine a young man belonging to a good family which has come down in the world. Being able and ambitious, he is taken on by a large enterprise owned by a distant cousin, and thirty years later we find him director of an impressive number of companies: vice-president of the country's principal deposit bank and of a building society, and also involved in industrial concerns in which the bank as such has no part, two of which manufacture glass and another fishmeal. In addition, he is president of the country's chief electrical enterprise. He is, moreover, a director of the largest credit institute, whose financial offshoots are in effect branches of the bank of which he is vice-president. He also plays a less prominent part in certain concerns which are customers of the bank and in which the bank takes an interest without directly controlling them. Clearly, a man who has collected all these trumps into his hand is not going to behave as a mere henchman. The *gens* which he has founded or revived may not be of the first order of importance, and he himself may not be of the highest calibre. But his relative dependence and the fact that he never becomes completely autonomous is in its way a source of strength: for he becomes a useful intermediary through whom his *patrón* can negotiate, or even penetrate spheres that would otherwise be closed to him.

Thus the Peruvian oligarchy is a network of families and their *clientèles*, it being understood that the family is a wider unit than the individual household. It is in fact an extensive and not a 'nuclear' concept; to which basic truth should be added the rider that the extension, as well as the cohesion, of Peruvian families is a variable quantity. In some cases the *gens* includes literally all the descendants of a common ancestor. In others, as I have said, each generation splits up into branches which are theoretically equal and autonomous but which concert their activities. Such families are, for practical purposes, clans whose separate but co-ordinated units cover very large sectors of economic life. I mentioned two brothers, one of whom is the president of the principal deposit bank while the second is the president of a bank associated with it. These brothers have two first cousins who are also brothers. Each pair of brothers constitutes a more or less firm alliance which also forms part of an alliance of the four cousins.

The activities of each clan are more or less specialised, and different types of clan may be distinguished by the twin criteria of specialisation and exclusiveness. As the shareholding lists reveal, certain families are especially interested in mining. To buy mining equipment and machinery from abroad, the family in question sets up an import business; and the financing of its enterprises enables it to create an investment bank. By contrast to this diversification, there is another clan which devotes itself almost exclusively to a single activity and operates as a self-contained unit, being the country's main producer and exporter of sugar. Some cousins and younger brothers of this clan figure on the boards of firms other than the main enterprise, but its wealth is essentially bound up in the sugar business, shares in which do not come on the open market. Its self-containedness takes two forms: firstly the small number of shares which its members hold outside the main business, and secondly its restrictive policy in the matter of marriages. This specialisation and isolation produce what may be called an encysted state of affairs. The clan in question plays only a marginal part in national life, its concern being merely to secure from it certain substantial but specific advantages.

At the opposite pole, there is the strategy of those clans which seek to maximise their overall power, to break into and permeate every sector of activity. The best example of this class is provided by the president of the third largest bank from the point of view of total deposits. He is listed among the directors of an insurance company, a building society, an oil refinery, a cement factory and a multitude of lesser concerns, all centring incidentally on the home market.

What Peruvian observers generally fail to notice is that such 'empires' are much less concentrated than they appear, being in fact rather loose federations of separate entities which are often not remarkable for good management. The growth of the so-called empire follows the course of bank investments, which does not seem to be dictated by a very selective policy but rather to be attracted by the promise of quick returns. The head of the 'empire' relies for his profit less on the sale of high-quality goods than on bounties and revenues of a monopolistic or speculative character. The dominant position which this or that firm belonging to the group acquires in a given sector is due to the support of the central bank of the 'empire', which does its best to discourage and eliminate possible competitors. The 'empire' may also strengthen its position by means of tariff walls–witness the textile industry in 1956, when Sr Juan Pardo Herren was Minister of Finance under President Prado. In the short term, the 'empire' will fix its prices abnormally high compared not only with those abroad, but with those of any home competitors; over a longer period, the nature and extent of its investment may be either excessive or inadequate. It is more concerned with speculative profits than with the fruits of monopoly; but its power crumbles once it ceases to enjoy the support and connivance of the administration. Apart from this, there are two limits to its growth. Firstly, the home market is still small and offers an insufficient number of customers open to exploitation; and secondly, the interests of export agriculture are too powerful and its position in support of free trade is too firm to permit the introduction of a prohibitive tariff which would turn the Peruvian market into the exclusive preserve of the nascent national industries.

The basic unit of the Peruvian oligarchy is the *gens*, in the same way as the unit of modern industrial society is the business organisation. The head of a Peruvian 'empire'–be it of the loose-knit, extensive kind or entrenched in the efficient production of an export commodity–is never a mere manager of anonymous capital. His attitude is not that of a technician or an organiser, still less an entrepreneur: it is most likely to be that of a banker or rather a financier. Certainly some families have succeeded, for a longer or shorter period, in achieving the status of *rentiers*. A specialised and exclusive clan which has carefully chosen its field of operations may entrust the management of its business to competent administrators. But, by and large, this situation is neither frequent nor lasting, and in any case it does not apply to the variegated 'empires' whose rulers are constantly in a state of alert. The search for foreign markets compels the oligarchy to vigilance. Tastes change, trade channels alter, and the shocks of international politics may endanger the best-protected interests. Anything which affects Egyptian cotton cannot be a matter of indifference to cultivators of long-fibre cotton in Peru. The oligarchy does not behave like a mere passive *rentier*: it makes its choice between cotton, sugar, zinc and lead, or pulls out of one investment in order to chase profits elsewhere. In short, the oligarch is a speculator; and while he is prepared to delegate most of the traditional functions of the modern businessman, such as technical management and administration, there is one to which he holds fast because it is linked with what may be called his propensity to speculation, and that function is the strategy of shareholding.

Is the oligarchy a financial one? Its members are farmers (but landowning has no mystic significance for them), mineowners, industrialists and something more. Should they not rather be called bankers? The banker is above all an arbiter: he chooses among the various possible uses of a given supply of capital, and plays the part of a sort of judge *vis à vis* potential investors. In this way it is largely he who mobilises savings and applies them to increase production. He may, of course, be led to take over control of this or that enterprise; but he is often dissuaded from doing so, not only by the resistance of the entrepreneur who wishes to remain master of his own affairs (and sometimes pays dearly for his more or less illusory independence) but also by the difficulty of effectively managing a large number of complex and varied undertakings. Thus a bank which takes up shares in a company is less interested in acquiring control and committing itself in the long term than in financial operations (amalgamation, regrouping, capital issue). What characterises business in Peru is that the saver, the banker and the investor are one and the same person. Capital is concentrated, but there is little or no distinction between the functions of saving, investment and administration. A Peruvian banker, investing his own money in a concern whose registered capital is in his hands and which is managed by his son, cousin, son-in-law or father-in-law, will not apply the same criteria of rationality as an American banker who collects liquid assets on the capital market to invest them in joint-stock organisations under non-shareholding managers.

Why has the oligarchy so far not turned towards industry?– because, at present, few of its members are entrepreneurs. For private enterprise to thrive, certain conditions are necessary which have not as yet been realised in Peru. In the first place, the role of new technical devices must not be excessive in relation to the human, physical and financial resources which can be brought to bear. As this condition is not fulfilled in a country like Peru, technical progress is, so to speak, imported or diffused from an external source.[1] Secondly, lenders must be prepared to back initiatives which offer only an uncertain chance of success, while choosing carefully the newcomers whom they decide to support. The Peruvian banking system is ill adapted to this, not only because the amount of long-term capital which it is capable of mobilising is chronically insufficient, but because the bankers' decisions are too often governed by motives of private solidarity rather than sound economic principles. Thirdly, the newcomer must be protected in one of two ways from foreign competition. Either he must make himself invulnerable by the size of his enterprise or the quality of his goods, or he must persuade his government to protect him by means of a tariff. And the Peruvian businessman is in general able to do neither of these things.

Nor is this all. While economic innovation still makes the fortune of lucky individuals, it is nowadays no longer a one-man affair. To be fully effective it must be relayed and, as it were, geared down by an elaborate marketing organisation. One of the drawbacks of the new Peruvian middle class is that the rise of ambitious individuals who make their way by luck, skill or personal virtues is a phenomenon which belongs to a bygone phase of the process of industrialisation. The traditional businessman (entrepreneur, in Spanish *impresario*) is being progressively replaced by the *gerente* or managerial expert. It is true that the oligarchical interests and foreign companies need such men; but can they find a place in the great national and foreign concerns?

The oligarchy seldom takes an interest in nascent industry, preferring to let others bear the initial risk. Let us take the case of an unusually speculative Peruvian industry—that of fishmeal—which, in the last decade, has yielded substantial profits to its pioneers. The initial investment is not very great: it involves paying wages, buying boats and equipping the factory in which anchovies are processed. Almost the whole product is exported, and the market is highly competitive. The capitalist who engages in this industry must be above all

---

[1] This was pointed out by Haya de la Torre in 1931, when he wrote: 'We use the machines that foreigners send us.'

a businessman and a speculator: the technical and organisational problems are relatively simple. What is needed is financial acumen and a thorough knowledge of the home and foreign credit market. Aptitudes of this kind are not uncommon, and the fishmeal industry has enabled some quite humble individuals to make considerable fortunes in a few years, either directly with the help of their own or borrowed money, or on a sleeping-partner basis. During this early phase the oligarchs remained on the sidelines. Naturally the hope of profit attracted too many ambitious but improvident newcomers, who fell into debt; whereupon the oligarchy intervened to concentrate and regroup the industry. As this story shows, industrial initiatives are not taken by the oligarchs but generally by newcomers, either recent immigrants or Peruvians of fairly low social status; after they have blazed the trail, the oligarchs appear on the scene to reap the profits.

The relationship between the oligarchy and the newcomers deserves to be looked at more closely. There is a widespread conventional view that the Peruvian oligarchy consists of the heirs of Spanish counts and marquises who have preserved the purity of their lineage and maintained the traditions of the Viceroyalty during the past century and a half of national independence. In actual fact, the great families of pre-independence days are scarcely represented in the business world of today, and few rich business families could go back more than a century to produce evidence of respectable bourgeois antecedents. We must also take into account the influx of foreigners: Italians, Germans and Yugoslavs, not to mention Arabs and Jews. In one insurance company, the chairman and two members of the board have Jewish names; and there is a fishmeal concern[1] in which no member of the board, including the chairman and vice-chairman, has a Spanish name. I may also mention two foreigners, one French, the other Italian. The former began as an engineer in a mining enterprise and managed to establish himself in national mining circles; he is now a director of various banking, insurance and mining concerns.[2] The other had a successful career in the electrical industry. But it is not sufficient to be accepted as rich: the next stage is to enter society. The *nouveaux-riches* or their children gain admission to the magic circle by marrying the right people, going to the right schools or having the right friends. The clever or lucky ones do not have to wait long; for, perhaps because the industrial sector is so

[1] Mentioned in the *Vademecum*, p. 284. [2] Ibid., p. 571.

under-developed, the two worlds of business and high society coincide almost exactly. This becomes strikingly clear if one compares the directors' yearbook with the list of members of the highly exclusive Club Nacional. Things are different in this respect at Buenos Aires or Santiago; and it is not certain that, even at Lima, this symbiosis between high society and big business will last many years longer.

The oligarchy and politics

There is therefore a Peruvian oligarchy, in the sense of a nucleus of powerful families who control the nation's wealth. Its members are not mere consumers, and while they may not themselves be producers or organise production, they determine its scope and direction. Is this plutocracy a governing class? The question is hard to answer. The power of a governing class is always difficult to define; the fact that such a class exists, however manifestly, does not mean that it governs everything. And in Peru, the problem of measuring the extent of the oligarchy's power is especially baffling.

Two equally unsatisfactory hypotheses may be put forward as to the relationship between the oligarchy and the world of politics. On the one hand, it is pointed out that the Presidency has generally been occupied by a military man. All the presidents were soldiers from 1824 to 1872, when the first Pardo was elected. They were, moreover, soldiers of fortune, usually of lowly origin and resentful of bourgeois creole society. General Odría, who headed the government from 1948 to 1956 and again stood for the Presidency in 1962 and 1963, is the latest representative of a tradition illustrated in the nineteenth century by Camarra and Castilla. The opposite thesis, developed by José Carlos Mariátegui,[1] is an article of faith among radical intellectuals. It holds that the *caudillo* is an accomplice of the oligarchy, even though he may seem to take demagogic measures against it. 'One way or another, the *caudillo* and the system of government by the military have fostered the development of the latifundia. This being so, it makes no difference that the Presidents are soldiers of mixed blood and that many parliamentarians are provincial *cholos* whom Lima society looks down upon. What counts is their docility towards the oligarchy.'

[1] José Carlos Mariátegui, *Siete ensayos de interpretación de la realidad peruana*, pp. 70–5.

Put in these terms, there is no satisfactory answer to the problem. Should we not simply recognise that the oligarchy and the political world are largely distinct but are nevertheless united by substantial ties? Is there in fact a political class in Peru, as there is in Colombia or Chile? If this implies the existence of a stable and specialised group of men, I doubt it. People at Lima, it is true, talk of 'politicians' (*los políticos*), usually in a scornful or contemptuous tone. But is politics a career? What strikes one about the composition of the legislative assemblies is their extreme instability. Between 1920 and 1963, each change of President was accompanied by an almost complete renewal of parliament. From one legislature to the next, between 80 per cent and 90 per cent of the deputies were replaced; the rate for the senate is lower, but must be at least two-thirds. There are of course a few parliamentarians who are practically immovable, and whom popular irony has christened '*sparadra*', or sticking-plaster. Two of these are Senators Alba and Mancheco Muñoz, from Cajamarca and Huancavelica respectively. Alongside these patriarchal fixed stars there are some intermittent luminaries. For instance, in the department of San Martín a certain individual, having served as senator from 1939 to 1945, went into a long eclipse and reappeared from 1956 to 1962. The explanation, to be sure, appears simple enough: the senator's two terms of office correspond to those of President Prado. Representatives seldom keep their seats from one parliament to another except in the senate, where they belong to one of two categories, being either local notables or the clients of some important figure on the national scene.

These notables are often dubbed *patrones*: they would be called 'caciques' in Mexico and 'bosses' in the United States. The *patrón* is the regulator of public favours: it is he who makes the rounds of the Lima ministries and ensures that a proper share of the heavenly bounty is wafted towards his department. On the one hand, he occupies a strategic position in the process whereby the needs and requests of distant areas are made known to the central power; on the other, it is to him that the great ones of Lima must apply if they wish to make contact with the provinces. At presidential elections in particular, it is he who mobilises the block vote of his faithful constituents, who are one and all in his debt. The *patrón*'s role is not too difficult to analyse. What he expects from the central government is to be granted a sort of suzerainty over his department: this he will achieve most easily if he happens to be a friend of the president's, or, failing that, if he has succeeded in keeping the authorities sweet and making himself indispensable to them. In this sense, the *patrones* with the greatest staying-power are independent: they are on terms with every regime and successive regimes must come to terms with them. But this is a rare achievement. A *patrón* needs a great deal of skill to become indispensable both to the central power and to his fellow-provincials; he also needs plenty of luck, for a new president may be tempted to get rid of a man who does not owe him everything and install a trusted henchman of his own. Thus, with few exceptions, the president's 'friends' do not outlast his own period of success. A president may of course come back for a second term, as did Sr. Prado; but between 1945, when he left office, and 1956, when he returned, a younger batch of clients had come to the fore. Thus only a few members of Congress, like the senator from San Martín whom I mentioned earlier, came back into office on the tide of his good fortune.

For a political class to come into existence, its members must enjoy a certain minimum of stability. This pre-condition applies, it would seem, to only a very few people in Peru. Moreover, the most stable politicians are not those who appear to concentrate on great affairs but rather those who have become effective champions of specific and narrow local interests. This is the more understandable in that Peru has, or had till December 1963, no elected local assemblies, so that the representation of provincial and departmental interests falls naturally to members of Congress, who tend to confine themselves to the role of canvasser and broker. But, apart from the two categories mentioned above–the clients of the great and the *patrones* entrenched in their provincial fiefs–we may distinguish a third class of politicians. Take the case of a certain senator for the department of Puno, who has been president of the senate. He began his career in 1924, under President Leguía, as deputy for the Lampa province in that department, and was elected to the same seat in 1939 during the first presidency of Manuel Prado. In 1956 he returned to Congress under Prado's second presidency, this time as senator for Puno. But it would be hard to see him either as a *patrón* whose parliamentary position is based on local influence, or as a mere cog in the Pradist machine. The man in question is a well-known mining engineer who has occupied several highly responsible administrative posts, such as the presidency of the Santa Corporation, and has represented his country at various international conferences, including a congress on

50

irrigation problems. His technical expertise and success in his profession confer on him a reputation beyond the limits of his department and mark him out for a political career. If he returns to Lampa as a 'favourite son' (*hijo predilecto*), he will be adorned by the prestige of wealth and reputation gained in wider spheres than the department of Puno. I might also mention another engineer, closely connected with the big mining interests, who is a director of several companies and at least one bank; after serving as Minister of Public Works (*Ministro de Fomento*) under the presidency of General Benavides, he became senator for Ica for a second term from 1945 to 1948, vice-president under General Odría in 1950–6, and finally ambassador in Paris during President Prado's second term of office. His career is instructive in two ways: it illustrates some of the links between the political and business worlds, and also the flexibility of the system of patronage which permits a single man to serve under such diverse administrations.

So far, we may distinguish four classes of Peruvian politicians. Firstly, the run-of-the-mill batch of 'president's friends', more or less hastily recruited, who do not outlive the chief executive's political fortunes. Till recently, the great majority of deputies and a smaller number of senators belonged to this class. Secondly–*rari nantes in gurgite vasto*–the *patrones* whose local strength has enabled them to survive fluctuations at the national level. Thirdly, the steady 'clients' who return to power in the wake of the leader who protects them or who gave them their first start. Fourthly, a small group of personalities whose success and prestige enable them to stand on their own feet and who, unlike the *patrones* of the second category, not only enjoy local authority but have succeeded in establishing themselves on the national scene as powers, albeit limited ones, in their own right. The difference between the second and fourth categories may be illustrated by pointing out that Senator Boza, when vice-president of the Republic in 1956, attempted to stand for the presidency–an ambition which would never have occurred to Don Octavio Alba, the senator for Cajamarca, whom I took as an example of the second class. This situation is changing inasmuch as big parties like Apra and President Belaúnde's Acción Popular have succeeded in imposing their system: between them, these two control two-thirds of congressional seats. In fact, the above analysis, based on the period ending with the elections of June 1963, is no longer valid today. If the present evolution continues, it will only widen the gap between the oligarchy and the political class. But the fact that these two are separate does not mean that they have become divorced and no longer have any interests in common. Even in the last century, the military *caudillos* did not surround themselves exclusively with their comrades in arms, but left room for the oligarchy in Congress, ministries and embassies. The heads of great families did not take a direct hand in the political game, but younger brothers and cousins were to be found in it, guiding the President's hand on the pretext of saving him from blunders. Except during the presidency of José Pardo and at the height of the 'civilianist' period–that is to say, roughly from 1900 to 1920–the great Lima families prudently avoided the limelight or were kept out of it by circumstances. The oligarchy followed the political drama closely and often directed it, but did not appear openly in the major roles.

The duality between the governing (or rather dominating) and the political class was characteristic of Peruvian political life from 1919 onwards. The *coup d'état* which brought Leguía to the presidency in that year spelt defeat for the civilianist (*civilista*) party with its dream of an aristocratic republic in which the great families would have kept under their tutelage the inert peasant masses, the soldiery and the Lima proletariat. Thenceforth, the attempt to create a large conservative party on Chilean lines was doomed to failure; and, to defend their interests, the great families were obliged either to come to terms with the military leaders, as they did with Generals Benavides and Odría, or to negotiate with popular tribunes like Haya de la Torre and his friends. The oligarchy is no longer in a position to govern openly: after the brief aristocratic interlude at the beginning of the century, the country suffered from alternate bouts of violent repression and anarchic turbulence. Yet, during this long period of instability, the oligarchy, without governing directly, managed on the whole to inspire and impose policies in accordance with its wishes and interests.

Seen in this light, the oligarchy gives the impression of a cynical, wire-pulling élite for whom its own interests are paramount. If it plays no overt part in politics, the chief reason is that it has no principles. As Hugo Neira has put it, the oligarchy 'lacks a consistent notion of its role, its position and its future ... Since Riva Agüero died, the Peruvian right wing has had no great ideologist ... Its face, so to speak, is half-hidden, visible only in blurred profile.'[1] In this young

[1] *Expreso*, 5 June 1962.

journalist's view, the 'right wing' which politically represents the oligarchy is blind and deaf to all civic responsibilities. It is interested only in the affairs of its own few families and is oblivious of everything else. Instead of patriotism, its values are inspired by 'health and sport' and the various pleasurable ways in which rich and well-brought-up people can expend their resources. At the same time, the oligarchy is timid, and in order to prevent explosions it is ready to call in a gendarme at any time, to whom it 'willingly entrusts the responsibilities of power'. It engages 'local Cæsars' to do its dirty work and 'use violence on its behalf'. Its status is that of a 'parasite', maintained by 'feats of wire-pulling which it regards as the sum-total of political wisdom'.[1]

This severe judgment of the oligarchy is not found only among writers who may be generally described as left-wing: it has never been better expressed than by the author whom Neira justly calls the great ideologist of the Peruvian right, and who roundly condemned his fellow-oligarchs fifty or more years ago. In his *Paisajes peruanos*, José de la Riva Agüero, in an admirable meditation on the battlefield of Ayacucho, spoke in these terms of the different categories which made up the Peruvian élite:

'Who were those that set up to govern the new-born state? The poor, silly colonial nobility of Lima, incapable of effort and destitute of ideas? Their ineffectiveness left a void which was filled by the military *caudillos* . . . Shoddy rhetoric and pompous attitudes were not sufficient to disguise the chieftains' true character and the vulgarity of their appetites . . . How slack and feeble was the patriotism of the creole bourgeoisie! In the souls of these newly-rich merchants, what unawareness of ancient Peruvian traditions, what stupid and suicidal contempt for the nation, what sordid, Levantine egotism!'[2]

Thus the grandson of the first President of the Peruvian republic, bearing one of the greatest names of the colonial tradition, condemned the oligarchy outright on two grounds: political ineptitude and selfishness. We are not concerned for the moment with the bases of his argument and the justice of the verdict: I wish merely to point out that he denies any legitimacy to the groups which economically dominate the country.

The charges of egotism and indifference to the common weal (*falta de sensibilidad*) which are levelled against the oligarchy by the right as

[1] Ibid.   [2] José de la Riva Agüero, *Paisajes peruanos*, Lima, 1955, pp. 117–18.

well as the left are summed up in the widespread view which dismisses it as a mere plutocracy. In contrast to this gloomy picture, some conservative writers look back with nostalgia to a past, unhappily gone beyond recall, in which the better classes, if they did not govern the state, were at least prominent in their native towns. In the volume of his memoirs describing the town in which his family lived and in which he grew up,[1] Víctor Andrés Belaúnde paints the picture of a provincial oligarchy which, as he sees it, is an authentic aristocracy. The 'good' families of Arequipa, which are not exactly the 'great' Peruvian families, since wealth and power became concentrated in Lima, did not live in luxury: they displayed, among other virtues, decency, moderation and economy. 'The home was the cornerstone of life at Arequipa: the family was an ethical and economic unit . . . the city was really a confederation of families.' Later, the author goes on: 'Arequipa was a democracy of gentlefolk (*hidalgos*), each one of them equal to the king except for his money, as the Castilian proverb has it.' Money did not help one to enter society or achieve recognition: 'all that was needed was the fellowship of Catholic faith and good breeding'. These families, interlinked by marriages and cousinships, were large communities, governed by stern yet generous patriarchs. When José Gómez de la Torre dies, his brother, the writer's uncle, takes the widow and her six children into his household, and thus, 'in the old house in Merchants' Street, counting all the relatives and their children and grandchildren, over thirty people sat down at the same table every day'. And, as the writer piously adds, the uncle's lucrative practice as a lawyer enabled him to go on maintaining this enormous family. Finally he exalts the civic and Christian virtues of the Arequipa gentry in the following, no doubt somewhat idealised terms:[2] 'Model heads of families and exemplary citizens, hard-working, courteous to all and supremely dignified at all times of their lives, a single word sums up all their qualities: authority (*señorío*). The *señor* is conscious that authority belongs to him; but this consciousness is not proud or arrogant, it is the humble awareness of a mission to be fulfilled, a duty to be accomplished . . . It is not a claim to the exercise of power or the enjoyment of privilege.'

[1] V. A. Belaúnde, *Arequipa de mi infancia*: chap. 10, *El ambiente familial*, pp. 217 et seq.
[2] A very different picture of Arequipa society is given us in Flora Tristan's *Mémoires d'une paria*. The greed, cunning and duplicity of Tío Pío contrast with the virtues of the 'Christian *hidalgo*'.

This Christian hidalgo's motto might well be *'noblesse oblige'*. The galaxy of virtues that Belaúnde ascribes to him may be grouped around two main themes. First, that of dignity: his home is imbued with a sense of decency and restraint, and any who fell short of these qualities would be firmly recalled to order. It is the mother who maintains the purity and sanctity of the household. 'The lady of the house played a triple role: she was the guardian of the moral tradition and embodied the virtues of self-sacrifice and purity as well as those of charm and grace. Thus our families, like those of Spain, were dominated by a matriarchy which enshrined both moral and aesthetic values.' This austerity tempered by the matron's smile found expression in the family gatherings (*tertulias hogareñas*) which, the writer tells us, were 'worth more than meetings in other people's houses or in the elegant but conventional world of clubs ... These gatherings were marked by tenderness, dignity, discretion and reserve–sometimes even by a silence which had its own meaning.' The Christian hidalgo's second main characteristic was devotion to others. He devoted himself to his family, his servants, his far-off relatives, his home town and the nation itself. At all times he was vividly aware of his duty and responsibilities. While the oligarch at Lima thought only of his interests and pleasures, the good citizen of Arequipa felt bound to help all those who stood in need. But, being a Christian, he was modest and took care to purge himself of all boastfulness; or rather, he was proud only of his modesty.

This provincial aristocracy as Víctor Andrés Belaúnde describes it has a flavour of archaism. One of the bases of its power has disappeared, namely its money. This appears from the history of the Belaúnde family itself. Víctor Andrés's father was, we are told, 'by his own and his wife's inheritance' the owner of several haciendas in the Majes valley in which Arequipa lies. These estates should not be confused with the *latifundios* of Puno or Cuzco: even the biggest of them are small in area, devoted to cattle-raising, mixed farming and viniculture. 'At that time,'[1] Víctor Andrés goes on, 'the brandy produced in the Majes valley fetched a high price and brought in a useful profit'. But then came misfortune: 'The southern railway line[2] was built, and brought to our part of the country the cane-sugar brandy which is made around Cuzco: so that ours, though of far

[1] I.e. about 1860, just before the construction of the railway, which was made possible by the fabulous profits that accrued to the Peruvian government between 1850 and 1870 from the sale of island guano in Europe.
[2] Running from Cuzco to the port of Mollendo, through Puno and Arequipa.

better quality, suddenly fell to one-sixth of its value.' To weather the storm, Víctor Andrés's father turned himself from a wine-merchant into a dealer in alpaca and vicuña wool, which he bought in the Puno and Cuzco areas to the north. 'He opened an establishment for scouring wool (*lavandería de lanas*) and extended his business as far as Puno and Cuzco.'

Arequipa is not in fact the most typical place from which to illustrate the decay of the regional aristocracy which set in after about 1860. It is true that this southern city grew less important as the political and economic dominance of Lima increased. But, late in the nineteenth century, Arequipa still gave the republic such great men as Nicolás de Piérola, and its principal families, small as their fortunes were compared to those of the Lima plutocracy, furnished in each generation their quota of able men. The career of Víctor Andrés Belaúnde himself–writer, orator, scholar, diplomat, enjoying the highest prestige at home and abroad[1]–illustrates this tradition of the country squirearchy, a class into which the most opulent families of the capital are glad to marry and which is capable of filling the highest public offices with dignity. But diminishing wealth and the loss of power and prestige imposed heavy sacrifices on the less fortunate.

Trujillo and its aristocracy suffered a similar decline. In his biography of Haya de la Torre, Felipe Cossío del Pomar describes the aristocratic atmosphere in which the future leader of Apra was brought up. 'Powerful Trujillo families, with all of which Víctor Raúl Haya de la Torre was connected, were prominent both in colonial times and after independence. His ancestors on both sides (his parents were first cousins) are also to be found in the royalist, anti-independence camp, fighting for King Ferdinand VII.' In whichever direction we turn, whether among the royalists or the liberators, we find the ancestors of great patrician families listed by Cossío: those of Cardónez, Bracamonte, marquis of Herrera and count of Valdemar, Lieutenant-General Martínez de Pinillos and the Urdapilletas . . . This society with its respect for nobility is no less bent on maintaining the principles of honour (*honorabilidad*) than that of Arequipa. 'The women are devout, strict and attached to tradition.' The Trujillo gentry could give points to those of Arequipa as regards honour, dignity and respect for oneself and others. But, at the turn

---

[1] He is a former president of the General Assembly of the United Nations, and the uncle of the present president of Peru, Sr. Fernando Belaúnde Terry.

of the century, things changed at Trujillo too, and in a much more radical and dramatic way than at Arequipa:

'Suddenly the big limited companies and corporations made their appearance, the banks and great export firms which sold abroad the sugar produced in the Chicama valley. Foreign firms gradually took over haciendas, mines and commercial enterprises. Titled families found themselves in increasing distress. The former masters of the land, dispossessed and discomfited, took refuge in administrative jobs which, minor as they were, could be accepted without loss of face and without compromising rank and dignity.'[1]

When the influx of cane alcohol ruined the wine-growers of the Majes valley, the father of Víctor Andrés Belaúnde restored his fortunes by going into the wool business. But to the aristocrats of Trujillo, any such resort to commerce would have been a degradation: the only course open to them was to engage in some respectable but ill-paid employment such as the legal profession. Their society had received as it were a direct hit, of a different magnitude to that which affected Arequipa. The exploitation of the hydraulic resources of the Chicama valley involved a rapid concentration of land in the hands of a few foreign companies; and the ruin of the former landowners was completed by the installation of powerful factories for the processing of huge quantities of sugar-cane. The big business interests having thus secured control of all local sources of wealth, the Trujillo gentry had no other recourse left than to go into exile at Lima or to remain, dignified but resentful, at home.

'Of course', as Cossío del Pomar observes, 'some of these great families managed to preserve their patrimony intact; but very few were able to adapt themselves to modern economic methods and to adopt the invaders' techniques without losing the tradition of chivalry and dignity (*sin perder la tradición caballeresca de la dignidad*)'. It was amid the ruins of this traditional society that Haya de la Torre spent his youth. 'When Víctor Raúl began his rebellious life at Trujillo, the foreign companies were working without respect for God, for the country, for their human capital or for any law except that of maximum returns. Fantastic concessions, such as a free port, were made to them by those in power. It was a policy of surrender (*entreguismo*); the populace, ruthlessly abandoned to its fate, contemplated with indifference and apathy the state of public affairs, conducted by ineffectual authorities.'

[1] Felipe Cossío del Pomar, *Víctor Raúl*, p. 22.

2

The Dependence of the Middle Classes

The Spanish term *clase media* is no clearer than its equivalent in other languages. To give it any sort of definition, we must realise that it refers to a hierarchical conception of society. Peasants are those who till the land and artisans those who produce useful objects: the status of these social groups derives from their activities. Marxian sociologists define the worker in terms of his 'situation': he provides the labour force but has no say as regards its use and no control over its product. The denomination 'middle' indicates that those who apply it to themselves, or to whom it is applied, are primarily concerned with their relationship towards those above or below them. Being neither at the top nor at the bottom, they define themselves negatively: they do not belong to the governing class, yet are distinguished from the masses. In a country where the oligarchy is so sharply distinguished as in Peru, the middle class may be expected to define itself by its exclusion, whether forced or voluntary, from the élite. And, as the country also comprises a large percentage of illiterate Indians, the middle class is bound to be conscious of all that distinguishes it from them: the more so as the hierarchic scale is symbolically reinforced by the racial and cultural distinction between Indians and non-Indians.

If, by the term 'middle class', we understand those groups which, although they do not take part in great political decisions, have opinions about these and express them whether they are asked to or not, such a social class cannot fail to carry weight in the nation's political life. It makes a great deal of difference whether the middle class is disposed to make any contribution or merely to play the role

58

of a *tertius gaudens*, and whether or not it is prepared to enter into a coalition with the oligarchy. If the great ones can succeed in keeping it in a state of dependency, they are assured of perpetual power; if it resists or refuses, their primacy is jeopardised. But this tidy description runs into difficulties. In the first place we must define or at least identify the groups that we elect to call 'middle' in terms of power and prestige. On this, observers are far from unanimous: some regard the middle class as small and weak, while others on the contrary emphasise the rapidity of its expansion.

The numerical increase of the middle class, the variety of its composition and the ambiguity of its values

The first of these two views held the field at the end of the last century. It can still be found in '*Perú, estructura social*', a lecture delivered by the ex-President Bustamante Rivero during the first *semana social* ('social week') in 1959; but it is noteworthy that Bustamante combines it with the second view. 'Until the last few years, it may be said that we had no real middle class. Our population was divided into two groups: that of the rich ruling class and that of the poor and downtrodden.' This dualistic approach is qualified by a remark on which the speaker did not elaborate: 'Certain groups which might be regarded as intermediary, such as bureaucrats and skilled employees, had no class characteristics, but were parasitic appendages of the governing class.' A small body without class-consciousness, dependent on the rich and powerful–such was the description of the Peruvian middle class given by Bustamante, who adds: 'Moreover, their means of livelihood ranked them with the broad masses of the population.' However, after analysing with much insight the causes of the slow development and atrophy of the middle class, he continues: 'But new factors are already transforming the scene. Demographic growth, industrialisation, the modernisation of firms, the increasing scale of public administration and the development of transport ... have swelled the ranks of the middle class with newcomers who possess a certain degree of education and training.'

At this point, the reader is inclined to put the point-blank question: is the middle class too small or too large? It must be one or the other. Let us begin by giving a few figures for the various elements which make up the middle sector of society. Take the liberal professions. There are in Peru 3,000 doctors and 2,000 chemists. The legal profession is much more numerous in the sierra zone, for reasons I have analysed elsewhere.[1] The proportion of lawyers to doctors there is at least five to one, and the former figure would be doubled if we were to include the class of *tinterillos*–more or less unqualified pettifoggers whose forensic talents are at the disposal of the vast body of litigants. The state maintains 40,000 primary schoolteachers and 10,000 teachers in secondary schools, including technical colleges.[2] Non-state education, which is by no means wholly in the hands of the church, employs 5,000 teachers in grammar schools, that is to say about as many as the state, but is a good deal weaker on the technical side. Higher education, which is self-governing and not covered by official statistics, employs between 2,000 and 3,000 professors, lecturers etc., working more or less full-time. It is estimated that the number of teachers of all kinds has at least doubled in the last ten years.

But, since the beginning of the century, a new factor has developed which makes it inappropriate to define the middle class by purely educational criteria: namely the mass production of consumer goods for an ever-widening market. Even in poor countries–those where the *per capita* income is low and very unevenly distributed–goods which were once the exclusive privilege of the few are becoming available, if not to the whole population, at least to that large part of it which belongs to the modern economic sector. Cars, refrigerators, radio and television sets are not reserved for the oligarchy, but are within the reach of customers who, by their income or training, belong to the middle or lower class of town-dwellers.

This is shown by the fact that the number of cars owned in Lima alone rose from 15,000 in 1945 to 85,000 in 1961. The total number of private cars and lorries for the whole country in 1961 was about 155,000, and the annual increase is said to be 8–10,000.[3] A similar story holds good for radios, and in Lima alone there are over 160,000 television sets.

The distinctive feature of the old-style middle class, the smallness of which was deplored by liberals and positivists at the end of the last century, was its degree of professional qualification. This criterion

[1] F. Bourricaud, *Changements à Puno*, pp. 52–5.
[2] Cf. *Boletín de estadística peruana*, 1962, pp. 780–94.
[3] Based on the estimates in *Análisis de la realidad socio-económica del Perú, Primer borrador*, mimeographed, August 1963.

has not lost all its force: to belong to the middle class, one must have had at least a year or two's secondary schooling. But opportunities are not the exclusive preserve of *doctores* or graduates: they are available in some degree to the whole urban population, including its most under-privileged members, and the inhabitants of shanty-towns (*barriadas*) are, from this point of view, closer to the petty bourgeoisie of officials, clerks etc. than to the native rural population from which they have sprung. This suggests that we should distinguish, within the middle class, a narrow sector of the old type and a larger, more modern one. The former would comprise the liberal professions, officers and officials of middle and lower grades, including teachers and technicians. The second group, defined by its level and style of consumption, comprises a large slice of the urban population, especially that of Lima. The distinction between the two groups has its origin in the increasingly rapid development of the educational system, which we should now consider.

An analysis of the Peruvian schools system soon reveals the ambiguity of the middle class's scale of values. An instructive debate took place on this subject at the beginning of the century between Deustua and Villarán. The former contended that: 'Work and character formation, morality and egotism are inseparable parts of the educational process . . . Work itself does not educate: it enriches, makes men alert and encourages good habits, but it is bound up with selfish motives which keep them in slavery. The sense of vocation which makes work happy and pleasant is an egotistical one . . . Liberty is not the result of work in itself . . . but of moral and aesthetic values . . . So-called logical values, and learning in general, do not suffice to confer upon work the extra dimension of freedom which is the essence of human personality.'[1]

Deustua's thesis is not so easy to interpret as it may at first seem. It is based on the theme of liberty and human dignity: systems of education are to be judged by their contribution to individual perfection. This appeal to transcendent values is the prelude to a condemnation of the pragmatic approach which sees education as nothing more than professional training. Basically, Deustua seeks to preserve 'humanist' values. The Christian hidalgos whom V. A. Belaúnde describes are prepared to recognise, on a level with themselves or slightly lower, the mass of respectable, able, hard-working

[1] *A propósito de un cuestionario sobre la reforma de la ley de instrucción*, Lima, 1914 (chap. 4), quoted in Mariátegui, *Siete ensayos*.

and somewhat hidebound professional men, who, given proper education, will learn to respect and observe the usages of good society. Mariátegui, for his part, dismisses this as a 'purely aristocratic' point of view, and castigates Deustua for not understanding that the basis of modern society is work.

Villarán, whom Mariátegui describes as an 'orthodox bourgeois', put forward the opposite thesis, according to which the content and methods of education should be dictated by social needs. However, Villarán was not a positivist but rather a disciple of the pragmatists. In 1908 he wrote, in *El factor económico en la educación nacional*:

'The main function of the school is not to instil morality: that is a task for religion and the family . . . The school is there to supply, not education in the wider sense but rather instruction, which Alfred Fouillée called "the abstract, universal instrument of work" . . . By so doing, it develops industry and economic effort, the fruits of which are of undeniable educative value . . . In this indirect fashion the school performs its true moral function, namely that of endowing the mass of the population with sufficient political strength to deter the governing class from abuses and preserve the equity of social relationships.'[1]

But here comes the main argument: 'From the point of view of increasing wealth, no profession can be compared with industry. Throughout human history there has probably never been a more powerful group of rich men than the New York or Chicago millionaires whose wealth staggers our imagination–and did they not all make their fortunes in business?' Villarán's utilitarianism is naïf rather than cynical: it rests on the premise that he who enriches himself enriches the community. 'While the doctor gives us health, the teacher knowledge, and the lawyer and soldier their protection, it is the farmer, the businessman and the manufacturer who give us our daily bread, house and feed us and provide us with enjoyments of every kind.'

While there is something to be said for the pragmatic line advocated by Villarán and others, it is doubtful whether it has attained the objects claimed for it. Classical studies are taking a back seat, but is professional education improving? What is certain, however, is that from the 1920s onwards the educational system, both secondary and higher, has embraced an ever larger sector of the population.

[1] Manuel Vicente Villarán, *Páginas escogidas*, Lima, 1962, p. 338.

By so doing it has become an unrivalled centre of communication and, as a result, is involved in a state of continuing crisis.

The university reform movement which was launched in 1917 at Córdoba in the Argentine spread rapidly to Peru. The principal demands put forward at Córdoba were endorsed at a students' congress at Cuzco in 1920, which was attended by the young Haya de la Torre. Describing pre-reform conditions, Mariátegui wrote: 'The colonial spirit in Peru was entrenched in the university.'[1] The same remark was made from a different viewpoint by the staunch Catholic V. A. Belaúnde, who described the university as the 'link between the Republic and the former colony'. The crises of the 1930s, which twice led to the closure of the San Marcos university at Lima, brought about radical changes in the composition of the faculty, the student admissions system and the methods and spirit of the institution. The reform movement took as its main slogans *asistencia libre* and *co-gobierno*, and its principal weapon was the *tacha*, to be described below. The purpose of the demand for *asistencia libre* was to exempt the student from putting in a prescribed number of attendances at lectures. This was, at first sight, a minor disciplinary question, but it tended in fact to alter the image of the traditional student. The *señorito*–the young man of good family–could spend all his time at the university because his parents and relatives sheltered him from material cares. But the *cholo* from the provinces, who must eventually work for a living, expected his teachers to equip him for a profession, and was less attracted than his predecessors by the beauties of classical culture. The object of *co-gobierno* was to associate the student with the conduct of university affairs. Between 1945 and 1948, and again under the university law of 1960, the students secured the right to be represented by delegates on the councils of the university and the various faculties in a proportion of one to two, and to take part in the elaboration of syllabuses and the election of professors and lecturers. Naturally, elections to the students' unions had a distinctly political character, the parties vying to secure control of San Marcos and other institutions. Apra dominated the university from 1945 to 1948, but their adversaries combined against them, and after Dr. Prado again became president in 1956 they did not succeed in re-establishing their former monopoly of influence.

Such a drastic change in teacher-pupil relations naturally excited fierce resistance from the old guard. The students retaliated with the

---

[1] *Siete ensayos*, chap. 4.

unconventional weapon of the *tacha*. This word signifies 'censure': if a professor is *tachado*, it means that his students have declared him unworthy to teach and outlawed him from the university. The students were careful, in using this procedure, to base themselves on academic grounds; but the victims were not slow in branding this as hypocrisy, and they were often justified in accusing the students of petty spite and mean revenge. The university became a battle arena, with the strike as one of its most typical institutions. If a newly-elected rector was unpopular with a majority of the students, or with the best-organised and most turbulent group amongst them, the student body would go on strike for an indefinite period.

University reform has accelerated the process of social mobilisation, which is not to say that it has made it as complete and effective as it ought to be. The heirs of Manual Vicente Villarán may well lament that the termination of the classical and humanistic monopoly, instead of leading to the formation of a technical élite, has merely helped to submerge the old colonial-style university under a wave of *cholos* from the provinces. At all events, the barriers are down, as will be shown by a few figures. In 1962 the number of pupils in public and private secondary schools amounted to 158,000,[1] to which must be added 40,000 from the industrial, commercial and agronomic branches of technical education. As regards higher learning, on 19 June 1957 San Marcos, which recruits from the whole country except for three provinces, had in its various faculties a total of 10,442 students.[2] It is true that 42·48 per cent of these belonged to the Lima agglomeration; but this is not excessive considering that Lima, which contains about 20 per cent of the country's population, offers by far the greatest opportunities of qualifying for university entrance. Thus we see that the university exerts a massive attraction outside the capital and the other urban centres. The objection that students come to Lima in such numbers because of the inadequacy of provincial universities will not hold water: for example, Cuzco, where there is an ancient and very vigorous university, sends only 140 students to San Marcos, or 1·3 per cent of its total student body. Every second Peruvian student attends a provincial university at least for his first two years. Nor is it only San Marcos which is opening its gates, or yielding to the pressure of young men and women

---

[1] Cf. *Boletín*, p. 783.
[2] *Censo del alumnado, Comisión coordinadora de la reforma, oficina central ejecutiva*, p. 17.

from up-country: provincial universities are springing up at Huamanga (Ayacucho), Huancayo, Ica and even Puno.

Another way of evaluating the rush to the universities is to investigate the students' social origins. In an enquiry carried out at San Marcos in 1957, 37 per cent of those questioned did not indicate their parents' profession. Of the remaining 63 per cent, 20 per cent were the sons of managers or skilled employees, 15 per cent of farmers and 12 per cent of artisans and day labourers (*jornaleros*). We should examine further the connotations of vague terms like 'farmers' and 'employees'. A 'farmer' may be an estate owner, a peasant or even a native *comunero*. On pages 90–1 of the census, under Group IV (agriculture), we find that out of a total of 993 replies, 878 relate to the sons of small farmers (*agricultores de pequeña escala*), as compared with 21 sons of big landowners (*hacendados*) and one son of an agricultural labourer (*peón*). Group I (*profesionales*) tells a similar tale: out of 1,216 who stated their origin, 210 were sons of primary school teachers (*normalistas y profesores de primaria*), 81 of secondary school teachers, 215 of lawyers, 119 of doctors and 185 of accountants. In Group III (*vendedores*) we notice the large proportion of sons of independent merchants or businessmen–1,025 out of 1,485, as against 35 sons of clerks and shop assistants (*dependientes en tiendas de comercio*). These figures amply confirm the impression I myself had as a teacher, that the students belong to the middle class (middle-middle or lower-middle) and are to a large extent provincials and *mestizos*. Adjustment is no easy matter for those who have had to make a brusque transition from traditional to urban life, and who are burdened in addition with an ambiguous cultural heritage.

The complex of problems linked with the mobility and 'marginality' of the middle class may be illustrated from the situation of the *cholo*–by which term I shall denote the half-caste on the way up, with a smattering of education, some experience of urban life and the ambition to make a career in the tertiary sector (that of the service industries). I am well aware that this formulation of the problem is open to question. It makes too exalted a figure of the *cholo*, and tends thereby to depreciate the middle class in general: a doctor or a schoolmaster is not a *cholo*. Nevertheless, a study of the latter's condition may help us to grasp the psychological and cultural problems of social mobilisation.

Mobilisation in a Dualistic Society

The marginality of the 'cholo'

The first point to notice is that, although the term *cholo* has been in current use ever since colonial times, the type which it denotes today is a modern one, not to be confused with the traditional half-caste who is still to be found here and there in small sierra towns. Here is a description of an artisan, one might almost say an artist, from the city of Ayacucho. 'Don Joaquín López Antay, though of Spanish origin on his mother's side, was an Indian: not a low-class Indian, but an owner of property in a small way.'[1] By reason of his artisanship, he enjoyed a respectable position. His fellow-townsmen treated him with the consideration due to an acknowledged master of his craft, and the gentry came all the way from Lima to buy the altarpieces that he carved and painted by the methods his grandmother had taught him long ago. Don Joaquín was not one to put up with disrespect. When, as Arguedas tells us, a visitor made fun of his accent, he rebuked him with: 'Each one of us talks in his own way, *señor.*' His dignity being respected by all, he bore no grudge or resentment against the traditional society in which he occupied a strictly defined but honourable place.

The old-style *mestizo* of this type neither merged with the Indian masses nor aspired to the society of the notables, the *vecinos* who owned the land and exercised local authority. Alongside the artisans and in a similarly intermediate position, the old society recognised men of law–magistrates, attorneys and *tinterillos*. (This last term, from the word for 'inkwell', denotes, with a touch of contempt, the small-town lawyer who, without being formally qualified and enjoying the magic title of 'doctor', is allowed to plead in court on certain conditions). The overcrowding of the legal profession has long been denounced as a vice of Peruvian society.[2] But, while the artisan is honoured for his skill and professional standing, the pettifogger (*leguleyo*) is an object of mistrust, a person from whom any kind of trick may be expected.

When the *comuneros* of Rumi, under their chief Rosendo Maqui, have to defend themselves against the *gamonal*, Don Alvaro Amenábar y Roldán, they soon find out the meaning of red-tape and

[1] José María Arguedas, 'El arte popular y la cultura mestiza', *Revista del Museo*, Lima, 1958, p. 150.
[2] Cf. the speech by Villarán (*Páginas escogidas*, pp. 316–17) in which the famous jurist lamented that there were more students of law than of medicine.

bureaucracy. 'These diligent functionaries rarely functioned and they spent their time passing on to their inferiors or superiors harmless communications . . . The judge was buried from sight behind mountains of stamped paper.'[1] The *comuneros* are defended by the *tinterillo* Bismarck Ruiz, whom Ciro Alegría depicts as a vulgar sensualist, drinking and roistering while his mistress, the *costeña*, wheedles money out of him. When the *comuneros* go to Ruiz's house, his wife greets them with the cry 'That man stays at La Costeña's. He's there all the time . . .' Sure enough, there they find him. There were a great many people there, and the sound of laughter, songs, and the merry strumming of guitars could be heard.'[2] Bismarck–'his eyes were bleary with drink and he reeked of brandy as though he had been soaked in it'[3]–offers beer to his clients, who have never drunk anything but the local *chicha*, and asks for an advance of fifty soles to be going on with . . . But in the end he is easily circumvented by Don Amenábar and the latter's lawyer. 'It would take too long to tell all Bismarck Ruiz's lies and promises, all the judge's and clerks' subtleties and chicanery, all Amenábar's scheming.'[4] The *tinterillo* takes his clients' money and abandons them to their enemies.

While the half-caste is often depicted as a traitor, the typical *cholo* figures as an intermediary. His dependent position is well analysed in *Yawar Fiesta*, by José María Arguedas. This novel is set in the town of Puquio in former times, with the *cholos*–or, as they are locally called, *chalos*–occupying a position between the Indians and the *mistis* (whites). 'The *chalos* are sometimes found amongst the *vecinos*, sometimes amongst the Indians in their *ayllus*. They do not live in the *mistis*' quarter, but in alleys adjoining it. Whether they like it or not, they are reckoned as belonging to the *ayllu* from which they originally came . . . The head of an *ayllu* is appointed by the prefect from among the *chalos*.' This passage illustrates the 'marginality' of the *cholo*, who is neither fish nor fowl. He no longer lives in the Indian quarter, but is liable to be reminded at any time of his Indian origin, of the fact that he belongs to this or that *ayllu*. He is chosen by the prefect or subprefect to exercise authority among the *comuneros*. As a go-between he is suspect to both *mistis* and Indians, for he is 'sometimes with the one and sometimes with the other'. This is illustrated by the following detail. 'When night fell, the half-castes clustered round the doors of taverns and cafés to see what the *mistis* were drinking and

[1] *Broad and Alien is the World*, chap. 3, p. 68.   [2] Ibid., pp. 69–70.
[3] Ibid., p. 73.   [4] Ibid., p. 200.

what games they were playing. Sometimes they would go inside and watch, standing against the wall so as not to be in the way.'[1] The half-caste *cholo* does not share in the *misti*'s social life. He does not drink with him, or get drunk on the same tipple. In another passage, the notables offer the subprefect a glass of champagne, while the *cholos*, who are not invited, repair to the tavern to drink beer. The *cholo* also shows his deference by standing against the wall 'so as not to be in the way'.

How does the *cholo* earn his living? Arguedas distinguishes two types. Firstly the servant: 'On rainy days, people of consequence would call up a *cholo* whom they happened to see passing in the street and send him to fetch their coats and umbrellas or to perform any kind of errand.'[2] But there is also the commercial type of *cholo*, hard-working and a great traveller. 'They do business on the coast, where they exchange meat, wheat and cheese for contraband liquor, soap and candles.' This second type is distinguished by his mobility and his function of trading the products of the sierra for those of the coast. Arguedas adds a final touch: 'Many of these half-castes have friends in the *ayllus* and stand up for the Indians, who call them Don Norberto, Don Leandro or Don Aniceto.' The *cholo* is in between the Indian and the *misti*: he may either throw in his lot (*entregarse*) with the latter or set up as the former's protector, in which case the notables will look on him as a firebrand and troublemaker (*cabecilla*).

Ten years pass. The next generation of *cholos* migrates to Lima. A road has been opened from Puquio to the coast, and 'by it more than two thousand people from Puquio, Lucanas and Coracora reached Lima, while others streamed to the capital from the northern, central and southern sierra'.[3] This first migration of the 1920s was directed towards the tertiary sector of the economy: *serranos* flocked to the university and schools, factories and business houses of all kinds. How did the new arrivals ensconce themselves? Those who had come early on, for instance as the servants of Puquio notables who were rich enough to maintain a house in the capital, 'looked after those who arrived later by road . . . Without being organised by anyone, the arrival of the *serranos* from Puquio and elsewhere took place in an orderly fashion, with one *cholo* helping another . . . The *mistis* helped the people of their own class, introducing them into "society". Students helped one another as far as their allowances permitted: the

[1] Arguedas, *Yawar Fiesta*, pp. 17–18. [2] Ibid., p. 18.
[3] Ibid., p. 91.

poorer ones found an attic near the university or the school of mining, or a servant's room at the end of a corridor or under a staircase, or else they lodged in one of the old mansions which are nowadays on the point of collapse and are let out, room by room, to workmen and destitute people.'[1]

It will be noted that the scale of the migration was fairly limited, affecting as it did only 2,000 people from the Puquio area; and also that it took place in a systematic fashion. There are three aspects of this. In the first place, the forerunners spy out the land for their friends and relatives who have stayed at home; then, within each category—*cholos* and *mistis*—the pioneers control and regulate the flow; finally, the newcomers are looked after by those who have come to the capital ahead of them and have urged them to follow suit. After the provincials have reached Lima, they continue to live in local groups. Those from Puquio, for example, 'gravitated to the Mascona quarter, where they founded a club—the Centro Unión Lucanas'.[2] There is an ample literature about these provincial clubs at Lima. Arguedas' description brings out two points. Firstly, their variety of ethnic composition: although the bulk of the members of the Centro Unión Lucanas are natives of Puquio, the captain of the club's football team is a Lima negro. Secondly, the moving spirits are students whose closest associates are a community of small artisans. 'When the officers of the Lucanas Club decided to turn it into a sporting and cultural centre . . . they met as usual in Gutiérrez the tailor's room, under the chairmanship of the student Escobar.'[3] There is a list of their names and offices: Escobar was elected president; the student Tincopa, secretary; the *chauffeur* Martínez, assistant secretary; the *tailor* Gutiérrez, treasurer; the *bus-driver* Rodríguez, the *workmen* Vargas and Córdova, and the *clerks* named Guzmán . . . were elected members of the committee.[4]

Escobar proceeds to make a speech defining the aims of the new society. 'There are today hundreds of provincial associations at Lima, defending community interests against the encroachments of landlords, government authorities and priests.' The club is primarily an 'organisation for the defence of indigenism'[5] and of the Indians; but, not content with defending *comuneros* against tyranny, their founders seek to 'raise the cultural level of members by organising

---

[1] Ibid., p. 93.   [2] Ibid., p. 94.   [3] Ibid., p. 94.   [4] Italics added. F. B.
[5] The name of an association which historians regard as the origin of indigenism. Cf. Mariátegui, op. cit.

lectures, building up libraries and even publishing reviews'. This cultural function is performed in two ways: the leaders teach new arrivals to fend for themselves and survive, but also give them a chance to 'keep alive the memory of their native soil by forming bands of musicians and organising *fiestas* such as they used to hold in their villages'.[1]

Having situated *Yawar Fiesta* in space and time, we may briefly indicate the plot of the novel, which illustrates the *cholos*' relationship to the authorities on the one hand and the Indians on the other. By a decree of the Ministry of the Interior, the Puquio authorities are forbidden to allow the Indians, as hitherto, to take part in the *corrida* held on the national day, 28 July. This decision provokes different reactions among different social groups. The notables (*alimeñados*), who wish to curry favour with the subprefect, applaud. 'All thinking people agree with you, *señor subprefecto*. Up to now the Puquio bullfight has been a scandal, a disgrace to our town. African savages could not have behaved worse. But we, *señor subprefecto*, are not like the *cholos* who have no idea how to fight a bull but throw themselves on its horns as soon as they have a drop of drink inside them.'[2] The Indians, however,[3] have their own ideas: they have determined to capture a fierce bull (*toro bravo*), the famous Misitu whose strength is a byword throughout the countryside. Their challenge is in fact aimed less at Misitu than at the bull's owner, a rough-spoken member of the local gentry, Don Julián Arangüena.

To organise a civilised *corrida*, '*a la criolla*', a matador is needed. So 'at the beginning of July, the chairman of the Centro Unión Lucanas received the following telegram: "Please engage *torero* on behalf municipal council. Letter follows." ... The student Escobar was astonished that the Puquio gentry should be giving up their Indian-style *corrida* of their own accord.' However, he enquires at the Ministry and finds that this is indeed the government's wish. Escobar felt reassured. 'The Centro will see to it that the government's circular is carried out. We'll go to Puquio! No longer will Indian blood be shed in the arena to amuse the *mistis*. This time they're scuppered (*están fregados*). The government's on our side—this is our day of victory!" '[4] Thus the first impulse is one of triumph—the government is on our side, it is we who hold the whip-hand. 'This time they'll see

---

[1] Arguedas, op. cit., p. 94.   [2] Ibid., p. 54.
[3] *Cholos* is used indiscriminately in this passage for the *ayllu* Indians and the *cholos* properly so called.
[4] Op. cit., p. 97.

what we're made of–they've laid the knife to their own throats. It's a miracle! Even if I have to dress up as a policeman and take pot-shots at them, it's we who represent the forces of law and order.'[1] Escobar's delirious wonder at the 'miracle' brings out the ambiguity of the *cholos'* position, resting as it does on borrowed power. But all doubts vanish at the turn of events which turns the rebels of Lima into defenders of public order at Puquio, and the scene ends on a note of rejoicing. After the meeting, Escobar gets up and walks over to the portrait of Mariátegui, the communist leader, whom he addresses as if he were there in person: 'Master, you will be pleased by what we are going to do: your words were not in vain, we are going to bring them to life. Have no fear, we shall not die before we behold the justice that you predicted.' Thereupon a member of the group, the 'bishop', takes up his guitar, and 'all seven of them gathered under the portrait and began to sing in Quechua:

> *"They say that all men are afraid*
> *When death approaches;*
> *But have courage, brother, and do not weep."* '

The Centro Lucanas decides to send representatives to Puquio with the *torero*: but already things are going wrong. Don Julián Arangüena, the owner of Misitu, is doing all in his power to see that the government circular remains a dead letter. On the other hand, the parish priest, the mayor and some of the gentry are on the sub-prefect's side, and so our *cholos* find themselves in the same camp as the notables whom they regard as their enemies. 'We know that lot– Don Demetrio, Don Antenor and the *cura*. If they're in cahoots, we'd better watch out. Any agreement between them is bound to be bad for us.' Especially as a certain Don Pancho Jiménez, to whom they are attached despite his brutality, has got on the wrong side of the subprefect and has been put in prison. 'Let's go and see for ourselves.'[2] So the *cholos* of Centro Lucanas arrive in Puquio on the very day on which the Indians win their bet with Don Julián and succeed in capturing Misitu, whom they bring 'like a puppy on a lead' from his mountain lair towards the village.

Escobar and his friends first meet the Puquio notables in the subprefect's office. 'Don Julián caught sight of the student Escobar, the chauffeur Martínez, Tincopa, Vargas and all the other "damned *cholos*" (*cholos renegados*) as he termed them, the ringleaders of the

Centro Unión Lucanas. Infuriated by their presence, he growled "What are these riff-raff[1] doing here?"' A conversation ensues between Don Julián and the subprefect, interrupted by Escobar. Someone having pointed out that if the bull arrives in the village, even on a tether, there may be a panic among the schoolchildren who are to parade on the eve of the national day, Escobar exclaims to Don Julián: 'I suppose you think our schoolboys are like you, such thugs that they wouldn't be afraid of a wild bull!' The other replies: 'You've forgotten your childhood, my young friend. I expect you'd have peed with fright, but our youngsters aren't such milksops.' At this point the chauffeur Martínez pushes to the fore and stands beside the subprefect. 'As for you, Don Julián,' he cries, 'you're nothing but a crook and a blackguard.'[2]

In this way the *cholos* stand up to Don Julián and his companions.

'Don Antenor and Don Demetrio were speechless with amazement, and looked confusedly at each other. So these *cholos* had no sooner set foot in the village than they treated the subprefect as an equal, not to mention themselves, the representatives of the oldest families in Puquio! ... At the back of the room a little crowd of half-castes were craning their necks to look at Martínez, Guzmán and Escobar the student, who had actually dared to interrupt Don Julián and call him a thief to his face, and before the subprefect too! They felt like rushing forward, embracing Escobar and triumphally chairing this Indian who had learnt Spanish so that he could give a piece of his mind to the cruellest *gamonal* in Puquio.'[3]

Escobar had indeed displayed courage in bearding Don Julián ... But after leaving the subprefect, the *cholos* go off to meet the Indians who are leading Misitu down from the mountain. The tone of the story changes. Night falls, and the mood of triumph subsides. 'There was no-one to be seen around the fountain of the Chaupi quarter, and beyond it all was dark, except for a night-light encased in leather which hung from the lintel of the chapel door.'[4] Guzmán and Escobar begin to talk:

' "It would take us a thousand years to cure the Indians of their superstitions," said Guzmán, gazing at the square which, on this eve of the festival, lay dark and deserted.

' "It all depends. If we had a decent government, a government of our own, it wouldn't take so long to stop them being afraid of the

---

[1] The Quechua term *k'anras* is much stronger and almost untranslatable.
[2] Op. cit., p. 150.   [3] Ibid., pp. 151–2.   [4] Ibid., p. 155.

earth and the sky, ravines and rivers . . . But what can you expect of the sort of government that backs up *gamonales* like Don Julián? . . . They're the people who keep the Indians enslaved to darkness and fear and 'mythical terrors', as we call them at the university . . . But if we had the power, then things would be different. We'd do away with the causes that have kept atavism and slavery alive for all these centuries." '[1]

At first sight this passage is not particularly striking. Its theme is that of 'enlightenment', of which the *cholos* see themselves as the apostles and which is opposed to 'mythical, atavistic fear'. But there are some interesting *nuances* beneath the surface. To begin with, the condition of progress is a 'strong government', and as soon as this government 'of our own' is installed, everything will go quickly and easily. We, whose historic task is to liberate the Indian, are powerless as long as stony-hearted *gamonales* like Don Julián are at the head of affairs; but all this will change tomorrow when we have taken their place. Guzmán's reply is a challenge to this over-simplified view and to the crude intellectualism of Escobar, who sees the Indian as a child to whom the *cholo* is to bring enfranchisement. 'When I heard' says Guzmán, 'that the K'ayau Indians were going up into the mountains to fetch Misitu, I felt angry and sorrowful because there was going to be another massacre of Indians after all. And yet, now that we are on our way to meet the *ayllu* people, I feel like shouting for joy.' Why this change of attitude? He explains:

'Do you realise what it means that the K'ayaus should have the courage to go chasing Misitu in the Negromayo forest? They've done it out of pride, as a challenge, to show their strength, the strength of them all combined when they choose to work together. It was the same thing when they made the Nazca road. Of course there were intellectuals at Lima who said "These Indians are crazy–they're working for their exploiters". And yet today it was on that road that you and I came from Lima . . . and it's their example which made me understand and decide to defend their cause, when I travelled to Lima myself by the road they made for us . . . And today, do you realise it, Martínez the chauffeur, who was born in an *ayllu* in Puquio, Martínez the Indian has put the most powerful *gamonal* in Lucanas in his place and humiliated him for good and all–the famous Don Julián who calls us "damned *cholos*"!'

The enthusiasm of Guzmán, declaiming on an empty square in

[1] Ibid., p. 156.

Puquio, is comparable to that of Escobar in Lima under the portrait of Mariátegui: 'Our day will come.' His optimism springs from two convictions. Firstly, the native masses are inspired by an irresistible force, driving roads and–literally–moving mountains; and when Martínez speaks his mind to Don Julián, what strikes Guzmán most is that he is an Indian, born in an *ayllu* at Puquio. But the Indians' strength belongs to the realm of the unconscious: they do not themselves know what they are doing or why, and least of all do they know, or perhaps even wish to know, the consequences of their acts. Why have they gone to fetch Misitu? Objectively, their action is absurd, and yet it may be of the greatest symbolic importance: by capturing Misitu they have 'killed an *auki*',[1] one of the gods whom, in their fear and imagination, they believe to dwell in the heart of the mountain. Without knowing it, they are moved by elemental forces: the desire to assert their power, to hurl down and accept a challenge. This spontaneity is beyond the grasp of intellectuals, who take fright or mock at the 'stupid Indians'; yet it is these stupid, obscurantist Indians who have opened up the way for Escobar, Guzmán and their friends to tread.

If we compare Guzmán's speech to Escobar's, we see that it inverts the relationship between Indians and *cholos*. In Escobar's eyes, the *cholo* is called on to liberate the Indian; to Guzmán, revolutionary strength resides in the mass of the *comuneros*. But the two classes of Indians and *cholos* are not rigorously distinct. The same individuals feel themselves, and are felt, now to be *cholos*, now half-castes and now Indians. We have seen that Guzmán calls his friend Martínez both the 'chauffeur' and the 'Indian'. But the following remark of his is even more revealing: 'On the day when *they* (the Indians) become what *we* already are, *cholos renegados* as Don Julián calls us, we shall lead the country to such greatness as no-one can imagine.'[2] In short, the two groups must exchange qualities and merge into each other. The Indians will provide strength and the intellectuals light; and the mixture of the two will be the 'dirty *cholo*' who demands, provokes and glories in the domination exercised over him by Don Julián and the other 'stony-hearted *gamonales*' ...

After thus discoursing about the Indian and his strength, our *cholos* come face to face with the *comuneros* who are bringing Misitu down from the mountain. After the first joyful meeting, 'the Indians started asking questions about the road to the coast, and life down

¹ Ibid., p. 157.   ² Ibid., p. 157.

there; some even wanted to know about Lima. The *cholos* answered to the best of their ability, after which they tried to explain to the Indians that if they had captured Misitu it had nothing to do with an *auki*, the mountain deity to whom they ascribed such power: it was because they were brave and "man can always conquer the animals". The Indians pretended to believe them.'[1] This didactic approach of the *cholos*, taking seriously their role as bringers of enlightenment, contrasts with the sudden impulse of Martínez the chauffeur, who springs towards the Indians who are leading the bull with the words: 'Here, I'll pull it on behalf of the Centro.' – 'Why shouldn't I?' – 'No, you'll hurt your hands. Besides, I've a right to because I'm more Indian than you are.'[2]

I need not describe in detail the rivalry between the two comrades as to which of them is 'more Indian'. But it is interesting to note how, after adopting a detached attitude towards the natives' excitement, Martínez and Escobar plunge headlong into it. Martínez is set on making a triumphal entry into Puquio. 'The bull was pulling hard and the halter scorched his hands, but as he walked along shoulder to shoulder with the Indians he felt full of pride . . . his arm was strong enough for the task and he pulled lustily.'

The *cholos* were cock-a-hoop; but next day they had to change their tune. For was it not Escobar, Martínez and his friends who had hired the *torero* at Lima and brought him to Puquio, in order that the subprefect and notables might give effect to the circular forbidding amateur bullfighting? And had they not, by so doing, placed themselves in the authorities' camp and cut themselves off from fellowship with the Indian masses, dear as this was to them? Next morning, before the *corrida*, Martínez and his friends try to gild the pill for the *comuneros*, who are curious about the former's companion, the fair-haired young Spanish *torero* from Lima. Martínez, who is asked to explain, starts to equivocate: 'He's a chap from Lima, the *mistis* sent for him. They say he's a good *torero*, but of course he'll be no match for Misitu.' The Indians, who are still tipsy after an all-night carousal, are not convinced. The *cholos* debate among themselves. 'It's no use, they're determined to get their necks broken, what can we do about it?' After arguing this way and that, making excuses for the Indians' pig-headedness ('We went about it the wrong way . . . we didn't explain properly . . . it would have been better to call off the bullfight altogether'), Escobar and his friends go and see the subprefect. 'It's a

[1] Ibid., p. 161.   [2] Ibid., p. 162.

bad business', Martínez explains. 'The *comuneros* say that they brought Misitu here and no-one else has the right to fight him . . . It's hard to make them see reason.'[1] The subprefect is not at a loss. 'The only argument these brutes understand is force.' And he orders the police to make it known that the first Indian who jumps into the arena will be fired on.

The *cholos* have come to the end of the road. Unable to move the subprefect or to persuade the Indians, they resign themselves to watching the latter try conclusions with Misitu. Their last hope of averting the slaughter rests on the little *torero* from Lima. 'If he shows up well at the beginning and makes some good passes, perhaps the Indians will stay quiet behind the parapets–he'll magnetise them.'[2] But the inevitable happens, and once again the *corrida* of 28 July claims its toll of disembowelled Indians.

Thus the *cholos*' failure is complete. Without considering how far Arguedas' pessimism is justified, I would point out that it belongs to a tradition of Peruvian literature. In *Broad and Alien is the World* the *cholo* type is represented by two characters, the proud brigand Vásquez and Benito Castro, who both come to grief and are murdered. The aspect of Arguedas' portrait of the *cholo* to which I wish to draw attention is that of inner conflict and contradiction. Born and brought up in the native quarter of Puquio, Escobar and his friends belong both to the traditional society and to the modern world which was taking shape in Lima in the 1930s. They see themselves as distinguished by unalterable hostility towards the gentry, the *gamonales*. But their ambivalence is best expressed by their attitude towards the Indians. They see themselves as defenders of the oppressed *comunero*; and as well as their mission as bringers of justice they are trying to affirm and proclaim their own personal identity, which they first displayed in opposition to the *gamonales*. But they are nonplussed by the Indian, because they do not know what he is or what they are themselves. Are they to civilise the *comunero* and rescue him from his ancestral fears, at the risk of turning him into a half-caste like themselves, a *cholo renegado*? Should they trust his spontaneity to discover new ways and discern its own objectives? In the end, neither course is open to them. For their task of education to succeed, time and a friendly government are needed, and there is no guarantee of either. If they leave the Indian to himself, making an act of faith in his spontaneity, that elemental

---

[1] Ibid., pp. 170–1. [2] Ibid., p. 175.

strength may not only turn against them but destroy itself. In the final scene of *Yawar Fiesta*, the *comunero* Hualpa–deaf to advice, stubbornly disobedient and fuddled by alcohol, impelled by the death-wish to assert himself by a supreme act of denial–leaps into the arena and impales himself on the bull's horns in a mad, sublime sacrifice which may be called suicide.

Violence, cunning and cowardice

The *cholo*, at bottom, is well aware that he has little chance of shaping the world as he would like it to be. Since, however, he cannot accept the existing order of things–the position to which he is condemned and the ignominious treatment of the wretched Indians–he is the victim of an agonising conflict. By making a frontal attack he not only courts failure but is likely to bring the worst calamities and retribution upon others, above all those whom he seeks to defend. Can he then resort to subterfuge, using craft instead of violence?

The quality of *viveza*, which denotes a mixture of mental agility and cunning, is never attributed to the Indian, whereas *vivo* is a stock epithet for the *cholo*. It so happens that in *Yawar Fiesta* we are not given a picture of the type of *cholo* who wins through by a combination of luck and skill. True, Escobar and his friends enjoy the brief illusion of having played their cards skilfully, when they are able to congratulate the subprefect on throwing Don Julián into gaol. But they are mistaken as to the former's motives in thus disciplining the most reactionary *gamonal* in Puquio. 'Our congratulations, *señor subprefecto*: it is not every day that we meet so just and energetic an official.' But the subprefect is not a philanthropist, and the *cholos* are soon undeceived. Next day, when it is clear that the Indians will not listen to reason and insist on their free-for-all *corrida*, the subprefect interrupts impatiently: 'That's all rubbish (*vainas*)! The only answer to these brutes is force.' Arguedas does not present his *cholos* as particularly cunning or even particularly enterprising. Indeed, they take scarcely any initiative whatever: and the fact that they take any part in the action at all is due to the Puquio notables asking them by telegram to find a *torero*. At the dénouement they are as passive as at the beginning–drifting with the tide, at the mercy of circumstances.

Let us go down a little in the social scale and see how Benito

77

Castro, one of the *cholos* in Alegría's novel, gets out of difficulties. Benito, who is the adopted son of the wise old Rosendo Maqui, has had to leave his native village. For reasons that do not concern us here, he has parted company with his *patrón*, and, having no desire to fall into the latter's clutches again, has embraced the wandering life of a *cholo* and become a muleteer. 'Heading south, against wind and destiny, . . . one day he reached a place called Pueblo Libre.' It so happens that, as he stands in the main square, a small-town demagogue named Pajuelo, 'a dark man, about thirty years old, in a worn, dark suit but wearing a necktie',[1] is making an electoral speech to his supporters. The police come and break up the meeting, and Benito finds himself arrested. He is taken off to the subprefect of the province, who, when he finds him to be a stranger to the village, asks where he is from. He replies 'I'm from Mollepata'[2]–which is not true. He lies because, if he said who he was and where he came from, he might be sent back to his *patrón*. In order to cover his tracks he pretends to come from Mollepata, far off in the northern sierra: if the ruse is not detected, he is safe.

The subprefect, who is no fool, realizes that Benito is trying to deceive him. 'You are a smooth one. What are you doing around here, then?' Benito's first lie leads him to invent another. 'I was waiting here to drive some cattle to the coast for Don Mamerto Reyes.' Benito is now running a double risk. If the subprefect succeeds in contacting Don Mamerto, a well-known merchant, he is done for. But luck favours him: Don Mamerto cannot be traced, and the subprefect gives up the attempt to find out whether Benito–who does not give his real name–is known at Mollepata, since (thank God!) the telegraph line does not reach that out-of-the-way spot. So Benito has saved his bacon at the cost of two lies, which fortunately were not discovered. How far does he deserve the subprefect's description of 'smooth' (cunning, *vivo*)? Certainly he gets out of trouble, but how? When the subprefect questions him about Pajuelo's subversive speech, he 'plays dumb' and evades the issue: he has no idea what Pajuelo was talking about. Then he invents two convenient lies and sticks to them. Actually the subprefect is not wholly taken in, but, being lazy or cynical or both, prefers not to waste time clearing up such a trifling matter. Benito's cunning is revealed in several ways: he pretends to be stupid, he lies and does not give himself away; finally, he is lucky. Also, though the author does not dwell on this,

[1] *Broad and Alien is the World*, pp. 151–2.   [2] Ibid., p. 154.

his cunning itself appeals to the subprefect and induces him to wink an eye: Benito's good fortune is not due only to his lucky star but also to the connivance of the authorities, who let him go as summarily as they arrested him, because he 'seems a decent chap'.

Cunning is the weak man's response to a situation where, institutionally, he is at a disadvantage. But there is a major difference between the cunning of the *criollo* and that of the *cholo* Castro: the former can mobilise his subordinates and make them stand in for him, while the latter has only himself to rely on. The subtlest form of cunning, *viveza*, is to make someone else act for one at his own risk— to pull strings without the risk of oneself being compromised. There is an excellent example of this in *Yawar Fiesta*, where another subprefect, described as a boaster and embezzler, has a set-to in his office with one of the Puquio notables, Don Pancho Jiménez, whom he suspects of covertly encouraging the Indians in their desire for a free-for-all *corrida*.

In this dialogue between the subprefect and Don Pancho, I would draw attention to the ways in which aggressiveness is manifested. To begin with, the personal challenge is veiled and the target a fictitious one: the subprefect does not attack Don Pancho directly but launches out against the 'Indian riff-raff (*indiada*), with which he associates Don Pancho by implication. The latter realises that it is he who is being attacked, and reacts accordingly. The tension mounts by stages, of which three may be distinguished. In the first, Don Pancho, though in general he is wise enough to keep in his place and give the authorities a wide berth ('*con Vd. no me meto*'),[1] loses patience with the subprefect's groundless accusations and jumps to his feet in a threatening manner. They are prevented from coming to blows by a police sergeant who steps between them. But the calm is short-lived. Suddenly, for no apparent reason, the subprefect moves towards Don Pancho as if to strike him, but instead offers him his hand. The third phase is as follows. Don Pancho has left the subprefect's office and is half-way across the square. ' "Come here, sergeant. You can see him there, on the shady side of the square. He's escaping. Don't you understand, the bastard's escaping! Why don't you fire? You could shoot him down like a dog!" ' The subprefect spoke slowly, in a low voice; he was trembling all over.[2] The sergeant does not move. When Don Pancho is out of range, the subprefect lashes out: 'You have behaved like a coward.'

[1] *Yawar Fiesta*, p. 60.   [2] Ibid., p. 77.

It is dangerous to give way to violence. One may, of course, be no longer master of oneself. The crisis occurs when one's will is thwarted by circumstances or by someone else's hostile design. When a man in authority is foiled by one still more powerful, he will either turn against the weak or get another to wreak vengeance on his behalf; but in the first case he risks appearing ridiculous, and in the second odious.

Of another notable, Don Jesús–a real fox who has nevertheless fallen into the subprefect's toils–Arguedas says: 'All the way home, he went on cursing, and at lunch, for no reason at all, he flung a plate at his wife's head by way of venting his wrath against the subprefect.'[1] In this way, violence is exercised on a substitute: the wife pays for the offence of another. We may compare Don Jesús' conduct with Benito's and that of the subprefect who tries to have Don Pancho murdered. Like Benito, Don Jesús is in a position of inferiority *vis à vis* the representative of authority, who always has the last word. But while the *cholo* manages to talk his way out of the situation, Don Jesús, who is a person of some consequence, is made a fool of by the subprefect, and vents his exasperation on his defenceless wife. As for the subprefect in the scene with Don Pancho, he cuts an odious figure as the instigator of a crime which he dares not commit himself but seeks to execute through a subordinate. The sergeant retorts effectively: 'I am not a murderer, *señor*. The only people I have shot in the back have been highway robbers.'[2]

The episode is an interesting example of displaced aggression. This term usually denotes the replacement of one target by another, symbolic one–as when, at the outset, the subprefect raves against Puquio instead of directly attacking Don Pancho. But in the third stage, what is suggested is a different aggressor and not a different victim. We may discern the initial impulse of anger with Don Pancho, who has put obstacles in the subprefect's path and refuses to give in. This impulse, after being checked, returns in full urgency at the sight of Don Pancho, unprotected in the no man's land of the empty square. Prudence can be forgotten for a moment: after all, an 'escaping prisoner' runs the risk of being shot down. Arguedas shows us the subprefect gloating sadistically as he imagines the death-throes of Don Pancho, pitilessly struck down from behind. But, lacking the courage to fire himself, he falls back on incitement, urging his subordinate to perpetrate the deed which he ardently desires but which

[1] Ibid., p. 122.   [2] Ibid., p. 78.

caution and weakness prevent him from executing. And his guilty conscience finds expression in the charge of cowardice which he flings at the sergeant lest it be applied to himself.

The 'acting out' of violence is dangerous even for those in power; and it is avoided even more by those in a position of dependence. With them, it seems to be held in check both by practical considerations (*no meterse*) and by a deeper form of repression, consisting of panic horror at what would happen if all controls were to give way. Thus, still in *Yawar Fiesta*, Don Pancho Jiménez has an altercation in front of the subprefect with a notable of greater dignity than he, Don Demetrio Cáceres. Don Pancho, who is the worse for drink, hurls the coarsest insults at his adversary (*chosco, carajo, adulete*) and for good measure flings the contents of his glass in his face. This is presented as a normal outburst: perhaps because he is drunk, Don Pancho can let off steam and tell the other what he thinks of him. Apart from the excuse of drunkenness, his action is not really as bold as it seems: Don Demetrio, for all that he is a man of consequence, is no match for Don Pancho. He is a stuck-up good-for-nothing, probably the less well off of the two, and Don Pancho is running no great risk by his conduct. But then the subprefect intervenes. 'The subprefect, who had entered the shop, gave Don Pancho a warning shove. The latter exclaimed: "All right, *señor subprefecto*, push me around if you want to. I'm not getting involved with you! (*Con Vd. no me meto*)." And he lifted an arm to protect his face.'[1]

Without enquiring whether there is an element of deliberate farce in Don Pancho's action, we may note that by this almost ludicrous demonstration of respect for authority he becomes, as it were, invulnerable. The rule of avoiding trouble with those stronger or more powerful than oneself may, if followed in all circumstances, enable one to keep out of disagreeable situations. Those who are important enough not to fear retaliation may take out their vexations on lesser fry. The others do well to bow to the storm.

The first principle of wisdom is to have as little as possible to do with those who are in a stronger position than oneself. Even in the reverse case, one should handle others with the utmost circumspection. The prudent maxim that one should know one's place and stay in it is suspended only during brief moments of holiday. Arguedas' *cholos*, for instance, twice indulge in what may be called displays of triumph: at Lima, under Mariátegui's portrait, and at Puquio on the

[1] Ibid., p. 60.

evening of their arrival. But on both occasions their exultation is due to the belief that the authorities are on their side: they are keenly conscious of their strength, but also of the fact that it is borrowed. On both occasions, too, their triumph turns to aggression, if only verbal and long-range, against the *gamonales* and the great ones of Puquio and Lima. And, finally, their sense of fulfilment is short-lived: duped by the subprefect, they return to a reality of humiliation and disappointment. The lyric intensity of their triumph is some compensation for past rebuffs and failures, but it prepares the way for future ones. It suggests, to my mind, that the *cholo* is at bottom incapable of assimilating the gloomy principles of self-protection, because they would involve an unbearable deflation of his ego and would, in the last resort, oblige him to hate himself.[1]

The rigour of the doctrine of prudence, tempered though it may be by occasional outbursts, is offset by what I may call the integrative function of creolism (*criollismo*), which imparts a tinge of legitimacy to the drab realism of practical caution. The creole is, first of all, the Peruvian as opposed to the foreigner, and also the *costeño* or man of the coastal zone as opposed to the *serrano*. For example, on sugar plantations and cotton estates, it is customary to distinguish between *serranitos* (the term denoting workmen who have recently arrived from the sierra) and creoles (*criollos*), who were born on the coast or have lived there for some time, speak Spanish and have adopted local standards of food and dress. The term *criollo* also applies to people of the best society—for example, the head of some rich and powerful family who maintains an expensive stud of fighting bulls. It denotes a complex of cultural features rather than a stage in the social hierarchy. But the concept of *criollismo* is not very clearly defined. It is based on an antithesis between two pairs of values, one positive and the other negative. In the first place, it denotes subtlety and sensuality: a nostalgic, rather languid sensuality, a voluptuous laziness which finds pleasure in contemplating its own sterility. The reverse side of this picture is the dashing cavalier (*jinete*), plucking his guitar and trolling a ballad. The second set of values presents the *criollo* as sly and cunning, a schemer and intriguer, and, at the bottom end of the scale, as a coward. These attributes are summed up in

---

[1] *Yawar Fiesta* ends with a suicide—but, curiously enough, that of a pure Indian and not a *cholo*.

The Dependence of the Middle Classes

what, at Lima, is called *cundería*: the talent for dodges, intrigues and machinations of all kinds.

It would be a mistake to define Peruvian culture exclusively in terms of an antithesis between ostentatious virility and effeminate aestheticism: Lima is neither Castile nor Andalusia. But we should recognise the integrative and conservative force of these images, which have their place in the reassuring myth of what Sebastián Salazar Bondy calls the 'colonial Arcadia'. Discussing the *Tradiciones* of Ricardo Palma, Mariátegui in his time denounced as *perricholismo*[1] his compatriots' nostalgia for the days of the Spanish viceroyalty, a mood in which he detected an intention to deny or minimise the importance of the native element. Salazar Bondy agrees with this diagnosis and mentions also a sensualist strain and a vein of amoralism, or quietism if the term be preferred. In the context of the 'colonial Arcadia', these fantasies are taken for reality. Happiness is behind us, but it did exist at Lima in the time of the viceroys–*una Lima que se va* (a disappearing Lima), to quote the title of a well-known book by José Gálvez. What is left now are traditions, or rather Tradition, embodied not only in festivals and a way of life but in a social hierarchy which is thought of, not as efficient and respectable, but as gracious, sensitive and decorous.

The values of creolism are far from commanding the respect of the entire middle class. Salazar Bondy himself speaks of the 'colonial Arcadia' only to denounce it as an aberration: in his book *Lima la horrible* he aligns himself with the rebels and dissidents. But in between acceptance and rejection, it seems possible to discern a middle-of-the-road attitude on the part of some who ascribe the less desirable features of creolism to themselves while crediting the oligarchy with all its virtues. The terms *criollada* and *criollazo* are used to denote the coarse behaviour and tricks of the vulgarly ambitious: neither expression would be used of the gentry (*la gente, nuestra sociedad*), but they spring up unbidden when it is a question of a venal journalist, a politician or a sharp lawyer–all middle-class types. The distinction of the *gesto bien criollo* (true creole behaviour) is at the opposite pole from such concepts. From this point of view the oligarchy may appear as a race of Olympians (to use Edgar Morin's term) who achieve effortlessly, with grace and decorum, what others can only dream of and enact in a small and petty way. These

---

[1] From La Perricholi, a celebrated creole and mistress of an eighteenth-century viceroy. (Translator's note.)

Olympians, in short, represent the quintessence of social life. They have only to be as they are in order to justify a society that was made for them; and their existence sheds a reflected glory on the middle class.

The foregoing analysis may be summed up in two main points. In the first place, the members of the middle class are, objectively and subjectively, mobile: the criterion of mobility being that they have received the minimum of formal education enabling them to leave the traditional sector of society and enter the modern. The second point is their aggressiveness towards the established order and its representatives: an aggressiveness which is however canalised, transferred and sublimated. It is canalised in the sense that realism compels the 'mobile' individual to see the world as a dangerous place in which caution is essential. It is transferred because instead of being directed against appropriate objects it is vented on substitutes, and through channels so devious that the individual achieves his ends without having to reveal himself.[1] Finally, it is sublimated inasmuch as, thanks to the image of *criollismo*, cunning and caution assume the guise of a refined and sceptical wisdom.

It may be objected that the dependence of the middle class is also a cliché of European societies. But in Europe, among the various groups covered by this term, the autonomy of the individual is great, whereas in Peru it is very small. With us, independence is a constant demand of the liberal professions. Government officials, more especially in the lower ranks, while they are not independent like doctors or lawyers, are protected against improper or arbitrary treatment by a statute which strictly lays down the terms of recruitment, promotion and dismissal. The businessman or small industrialist, who also belongs to the middle class, enjoys independence based in his case not on professional qualifications or an official statute, but on the possession of capital. In Peru, by contrast, there is no bureaucracy guaranteeing to its members impartial recruitment and regular promotion; and the oligarchy's control over national resources has hitherto been such that the chances of an adventurous newcomer pushing to the fore while maintaining his independence were small indeed.

[1] '*Tira la piedra, pero oculta la mano*' – he throws the stone but hides his hand.

The Dependence of the Middle Classes

The prospects for the managerial class ('gerentes')

However, this state of affairs has to some extent altered. The rapid growth of industry since 1960 favours the development of medium-sized enterprises or production units. Even though the 'establishment' maintains close control over the industries which are springing up around Lima, the role of technicians and administrators is bound to increase. This affords scope for the *gerentes* – often spoken of as 'the younger men' – of whom more and more has been heard during the past few years.

Let us outline the career of an imaginary typical member of this class. He was born between 1925 and 1940, probably at Lima; his father, a provincial who had recently settled in the capital, was a minor clerk of some kind. After the normal secondary schooling he became a student in one of the faculties of the University of Engineering. The turning-point was when he obtained a scholarship to study abroad – in the U.S.A., if he was one of the luckier ones. (A stay in France carries great prestige for intellectuals but was until recently less popular among technicians, especially in industry.) Back in Peru, he is taken on by one of the big U.S. or Peruvian-owned companies. But whichever it is, although he has probably had first-class technical training and has learnt something about large-scale modern organisations – either during his foreign studies or as a trainee, perhaps with the U.S. mining firm by which he is now employed in Peru – he will be confined to executive and managerial functions and will have little chance to take part in real decision-making. In the U.S. companies, he will find it difficult to rise above a certain level: the chairman and the senior directors are all North Americans,[1] though a few seats are kept on the board for Peruvians who are useful because they belong, as a rule, to good society and are able to exert influence in ways which are suitably rewarded. In a Peruvian firm he will be no better off. In the first place, he will have to meet competition from colleagues who have not got in on their merits, as he has, but on personal grounds: the plums are reserved for friends, relatives and protégés of the boss's family. Moreover, the business is probably run by methods which his mentors in the U.S. have stigmatised as immoral and uneconomic. He will be sickened at the waste and favouritism,

[1] In August 1964 a Peruvian became president of the Cerro de Pasco Corporation.

the success of colleagues who excite his envy but not his respect. He is consulted and allowed to express opinions, but only on condition that he 'knows his place'. Inevitably he is resentful of a system which he has good reason to condemn as immoral, unfair and inefficient. What means has he of altering it?

As to his political leanings, they are uncertain except on one point: he is a *desarrollista*,[1] a believer in 'development'. This term connotes a general sense of urgency rather than any specific objectives. Development, as everyone agrees, means the increase of the national product and of *per capita* income. Beyond this, the *desarrollistas* vary widely among themselves. Those who may be called 'orthodox' put their trust in the economic liberalism of which *La Prensa* is the mouthpiece. Others see development as a process of cautious and gradual industrialisation, and, being less associated than the first group with the traditional oligarchy, look forward to the growth of a national bourgeoisie. A third group, openly hostile to the old oligarchy and sceptical as to the possibility of industrialisation by classical means, hankers after planning and state control, for ideological rather than technical reasons.

However, all three groups are united by the conviction that something must be done, and that Peru's future depends on economic progress. What the advocates of change need is a lever to set the country in motion. Who is likely to take the lead? Behind the hostility felt towards the oligarchy by the various groups known collectively as the middle class, there is a basic ambiguity of attitude. At times they denounce the oligarchy's exercise of power as immoral and unjust: this was the main theme in the 1930s, when 'indigenist' writers let fly at the inhumanity of the *gamonales* as typical specimens of the ruling class. At other times, such as the present, the oligarchy is attacked as backward and inefficient. The *cholos* in Arguedas's novel have already lost the half-caste's traditional respect for the gentry, *los principales*. But while they make no bones about their desire to make a clean sweep of the *gamonales*, they are obliged in the end to admit failure. Their cunning is not equal to that of the foxy subprefect, who has little trouble in outwitting them; and at the same time they lack the strength and instinctive vitality of the true Indians. This form of impotence due to the *cholo*'s marginality and the contradictions it imposes reappears, *mutatis mutandis*, in the new middle

[1] In this connection, an interesting study might be devoted to a group which has adopted the slogan *Acción para el desarrollo*.

class. When we say that its members are dependent upon the oligarchy, this does not mean that they accept the latter's power as legitimate. They have, it is true, assimilated certain of its values, particularly as regards style of living and consumption standards. But they are all the more resolute in denying its legitimacy and its right to go on managing the country's affairs.

The possibility of some radical change is at once inspiring and disquieting, attractive and fraught with the risk of subversion and disaster.[1] Against it stands the caution and realism of those who have learnt that provided they attend strictly to their own interests and do not openly challenge those in power, they have a fair chance of making ends meet and perhaps bettering themselves. It is this which, in the last resort, ensures the 'neutralisation' of the middle class. Having failed to evolve a system of values which they could hope to impose on society as a whole, and being as yet only half-prepared for tasks which might enable them to assert their autonomy *vis à vis* the oligarchy, the middle classes perforce remain in an attitude of resentful compliance.

[1] Cf. Part II, chap. 3.

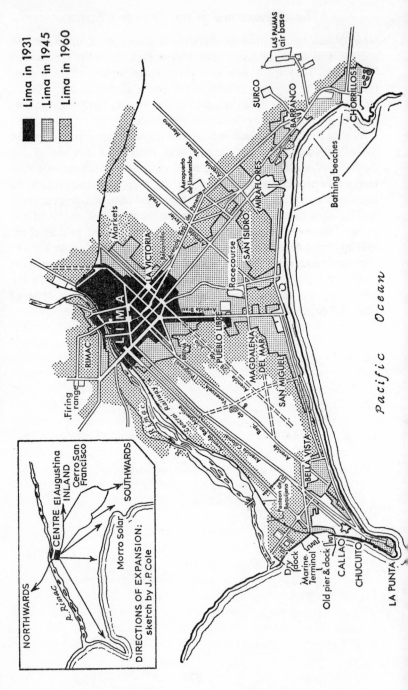

The development of Greater Lima

Lima in 1931
Lima in 1945
Lima in 1960

NORTHWARDS

R. Rimac

CENTRE El Augustina INLAND

Cerro San Francisco

Morro Solar

SOUTHWARDS

DIRECTIONS OF EXPANSION:
sketch by J. P. Cole

Firing range

RIMAC

Markets

LIMA

LA VICTORIA

BREÑA

PUEBLO LIBRE

Avenida Brasil

Raceourse

MAGDALENA DEL MAR

SAN MIGUEL

Av. de Venezuela

Rap. de Venezuela

Avenida Rep. Argentina

Avenida Colonial

Central Railway

Callao-Ancón Railway

Panteon de Bequiano

BELLA VISTA

Dry dock

Marine Terminal

Old pier & dock

CALLAO

CHUCUITO

LA PUNTA

SAN ISIDRO

Raceourse

Balconcillo

Av. de Venezuela

Aeropuerto de Limatambo

Prado

Javier

Avenida Tomas Marsano

MIRAFLORES

SURCO

LAS PALMAS air base

BARRANCO

CHORRILLOS

Bathing beaches

Pacific Ocean

3

Los Olvidados—*the Violence of the Have-nots*

As applied to the mass of the Peruvian population, the phrase *'los olvidados'* (the forgotten ones) connotes first of all the inferior position of the illiterate, who are disfranchised, and in general all those whose archaic methods of production, low output and beggarly income exclude them from a share in modern life. The paradox of a regime such as that of Peru is that the majority is relegated to the state of a permanent minority. The confinement of the Indian masses in a sort of forced-labour reservation continued until quite recent times: in the 1920s they were still obliged to live in their own settlements. The character of Rosendo Maqui in Alegría's novel illustrates the relations, or lack of them, between the old-style Indians and the public authorities. Old Rosendo recalls that in his youth 'For a long time there had been talk about a war with a person named Chile. People said Chile had won . . . The villagers didn't see the war, because it never came their way . . . They had believed that Chile was a general until the damned Blues came. Their captain heard them talking once about General Chile, and he growled at them: "You ignorant fools, Chile is a country and the people there are the Chileans, just the same as Peru is a country and we are Peruvians." '[1] The only representatives of the state whom the Indian saw were the recruiting-sergeant, the tax-collector and the magistrate, who naturally always backed up the *gamonal* against the villagers.

From time to time an Indian revolt broke out at one place or another; the cause was generally purely local and no-one outside the area was affected, so that repression was not difficult. The famous

[1] *Broad and Alien is the World*, p. 21.

Mobilisation in a Dualistic Society

rising led by the chief Atusparia in the department of Ancash in 1885 is thus described by Alegría:

'The Indians were groaning under the yoke. They had to pay a poll tax of two soles twice a year, and they had to do free "work for the Republic", building roads, barracks, cemeteries, churches, public buildings. And the rich were wiping out the communities, the *ayllus*. The Indians had to suffer in silence . . . They presented a protest to the prefect of Huarás . . . Pedro Pablo Atusparia, the first signer of the protest, was put in prison, beaten and mistreated. Fourteen mayors came in protest against this injustice. They too were put in prison, beaten and mistreated . . .

'[The Indians] pretended to give in, and on the first of March came down to Huarás carrying bales of straw to thatch a roof that was "work for the Republic". At a given moment they pulled out of the bales the machetes and iron bars that were hidden in them, and the fight was on . . .

'Huarás was besieged. The next day it fell . . . The revolution spread. The Indians . . . attacked Yungay by surprise . . . All the towns were taken . . . The Indians had a few rifles, forty cases of dynamite, and eight barrels of powder that Uchcu Pedro took out of the mines . . . The rest had to use iron bars and machetes . . . Uchcu took command of the important passes of the Black Range . . . They sent messengers to the departments of La Libertad and Huánuco, asking for help, asking them to join the revolution. But the battalions of the government were already there with good rifles and cannon. The Indians died like flies . . . Atusparia, wounded in the leg in the fight at Huarás, fell and over him fell the corpses of his guard.'[1]

From the beginning of the present century the Indian, the forgotten man, began to be talked about; but what weight does he carry in Peruvian society today? In the 1930s he was thought of as a lethargic character, who needed rousing. Alegría's novel illustrates this clearly. The life of the wise old chief Rosendo Maqui is, in fact, nothing but a series of failures. He is powerless to protect his village against Don Alvaro's designs; he does not see through the pettifogging Bismarck Ruiz until it is too late; and when he dies in prison his community is destitute and his family and friends dispersed. Benito, his son, is a failure too, and the last pages of the book describe his violent death. But in the early part of his life, roaming the world on muleback, he acquires some sophistication. If disaster and death overtake him in

[1] Ibid., pp. 158–9.

Los Olvidados – *the Violence of the Have-nots*

the end, it is perhaps because he departs too soon from the cautious attitude of the wily *cholo* and tackles a stronger adversary head-on.

The *indigenistas* of the 1930s presented the Indian not only as a victim but as an agent of retribution who would come down from the mountains, sweeping all before him. As Luis E. Valcárcel put it in *Tempestad en los Andes*, 'the Indian proletariat awaits its Lenin'. Mariátegui, in his preface to Valcárcel's book, expressed the same idea more soberly. 'Faith in the resurrection of the Indian people does not depend on the gradual westernisation of the Quechuas. What is bringing the Indian to life is not the white man's alphabet and civilisation but the myth, the ideal of socialist revolution. Revolution is the quintessence of his hopes.' But Mariátegui's 'socialist revolution' has not come about, nor has the restoration of the Quechua republic of which Valcárcel dreamt in the 1920s.

For the past ten years or so, the Indian has ceased to be the sole target of observation and centre for the hopes of all men of good will. Internal migration and the growth of cities, especially the Lima conurbation, have aroused interest in urban problems in general, which may be regarded as a sign that Peru has entered a new phase of development in which urbanism is the essential feature.

Thus the Indian is no longer the 'forgotten man' *par excellence*: other social categories have come into the picture which, though confined like him to the fringe of political society, are less resigned to being excluded from it. The mass of second-class citizens and 'outsiders' is today of mixed composition, including not only the traditional sector but part of the urban community. The term 'proletariat' is not out of place, provided one recognises the obvious differences between the inmates of the *barriadas* (shanty-towns) and the French or English workmen of the early nineteenth century. For one thing, the urbanisation of Peru is proceeding faster than its industrialisation: so that a great many 'proletarians' are not only unemployed but are unlikely ever to become producers in any real sense. If one speaks of an 'industrial reserve of labour', it must be with the recognition that many of its members will never take part at any point in the economic cycle. Many, indeed, though they live in cities, are out of place in industrial society. Secondly, the period during which the *serranos* have poured into Lima is that of mass media and mass production. Not all shanty-dwellers have to do without radio, television and motor-cars. Thirdly, and this is the main point, the first provincial influx in the 1930s took place at a time when there already existed a rudimentary form of workers' organisation, which will have a difficult task in adapting itself to the second wave which is now filling the *barriadas*. In the Lima urban region a general strike of public transport employees took place as early as 1919, under union leaders who seem to have been anarcho-syndicalists.

I have already made use, in the social context, of the distinction between ancient and modern: for instance, the old-style middle class contrasts with its modern successor, albeit both are equally dependent. Within the governing class, too, one may distinguish a traditional group, corresponding to what we have called the oligarchy, and an embryonic 'national bourgeoisie' whose attitude towards development differs from that of the oligarchs. A similar distinction might be drawn in regard to the 'forgotten' masses. Let us imagine a working class with traditions which are all the more pronounced because of its physical isolation (for instance in mining camps) or because of strong corporative influence, as among railwaymen. What will happen when this class is swollen by a flood of newcomers straight from the farm, in whom class-consciousness and the thirst for justice are less developed than in their predecessors? The rustic migrants of Peru, bred in the paternalistic atmosphere of tradition, were wholly unprepared for the slavery of industrial discipline and the ways of urban life. In these novel surroundings they look for protectors and spokesmen, and feel lost if they do not find them.[1] No gulf could be greater than that between the life of the sierra and that of the shanty-town. Lack of professional skill and suitable education is not the only bar to assimilation: for many Indians, learning to speak Spanish fluently and correctly is no easy task. A further point is that before the mass invasion from the sierra, the Peruvian working class was very small, lacking in self-assurance, and, since as far back as the 1920s, hopelessly divided by the conflict between Apristas and communists. Thus the present situation is characterised not so much by the opposition between the old working class and the new working masses, as by that between the organised and unorganised sections of the underprivileged population, whether urban or rural.

In using the term 'organised' I do not have in mind simply the

---

[1] Gino Germani, in his analysis of Peronism, lays great stress on the disruptive effect of the invasion of Buenos Aires by masses of primitive peasantry seeking work. Uprooted from their traditional life and ill at ease in the new society, unable to find work and so enjoy the protection of its long-standing union organisations, these peasants fell an easy prey to Peronism with its 'authoritarian' propaganda.

existence of trade unions, but the general ability of particular groups to identify, express and defend their members' interests. The manner in which claims are put forward varies with the type of organisation. The miners have fairly articulate unions which achieve some measure of their demands by complicated methods involving negotiation, blackmail and the strike weapon. Take, again, the Indian communities of the central area, which have given proof of their strength in their efforts to recover land of which they claim they were dispossessed by big national or foreign firms (e.g. the Cerro de Pasco Corporation). Having formulated their case more or less clearly, they appeal to the courts or political authorities; but if these fail to grant their wishes, they tend increasingly to squat on the lands in question and thus get their way by force. Finally, the poor wretches who vegetate in the shanty-towns offer an illustration of the principle that it is organisation which counts. By reason of the general character of their protest and the difficulty of righting their wrongs immediately and completely, they seem condemned to remain 'forgotten' for ever –unless they should succeed in arousing public opinion and thus exerting pressure on the government, or unless they become the vanguard of the revolution and bring all down in ruins.

To assess the degree of organisation of a particular reformist movement, many factors have to be taken into account. The first step is to analyse the working of the institutions which represent the wishes and aspirations of the underprivileged. One point is decisive: a claim for the redress of grievances may, according to its nature, be confined to the context of bilateral negotiations or, on the contrary, extend into the field of politics. The better 'organised' a movement is, the more skilled its leaders will be at gauging their attacks, keeping them on target and not allowing themselves to be swept into extreme courses. My object in this chapter is to show not merely that violence is bound to occur but also why it is that the explosions remain sporadic, so that we are left with the conclusion that the worst is not inevitable.

Miners on strike

Peruvian mining is concentrated in two main areas. In the south of the country, copper mines were recently discovered and are worked by an offshoot of the U.S. companies.[1] But throughout this century,

---

[1] I shall not here consider the southern area.

in the central region some hundred and twenty miles north-east of Lima, deposits of lead and zinc have been exploited by the Cerro de Pasco Mining Corporation, whose headquarters are in the U.S. and which is often regarded in Peru as a symbol of international capitalism. A French company is also active in the same region–the Mines de Huaron, linked with the Barque de l'Union Parisienne. Though it occupies second place, its output is far behind that of the Corporation, which accounts for three-quarters of the national production of lead and zinc; moreover, the Corporation is the only concern which refines the metal and exports it in the form of ingots.

To understand the formation of an old-style working class in Peru, we may study the growth of the syndicalist movement in the Cerro de Pasco encampments. From 1930 onwards–especially during the difficult months after the fall of President Leguía, when the U.S. depression brought about a slump in mining activities–the parties of the extreme left gained a firm foothold in this area, and rivalry between Apristas and communists was particularly strong. The organisation of miners' unions appeared in full strength in 1945, but for three years only. During the eight years of General Odría's rule the union leaders, most of whom belonged to the proscribed Apra party, were hunted by the police. After 1956 they came to the fore again under the civilian regime of Dr Prado, and in each successive year they have measured their strength against their employers in the discussion of the collective agreement (*convenio colectivo*).

Some features of these unions may be noted. In the first place, their bargaining tradition is an old one: their founding fathers were militant revolutionaries, Apristas or communists. No doubt the present-day leaders have drawn in their horns, and above all learnt to negotiate; but the tone of their claims is sharp, the more so as the 'class enemy' is a foreign company. Secondly, what proportion of the workers are unionised? Here we must distinguish between white-collar workers and others. At Cerro de Pasco, all the miners and smelters belong to a union, which however does not exert specially close control over them.[1] In the small mines and such medium-sized concerns as Huarón, the degree of unionisation seems to vary according to the scale of the enterprise and the nationality of its

---

[1] On the other hand, employees (*empleados*), who under Peruvian social legislation enjoy a different status from workers as regards holidays, pensions and dismissal, do not show great eagerness to form unions, at all events in industry: banks and the public service are a different matter.

capital; and the nationality of the local managers is as important as that of the ultimate owners.

Finally, with what matters are the trade unionists–i.e. both the leaders and the membership as a whole– expressly concerned? First and foremost, with wage levels. These are generally fixed from year to year as a result of negotiations which involve not only the employers and wage-earners but also the Ministry of Labour, whose representative acts as a mediator and, if need be, as a quasi-arbiter.[1] The negotiation may be short or long; sometimes agreement is reached directly, at other times not without the threat or reality of a strike, which may be peaceful or violent. The complexity of the discussion is increased by the variety of interests represented on the employees' side. Since 1957, when the prices of non-ferrous metals on the U.S. market declined, wage negotiations have been implicitly linked with discussions on the volume of employment. The firms' object is to reduce costs by raising productivity, and while not resorting to dismissal they have limited recruitment. At the same time, they are concerned to step up training and thus enable the workers to make better use of the large quantities of costly equipment. This policy on the owners' part will oblige the unions, willy-nilly, to interest themselves in other problems besides wages. They are in a dilemma: either the workers want stability of employment, in which case they must be 'reasonable' over wages, or else they may stand out for high wages at the risk of being unemployed. There is another difficulty. For a long time, the miners regarded their wage as a supplementary source of income only: many were still peasants, and went down the mine when they could be spared from the fields. This was especially the case with the medium-sized and smaller mines. For many years past, Cerro de Pasco has endeavoured to keep its personnel on a permanent footing, whereas Huarón, for example, was not unduly perturbed by a very high turnover. But as the need for qualified workers increases, the firm which has paid for their training will want to keep them for itself and to have their services full-time. Problems of industrial discipline are thus likely to become increasingly difficult, as is the unions' choice of bargaining strategy. In the first place, the types of worker whom they set out to represent are more and more diverse. Secondly, the political and ideological cleavage between those for whom stable employment is all-important

---

[1] 'Quasi', because the arbiter has no way of enforcing his decision, except indirectly, in certain circumstances, by declaring the strike illegal.

and those who refuse to compromise becomes steadily greater, so that each negotiation on wages turns into a trial of strength between moderates and extremists.

These facts were illustrated by the negotiation of 1959, which took place under the shadow of a serious incident reported as follows in the Aprista newspaper *La Tribuna* of 23 November 1958:

'On Wednesday 19 November, at 3.40 p.m., a gang at the Lourdes mine came off duty . . . Fràncisco B. was returning to his quarters, carrying a dinner-pail . . . As the foreman O., who was tired and in a hurry, walked past him, Francisco, meaning no more than a childish joke, aimed a blow with his pail at the foreman's back. The engineer D., seeing this and believing the attack to be in earnest, ran to the help of O., who was defending himself. He also took the affair seriously, and went with D. to the office to get B.'s cards and discharge him. While there they met another engineer, T. The miners, who were coming up from the pits in large numbers, gathered round the building to find out what was going on. The shop steward appeared and was greeted with cheers, but the mood at this point was of no more than curiosity and expectation. A detachment of militia arrived under Major P. Meanwhile a quarrel developed inside the building between T. and the shop steward . . . The militiamen tried to calm the parties down and induce them to settle the matter amicably without involving higher authority. But when a police inspector who was also present reached for the telephone, a scuffle arose and the miners broke into the office. The engineers fled, fearing for their lives, while the miners pillaged the building. The prefect, who came on the scene soon afterwards, declared that the matter would be settled equitably but that those guilty of violence would be punished. He succeeded in rescuing the three engineers, who were in a serious condition, and drove them off in his car.'

So far, the outbreak of violence had only affected an office building; but it now spread to the whole town:

'At 6.30 p.m. the miners coming off duty heard what had happened and without any encouragement from their official leaders (*dirigentes legales*) flocked to the elegant residential quarter of Bella Vista which contains the homes of senior officials of the company, many of them foreigners. Some union leaders and Apra members tried to restrain the crowd, but they paid no attention and began throwing stones at the houses. The luxurious golf club–home of a sport so dear to the North American's heart–was sacked; food, stoves and furniture disappeared. Apart from this the damage was limited: a Volkswagen was burnt, and some wives and children of officials were hit by stones thrown into their houses. At 9 o'clock the miners held a general meeting, though the chief secretary of the union did not appear and his deputy had to take his place. (Neither official is a militant of our party.) Later in the evening it was announced that the three engineers had resigned, which did much to appease the miners.'

Next morning the town was quiet, but the miners found themselves unable to get to the pits: the firm's answer to the night of violence was a lockout. In a statement to this effect published in *El Comercio* on 21 November, the U.S. firm described the incident in terms identical to those of *La Tribuna*'s report and added:

'Many of the rioters were unidentified, which suggests that the incident at the mine was of no importance in itself but was exploited to create an atmosphere of subversion and disorder ... These acts of vandalism, which our firm is unwilling to ascribe to members of its own personnel and is inclined to attribute to foreign elements who have an interest in provoking such crimes, are being investigated by the national authorities. Meanwhile, and until further notice, the Cerro de Pasco Corporation is obliged, to its great regret, to suspend operations until calm is restored, since it would be a very grave responsibility to expose its senior staff and their families to harassment and personal violence.'

The miners were anxious to get back to work, but the Corporation was in no hurry to comply. The day passed in argument at the prefect's office, and the union leaders, embarrassed by strong pressure from below, expressed indignation against the firm while repeating that they condemned all violence. The miners stood about the streets talking, and old grievances were revived. 'In particular, they frequently refer to the one-hour break for refreshment to which the firm had agreed long ago, a concession which the older union officials were especially proud of having secured. It so happens that some days ago the engineer T. issued an order reducing the break to half an hour; moreover, he has been displaying a list of two hundred miners who, he claims, ought to be dismissed.'[1] ... At last, during the night, agreement was reached between the firm and the unions, after violent clashes on several points of procedure. The head of the department of industrial relations refused, in particular, to allow the union's legal adviser to attend the meeting, saying that 'while he had

[1] *La Tribuna.*

the greatest respect for labour unions, he could in no circumstances agree that an outside person who was neither an employee nor a workman in the firm's service nor a member of the administration be allowed to take part in the debate.'[1] The miners yielded on this point and also agreed that the three engineers should retain their posts, their letter of resignation being returned to them by the union.

This episode prompts certain observations. Firstly, the ease with which violence is triggered off by a minor incident. Secondly: the unions, in *La Tribuna*'s version, play a moderating rather than a leading role. Again, the Corporation stands firm and refuses to budge on certain principles, being determined to protect the authority of its senior staff. But the whole affair is fully comprehensible only in the context of the negotiating process and the forthcoming collective agreement. On 3 December 1958 a communiqué appeared in *La Tribuna*: this did not commit the Miners' Federation for the central area, but was signed only by some unions on behalf of individual pits. Their claim was for a wage-increase of 50 per cent, back-dated to 19 November, and a cost-of-living allowance based on the official retail price index. During December and January the other unions ranged themselves behind the demands of the pilot group. Attempts at direct negotiation failed, and recourse was had in vain to the Junta de Conciliación, a board composed of two owners' and two workers' delegates, chaired by a representative of the Ministry of Labour. Meanwhile tension was growing. After a serious incident on 27 January 1959 at the San Cristóbal mine, which also belongs to the Cerro de Pasco Corporation, the workers demanded the dismissal of the manager and a member of the administrative staff. Finally, on 23 February the Miners' Federation for the central area called a strike, on the following grounds:

'The Regional Federation . . . has failed to obtain satisfaction of its claims by direct negotiation (*trato directo*), a setback due entirely to the company's intransigence. When the matter was referred to the Ministry of Labour, the company declared that it could not grant a rise of more than 7 per cent, whereas the unions stand on their demand for 50 per cent. The Ministry, as a compromise, proposed an overall increase of 22 per cent: this is quite inadequate, being lower than the minimum rise of 25 per cent granted to civil servants on 29 May last. Miners' wages in Peru are the lowest in the world, and

[1] Ibid.

Los Olvidados—the Violence of the Have-nots

thanks to the depreciation of the sol in terms of the dollar, the companies have made huge profits while real wages decline. For these reasons, the Federation hereby declares a general strike for an indefinite period.'[1]

In view of the wide gap between the rise demanded by the miners and that offered by the company, it was clearly no easy matter to effect a compromise. In proposing to split the difference at 22 per cent, the government probably did not expect either party to agree at once. The unions, for their part, were concerned to demonstrate their good faith: the miners had availed themselves of every legal recourse, and if they turned down the Ministry's offer it was because this constituted unfair discrimination in view of the civil servants' rise of 25 per cent. On the substance of their claim, they put forward an argument likely to appeal to public opinion: the profits realised by the companies as a result of the fall in the value of the sol should enable them, if their directors were concerned to do the decent thing, to raise nominal wage rates and so make up for the drop in real ones. Here we may distinguish the solid nucleus from the obscure penumbra. The unions, though not necessarily the workers, attached great importance to the difference between real and nominal wages. At the same time, they refused to admit that the depreciation of the sol was in line with the collapse of ore and metal prices on the North American market, which had cut into the companies' gross profits for 1957 and 1958. The Cerro de Pasco Corporation pointed this out in its first communiqué:

'As public opinion is aware, the mining industry is going through a crisis due to international factors outside our control. In these circumstances, to increase overheads by a rise of 22 per cent in basic wages, plus additional welfare charges of all kinds . . . would endanger the stability of the firm and the security of its employees, whose leaders are, whether consciously or not, demanding wage increases out of all relation to practical possibilities and are seeking to impose them by means of strikes.'

In a second communiqué on 23 February the firm recalled that since 1952 they had granted cumulative increases of 71·25 per cent, so that their wages were 'among the highest in the country'. As for the argument that the miners had suffered discrimination by being excluded from the 25 per cent increase decreed in 1957 by Dr. Prado's government, the company pointed out that the decree had

[1] *La Tribuna*, 20 February 1959.

expressly made this exception 'on account of the particular situation confronting the mining industry', and that the unions had made no protest at the time. To the latter's complaint of the rise in the cost of living, the company replied that 'it could not consider freezing the prices of essential goods sold in its canteens and co-operatives, since this would involve an unacceptable burden'. This was a double-purpose formula. Its immediate object was to make clear that the prices of goods sold in the company's canteens and shops would not be frozen but would be allowed to rise in conformity with the general market: the company was not rich enough to offer costly subsidies to its employees. But in addition, the company's formula ruled out any question of a sliding scale and reserved its position as regards the freezing and control of prices in general. The company also enlarged on the industry's difficulties:

'In the U.S., the price of lead in November 1957 was 13·5 cents a pound, and that of zinc was 10 cents; in Europe, the figures were 10·4 and 8.4 cents ... In May 1958, when the government excluded the mining industry from the general pay rise, lead had fallen to 11·5 cents in the U.S. ... Now, in February 1959, lead stands at 11·5 cents in the U.S. and zinc has climbed slightly to the same figure ... The Corporation also points out that by reason of its quota system the U.S. imports only 40–45 per cent of the Peruvian output of lead and zinc, the rest having to be sold in Europe at lower prices which leave no margin for increased costs.'[1]

Meanwhile the unions on their side were not idle. On 4 February the C.T.P. (Confederation of Peruvian Workers) published in *La Tribuna* a wide-ranging memorandum drawing the moral from the San Cristóbal affair. This, be it noted, is not an individual union or regional federation but the supreme organ of the national trade union system. Points 1 and 2 of the memorandum advanced specific claims and accused the company of not having issued the miners with oilskin clothing as promised, and of equipping them with inadequate tools. Point 3 further charged the company with bad faith in the manipulation of wage-rates. But the main complaint was in point 5: 'The firm has not respected the rights and functions of the trade union organisation, which must remain independent of managerial interference. It has intervened in the union's affairs, creating difficulties for the secretary-general and endeavouring to cast doubt on his capacity and merits.'

[1] *La Prensa*, 19 February 1959.

Los Olvidados—*the Violence of the Have-nots*

The strike went on, and an appeal was made to the President of the Republic in the hope of breaking the deadlock. On 25 February Sr. Prado received the miners' delegates, who handed him a three-point memorandum. This began by contemptuously rejecting the Ministry's offer of 22 per cent as a 'so-called nominal increase', whereas the unions stood by their demand for a 'real wage in accordance with the promises given' (*salario real tal como se pactó*)—an ambiguous formula which offered some hope of progress. The miners' first demand had been for a rise of 50 per cent in nominal wages, but at the same time they made play with the notion of real wages and of maintaining parity with the standard of 1957. By not mentioning the 50 per cent claim to the President but confining themselves to the 'real wage' argument, they facilitated his task of arbitration, both by not confronting him with a specific claim and by taking their stand on the principle of the maintenance of purchasing power. They also made much of the threat of mass dismissal to which certain workers were allegedly subjected by the company.

The President's reply was no less subtle than the unions' demand. At first sight it appeared completely negative: Dr. Prado stood firm on the 22 per cent proposed by his Ministry and endorsed the company's arguments about the overwhelming burdens that the mining industry had had to carry since 1957. But he hinted that the government would not allow the company to dismiss workmen *en masse*. According to *La Prensa*, the President said that he was not aware of this possibility, but that if it occurred 'the government would step in'. It was not clear whether this expression denoted a promise, but in any case it served to appease the union leaders and enabled them to save face, since they could return to the rank and file with a more or less definite promise that the President would not allow them to be turned out of their jobs.

As the strike had been going on for more than a week, the workers' reserves were exhausted. But the elements of a solution were now at hand: the company would not go beyond 22 per cent or freeze the prices of essential goods in the shops run for its employees, but on the other hand it realised that it could not carry out any dismissals for the present. The only outstanding question was when the men would go back to work. The first to give in were the foundry workers. 'After the delegates had reported on their interview with the President, more than thirty speakers urged that the strike should be called off but that the union should maintain its demands for security of employment

101

and price-freezing for essential goods, and should reopen negotiations on labour conditions and discipline as soon as possible.'[1] The two latter stipulations had little or no hope of being accepted, but one never knew; and a new round of talks on labour conditions would enable the unions to maintain contact and keep up the pressure. But the Corporation, having decided how far it was prepared to go, put its foot down: it issued a communiqué stating that work would not be resumed unless it was first clearly understood that all the provisions of the existing collective agreement, other than the wage-rate, were prolonged without alteration. The unions finally gave in, and the pits reopened at the beginning of the following week, on 4 March.

The men had demanded 50 per cent and were putting up with 22 per cent. The company offered 7 per cent and raised this to 22 per cent, while asseverating that they could not afford to do so. Agreement was only reached after a period of intermittent threats, blackmail and violence. This last may take different forms. It may, for instance, break out spontaneously over some trifling incident, such as the horseplay of the Cerro de Pasco miner at his foreman's expense. When this happens, the problem for the union leaders is to keep matters under control and not allow rioting to develop to a point where it leads to police repression or reprisals by the firm. They have all the more reason to fear the spread of anarchy in that they are for the most part Apristas and, as such, are apt to be overtrumped by rivals who accuse them of moderatism. But the union leaders need the workers' strength, if not their violence, in order to prove to the capitalists that they are ready to endure the sacrifices that a strike of several weeks may entail.

The union leaders' power depends on their keeping the workers in an aggressive yet disciplined state, for which purpose they must possess their confidence. I mentioned above a case where the firm laid the responsibility for disorders on 'ringleaders from outside the area'. The union leaders themselves use this formula to discredit a movement which is slipping out of their control: all they need do is to replace the term 'agitator' by 'provocateur'. In any case, the strike described above was not unleashed lightly. The company, on its side, did not accuse the union leaders of having fomented it, and the latter remained in close touch with their membership throughout the negotiations. The strike began and ended with a vote by the miners themselves. Such votes and consultation may indeed not afford every

[1] *La Tribuna*, 28 February 1959.

possible guarantee, but they do provide for liaison and mutual restraint on the part of the represented workers on the one hand and, on the other, the union leaders who are responsible to them and, it would seem, neither desire nor can afford to take undue risks.

Did the strike pay off? A rise of 22 per cent was not to be sneezed at, making up as it did for the rise in the cost of living between 1956 and 1958. Three weeks' wages had been lost; but, on the other hand, the company had implicitly agreed to dismiss no one. This, of course, did not prevent it from suspending recruitment–a weapon of some consequence in an area where the company controls the main source of income. On 28 February 1959, before the resumption of work, *La Prensa* published an article entitled 'New mining policy for Peru', with a sub-heading 'Proposed aid for mines, excluding those of lead and zinc'. Indeed, the company possesses various ways of countering labour claims. To begin with, it can suspend recruitment and thus fix employment at its existing level, while making every effort to replace workers by automated permanent equipment; and, as far as the future is concerned, it can divert production to more lucrative commodities such as copper. Thus the firm and the union confront each other in a tactical war; the workers obtain solid concessions, but have to compromise for fear of prejudicing their own situation. Nevertheless, while the adversaries on this occasion knew they would have to make concessions to each other, they did not succeed in reaching agreement by direct negotiation: the Ministry official was to all intents and purposes an arbiter, and the 22 per cent recommended by him was the figure finally agreed on. The official has an effective weapon against the unions at his command in that, if they refuse mediation, the strike will be declared illegal, and the firm is then free to dismiss its employees at will. Is the official biased on one side or the other? Rather than discuss whether he is 'objectively' the company's ally, I would point out that while it is quite likely that given their initial positions the managers and the union leaders would, without much deliberation, have realised that the figure of 22 per cent was that on which they would have least difficulty in reaching agreement, they would still have taken longer to do so if the figure had not been named by a third party. The union leaders could explain that it was forced upon them by the state, and the managers could represent that in accepting it they were not yielding to workers' pressure but making a sacrifice for the public good. Thus neither side lost face. It is true, however, that if they had not from the outset been able to count on the state's good offices, the miners would not have stepped up their claim to 50 per cent nor the managers offered a niggardly 7 per cent.

The miners, in general, have an efficient organisation with which to defend their interests. On the local level they are represented by unions capable of making themselves directly heard by the managerial personnel. These lesser bargaining units are combined in a fairly well-integrated regional federation: if the miners of a particular pit or area seek redress, their efforts will probably be followed and supported by the whole region, except in the case of a wild-cat outbreak which will probably die a natural death, unsupported by the unions. Control is exercised by each union on the one below it: firstly at the regional and federal level of miners' organisations, and ultimately at the 'confederal' level by the C.T.P., to which all wage-earners are in principle free to belong. But this control is not over-strict: the secretaries and officials of each union, who are elected more or less regularly, seem to possess considerable freedom of movement *vis à vis* the authorities of the next higher body. Still, their autonomy has its limits: for the lower bodies need the higher to ensure consideration of their demands by superior authorities on the national level. Trade union demands are reinforced by parties and the political system. The strength of Apra between 1956 and 1962 was due to its success, in various branches of industry, in asserting itself as an indispensable intermediary between demands from below and the power of arbitration possessed in some measure by the state apparatus.

A strike of bank employees, or the dangers of politicalisation

To correct the over-optimistic impression which may be given by the foregoing example, I propose briefly to examine the question of conflicts between the banks and their employees.[1] The annual banking strike, like the university strike, is a Peruvian tradition. Let us take the case of April-May 1959, when the banks remained closed for over five weeks. At the outset, the unions demanded an increase of 30 per cent on the lowest salaries and lesser increases on the medium and higher ones, while the banks offered, as in previous years, an overall increase of 5 per cent. When negotiation failed, the parties appealed

[1] I have chosen the bankers' strike for discussion because they are employees and not workmen and because their unions are much less strongly entrenched than those of the miners.

Los Olvidados–*the Violence of the Have-nots*

to the Ministry of Labour, which proposed 9·15 per cent. The employees rejected this, while the managers took a subtler line. In a statement issued on 17 April they declared that they could not afford such 'extravagant' increases but that, whatever the cost, they were prepared to abide by the Ministry's decision. They then drew attention to the number and value of the concessions they had already granted their employees: bonuses for wives and children, widows' pensions, subsistence allowances for those sent to work in the sierra or the Amazon basin, profit-sharing, a special allowance for cashiers (*por manejo de efectivo*), an annual salary calculated on the basis of $14\frac{3}{4}$ months instead of 12, allowances representing 50 per cent of school fees and of the cost of children's journeys to school, and three months' paid leave after 25 years' service. The object of this statement was of course to represent the bank employees to the public as a privileged class, and one moreover which was guilty of sabotage by engaging in a prolonged strike which paralysed business and inconvenienced the public. A government statement of 16 April 1959, which we shall examine a little later, made similar accusations against the bank workers' unions, whose policy, 'directed towards paralysing trade and industry and fomenting an atmosphere of discontent and unrest . . . has accounted for twenty work stoppages in the past year . . . thus reducing to 195 the number of days worked in this branch of the economy, which is far below that worked by other employees'.[1]

The unions for their part insisted on the banks' greed and disputed the notion that their employees were privileged. In *La Prensa* of 19 May 1959 a statement by a tiny group of the extreme left, the Movimiento Social Progresista, to which some of the union leaders belong, declared that 'bank employees are in no sense a privileged section of the working class'. However this might be, they did not follow their unions unquestioningly. In a statement of 29 May, their last in connection with this strike, the managers pointed out that in some public or semi-public credit associations, like the Agricultural Credit Bank, the Reserve Bank and the Mining and Industrial Bank, the employees had not conformed to the line laid down by the unions. On 11 April, *La Prensa* (Sr. Beltrán's organ) published figures according to which between 10 per cent and 50 per cent were still at work, with 100 per cent at the Reserve Bank. To discourage such blacklegs, the strikers resorted to violence. 'A number of scuffles

---

[1] *El Comercio*, 17 April 1959.

105

took place yesterday at the doors of banks between strikers and those who wished to return to work. The police intervened to protect the latter and kept some of the more hot-headed strikers under arrest for a few hours.'[1] When the return to work could no longer be delayed, the unions aggravated the backlog by giving the order to 'go slow', thus prolonging the paralysis of banking operations by several days. The managers were prompt to condemn this attitude as a 'long-thought-out plan to prevent business returning to normal'. The issue at stake was in fact that of payment for the period of the strike, which the unions demanded and the bankers refused–with, in the background, the threat of dismissal which could not yet be put into effect as the Ministry of Labour had taken care not to proclaim the strike illegal. 'The employees' federation is endeavouring indirectly to secure the payment of salary for the days lost by the strike, on the pretext that special remuneration is due for the work which has accumulated over the period. The banks, for their part, are prepared to suspend the issue of letters of dismissal, to grant advances on salary and to pay for overtime whenever necessary.'[2]

In short, the unions aimed at eliminating any suggestion of sanctions in respect of the strike and recovering the total of unpaid salary in return for making up arrears of work; but the managers, while ready to help employees who were short of cash, insisted on doing so as an act of grace by means of repayable loans, supplemented if necessary by overtime. The intensity of this rearguard action reflected not only the animosity between managers and clerks: the strike leaders had a special incentive to get their own way because a fierce struggle had broken out within the unions between adherents of the C.T.P., which was closely linked to Apra, and those whose inspiration and directives came from circles further left, whether communist or Castroist.

Analysing the 'lessons of the strike', *La Tribuna* on 7 June 1959 spoke of 'unconditional surrender . . . due to the movement's political deviations and the disastrous activity of its leaders, communists in disguise who pull the wires of the trade union organisation'. We need not necessarily follow the Aprista newspaper in its talk of 'unconditional surrender' or in dismissing the organisers of the strike as 'strategists of defeat': both these judgments appear open to question. What is of interest here is the specific form of government intervention in a 'politicised strike', as compared with that of the Ministry of

[1] *Crónica*, 15 April 1959.　　　　[2] *La Tribuna*, 28 May 1959.

Los Olvidados – *the Violence of the Have-nots*

Labour and President Prado on the occasion of the miners' strike. In both cases, the dispute was only settled under pressure from the public authority. But the bank employees, unlike the miners, had no single union which indisputably represented them. Their federation, the F.E.B., dissociated itself at the outset of the strike from the C.T.P., professing allegiance instead to a more or less bogus organisation, the F.U.T. (*Frente Unido de Trabajadores* or United Workers' Front), which the Apristas with some reason looked on as an offshoot of the communist party. The unions also instigated street demonstrations in which the government was attacked without restraint. The Ministry of Labour responded by taking a tougher line: when giving its verdict it did not, as with the miners, merely indicate the level of increase it judged reasonable, but ordered the employees to go back to work within three days, failing which the strike would be declared illegal. Having made its attempt at mediation the government let matters take their course, being apparently well content that the strike should run aground and its leaders become discredited. On 15 April, after issuing its suggested award, the Ministry declared that it had said its last word and that 'if the parties wish to reach agreement by themselves, they are welcome to do so'.[1] The date of this off-hand announcement may be noted. On 16 April the President of the Republic exercised his right under Article 70 of the Constitution to suspend for thirty days the guarantees afforded by Articles 56, 61, 67 and 68, which concern powers of arrest and search, freedom of movement and the right to hold meetings. The President's decree was based on a long list of grounds. 'Not only have the leaders of the Federation of Bank Employees ignored the decision taken by the Ministry of Labour, but they have abused their power so as to paralyse the national economy and have embarked on a movement of agitation under the direction of individuals unconnected with their profession.'[2] Next morning, twenty-eight union leaders were arrested at Lima and the unions' premises at Arequipa and Trujillo were occupied and closed down. In this way the government seized the opportunity presented to it by the 'politicalisation' of the strike. The game was not yet won, since on 23 April the F.U.T., in protest, called a twenty-four-hour general strike. This had little effect, but the banking strike dragged on till the end of May, by which time the employees resigned themselves to the idea of going back to work without being paid for the days they had lost.

[1] *La Prensa*, 15 April 1959.   [2] *Crónica*, 16 April 1959.

The outstanding aspect of this affair is the extent to which the bargaining process was 'politicised'. The union leaders were described in the Aprista press, rightly or wrongly, as either communists or Trotskyists. When the President used his powers under Article 70 the Apristas and the C.T.P. did not protest—far from it. 'An inefficient and misguided movement has supplied the executive with the pretext it needed to suspend republican guarantees. A strike which went beyond the reasonable limits of collective bargaining has, as was inevitable, provoked the government to security measures.'[1] In short, the Aprista party and the supreme trade union body disowned the bank employees' union. When, towards the end of the strike, the latter body sought to renew relations with the C.T.P. to revive its flagging morale, *La Tribuna* (in an article by Richard Temoche) contemptuously rejected the appeal, at the same time reminding the F.E.B. leaders of the insults they had poured on the Aprista trade unionists:

'How can any sensible person dream of co-operation with a "treacherous institution" run by "blackguards"?—to use the terms in which the leaders of the Trotskyist faction of the F.E.B. were recently alluding to the C.T.P. and its leaders . . . Naturally we deplore the fact that these gentlemen have succeeded in bamboozling over three thousand workers and keeping them out on strike for forty-eight days . . . But for the present, the only thing to do is to prepare the way for an effective and cordial reconciliation, from which will arise the united force which we need to tackle the grave problems of the hour.'[2]

Disturbances at Chimbote

The conditions in which violence is apt to break out may be studied in the Chimbote episode of June 1960. Chimbote is a port, some 240 miles north of Lima, whose population was 4,200 at the 1940 census but is said now to number 65,000. There are two reasons for this extraordinary increase. An iron and steel plant was built there about 1950: coke and ore are brought to it by sea, and power is supplied by hydro-electric works in the valley of the Santa, a small river which flows into the Pacific near Chimbote. This investment, which was announced proudly as a decisive step towards the country's economic

[1] *La Tribuna*, 17 April 1959.   [2] Ibid., 24 May 1959.

liberation, has not had the most fortunate history. The company which runs the Chimbote works on behalf of the Peruvian government produces, at high expense, about 100,000 tons of steel a year and employs between 1,200 and 1,500 workmen. Had the iron and steel works been the only factor, Chimbote would probably have remained a minor port like many others on the grey, sterile Peruvian coast. But from 1956 onwards fishmeal canneries began to increase and to attract labour in large quantities. These workers, who were quite well paid, brought their relatives with them, and formed settlements around the town in *barriadas* which have grown like mushrooms.

On 12 May 1960 the iron and steel workers went on strike. They had been in conflict for some weeks with their employers, the SOGESA company, over their demand for a pay rise of 5 per cent, based on a cost-of-living clause in the collective agreement which was then about to expire. Thus the unions were asking for nothing more than the execution of a contract which the company had freely signed. On 14 April they published a statement accusing the company of 'refusing to improve on its initial proposals concerning night work and overtime rates and in particular the adjustment of wages to the cost of living', and adding that 'it is thus responsible for the strike which its intransigence obliges us to declare'. On 14 April *La Tribuna* summed up the positions of the two sides as follows. 'As regards night work, SOGESA offers 3 soles and the unions demand 8; for overtime, the company offers a bonus of 25 per cent and the unions ask for rates of 50 per cent, 75 per cent and 100 per cent according to wage-level. As regards actual wages, the company offers a rise of 6 soles for those receiving between 22 and 26 soles, while the unions want a rise of 8 soles at this level and 7 soles for those receiving more.' Agreement might have been possible, but negotiations foundered on the cost-of-living clause, to which the unions clung tenaciously and which provided for an automatic rise of 5 per cent if retail prices had gone up by more than 10 per cent in the previous twelve months. This claim, however, was not only inconvenient for the company but also unwelcome to the government of Sr. Pedro Beltrán, which was engaged in a 'stabilisation' campaign. The Minister of Labour turned a deaf ear to the unions, who declared that 'twenty-three days after the conflict began' and a week after the unions had apprised the Ministry of a complaint against SOGESA for 'violation of the collective agreement', the government had vouchsafed no reply. The statement went on: 'We are making public our profound surprise at the silence of the Prime Minister, whom we requested for an audience a week ago, and who, if we are to believe the company authorities, is firmly opposed to the execution of the cost-of-living clause embodied in the collective agreement.'[1]

It is not clear whether the company and the authorities had decided to let the strike come to a head; it may be that the former were prepared to accept most of the claims, but that the Prime Minister – whom the opposition accused of coldness and inhumanity (*falta de sensibilidad*) – would only consent if the unions dropped the vexatious principle of the sliding scale. In any case, and whatever Lima's intentions, the local situation was taking an ugly turn. Protest meetings were called in which all the workers of the area participated, and a large rally was organised. Meanwhile the company kept some of its shops going on a makeshift basis with the aid of the navy. The local police was reinforced by troops, and a warship with marines on board patrolled the harbour-mouth. On 10 June, the Workers' Union of the Santos province, in which Chimbote is situated, addressed an open letter to the President 'respectfully begging his august personal intervention in order to compel the company to fulfil the obligations in regard to the automatic adjustment of wages which it assumed *vis à vis* its employees on 2 and 16 April 1959'. The signatories declined responsibility for the 'unforeseeable consequences that may be provoked by the company's obstinacy'. They referred once more to the sanctity of contracts, and emphasised that 'trade unions would have no reason to exist if their essential objective, namely the conclusion of collective agreements, could be nullified by the obstinacy or intransigence of a company which does not consider itself bound by its pledges'.

This appeal produced no official reply except from the acting Minister of Labour, who, on the ground that he was insufficiently informed, said that a decision would have to wait until his principal, then in Geneva, returned to Lima. On 10 June, nineteen workers went on hunger-strike, and on the same day a general strike was declared at Chimbote. On the 14th, an incident occurred which destroyed the hopes of a reasonable solution. *La Prensa*'s report of the 15th was, broadly speaking, confirmed by the rest of the press. 'On the fourth day of the general strike called by the local trade union, the town was in a state of extreme tension. Early in the day the strike was still only partial, but the leaders were determined to

---

[1] *La Tribuna*, 5 June 1960.

Los Olvidados – *the Violence of the Have-nots*

paralyse all activity . . . Groups of workers placed enormous boulders on the Miramar bridge, which commands the southern access to the town, and the José Gálvez level crossing to the north.' The military were ordered to clear the roads; on the southern side they met with no resistance, but on the north there was trouble. 'About a thousand men stood on the road to block it. Several dozen motor vehicles, with three lorries of the Lima-Tumbes line at the head of the queue, demanded passage: the lorry-drivers hooted louder than any, but without success. At this point a van drove up containing six policemen under the command of a major: they attempted to get through, and a scuffle unfortunately developed between them and some of the workers.' The newspaper described the fight and added: 'The police were obliged to give way and, to cover their retreat, fired some shots in the air, after which they got into their van and drove off.' Half an hour later the police returned, this time over a hundred strong. Stones began to fly; the police fired back and continued shooting sporadically for thirty minutes, killing four men and wounding fifteen others.

That afternoon a largely spontaneous demonstration took place, and according to *La Prensa* the crowd numbered between three and four thousand. Some food-shops were sacked, and others protected themselves by locking their doors. Stones rained on hoardings and shop-windows, and a shoe-shop was demolished. The demonstrators were about to attack a car when its owner emerged from his house and held them off with gunfire. Four other cars, parked outside the main hotel, were overturned and set on fire. The fire brigade were prevented from intervening by the angry crowd: several firemen were manhandled and their engines and hoses damaged.

However, things went no further, and calm was restored by the arrival of police reinforcements. The episode is, however, typical, both in the sense that it might happen again and in that it presents characteristic features of the sort of riot which Lima students sometimes call *quiebraquiebra* (from *quebrar*, to break). The Chimbote incident was provoked by the 'hard core' of strikers who wished to impose a complete stoppage and to intimidate those of the population who were indifferent to the strikers' aims or annoyed or inconvenienced by their activities. Once the small group of men determinedly blocking the road clashed with the police, the temperature rose and a miscellaneous crowd became involved. This led to the second skirmish with the police, in which some demonstrators were

111

killed or wounded, and which was followed by a few hours' pause. All afternoon, the town was occupied by a crowd, probably not more than 5,000 strong, which worked off its aggressiveness in acts of pure violence and others of a more self-seeking type: on the one hand setting fire to parked cars and preventing the firemen from doing their duty, on the other plundering shop-windows and stalls.

How much control did the 'hard core' exercise over the mass of rioters; or conversely, how spontaneous was the outbreak on the afternoon of the 14th, and how deliberate was the decision to interrupt traffic into and out of Chimbote? These questions have a bearing on the likelihood of a *bogotazo*[1] taking place in one or another of the growing towns surrounded by a ring of *barriadas*. There are few data which would enable us to answer them, but at all events there is a wide belief in the seriousness of such a threat. *El Comercio* and *La Prensa*, for once in agreement, underlined the horrors of the Chimbote riot. *El Comercio* on 16 June 1960 published a leader entitled 'The bloody events at Chimbote', which deplored 'the attacks on private property and personal violence that inflicted hours of terror on Chimbote and have filled the country with forebodings of insecurity'; while *La Prensa*'s headline ran: 'Arson and pillage: 4 dead, 27 wounded.'

The union leaders, for their part, were careful to disclaim responsibility. During the week after 14 June, a series of statements by the state authorities, the unions and Apra blamed the disaster on 'outside agitators' and 'communists'. On the 16th, the secretary-general of the union of SOGESA employees declared, according to *La Prensa*'s report next day: 'We must regret the intrusion of politics and demagogy into our trade union struggles . . . Since when have strikes been accompanied by the daubing of hammers and sickles on walls? We do not need the intervention of forces alien to our movement . . . The strength of the workers' movement is its unity.' Naturally, the acting Minister of Labour and the Minister of the Interior took up the theme and asserted on 18 June that 'beyond any doubt the incidents were deliberately provoked': the more so as 'when the riots broke out, a settlement was on the point of being reached'. This attempt by the government to save its face did not meet with immediate response, but, as we shall see, the union leaders eventually

---

[1] This term is an allusion to the celebrated and destructive riot which swept through the centre of Bogotá one afternoon in July 1948, when news was received of the murder of the liberal leader Eliecer Gaitán.

accepted the official version. On the day after the riot, the Ministry of Labour issued a communiqué which went a long way to meet the unions' month-old demands in regard to overtime and night-work, while suspending for a year the application of the cost-of-living clause. On 18 June, the two Ministers concerned issued statements in *La Prensa*, indicating that the police had done its duty though perhaps with too heavy a hand: 'I consider', said the Minister of the Interior, 'that the police acted with skill (*tino*), firmness and decision.' The Minister of Labour, for his part, declared that the 'claim presented by the unions had taken its normal course.'[1]

The unions did not agree. On the evening of the 14th they issued a statement accusing the acting Minister of having shown 'callousness and indifference towards the search for a settlement'. But they soon ceased to pillory the government and concentrated their attack on 'irresponsible and provocative elements'. On 16 June, the provincial union enlarged on the above-quoted personal statement by the secretary-general of the SOGESA union. 'In view of the grave events provoked by irresponsible elements which, having infiltrated among the workers, have engineered a series of incidents completely foreign to the ethical and social standards of the working-class movement, [the union] regrets and condemns these acts of bloodshed ... which have no other purpose or effect than to prevent the state from granting the workers' just demands.'[2] A statement of 22 June repeated the same theme. 'The tragedy at Chimbote was provoked by demagogues who wished to make capital out of (*traficar con*) the victims' corpses.'[3] Finally, on 26 June an association, whose representative character is open to some doubt, called the Federación Única de los Barrios Marginales de la Provincia del Santa (i.e. the slums of Chimbote) denounced a certain Cupertino Foronda Macedo, a 'well-known agitator' and 'exploiter of the needy', as having exceeded the orders of the SOGESA union and instigated the general strike which led to the clash of 14 June, at a time when 'negotiations at Lima between the Ministry of Labour and the union leaders *were on the point of achieving a satisfactory solution*'.[4]

Thus the account of the matter given by the acting Minister of Labour in his interview of 18 June was, after the lapse of a few days, endorsed by the union leaders who, on the 14th, were accusing him of 'callousness'. This instructive evolution may be interpreted in

[1] *La Prensa*, 18 June 1960.   [2] Ibid., 16 June 1960.
[3] Ibid., 23 June 1960.   [4] Author's italics-F.B.

various ways. On the simplest and most cynical level, we may see in it a realistic desire by the union leaders to 'cut their losses' and wash their hands of a bad business, or, as they say at Lima, 'get rid of the corpse' (*no cargarse del muerto*). The second stage of the operation is to shift responsibility from oneself on to one's adversary. 'It was those irresponsible, hot-headed elements who spoiled everything, just as we were about to reach agreement after long and delicate negotiations, thus proving the zeal with which we defend our members' interests.'

The cynical interpretation should not be pressed too far: account must be taken of the fear and horror that scenes of violence inspire, after the event, not only in those who were mere spectators but in those who took an active part. In *La Prensa*'s report of 16 June, we may note a remark by the secretary of the Chimbote association of trade unions (to be distinguished from his colleagues of the provincial and the SOGESA unions): 'We workers didn't set fire to the cars: it's not a thing we would do, we aren't incendiaries.'

To assess the risk of violence which threatens Peruvian society, we should distinguish, as it were, the detonator from the explosive. The workmen or employees whose organisations are of long standing, such as miners or even bank-clerks, have some experience of discussions with their employers; and while these may at times be stormy, they are nevertheless likely to lead to a broadly acceptable compromise. More serious accidents may occur when previously inert masses are exposed to intense though transient excitement: the Chimbote episode is a good example of this type of convulsion, breaking the thread of everyday life. If for any reason a spark of conflict should fall into the midst of a tense and over-heated atmosphere, may we not fear that the whole, or a large part, of the social edifice will be affected by the resulting blast and may collapse?

The 'barriadas', or the second wave of social mobilisation

This fear, at all events, assails conservatives who reflect on the problem of the *barriadas*–the shanty-towns around Lima and other cities which have grown so rapidly in the last fifteen years. The flood of migrants from the sierra since 1950 constitutes what may be called the second wave of social mobilisation, distinguished in both quantity and quality from the migration which took place in the late

Los Olvidados—*the Violence of the Have-nots*

1920s. The second wave is more massive than the first and comprises for the most part an unskilled population, very different from the clerks, artisans and day-labourers whose migration from Puquio to Lima was described for us in *Yawar Fiesta*. Most observers find the second wave of migrants a distressing spectacle. 'It is scarcely conceivable', writes a former President, José Luis Bustamante y Rivero,[1] 'that at this stage of history and in the very centre of our capital city, we should witness such a grievous conjunction of human wretchedness and lack of social conscience'. But shame rapidly gives place to fear. 'This phenomenon, which the authorities have been powerless to remedy . . . has recently led, near Lima, . . . to the occupation by more than 15,000 persons of lands surrounding the village of Atacongo, where the squatters have founded the celebrated "city of God" (*ciudad de Dios*).'[2]

These squatters who install themselves in small groups, under cover of night, on vacant lots that are frequently of doubtful and contested ownership, seem fitted for the role of an 'internal proletariat', a blind force which, if directed by a revolutionary will, might one day sweep all before it. The new proletarians may well be seized by the 'desire to destroy everything that is worth anything, because they have no sense of value and because all they know is that they are capable of seizing the good things which are unjustly denied them and, paradoxically, are reserved for those who have turned them into pariahs'.[3] To the well-intentioned observers who desire its redemption, the proletariat appears first and foremost as the victim of an injustice which reflects disgrace on the governing classes. But it also appears as a formidable threat, not only to the beneficiaries of the existing order but to the traditional values of Christian civilisation.

Apprehension of a barbarian onslaught in what may well be the near future, coupled with an awareness of the inhuman conditions of life in the *barriadas*, leads to reformism in some quarters and a revolutionary attitude in others; but both groups are united in feeling that the situation is intolerable and that 'something must be done'. Is the viewpoint we have described borne out by the conclusions of ethnologists, economists and sociologists? Information about the Lima *barriadas* is extensive but not always reliable. Estimates of their population vary considerably, from 10 per cent of the city's

---

[1] *Mensaje al Perú*, Editoria universitaria, Lima, 1960, p. 67.   [2] Ibid.
[3] Lino Rodríguez Arias, *La democracia cristiana en América latina*, Lima, 1961, p. 72.

total to 300,000, or nearly 20 per cent. A commission set up by the Prado government in 1956 caused a report to be drawn up by the ethnologist José Matos: this has not been published but can be consulted in the library of the San Marcos university, and its main conclusions have been embodied in administrative memoranda which have received limited distribution. Some of Matos's facts are probably now out of date, since his enquiry was carried out between October 1956 and July 1957; but his broad conclusions seem to me of permanent value in correcting many errors and prejudices. Until we possess a work comparable to Oscar Lewis's study of the slums of Mexico City, Matos's report will retain its importance as a description of 'poverty culture' in the Lima *barriadas*.

We may consider the slum population from three points of view: those of origin, education and means of livelihood. The great majority of Lima slum-dwellers seem to be provincials, though a number were born in the department of Lima or the city itself: many of these seem to have moved from hovels in the centre of the city, finding it easier to install themselves in the shanty-towns. Thus the inhabitants of the latter are not all newly-arrived *serranos* but include some *criollos* too. The degree of assimilation of the newcomers may be gathered from their educational level. 90 per cent of those questioned in the 1957 census claimed to have attended school for a longer or shorter period; of the 10 per cent who were illiterate, three-quarters were women. Taking into account only men, the level of education in the *barriadas* is higher than the average for the whole country. It is true that school attendance was in general extremely brief: less than 1 per cent went to a university, 10 per cent to grammar school, and the remaining 90 per cent went through only the first two years of primary school. As regards occupation, nearly 60 per cent were artisans and workmen; 15 per cent were servants, janitors and watchmen; another 15 per cent were travelling salesmen; 5 per cent were transport workers and 2 per cent worked in offices. Nurses, midwives, teachers, accountants etc. made up nearly 1 per cent. Of the total, 70 per cent were in what the investigators called 'stable' employment, earning (according to their own statements) an average monthly wage of 617 soles, or about $31 at the then rate of exchange.[1] (The average daily wage for all those in employment was 30 soles or

---

[1] The average income per annum would thus be about $370 for a wage-earner in the *barriadas*, while the average for the whole of Peru, counting wage-earners and non-wage-earners alike, was at that time probably about $120.

about $1.50.) This figure must be considered in the light of two facts. Firstly, the proportion of wage-earners was very high: only 1 per cent of those questioned declared that they were unemployed. Secondly, even the youngest adult member of every household was a wage-earner.

What may we conclude from these facts? In the first place, by 'stable employment' the investigators mean employment lasting at least one month. As regards qualifications, they define these in terms of broad categories such as artisan, workman etc. Two main points emerge, however. Firstly the importance of the tertiary sector (that of service industries). Itinerant salesmen, servants of all kinds, drivers and clerks account for 37 per cent of the wage-earners. Secondly, a breakdown of the majority group of artisans and workmen shows that the latter make up only one-third of the group, or about 20 per cent of the wage-earning population.

It appears difficult simply to identify the *barriada* population with the proletariat: certainly we cannot do so if we understand by this term the industrial working class. If by 'proletariat' we mean the under-privileged, we should bear in mind that the inmates of the *barriadas* are not so badly off in terms of income by comparison with the average Peruvian, let alone the most destitute of the Indians. This throws light on the fact, which surprised many observers, that the great majority of those questioned declared themselves satisfied by comparison with their previous lot, whether they were peasants straight from the sierra or townsfolk from the slums of central Lima.

The 1957 enquiry also provided a surprise for those observers who expected that material conditions in the *barriadas* would lead to promiscuity or to moral and psychological anarchy. On the contrary, the strength of family ties was much in evidence. 62 per cent of those questioned lived in basic domestic groups, i.e. composed of parents and children only, and 26 per cent in wider units comprising also relatives or friends on a more or less permanent basis. In 5 per cent of cases the family consisted of one parent with his or her children, and only 2 per cent of those questioned lived alone. (This is not quite the whole story: many, perhaps most, couples are unmarried, and it would seem that about 40 per cent of births are illegitimate.) The nature of the primary social ties which are thus preserved has not as yet been sufficiently analysed, though it is of interest both to ethnologists and to psychiatrists. The former have sought to discover whether traditional forms of mutual aid survive in the *barriada*

117

setting. Here there are two institutions of importance: that of *compadrazgo*, whereby godparents and godchildren owe one another help and protection throughout life, and occasional specific forms of solidarity, for instance in house-building. But the primary group in *barriada* society is exposed to a good deal of strain. Broadly speaking, the individual may choose between confining his sights to the family group, identifying with those who come from the same area as himself (*paisanos*), or establishing more or less close relations with his neighbours. His personal equilibrium will be very different according to which solution he adopts.

This is illustrated by the work of Peruvian psychiatrists. Drs. Caravedo, Rotondo and Javier Mariátegui[1] have noted the frequency of attitudes of isolation and distrust. 'Several of the inhabitants of Mendocita told us that no one had ever visited them; about a third of the population had no contact with its neighbours or with people elsewhere . . . The majority have very few acquaintances and connections, the most isolated being those newly arrived from the sierra, who often have as many friends from their native village as from their present neighbourhood.'[2] Not only do many individuals take refuge in their family circle, but in addition they are confined by ethnic barriers. Mutual prejudices exist between *criollos* and *serranos*, and the latter tend to live in groups according to their place of origin. Their reaction to this situation is to mistrust the people around them, whom they suspect of envy and ill-will, and to adapt themselves cautiously to the surrounding hostility. 'The quarter I live in is a bad one, full of crooks (*rateros*): I'm afraid to go out at night . . . Lots of the negroes are up to no good . . . People look sideways at me because I'm poor and because I've got a small bit of land that they'd like to get their hands on.' However, it is not only the world of the *barriada* that is seen as hostile and malevolent: things were the same back in the sierra. 'Up there they tried to take everything away from us—fields, springs and all. So I left my village, and I've no wish to go back. The only way to defend yourself is to clear out.'[3]

Here we recognise the same theme as in the case of the middle-class *mestizos*: *no meterse*, or 'Don't go looking for trouble'. To adjust to shanty-town life, the individual organises a system of minimum security based, according to circumstances and to his emotional requirements, on his immediate or wider family and/or his

[1] In *Estudios de psiquiatría social en el Perú*, Lima, 1963.
[2] Ibid., pp. 115–20. [3] Ibid., p. 306.

neighbours. But how does he apply the principles of caution *vis à vis* his present surroundings? This the psychiatrists fail to tell us; and, for lack of analysis of the way in which the man of the *barriadas* seeks to adjust to a hostile *milieu* of which he is largely ignorant, they have probably exaggerated the passive and regressive aspects of this 'poverty culture'. Yet the *barriada* has its own collective life and is not merely a collection of self-contained individuals, indifferent to the outside world. Is that world as 'broad and alien' to them as it is to Alegría's Indians? In point of fact, the more alert of the 'under-privileged' view society in terms of problems whose solution depends on their getting on the right side of the authorities, and, in the case of the abler and more ambitious, being appointed chairmen or secretaries of the *Juntas de Pobladores* or settlement committees.

The *barriada* population's first problem is to defend itself against the real or self-styled owners of the land it lives on. The *pobladores* are often involved in interminable lawsuits; and if the land is recognised as belonging to someone living outside the *barriada*, the problem of rent arises. Once the shanty-town is firmly established, the *pobladores*' task is to persuade the authorities to install a minimum of facilities. First, water will be laid on at a few points, and later electricity; but long after this has been brought to the shanties, the unmade roads along which they cluster (some little more than tents, others made of adobe bricks and some few of solid material) remain pitch-dark at night. Sewage and street-cleaning are the inhabitants' responsibility, at least until the new quarter is transformed into a borough or urban district. When that day comes, teachers will be sent and a school built, usually on the initiative and with the help of the *pobladores*. As the *barriadas* spread further and further from Lima, transport must be organised for those of the inhabitants who work in the city.

The achievement of these elementary facilities is the task of the organisations of *pobladores*, whose leaders make the necessary contacts with the political and administrative authorities. In general the settlers seem to regard the organisations as valuable, though they are frequently caustic on the subject of the leaders – chairmen and secretaries – who are generally mistrusted by the *barriada* folk as self-interested and too clever by half. None of them, as far as I know, has ever become popular outside his own quarter, and even within a given organisation few seem to remain in authority for long. These 'leaders' are in fact middlemen, who seek favours for themselves and

119

their clients, offering in return votes and the acclamation of those who have received benefits. But while they see to it that their services are recompensed, none of them so far seems to have become autonomous and set up as an independent agent. In the 1962 election, some *barriada* leaders who considered that they had been badly treated by the heads of the main political parties formed a list of candidates, but none of them was elected. Thus most of this class, insecure in their middlemen's role, take care not to commit themselves irrevocably and to be in a position to treat with the highest bidder. No party can be sure in advance of the *barriadas'* votes, and, as we shall see,[1] it was probably the most expensive error of the extreme left to assume that it could conquer the 'under-privileged' vote by a radical campaign in the Castro manner.

The importance of the *barriada* vote at Lima was first evident in the presidential election of 1956. According to the account by Guillermo Ramírez y Berrios,[2] Dr. Manuel Prado received his supporters 'in the presence of large groups from several populous *barriadas*, . . . whose leaders, despite their distance from the city, had made a praiseworthy effort to appear before the candidate's house'. By way of confirmation, the author reproduces a photograph of himself presenting to Dr. Prado 'a humble inhabitant of the remote *barriadas* of the Agustino quarter'. While in power, Dr. Prado nursed his relations with the shanty-town folk and was often seen, accompanied by his wife, the high-born Doña Clorinda, opening schools and dispensaries in the most tumbledown quarters, where the presidential couple invariably appeared in the most elegant outfits amid the respectful and delighted murmurs of the inhabitants. *La Prensa* thus described, with a front-page photograph, how Sra. de Prado opened two schools in the *barriada* of San Cosme on 19 November 1961. 'The pupils presented bouquets to the First Lady, recited a complimentary speech and greeted her with the utmost respect and cordiality. The chairman of the settlement committee expressed gratitude to Her Excellency on behalf of all the head of families who were present and emphasised that the government had kept its word by endowing the *barriada* with six primary schools, a kindergarten and three fully-equipped sets of premises.'

All this is a long way from the image of a flood of barbarians engulfing the city. The potential explosiveness of the *barriada* is in

[1] Cf. Part II, chap. 3.
[2] *Grandezas y miserias de un proceso electoral en el Perú*, p. 165.

Los Olvidados – *the Violence of the Have-nots*

fact very hard to measure. There is no guarantee that incidents such as those at Chimbote will not grow to such a pitch as to constitute a revolutionary situation, i.e. one beyond the control of organised political forces. At the outset of this chapter we called the masses *los olvidados*, the forgotten ones – a term which now appears only half appropriate. In the first place, these outsiders inspire fear and are talked about, and this is already an indication of their success. Secondly, and this is even more significant, they have managed, if not to become integrated in society, at least to occupy a certain place within it – for, under pressure from this vaguely threatening mass, the other classes are bound to take some account of their demands. The inmate of the *barriadas* is a second-class citizen in the sense that the society to which he belongs is still a long way from satisfying, and perhaps even unable to satisfy, his most elementary needs; but this is not to say that he is a complete outsider with no influence on events. Taking into account the frequency of contact and the continuity of negotiations between the 'forgotten people' and the administrative and political authorities, I am inclined to think that their influence is gradually on the increase and that their weight will not necessarily slide, or be cast, into the scale of revolution.

The pessimistic viewpoint seems to me the less plausible in that the revolutionary leanings of the *olvidados* do not seem to be clearly established. I can only give summary indications on this point and will confine myself to quoting from contemporary literature: the reader may thus compare the analysis which follows with that already devoted to the theme of 'dependence' in the middle class. Of late years, Peruvian literature has no longer concentrated on the Indian or the sierra: the broad canvases of the 'indigenist' school give place to the sordid picturesqueness of the *barriadas*. In a story entitled *The little boy who lived close to Heaven* (*El niño de junto al cielo*),[1] Enrique Congrains Martín relates the symbolic adventure of little Esteban, who has recently come from the sierra to live in one of the hillside *barriadas* outside Lima. Having come across a 10-sol note while out walking, he makes his way to Lima and falls in with a newsboy somewhat older than himself, called Pedro. The latter craftily persuades Esteban to lend him the note so that they can buy more newspapers and share the profit of selling them. Leaving Esteban in

[1] Included in Alberto Escobar, *La narración en el Perú*, Librería editorial, Lima, pp. 481–3.

121

charge of his stand, Pedro makes off with the money and Esteban never sees him again.

Various themes appear from this story. Firstly, the benevolent role of chance: 'For a completely unknown reason, Esteban had passed by the very place.' Or was it not rather Providence–'might it not be that the money (*aquello*) had found its way to him?' In any case, Esteban does not know what to do with his windfall, and when Pedro asks him he replies 'I don't know, I'll try to keep it safe some-where'. Pedro, for his part, at once sees the possibilities of the single banknote. 'He touched the note, fondled it, reflecting that this one might bring him another, and that other many more.' Pedro's business instinct is at work. 'There are lots of things we could do . . . We could buy newspapers and sell them in Lima, we could buy magazines and comics . . . If we bought ten soles' worth and sold them this afternoon, I bet you we could make fifteen soles.' Pedro hustles Esteban along to a newsagent. As he hands over the money, 'the child was seized by misgiving. Parting with the note was more painful than he had expected. He would rather have kept it in his pocket and been able to feel it as often as he liked.' But he yields to Pedro's insistence. 'He clutched the note desperately, then reluctantly withdrew it from his pocket. Pedro snatched it out of his hand and gave it to the newsagent.' They install themselves in the Plaza San Martín and sell off the papers and magazines rapidly. At four o'clock, when there is only one left, Pedro discovers that he is hungry and sends Estaban off to buy sandwiches, bananas and biscuits. He gives him two soles, keeping the rest of the proceeds. But when Esteban returns, having dawdled a little, he finds that Pedro has made off with the till.

Dr. Caravedo and his colleagues emphasise the theme of mistrust. The fear of being used and exploited does not relate only to those who enjoy power over us: we may at any moment be betrayed by our friends, by those in whom we confide. And this betrayal of a trusting child by a youth seems perfectly natural to the former. Esteban is grieved by it but is not surprised. The little *serrano* from Tarma sees the big city as a single obscure threat, a monster with millions of heads. 'A few days before leaving Tarma for Lima, Esteban had had a nightmare in which he dreamt of a huge beast with a million heads, and now every step he took seemed to lead him further into the animal's jaws.' What afflicted Esteban is not parental tyranny but neglect: his father died when he was a baby, and his mother, who has come to work in Lima, lives with a chauffeur who leaves Esteban alone but takes little notice of him (*no se mete conmigo para nada*). Pedro's treachery appears to him less as deliberate malice on the part of a false friend than as the way of the world, in which one must expect to be duped. Here is the description of Esteban's return to the meeting-place. 'He found himself on the pavement, twenty or thirty yards from where he had left Pedro. Could he have lost his way?... He looked around.' He thinks at first that Pedro may have been worried by his long absence and gone off to look for him; but his friend does not return. He asks passers-by what time it is. 'Esteban leant against the wall, motionless, with a packet of biscuits in his hand and his hopes in Pedro's pocket... motionless, trying with all his might not to burst out crying. So it was true, Pedro had cheated him. Pedro, his friend, had stolen his money. Was it not all the fault of the million-headed beast, and was not Pedro just a part of the monster? How could he tell? Anyway, it didn't matter. He stood up straight, and, nibbling at a biscuit, walked sadly towards the tram-stop.'[1] These few lines portray a mood of accepted disappointment with great psychological subtlety, apart from the somewhat banal imagery of the nightmare and the million-headed monster. The point I wish to bring out is that the frustration is accepted: nothing, not even revolt, is any use in a world in which your best friend is likely to swindle you and abuse your confidence to his own advantage.

Nevertheless, the *olvidados* are beginning to figure in the social scene. This does not mean that they play a full part in it, or that the rate at which they are being integrated affords a promise, still less a guarantee, of stability. Actually the old order, based on the cold-shouldering of the illiterate masses, is being replaced, not by genuine integration, but by the partial acceptance of more and more differentiated categories of persons who may succeed in organising in defence of their interests or becoming acknowledged factors in the political game. The walls which kept the *olvidados* excluded have already to a large extent been breached. Will they collapse altogether, or will it turn out some day, as with so many other fortresses, that they have been outflanked without their defenders realising it? Our best hope of answering these questions is by an analysis of rural life and the changes it is at present undergoing.

[1] Ibid., p. 485.

Agrarian unrest

The agricultural workers of the coastal zone have been accustomed to collective bargaining for a long time past. Take for instance the Chancay valley, about 60 miles north of Lima. The principal but by no means the only crop is cotton. In 1945, when Apra was first legalised, trade unions began to be formed, representing on the one hand the *peones* (farm labourers) and on the other the *yanaconas* (farmers paying rent in kind and enjoying a long tenure). After the eight years of General Odría's rule, the unions revived in 1956 with the policy of *convivencia* or 'coexistence'. During the next few years the valley was rent by violent conflicts. There were many subjects of dispute: claims about wages and norms of payment (*tareas*), work conditions and discipline, food and housing problems. But the principal controversy was over the legal recognition of the unions. Many estate-owners, seeing the unions as a weapon against their own power, sought to prevent their formation by forbidding the workers on their land to join them. The Ministry of Labour officials were under pressure from the estate owners, but the union leaders, who had plenty of legal advice at their command owing to the proximity of Lima, used every procedural device to further their claims. When these nevertheless failed and a strike broke out, the landowners had it declared illegal on the ground that the unions were not recognised. Some of the workers gave in, but the 'hard core' used threats and violence to discourage the strike-breakers; whereupon the *guardia civil* intervened to restore the right to work.[1]

The clash between strikers and 'blacklegs', followed by police intervention, is a pattern not confined to the cotton-growing valleys of the Lima area: a similar situation may be observed in the sugar estates of the north. We may take two examples, one of September 1959 and the other of May 1960. At Casa Grande, the biggest sugar-producing area in the country, there was a strike which lasted more than a week at the beginning of September 1959. The civil guard were patrolling the refinery to prevent it falling into the strikers' hands, and on the afternoon of the 8th, as reported by *La Prensa*, violent incidents broke out in the course of which the police fired on demonstrators who 'were continuing to maltreat two members of the

[1] I have drawn here on a manuscript by one of my students at San Marcos University.

civil guard who had been thrown to the ground'. In this affray four workers were killed and twenty-six injured, three of them seriously.

On 11 September *La Tribuna* gave a more detailed version of the affair, its tone being sharply hostile to the firm and favourable to the unions. 'Before describing how the massacre took place, we must refute the allegations of certain reporters [probably a reference to *El Comercio*, which in an editorial of the 10th accused the Apristas of being 'truly and directly responsible for the unrest pervading that section of the country'] who have given a distorted interpretation of the fact that the union had formed disciplinary units.' The Aprista journal justified the formation of these shock detachments as follows. 'Everyone knows that organised workers are a guarantee of the maintenance of order and the prevention of strike-breaking . . . The strikes in the Trujillo sugar-producing area have always been marked by exemplary calm, and the workers have always respected both property and persons.' To rebut *El Comercio*'s accusation that the Aprista unions were indulging in violence and fomenting civil war, the writer continued: 'These workers have never carried weapons, and the armlet they wear is nothing more than a symbol of dignity and calm vigilance.' Unfortunately, he went on, the managerial staff did not show the same discretion. 'As an indication of the employers' provocative attitude towards unarmed workers, we may note that a high-level official, in fact a sub-manager, ostentatiously carried a large pistol throughout the period of the strike.'

La Tribuna then proceeded to relate the episode of 8 September which we have seen briefly reported in *La Prensa*. 'On Tuesday afternoon, four "blacklegs" tried to bring in fodder for the cattle belonging to the estate. A group of women started to boo them for this anti-union activity, whereupon a platoon of the civil guard appeared on the scene and began to use tear-gas.' In the excitement and scuffle which followed, according to *La Tribuna*, 'the guard began to fire without orders'.

The 1960 incident took place on the sugar plantation at Paramonga, belonging to Messrs. W. R. Grace and Co. Here too, after a prolonged strike which had been declared illegal, a clash took place between police and demonstrators, in which three were killed and sixteen wounded. The strike on this occasion was due to the unions' refusal to agree to the installation of time-clocks (*relojes de control de asistencia*). The fight took place in two stages.[1] In the first, a group of

[1] Cf. the Chimbote episode, above.

'activists' attacked a van from which the owners' representatives were appealing to the men, through loud-speakers, to return to work.[1] The police intervened after some workers had been injured in the scuffle. According to *La Prensa*, they were met by a volley of stones, whereupon they used their firearms.

The Casa Grande and Paramonga incidents have two features in common. In both cases the dispute was between the union and the plantation authorities. The union claimed to represent and mobilise the workers as a whole and to impose its authority on waverers. The owners thereupon called in the police. Once the latter come on the scene, a clash is inevitable and there is some loss of life. But in neither case are matters pushed to extremes. The press, parliament and political circles deplore police violence—*La Prensa* in sorrow, *La Tribuna* in anger. But these violent interludes do not prevent the unions and employers from coming to terms on wage problems and, as we shall see, forming a united front on matters of concern to their industry as a whole.

Agrarian conflicts in the sierra are of a different stamp. We may distinguish two types. In the central departments, especially Cerro de Pasco and Junín, there are huge stock-farms employing very little labour. The animals are carefully selected, the pasture-land enclosed, and much expense has been devoted to protecting the meadows from drought and frost. The Cerro de Pasco Corporation owns two or three hundred square miles of land in the vicinity of its mines. The herdsmen being few, well trained and well paid, the landowners have little trouble with them; but the Corporation, in particular, is involved in endless boundary disputes with the Indian communities on the fringe of its immense domains. In May 1960, the Rancas community took possession of some pasture-land which it claimed on the strength of documents dating back to the eighteenth century. The police moved in to expel the squatters, and three *comuneros* were killed. The Corporation issued a statement on 3 May asserting that there had never been any dispute over the lands in question and that the community's claim had never been upheld by any court.

The second paragraph of the statement is interesting, as it reveals part of the reason for the Corporation's intransigence. The activity of 'well-known agitators' is mentioned, but what chiefly disturbs the company is the evidence which it discerns of a concerted plan

[1] *El Comercio*, 4 May 1960.

whereby the *comuneros*, by attacking without respite first at one point of the huge frontier and then at another, are endeavouring not merely to regain this or that strip of land but to erode the domain as a whole, nibbling at it from all sides. 'This subversive campaign began to bear fruit last year, when a first invasion took place, and another area was encroached upon at the beginning of January this year . . ·
It should be emphasised that the last attempt has taken place at a time when we were negotiating on the dispute which gave rise to the last invasion.'[1] No compromise is possible, since the *comuneros'* object is gradually to recover the entire area of the *haciendas* belonging to the Corporation. The conflict is not between employers and employed, but between landowners and squatters. We may wonder if there is any way out, and whether the Cerro de Pasco or another such corporation would be averse to re-selling its pasture-land to the government at a favourable price.

In the Cuzco area in the southern sierra, the position is different and more threatening. In the sugar plantations, as described above, the political exploitation of social conflict took a mild form because the Apristas, in accordance with the spirit of *convivencia*, did not push matters to extremes; while in the central area the *comuneros*, even if covertly encouraged by 'agitators', do not seem to have had any other object than to recover the disputed lands. It is a different matter when such agitation is inspired and directed by specialists in revolutionary action, as was attempted by Hugo Blanco in La Convención province in the department of Cuzco in 1961–2. Blanco began as a student of medicine, not at Lima but in his native town, and then went to Buenos Aires, where he was in contact with Trotskyist groups. He returned to Cuzco about 1960 and endeavoured to organise the peasants in one of the warm, damp valleys of La Convención. In this area a perpetual feud existed between the landowners and their *arrendires*, farmers whose tenancy is partly paid for in the form of services, and who themselves hire Indian *peones* who have been obliged to leave their miserable and infinitely subdivided plots. A double conflict seemed to be developing as regards the ownership of land and the use of labour. In 1961–2 Blanco managed to unionise both the *arrendires* and the peons; several pieces of land were seized, and the police who attempted to interfere were roughed up.

I shall discuss the political significance of this episode later. But

[1] Ibid.

127

Hugo Blanco's activity is interesting from another point of view, in that it enables us to follow the organisational process whereby a collection of distressed individuals is transformed into a social movement. Up to now we have seen how groups which are already organised defend their interests, more or less effectively. How such groups are formed is explained by Hugo Blanco in an article published by the Trotskyist review *Obrero y campesino* in August 1963, when he himself was in prison.

'The spread of agrarian revolution in Peru is directly linked with increased unionisation of the peasants, especially in the sierra and on the eastern slopes of the Andes.' Agitation has thus taken the form of unionisation: 'I consider that the essential task for the moment is to organise peasants' unions, and the party's efforts must be geared to this objective.' The emphasis on the sierra and the eastern slopes of the Andes is significant: the coast is not mentioned, although that is where most of Peru's agricultural wealth is concentrated. But the unions there, especially in the departments of Lambayeque, Libertad and even Lima, are for the present closely controlled by Apra. Consequently it is in the more destitute areas that revolutionary action on the landless masses appears most promising. 'We must first awaken (*despertar*) the peasants and instil in them a revolutionary spirit: they must begin to understand that the order which has endured for centuries can be changed to their advantage.' What changes are likely to appeal to these tradition-loving peasants and arouse their enthusiasm for a radically new system? The agitator must first 'present himself as an adviser (*asesor*) in matters of agriculture, sanitation, building, co-operatives and education'. To penetrate circles hitherto closed to him, he will endeavour to raise the peasants' standard of material life and culture by spreading information and furthering technical progress. Thus, the author explains, a double purpose is achieved. The peasants' confidence is gained, and 'other sections of the population, seeing the beneficial results of unionisation and revolution, will discover the latent power of the peasant masses which, if liberated, would display incalculable strength'.

The spread of technical and scientific knowledge is not, of course, an end in itself, but must be linked with a campaign of more and more specific demands:

'The party worker's activity has two aspects. It helps to raise the peasants' level of knowledge, but also to explain to them the true nature of the agrarian problem and the objective reasons for the injustice and loss due to the present system. For instance, if an estate-owner (*hacendado*) appropriates a certain area of pasture-land and so prevents the peasants from raising so many head of cattle, we must explain to those who can grasp the fact that this is why they have to pay high prices for imported meat instead of the country exporting it and lowering prices.'

A fresh stage is reached when strikes, combined with squatting, are organised against the *hacendado*. This is not easy, but requires long preparation. To begin with, the peasants of a particular *hacienda* are helped to defend themselves against the landowner's encroachments. On the basis of resistance groups for the defence of farmers' and smallholders' interests, federations are organised for this or that province. In the initial stage only the inhabitants of rural areas are affected, and revolutionary propaganda is confined to circulation by word of mouth; but once provincial federations are organised, methods change and written propaganda may come into play. Its content will not necessarily change: as long as only the rural population is involved, propaganda must be as concrete and specific as possible. 'In each particular case we must talk about potatoes, maize etc., or communications and industrial possibilities (in La Convención valley we talked to them about fruit-canning), or again about schools, colleges, universities, hospitals and clinics. But the point to hammer home on every occasion is that for Peru to become a great country, the peasant must own the land. We must impress on one and all that the choice is between land and death.'

Three points emerge from this article. Firstly, the author states clearly what conditions must be fulfilled in order that an agitation originally based on narrow and particular claims should be transformed into a genuine revolutionary movement. There must of course be a concrete basis, and that is why the agitator must talk about potatoes and wheat. But to avoid getting bogged down in minor local grievances, the movement must be provided with an enemy and a hope: the *hacendado*, and the cry of 'land for the peasants'. As Hugo Blanco astutely observes, the turning-point in the process of agitation is that at which the scope of activity is enlarged from the *hacienda* to the province. At this point a double evolution takes place: the peasants of different *haciendas* are enabled to co-ordinate their demands, and the agrarian movement comes into contact with the urban population. As Mr. Walt Rostow might say, the revolution is then at the point of take-off.

Mobilisation in a Dualistic Society

So far, the take-off has not succeeded. But in the second half of 1963 the wave of agitation redoubled, threatening this time to engulf the south as well as the central area. It began with *invasiones* affecting the big cattle-ranches of the central departments of Junín and Cerro de Pasco. These multiplied during August and September, and were described by *La Prensa* as 'an invasion by Indians who understand only primitive grazing-systems, and can only succeed in spreading havoc'.[1] The cattle-breeding estates of the two departments had in fact been modernised at great expense; the big Peruvian or foreign firms which had come into possession of them, sometimes by doubtful means, had introduced large numbers of pedigree cattle and sheep and re-sown and enclosed the pasture-lands. 'All this expense is now wasted; the Indians' inferior cross-bred cattle is mingled with the pedigree stock, the barbed-wire fences are broken down, and the pasturage has gone to rack and ruin.' Besides deploring this waste of wealth, *La Prensa* denounces the vandals who spur on the Indians. 'The real beneficiaries of these invasions are a few resourceful characters (*vivos*) who, of course, hope to secure the lion's share of the occupied areas.'[2] In these terms *La Prensa* hit out at the leaders, the *cholos renegados* as Don Julián called them in Arguedas's novel, who, in a pretended thirst for justice, make use of the Indians to further their own ambition. The article ends with an ironical passage on the 'spontaneity' of the invasions.

In November and December 1963 the agitation, which had calmed down after Blanco's arrest, revived in the Cuzco area. This time, observers were struck both by its spontaneity and by its degree of organisation. The Indian now appears as the member of a union. 'Let us make no mistake,' says the journalist Hugo Neira,[3] 'the Indian in his traditional *poncho* has learnt a lot and therefore changed a lot. The decisive factor is unionisation – a spark which may set fire to the whole of the southern sierra.' What are the objectives and the means of this 'peasant unionism', as distinct from that of the labourers on sugar or cotton plantations? The people of Cuzco are not fighting for higher wages but, as Neira emphasises, for the possession of land, which becomes more and more sought-after as the population increases. 'It is estimated', Neira writes,[4] 'that 60 per cent of the rural population of the southern departments consists of people aged twenty-one or younger'. The unions' weapon is 'invasion'. 'It is a

[1] *La Prensa*, 6 October 1963.   [2] Ibid., 11 October 1963.
[3] Hugo Neira, *Cuzco: Tierra y muerte*, p. 80.   [4] Ibid., p. 82.

130

Los Olvidados – *the Violence of the Have-nots*

peaceful occupation–invasion does not mean pillage, rape and arson, it is simply a process of taking possession of the private section of the *hacienda*. The owners can sit on their verandahs and watch their property changing hands, but no one threatens their lives.'[1] This moderation–for, according to Neira, nothing is more contrary to the Indian's ways than any form of licence (*desenfreno*)–is united with extreme prudence: the peasants take good care to avoid clashes with authority. 'Before recovering their lands, they send young men and sometimes women as an advance guard, and never take final action unless the police are elsewhere.'

The peasants' strategy has three principal aspects. As they only invade when certain of encountering no resistance, a game of hide and seek develops between them and the police. 'As there are more unions than police detachments, the police and soldiery are habitually baffled.' The prefect of Cuzco had to seek reinforcements from Lima to cope with the elusive forces which attacked everywhere at the most unexpected moments, as soon as his men turned their backs. But the peasants did not rely solely on the effects of surprise: their union leaders also employed psychological warfare. 'Often the peasants themselves come to the landlord and say: "There's going to be an invasion on Sunday, you'd better leave the *hacienda* and go and stay in your house at Cuzco." '[1] Finally, the union leaders have taken care not to adopt a hostile attitude towards President Belaúnde's government. 'Once the *hacienda* has been invaded, thousands of peasants wait patiently, sitting or standing, for the local authorities whom they have notified, to appear on the scene–showing by this gesture their confidence in the *viracocha* Belaúnde.[3] When the parliamentarians, officials and so on turn up, those of the peasants who speak Spanish will show them the land, saying: "Up to here is ours . . . What's left is the *hacienda* . . . We have taken back what belongs to us." '[4]

The peasants, as Neira emphasises, do not aim at occupying every *hacienda*, or the whole of any particular one, but only that part of the land to which they have a claim, valid or not. Their leaders are 'young people, including students and men straight out of the army'.[5] The students provide a link between the peasant organisations and the unions of textile workers, drivers etc. which have long been

---

[1] Ibid., p. 98.   [2] Ibid.
[3] In modern Quechua, *viracocha* means approximately 'lord' or 'master'.
[4] Neira, op. cit., p. 99.   [5] Ibid., p. 82.

established in the city of Cuzco. The students, too, are skilled at haranguing crowds, negotiating with the police or arguing a point of law with the *hacendado*, while the ex-soldiers 'know how to use fire-arms, submachine guns and so on'. This, Neira observes, is 'the result of a system of military training which weighs heavily on the peasantry while the young men of the gentry and middle class are practically exempt. This is what happens when the barracks are peopled entirely by Indians.'[1]

Do the peasant masses, thus led, already constitute a political force? Under revolutionary leaders united by a single doctrine and ideology, they could be efficacious; but as yet they lack unity of purpose. As Neira remarks,[2] it often happens that the union leaders are disowned by the rank and file. Thus, an *hacendado* offers the peasants who have invaded his estate 1,200 or 1,500 acres out of its total area of 5,000; the union leaders agree, the prefect gives his blessing, but the peasants themselves, or rather their wives, are not satisfied. '*Señor prefecto*,' says the union secretary, 'the villagers won't agree, their wives don't like it'. 'Then,' replies the bewildered prefect, 'you don't control your own people. What sort of leaders are you?' One of the peasants speaks up: 'We don't want the land because it's too far from our village.'[3]

If we bear in mind the obvious differences between a rising or *sublevación*, of which the Atusparia incident was a classic example, and the *invasiones* of 1963, we shall appreciate the importance of the organisational factor in the presentation of demands by the *olvidados*. In former times they resorted to violence, which was often touched off by a minor incident. Thus the affair was strictly localised and could be controlled and suppressed without great difficulty, and without attracting attention in the country at large. The 'invasions', on the other hand, are a direct challenge to the social order as a whole. We shall see[4] how they created difficulties for the new President and led to the early passage of an agrarian reform law. It is no longer a question of an explosion, of a violent but short-lived outbreak. The *invasiones* are conducted with prudence, method and a degree of understanding of the means of revolutionary action. If we agree with *La Prensa* that their leaders are 'agents of inter-national communism', we have to explain why it is that 'town-bred agitators' to whom no one would have listened thirty years ago are now finding a hearing. The reason is that native society has changed

[1] Ibid.   [2] Ibid., pp. 44–6.   [3] Ibid., p. 45.   [4] Cf. Part III, chap. 3.

and 'the Indian has become a peasant.' Co-ordination between the party apparatus of minute radical groups on the one hand and the peasant leaders on the other has been far less easy than the 'agitators' hoped, and this is no doubt why the movement, for all its scope, has remained a regional one. But the landless masses are no longer on the fringe of society: they too are taking a hand in the game.

PART TWO

WHAT IS TO BE DONE?

Modification of Dualism;
the Mobilisation Process

An oligarchy controlling at a distance a society with which it does not feel a sense of identity; a rebellious but prudent middle class; and a mass of under-privileged citizens who find an outlet by organising in defence of specific and narrow interests or by committing brief acts of violence whose political consequences have so far been abortive–such is the picture of Peruvian society presented by Part I of this work. We may add that this society is at once extremely mobile and extremely stratified, in other words that it is poorly integrated; or rather that the forces making for integration are becoming more and more problematical as society becomes more homogeneous or, if one prefers, less heterogeneous. We have seen ample proof that Peruvian society today is mobile, but it does not follow from this that it is open. The fact that *comuneros* come down in force from the Andes to settle in the *barriadas* does not in itself mean that the state is no longer run by the oligarchy. Rather, the combination of increased mobility at lower levels with unaltered rigidity at the top is a recipe for conflict, tension and possible explosions.

It is hard to see how the position of the oligarchy can remain intact in face of the confused but more and more insistent demands of the other sectors. But increasing awareness of these conflicts may promote a certain sense of national unity. As long as the masses remained on the fringe of society, the authorities had no trouble in repressing overt conflict, but the sense of solidarity and common destiny was very weak. At present the situation tends to be the reverse. Many conflicts are rising to the surface for the first time, but their solution is beginning to be envisaged in terms of collective action.

137

What is to be done?

What type of political regime is compatible with such a society as we have described? At the outset of this book I termed the Peruvian regime an oligarchy: the analysis in Part I justifies this description by showing to what extent the masses have been held at arm's length, as well as how difficult it is becoming to keep them there. On paper, Peru is a republic in which political power is based on the right of suffrage. The contrast between constitutional appearance and social reality is bound to throw light on Peruvian political life though the bare antithesis between appearance and reality should, in my view, be treated with caution. At all events, the classes excluded from power put forward demands that are very imperfectly attended to by the powers that be. And awareness of the discrepancy between society's 'demands' and the government's 'decisions' or 'solutions' is the first step towards political thought and action.

It may be pointed out immediately that, unlike the state of affairs in the nineteenth century, major political debates are not based ostensibly on constitutional issues, though in the aftermath of independence such matters as the extent of the executive power and the nature of parliamentary control were hotly debated. This fact, which is clearly brought out by Jorge Basadre in his monumental *Historia de la República del Perú*,[1] may be interpreted in either of two ways, both of which refute the common view that the great families succeeded, as soon as independence was proclaimed, in imposing a regime tailored to their wants. To begin with, the oligarchs of the period were deeply divided on ideological questions, and secondly they had to contend with so-called enlightened opinion – intellectuals, lawyers, journalists etc. By and large, the battle was won by the conservatives, or *autoritaristas* as Sr. Basadre calls them; and similarly the dispute between federalists and centralists was settled in the latter's favour. These debates, which throughout the nineteenth century were accompanied by much constitutional instability, led eventually to a practical outcome which today seems unchallenged. The Presidency is the corner-stone, but Congress, even when the President commands a majority in it, can make its views felt thanks to its power of censuring either the whole cabinet or individual ministers. In any case, the letter of the Constitution which has been in force since 1933 is at present attacked by no one.

[1] Cf., in particular, Basadre, op. cit., vol. I, pp. 197–201 and 347–59, on 'liberal constitutionalism and its paper barriers'; vol. II, pp. 520–3 on controversies concerning the right of suffrage; pp. 523–9 on the Presidency of the Republic; and 530–4 on Congress.

Modification of Dualism: the Mobilisation Process

But if oratorical jousts no longer take place on the merits of this or that constitution, two questions emerge which go to the root of political thinking. Firstly, however wise a constitution may be, how can one ensure that it will in fact be respected? To define rights is not enough: there must be a guarantee that they can be exercised. The second difficulty is this: even if the regular, or fairly regular,[1] functioning of institutions is assured, it does not follow that the needs of society will be satisfied. This leads to the concept of opposition between a legal–constitutional or quasi-constitutional–Peru on the one hand, and a real Peru–qualified by Basadre as 'deep' or underlying (*profundo*)–on the other.

The period of what Basadre calls the 'aristocratic republic' illustrates this clearly. Between 1900 and 1914, presidents and assemblies were elected in regular fashion. The army, reorganised by a French mission after the disastrous war with Chile, kept its proper place within the state. Conflicts of ideas and parties were fought out in a more or less orderly manner. And yet the gulf between society and the *civilista* (civilianist) regime was denounced at the very beginning of the century, by an intellectual, Manuel González Prada, who exercised a considerable and perhaps decisive influence on the generation which came of age around 1920. 'Peru is a sick body: wherever you put your finger, pus streams out . . . Quarrels and convulsions in the government; graft and prevarication on the bench; ridiculous shadow-boxing in Congress, and a people which has lost its faith.'[2] But although González Prada was read, admired and applauded, he did not succeed in becoming a political leader.

However, what González Prada brought to the fore in such a way that it could no longer be forgotten was the radical challenge, not to any particular aspect of the constitution, but to the whole social order. The birth of ideologies may be traced to the point at which traditional forms of legitimacy break down and the need is felt to 'think of something new' and above all to 'do something'. Every ideology owes its origin to some radical doubt. European socialists felt such doubt concerning capitalist society, based as it was on competition and the profit motive, and González Prada felt it concerning the neo-colonial oligarchy based on the exclusion of the Indian. But the ideologist's conscience is not content merely to challenge or even to combat. Once he feels obliged to close the gap between the

---

[1] Cf. below, Part III, chap. 1.
[2] Quoted in Basadre, op. cit., vol. VI, p. 2,853.

'demands' of society and the 'responses' of government, his first concern is to understand the reason for the gap, and therefore the kind of remedy which is needed.

The ideological brand of politics is distinguished by the absolute nature of the objectives pursued and the agent's total commitment to a line of policy. From this point of view, it signifies 'taking politics seriously', to the point where they are more or less explicitly treated as the supreme end of human behaviour. There is a striking contrast between, on the one hand, the *civilistas* as described by Basadre[1] ('united by friendship, interest and their collective predominance . . . they had little difficulty in manipulating the electoral machine and securing majorities') and, on the other, the Aprista leaders in the 1930s, persecuted but constantly returning to the fray, and imbued with their mission to 'save Peru'. Politics are no longer the art of compromise, the realm of sharp practice and cynicism – but a fight: González Prada's radical doubt and passionate reaction bore fruit in a radical desire, or at all events a claim, to engineer change.

This phase is distinguished by the name of Víctor Raúl Haya de la Torre, and by the birth of Apra. When we say that since the 1930s Peruvian politics have tended to become ideological, we are not of course asserting that the nineteenth-century conservatives and liberals were lacking in principle or were not serious politicians. But their principles were either the abstract ones of natural law, or particular and accidental customs treated as absolute. What was new in the ideological radicalism of the 1930s was the attempt to construct a political order adequate to the demands and the real or supposed needs of *all* Peruvians. In this sense, the various phases of the ideological awakening correspond more or less exactly to those of the process of social mobilisation.

The challenge to the old order and the framing of a radically new one, justified not in terms of abstract rights or the prestige of outworn traditions, but by the place it assigns to the 'forgotten masses' – such is the essence of the ideological revolution expressed in literature by the 'indigenist' movement and in politics by Apra and the various left and extreme-left groups. I do not intend to say much about the causes of this change in the manner of stating and feeling political problems, which has clearly a certain amount to do with the mobilisation and intensified racial mixture of the 1920s. It may be noted that at that early stage, ideology was the single common denominator

[1] Ibid., vol. VI, pp. 2,822–3.

Modification of Dualism: the Mobilisation Process

of the newly mobile classes. Poorly organised as they were, their only links – apart from origin in the same province or such institutions as *compadrazgo*-consisted in a more or less vague complex of attitudes. These 'mobile' individuals, as a result of having had some education, were much more accessible to ideology than their successors, the Indian peasants who have since poured into the *barriadas*.

The emergence of a radical ideology helped to modify the rules of the political game, the more so as it was based on a series of sharp antitheses. I shall try to illustrate the importance of the dualistic schema, particularly in Apra ideology, and to show the dangers of rigidity to which it led – until Haya de la Torre, in the search for greater flexibility, succumbed to the risks of opportunism. We shall also see how this dualism, marked as it was during the first phase of mobilisation, has weakened with the passage of time.

When André Gide was asked whom he considered to be the greatest French poet of the nineteenth century, he replied 'Victor Hugo – alas!' If, in Peruvian history, we are searching for the great divide – the point at which the political problems of mobilisation are stated for the first time, in the twofold guise of a radical criticism of neo-colonial society and a passionate call for national integration – then I do not see how Víctor Raúl can be denied the redoubtable honour of having pointed the way. I shall therefore try to analyse the main themes of the Apra ideology, in order to show how the problems and solutions which it propounded were taken up and reformulated by the conservatives to the right of Apra and the advocates of revolutionary violence to its left. Finally I shall examine the ideology of Acción Popular, not only because the leader of this movement, Sr. Fernando Belaúnde Terry, became President of the Republic in 1963, but because it displays certain signs from which we may augur the emergence of a new political style.

1

'Only Apra can Save Peru'

In 1931, a young man of thirty-six named Víctor Raúl Haya de la Torre stood as candidate at the election which followed the overthrow by Colonel Sánchez Cerro of President Augusto Leguía, who had been in power for the previous eleven years. At this time, Víctor Raúl already had ten years of political life behind him. As a student leader he played a large part in the strikes of 1919, and was exiled by Leguía. In 1924, in Mexico City, he founded a party which styled itself not Peruvian but American: the Alianza Popular Revolucionaria Americana (Apra). He attended a Comintern congress at Brussels in 1927, visited the U.S.S.R. and studied at Oxford and Berlin. Returning to his country after nine years of exile, he expounded his party's programme in a celebrated speech.

The Peruvianisation of Peru

The speech of 23 August 1931 portrays Peruvian society as a duality composed of rich landowners on the one hand and the masses on the other. This had been the state of affairs since before Peru gained its independence; and the present élite, descended as it was from the great colonial families which had continued to rule the roost throughout the nineteenth century, no longer possessed any legitimate authority. To begin with, it had 'never had any ideology of its own',[1] but had borrowed its ideas from various European and particularly French sources. This discredited élite had at the present day 'no claim to represent a majority of the nation, and [since] it lacks the

[1] References are to the five-volume edition of the works of Víctor Raúl Haya de la Torre, published by Ediciones Pueblo, Lima, 1961.

142

necessary strength with which to run the state, our political institutions have always been more or less decrepit'.[1]

Dualism is apparent not only in relations between the oligarchy and the rest of the nation but, on another level, in the contrast between the modern and the archaic sector of the economy. 'In agriculture or mining, for instance, we have companies that import capital, machines and technicians and introduce modern methods,'[2] while other concerns are small, weak and ill-equipped. As Víctor Raúl puts it: 'We have the tractor side by side with the wooden plough.'

Inevitably, this dualism is accompanied by dependence. The oligarchy dominates the nation and the modern sector controls the archaic sector. 'What else can one expect in an economy where on the one hand you have capital, technical skill, patronage, aids and guarantees of all kinds, and on the other only the most elementary means of production? Clearly the economy is weighted in favour of all that is stronger and better organised.'[3] This dependence is part of 'the law of progress . . . for the economic order has its own inexorable laws'.[4, 5] Dependence is thus 'predestined', or at any rate part of the nature of things, until such time as the dependent economy can attain to a stage of differentiation and higher development. 'We are not an industrial country; we did not invent machines, we only use those that come to us from abroad (*solamente manejamos la máquina que nos viene de fuera*).'[6] Again (p. 31): 'Imperialism, as defined by Hobson . . . denotes the use of the apparatus of government for the benefit of private national interests, chiefly capitalist ones, whose object is to secure profits in foreign countries.' Or, as Culbertson puts it, 'imperialism is the economic expression of modern civilisation beyond the seas'. By quoting these definitions, the speaker draws attention to two aspects of the phenomenon which he later carefully distinguishes. Imperialism, in the first place, is the export of capital, the spread overseas of the most up-to-date techniques and the expansion of the most go-ahead people. This spontaneous movement from the centre involves, or rather may involve, unpleasant political effects for countries on the periphery: the dominant society may take undue advantage of those whom it dominates.

[1] Haya de la Torre, vol. IV, *El Plan de Acción*, p. 27.
[2] Ibid., p. 29.   [3] Ibid., p. 30.
[4] These laws, according to Víctor Raúl, are of a mechanical or a biological type: the former leads to the notion of balance, the latter to that of development.
[5] Op. cit., p. 32.   [6] Ibid.

This expansion, no doubt, is as inevitable as that of a gas or a fluid: but may not the science which teaches us the laws of development also help us to control them? To Víctor Raúl, dependence is not a foregone conclusion. Certainly, as already noted, 'the economy is weighted in favour of all that is stronger and better organised'; but this is qualified by the hopeful phrase: '. . . until the interests of the most disorganised sector succeed in organising and in making themselves felt'. Thus Víctor Raúl opposes things as they are to what they would be if we set ourselves to change them. But who will take the responsibility of steering the country through this first phase of modernisation?

For 'we are not a homogeneous entity. Our economic and social development bears no resemblance to that of European countries which . . . have gone through a perfectly straightforward evolution. Ours is the country both of the Campa Indian in the Amazon basin and of the feudal lords of the sierra.'[1] Although at first sight Peruvian society appears dualistic, if one looks more closely the prevailing impression is of confusion (*desbarajuste*). No one social group is strong and homogeneous enough to govern the country: there is no national bourgeoisie and no proletariat. 'What social panorama is created by our economic situation? We are not an industrial country, and the proletariat created by our budding industry is in its infancy too.' Developing this theme, Víctor Raúl compares the proletariat to a child. 'This period, during which class-consciousness is being formed, may be compared with the development of a child's awareness and aptitudes. A child lives, feels pain and reacts to it, but has not the power to govern itself.'[2] This comparison suggests the present incapacity of the Peruvian working class – Víctor Raúl does not commit himself as to whether it is permanent – and thus marks off his position from that of the communists. Secondly, Víctor Raúl offers himself in the role of a mentor to instruct the sensitive, lively and spontaneous child in the art of governing its own affairs.

The working class being inadequate, can we count on the peasants to bring about the revolution? 'It has not been possible in our country to create a cultivated peasant class, and although the peasantry comprises a majority of the workers, still from the point of view of quality, having regard to the very primitive level of its techniques and culture, it is not itself qualified (*no está capacitada*) to dominate society and govern the state.'[3] As for the middle classes–

[1] Ibid., pp. 26–7.   [2] Ibid., pp. 33–9.   [3] Ibid., p. 37.

'the small property-owner, the mine-owner or businessman in a small way . . . these groups which perhaps make up a majority of the country'–they are equally ill-prepared for a political role.

Thus no class or group in Peruvian society is sufficiently mature to be entrusted with the nation's destiny. Whereas Proudhon spoke of the political capacity of the working class, Víctor Raúl denies this quality to workers, peasants and the middle class alike. None of these forces will organise of their own accord: only a political party can unite and lead them. Each of the three classes is impotent by itself, but they have a common interest in resisting 'the hold of the oligarchy and the minority'. Together they form the vast majority of the nation, yet at present they have no control over the state.

'If we look at the risk of encroachment to which the three classes are exposed by reason of their immaturity and incompetence, . . . we may fairly say, basing our political judgment on hard economic facts, that the state never has represented, and does not today represent, the interests and problems of the majority of the population . . . It is thus our duty to fight for the Peruvianisation of the state and the economic and political rehabilitation of the national majorities which constitute the nation's living force and whose numbers and quality entitle them to take part in conducting the national affairs of a democracy.'[1]

The problem is to 'regain control of the state for the majority of the nation' (*rescatar para las mayorías de la Nación el dominio del Estado*), and this political objective must be achieved by specifically political action.

'The duty of Peruvianising our pseudo-state falls upon us, the Apristas . . . As a political organisation, we represent the interests of the three "outsider" classes. We are a united front party (*partido de frente único*), created to solve the problems of the three classes which are united by common interests and by the political and national problems which they symbolise. These groups are prepared to pass over disputes that are not of immediate significance (*sacrificando las diferencias que no son de inmediata significación*) and to give priority to the great problem of the salvation (*salvación*) of the national majorities. Under the organic discipline of the party, they will take over the state (*tomar el Estado*) and turn it into an instrument capable of rescuing us from the economic imbalance in which we

[1] Ibid., p. 40.

145

live, and which is the main cause of our political and social inequality.'[1]

Apra, then, is not the party of a single class but represents a front –one might add, not so much a 'popular front' as a national one. The speech of 23 August 1931 lays more stress on the political task of creating a strong and independent state than on the demands of industrialisation. Víctor Raúl often refers to 'scientific policies based upon economics',[2] but the speech contains comparatively little on this theme: a paragraph on land reform, another on small-scale industry,[3] passages on 'monetary reform' and foreign capital, some references to economic regionalism[4] and comments on workers' claims.[5] In a manifesto published in February 1932, Víctor Raúl wrote: 'The industrialisation of the country, about which Sr. Leguía used to make speeches and which so many of our elderly politicians harp on today, is a meaningless phrase (*una vana palabra*).[6] 'It will be a long time before Peru can be industrialised like the United States, Britain, Germany or Japan, even if the whole world were to become socialist.' Víctor Raúl gives two reasons for this, the first based on the economic cycle–it is 1932 and the export of capital is at a standstill–and the second of a structural character: 'The costs of manufacturing at home prevent us from competing with the industries of developed countries.'[7] This disadvantage would still prevail 'if socialism were the dominant economic system of the world', for the constraints which arise from the international division of labour would still prevent or retard industrialisation.

The tasks of economic development and of remoulding the state are interconnected, but in the speech of 23 August the latter seems more urgent than the former. The objective which unites them is that of rationalising and functionalising social relationships, defining and reconstructing them on scientific principles. 'Our aim is to organise the state on a technical basis, to move towards functional democracy.'[8]

The speech of 23 August 1931 is a call for modernisation. The arbitrary domination of the oligarchy must be curbed, and the traditional sector of the economy freed from dependence on the modern sector, which is foreign or controlled by foreigners. Dualism, which means chaos and confusion, must be abolished. These exhortations are, or purport to be, based on scientific analysis. Science

---

[1] Ibid., p. 41.   [2] Ibid., p. 22.   [3] Ibid., pp. 52–3.   [4] Ibid., p. 56.
[5] Ibid., p. 57.   [6] Ibid., p. 122.   [7] Ibid.   [8] Ibid., p. 44.

teaches us the true nature of imperialism: 'If an expanding force encounters no resistance, it will continue to expand until it ceases of its own accord.' Science also teaches us that a living organism[1] cannot jump from one phase of evolution to another, and that a developing economy must pass in turn through each of the stages of social growth prescribed by history. This faith in science takes on a Marxist hue when Víctor Raúl stresses the importance of the technological factor in explaining Peruvian dependence on the outside world and the preponderance of the oligarchy, or at least its more modern sector.

The salient feature of this first great speech by the Apra leader is the combination of two tendencies which are present throughout his subsequent activity. The first may be called 'realism', the appeal to scientific data. Science has much to teach us about what we can do and what is to be expected from the historical process, for society has its laws of balance and development which are no less strict than those of the physical world. But everything depends on will-power – on the whole-heartedness, sincerity and tenacity with which we commit ourselves. The Peruvianisation of Peru will not take place of its own accord, but as the result of untiring and enlightened effort. This points to the second aspect of the Apra philosophy, which we may call 'voluntarism' – the appeal to the nation's energy.

Indo-America and symbols of identification[2]

In whose name does Víctor Raúl speak? In that of the masses, the 'national majority'. In 1930, the mass of the Peruvian population was still Indian. The sierra was more thickly populated than the coast, and the percentage of those speaking Quechua as their first or only language cannot have been much less than fifty. The intellectuals' interest in the Indian masses took various forms. Some felt pity for the Indian and the injustices he suffered: this attitude appears in literature at an early date, and is well exemplified in the novel *Aves sin nido* by Matilda Matos de Turner. Others were interested in native customs and folklore. The indigenist movement combined both points of view in its revolutionary demands and hopes. In Mariátegui's preface to *Tempestad en los Andes*, by Luis E. Valcárcel, who taught in the 1920s at Cuzco University, we read: 'Faith in the

[1] Ibid., p. 32. [2] Haya de la Torre, vol. I, *Indoamérica*.

resurrection of the Indian is not based on the external westernisation of Quechua territory. What gives the Indian courage is not the white man's civilisation or his alphabet, but the myth or idea of socialist revolution. The Indian's hopes are strictly revolutionary. Myths and ideas have been a decisive factor in the awakening of other peoples. Why should the Inca people, which devised the most elaborate and harmonious system of communism, alone be insensible to the movement which is stirring up the Chinese and the Indians of Asia?'[1]

We need not dwell here on the widespread but debatable claim that Inca society was a perfect model of socialist organisation. To Valcárcel–whose views were shared by novelists like Ciro Alegría and by many writers for the journal *Amauta*, which Mariátegui edited from 1925 to 1928–the Indian and the return to native tradition constituted the 'revolutionary myth' *par excellence*.

The Indian is ripe for revolution: as Valcárcel put it, 'the Andean peasant awaits a Lenin'. Can the socialism of the ancient Incas provide the central myth of Peruvian socialism at the present day? We may doubt whether Víctor Raúl ever took seriously Valcárcel's dreams of a return to the golden age of native Peru. When the former refers to the Indians in his 1931 speech, it is to emphasise that they form the bulk of the population and to demand that they should be treated as first-class citizens, or simply as human beings (*elevarlos al rango de hombres*). But, while Haya de la Torre was fully aware of the potential strength of indigenism, he also realised that its appeal was to half-caste intellectuals rather than to the Indians themselves. The Indian and his advancement were a banner around which the Apra leader rallied his partisans.

We should note his persistent rejection of such labels as Hispano- or Latin American. 'In my view'–he declared, taking up the theme of a lecture of 1927[2]–' "Hispano-Americanism" corresponds to the colonial period, "Latin-Americanism" to the republican independence movement, and "Pan-Americanism" to the domination of Yankee imperialism.'[3] This threefold analysis is presented as an example of the Hegelian dialectic. Marx, he observes, applied the dialectic to European societies, and it is now our task to apply it to the Americas. The result of course depends on the chosen point of reference. In the 1927 lecture, this was the pre-Columbian period,

[1] *Siete ensayos de interpretación de la realidad peruana*, Biblioteca Amauta, Lima, 1928, p. 39.
[2] '*El problema histórico de nuestra América*'.
[3] Haya de la Torre, op. cit., p. 18.

distinguished by its 'positiveness'. 'The primitive communism of the Incas was applied on an enormous scale . . . the unity of the empire extended over a huge territory . . . from south of Colombia to north-east of Argentina, with a population of twenty millions. Its basic unit was the *ayllu*, a native community closely knit by blood-relationship.'[1] The synthesis achieved by the Incas–like that of the Aztecs, which however was of a different kind and, according to Víctor Raúl, less 'positive' and coherent–is described by him as the 'negation of a negation', resulting from the imposition of a sovereign power on a mosaic of small clans to which it has brought the benefits of order and justice. This original system is opposed by the Hispanic antithesis, and the formidable (*tremendo*) collision between the Spanish invaders and native American society gives birth to a fresh synthesis, that of the colonial period. This system in turn breaks down, not as the result of an external shock but under the stress of conflict between creole society and metropolitan Spain. The winning of independence in the nineteenth century did not bring stability: the new states which had thrown off the Spanish yoke remained fragile and were exposed to aggressive Yankee imperialism. Thus, at the present day, America south of the Rio Grande is neither Hispanic, since the colonial society has been liquidated, nor Latin, since after the failure of Bolívar's great design the independence movement degenerated into a long period of anarchy; nor is it even Pan-American, since at the time of which Víctor Raúl is writing, continental unity could only be achieved by submission to 'Yankee imperialism'.

Hence, as early as 1930, Víctor Raúl adopted the term 'Indo-Americanism' as the 'expression of a new American revolutionary concept, subsequent to the Hispanic and Anglo-Saxon conquests and envisaging an economic, political and social organisation on a national basis. That basis will be constituted by the racial tradition and labour force of the exploited Indians, who since pre-Columbian days have been the true source of production and the backbone of our society.'[2] The Indo-American continent is inhabited by 'great national working masses, . . . the bulk of whom are Indian'.[3] Víctor Raúl here ascribes four qualities to the Indians. They are the 'source of production' (*la base de nuestra productividad*) and the 'marrow' of society (*la medula de nuestra vida colectiva*); they embody the true

---

[1] Ibid., pp. 54–5. [2] Ibid., pp. 18–19.
[3] Ibid., p. 29.

149

native tradition (*la tradición y la raza*), and they have been successively exploited by the Iberian and Anglo-Saxon conquests (*conquistas ibéricas y sajonas*). The Indo-American theory enables Víctor Raúl, who believes in 'the economic determinism of all historical phenomena', to throw scientific light on the themes of continental solidarity and the struggle against imperialism.[1] 'I propose to interpret in the light of historical determinism the discovery and conquest of America, the colonial period and the importation of Negroes, the independence movement and the establishment of republics, dollar imperialism, European and Asiatic immigration, the Mexican revolution and our own anti-imperialist movements.' Thus the struggle against imperialism is not mere 'aberrant sentimentalism' (*vagarosidad y sentimentalismo*) but 'a necessary consequence of the form and organisation of the capitalist system in force in the United States'.[2] Indo-Americanism, too, enables him to combine realistic claims and idealistic demands, based on a broad concept of the position of the masses living south of the Rio Grande. Providing as they do the only available labour force, and remaining firmly attached to their native traditions, their only hope of liberation consists in an effort of continental solidarity which must first be directed against 'Yankee imperialism'.

The Indo-American theme assumes many forms in Víctor Raúl's writings. He quotes André Siegfried and Keyserling on the importance of the Indian element, and writes with reference to the former's *Amérique latine*: 'Although this French traveller speaks of "white America" in opposition to "native America", he very properly recognises the importance and influence of the Indian strain in our race and our mentality.'[3] Similarly Víctor Raúl praises Keyserling for his perspicacity in discerning the 'essential Indianism' of the population of Buenos Aires; an 'optimistic sadness' which, according to the German philosopher, is the basis of Latin American culture.[4]

[1] Ibid., pp. 28–9.   [2] Ibid., p. 29.   [3] Ibid., p. 42.
[4] The conception of 'optimistic sadness' is developed in the tenth of Keyserling's *South American Meditations* (translation by Therese Duerr, Jonathan Cape, London, 1932). 'The original key in which humanity experiences life is not the major, but the minor' (p. 296). In South America, '*all* life and experience of any importance is passive' (pp. 297–8). 'In proportion to the readiness to suffer, the Ego is increasingly expanded. In the extreme case, it ends in a real inflation. And this hypertrophical Ego is inward-bent and exclusively self-observing . . . This Ego was not the Self, . . . which, when in-built into the whole of the psyche, leads to the integration of the whole man. Nor was it the Ego of the modern egoist' (p. 298). It consists of *ensimismamiento*, 'literally: "immersion in the Self" ' (p. 299) . . . 'I have seen Original Sadness in South America . . . Man . . . must yearn for liberation from the Hell of the incoherent

'Only Apra can Save Peru'

If the passages from Keyserling cited in the footnote to this chapter are compared with those used by Víctor Raúl, differences will be noted as well as a general resemblance. Firstly, the *ensimismamiento* to which Keyserling attaches such importance does not appear in Víctor Raúl's text; nor do the notions of passivity, dependence and the sense of guilt. On the other hand, the 'optimistic vitalism' perceived by Keyserling is presented as a distinctive feature. Whether it does in fact characterise all Indo-American cultures, including that of the Aztecs, is doubtful. It appears to me rather as the basis of a myth whereby Víctor Raúl and his party seek to express their hopes and their conviction that their cause will triumph in the end: sadness is for today, optimism for tomorrow ... The rejection of the tragic note may be taken as a sign of conviction that the game will eventually be won; indeed that it is won already, since, whatever the obstacles, the Indian's inner life is already imbued with revolutionary determination.

In Víctor Raúl's eyes, the 'myth' of Indianism is sufficiently powerful to inspire a revolutionary undertaking; and the indigenist theme also serves to bring out the uniqueness of the Latin American situation. Indo-America is not a mere extension of Europe or North America, but an independent social and cultural reality. Víctor Raúl, as we saw, provides a dialectical justification for this belief, which he has long held intuitively and which goes to the roots of his being.[1]

Early in Víctor Raúl's career, the dialectical approach led him to adopt relativist positions. 'On 11 May 1923 I published a polemical article in the Lima newspaper *El Tiempo* ... in which I attacked the

---

... but if ... the presentiment that self-determination is possible awakes within him, he must feel laden with guilt: he ought to have done better. .... That sadness which once was suspended becomes set in one direction as the cry of the creatures for their Maker ... And thus man first feels urged to strive not after self-determination, but after a determination by something that is outside himself. Hence the original urge to be allowed to obey.' (Pp. 302–3.) We may also quote Keyserling's remark that 'South American sadness is worth more than all North American optimism and all neo-European idealism'. (P. 304.)

[1] 'I remember that once, when the German archaeologist Max Uhle was visiting Trujillo, I heard him say at my parents' dinner-table that the Chanchán ruins were much more ancient than the empire of Manco Cápac.' Even more startling chronological statements were to be found in the textbook of world history by a certain M. Ducoudray, in which the young Víctor Raúl learnt under his French masters that 'in A.D. 1492, the Old World officially discovered the New'. .... 'Notwithstanding this statement, the Chanchán ruins suggested to me a different temporal dimension, in which our America was not a new world. When the Europeans discovered Chanchán it was already in ruins, so it must have belonged to a very old American world. But how could outsiders see it in this light?' (Haya de la Torre, vol. III, pp. 16–17).

false notion of unalterable truths and eternal principles, in an era profoundly marked by scientific revolution and the irresistible current of relativism.'[1] Continuing his autobiography, he relates that one of the works that most impressed him after his arrival in Europe was Hegel's *Philosophy of History*. But 'Hegel's interpretation left no room for the American world'; and when he read such words as 'World history moves from east to west: Europe is its end, as Asia is its beginning', or again 'Everything that takes place in America has its origin in Europe', he felt that Hegel had 'installed himself fairly and squarely in his Germano-European location', from which 'like an astronomer in an observatory whence only his own zodiacal hemisphere is visible, he studies the movement of the historical constellations . . . belonging to his world'.[2]

Does not relativism lead to a notion of history as a succession of isolated events? Víctor Raúl quotes Hegel to the effect that 'Each nation is in a unique situation: bygone events never coincide exactly with present ones, and circumstances are always completely original.'[3] Nevertheless there is such a thing as universal history; and Víctor Raúl understands the twofold aspect of Hegelian thought which on the one hand sees each culture as individual and on the other relates them all to a single historical conception. 'History is the idea of the Spirit (*Geist*)'; but 'the spirit of different peoples is manifested separately in space and time, and from this point of view account must be taken of the relationships of natural phenomena and human temperament, the natural and spiritual order etc.'[4]

By 'historical relativism' Víctor Raúl understands, as he tells us, a generalisation of the teachings of contemporary science; and his expression 'historical space-time' is an obvious allusion to Einstein. But it he means 'the continuum which links the objective field or geographical scene with man's subjective time-scale in relation to this area: the two being linked by a specific rhythm which, in social terms, may be defined as historic time.'[5] The relativist approach is based on

[1] Ibid., vol. III, p. 24.
[2] Spengler, whom Víctor Raúl also read about this time, represented a 'Copernican revolution', since although he too studied civilisations 'from the fixed viewpoint of the gravitational field of the old world', he took an interest in them for their own sake and ascribed to them an independent existence and value. Unfortunately Spengler did not always live up to this principle, and in practice, as an historian, he remained bound by a European perspective.
[3] Haya de la Torre, op. cit., p. 20.
[4] Quotations from Hegel are here given according to Haya de la Torre's Spanish version.
[5] Haya de la Torre, op. cit., p. 33.

the discernment of a subjective and human dimension, transcending the objective data of physics and mechanics. It shows us the link between space and subjective time–that in which the individual in question lives–as constituted by the objective rhythm of historic time. To understand what is meant by 'historical space-time' or 'objective field', we should note that the area in which civilisations live and die 'is defined not in physical terms alone ... but by the distance between different regions, especially those whose civilisations are respectively more or less advanced'. Space at first appears as a system of geometrical and physical relationships; but once we introduce the notion of distance, we see it as a series of routes between more or less differentiated areas. The distance between two countries is not simply a question of miles, but varies with the ease of communication between them; and this depends on economic links as well as social and cultural attractions and repulsions.

Similarly, time is not a succession of homogeneous moments following each other at a uniform speed. It may be more or less intensive, and periods may follow one another continuously or be more or less sharply separated. To take a relative view of space and time does not mean simply to acknowledge that they constitute frames of reference or viewpoints peculiar to each observer: it also means taking account of the situation of individuals and societies who live, not in a neutral receptacle or conveyance borne along at a steady pace, but within a qualitatively differentiated system of forces. The relativist viewpoint involves being aware not only of the subjectivity of the observer and the observed, but also of their interdependence.

As our author remarks, 'the Indian of the Andes, plodding along behind his llama or ploughing with primitive implements, his life geared to the rotation of the seasons, must find the day's work, and life itself, painfully long'. But, he continues, even though subjective time depends on objective conditions and there are thus as many time-scales as there are social and cultural systems, is it impossible to reduce this plurality to a unity? Is there no yardstick which applies to all systems alike? The relativity of space and time 'is not a source of disjunction and anarchy: ... it is fully compatible with a new, profound universality'.[1] If the Andean peasant or the Argentine *gaucho* seems to us to be living at a slow tempo, that is only because we are comparing his life with that of a city-dweller in Europe or

[1] Ibid., p. 34.

North America. The pace at which he lives and works is retarded 'in comparison with that of more developed peoples'.[1] The speed characteristic of each social and economic system thus 'depends on the progress (*pasos*) which each people has made in developing itself and in mastering nature'. Thus the relativist principle lays down not only that 'each social process must be considered in relation to every other such process', but also that they must all be 'related to a single scale which is that of the most advanced groups – the fastest, we might say, by analogy with the principle of physics according to which the speed of light furnishes an absolute criterion'.[2] Thus the basis of measurement is to be found in the rate of evolution of the most progressive economic and social systems, which influence the remainder through the objective framework of space and time.

What is the practical use of this cumbersome theoretical structure? In the first place, it serves to define the party's task: to 'Peruvianise Peru' is to enable the country to catch up with the most highly-developed nations. Secondly, it enables Víctor Raúl to make short work of Marxist dogmatism. 'From our point of view, Marx's historical dogmatism is in no sense a rule binding in all parts of the globe.[3] ... Marx's conception of the world is revolutionary and universal ... but Marx, for whom space and time are absolute frames of reference, is as much confined to his own observatory as Hegel ... both of them within the space-time continuum of European history.'[4] The aspect of Marx's teaching which Víctor Raúl explicitly rejects is the notion of history proceeding in a straight line and dominated by a single factor. But if one looks more closely, his objection is not so much to the rectilinear concept as to that of evolution from a single centre. 'History can no longer be centralised ... it is a universal movement which proceeds at varying speeds and by paths which are to some extent independent of one another. Everything is in a state of evolution, certainly, but not along a single line or by a strictly synchronised process. Historical facts are not links in a single great chain ... they have their points of contact and of interaction, but their importance and direction are by no means uniform.'[5]

Relativism leads Víctor Raúl to assert, following Hegel, that 'every philosophy is the philosophy of its own time'.[6] In other words, no philosophy and no ideology, be it Marx's or any other, is incapable of improvement. But while each philosophy and each ideology be-

---

[1] Ibid., p. 35. [2] Ibid., pp. 36–7. [3] Ibid., p. 36.
[4] Ibid., pp. 47–8. [5] Ibid., p. 49. [6] Ibid., p. 47.

154

longs to its own time, Víctor Raúl also lays down the complementary principle that each 'historical space-time' has its own characteristic philosophy. The schema of history that he presents to us is that of a plurality of more or less independent cause-and-effect sequences, a plurality of centres and poles which alternately dominate others and are dominated by them. But the number of these is not infinite, and each era is characterised by the effort of a particular region, continent or people to dominate, to assert its influence or simply to make itself known. The units of which the historic process is composed are those privileged communities—precarious and changeable though their situation is—to which Víctor Raúl gives the name of 'continental peoples' (*pueblos-continentes*).

This term makes its appearance in the Aprista vocabulary when Víctor Raúl sets about distinguishing and delimiting instances of 'historical space-time'. If history is an interaction or conflict between individuals and civilisations of varying importance, origin and duration, we have still to determine which of them have access to the stage of history, which civilisations count at a given moment and which do not. Víctor Raúl lays down the criterion that an authentic unit of space-time is constituted 'by the political expansion of a society on a continental scale'.[1] In other words, to be recognised by world history a civilisation must organise itself politically and control a large territory. Víctor Raúl emphasises that 'continental' is not used here in a purely geographical sense. He refers, it is true, to geopolitics; but 'historical space-time does not imply an exclusive link between politics and geography, but merely the conscious function of history in its sociological realisation, such as necessarily belongs to each continental people'.[2] The author thus seeks to clear his theory of two reproaches. It must not repeat the error of unilateral determinism, nor must it incur the charge of favouring imperialism.

Historical factors are localised in 'poles' which exert more or less powerful forces of attraction and repulsion on one another. Moreover, the boundaries of the 'objective field' are subject to constant readjustment. As Víctor Raúl puts it, 'A new India is on its way—why should there not also be a new Europe? and why not a new Indo-America in the regions where the old races of Iberia, Africa and Arabia came into contact with their contemporaries?'[3] Thus Indo-America enters upon the scene, and these are the good tidings in

---

[1] Ibid., p. 54.   [2] Ibid., pp. 65–7.
[3] Ibid., p. 54.

155

which we must have faith and which will justify the doctrine of 'optimistic sadness' and the space-time theory.

We must therefore do away with 'mental colonialism':

'Our political doctrines are, as a rule, merely the repetition of European formulae. Both on the right and on the left we find the same lack of creativity, the same servile imitation of foreign ways . . . Thus, more than a century ago, we copied the slogans of the French revolution, and today we vociferate those of bolshevism or fascism . . . This has led us into the false security of those who believed for centuries that the earth remained still and the sun revolved around it. To our ideologists and theoreticians of the right and left, it is not the Indo-American world that is revolving, but the European sun.'[1]

But the charge of 'mental colonialism' is not levelled only at conservative or reactionary thinkers, or at the *hispanizantes* who refer to Spain as the 'mother country': it applies equally to the communists.

'The communist party is, first and foremost, a class party . . . born of European economic conditions which are quite different from ours. Moreover, it is not a mere federation but a single, world-wide party, governed in absolutist fashion from its headquarters at Moscow . . . How can the communist party, with its seat of government at Moscow, lead Indo-America to victory against imperialism? Think for a moment, look at the map of the world; consider the history of our peoples and reflect seriously on our position.'[2]

His two objections to the communist party sprang from a common source. Firstly, it was the party of a class, and that class did not exist in Peru or Indo-America in 1932. To expect revolutionary action from a non-existent proletariat was the height of ineptitude. Secondly, Moscow's centralised control was incompatible with the recognition that history is not driven by a single force but is the end result of a large number of independent actions.

But was Indo-America, at this point in time, a 'continental people'? Two recent episodes are quoted to show that it was. 'The Mexican revolution, and the university reform at Córdoba in the Argentine, are the two chief events of this century on our continent, and both of them herald the Aprista movement.'[3] The Córdoba reformers attacked the 'mental colonialism' of the traditional universities and put to rout the *hispanizantes* and *europeizantes* with their enslavement to

---

[1] Haya de la Torre, vol. II, pp. 69–70. The passage dates from 1928.
[2] Ibid., pp. 64–6.   [3] Ibid., p. 131.

European culture. As for the Mexican revolution, it was presented by Víctor Raúl as early as 1928 as the precursor of the Indo-American revolution, which was to extend to the whole continent and awaken it to a sense of unity. 'To my mind, the Mexican revolution is *our* revolution. Its successes and failures, its mistakes and contradictions, its impulses and achievements–everything about it should be a source of the most fruitful lessons for our people.'[1] Twenty years later, Víctor Raúl added the following comment to what he had written in 1928. 'The Mexican revolution was the first social movement of the twentieth century, prior to the Russian or the Chinese . . . Nor was it only an agrarian and anti-feudal revolution: it was an anti-imperialist one also.'[2] But the main point was, as Víctor Raúl had already said in 1928, that it was a social revolution and not a socialist one. Instead of slavishly copying European socialism, it applied new remedies to a new situation: it invented as it went along.

Apra goes into battle

The ideology which the young Apra leader put forward on the eve of the presidential election of 1931 was, in the first place, a radical movement which aimed at replacing the old dualism by a genuinely integrated society. Secondly, it featured indigenist symbols linked with a largely mythical idea of the Indian.

The first difficulty here was that, while the Indians formed the bulk of the nation, they were excluded from it in practice and were scarcely conscious of this fact. At the beginning of the 1930s Apra, like indigenism itself, was a movement of half-castes (*mestizos*) who had, and could have, only a very indirect and limited influence on the Indian community. In those years, agrarian agitation in the sierra does not seem to have been very intense; and the Indians' method of putting forward their claims had not changed from what it was at the end of the nineteenth century, for instance, in the celebrated rising led by Atusparia.[3] Nor was it certain that the nascent party could count on the Lima working class (which still possessed only craft organisations), the Cerro de Pasco miners or the labourers on the sugar-cane plantations. These groups were few in number and geographically scattered; moreover, Apra's progress was hampered by its quarrel with the communist International.

[1] Ibid., pp. 129–30.   [2] Ibid., p. 131.
[3] For the phenomenon of *sublevación* cf. Part I, chap. 3, and Part III, chap. 3.

What is to be done?

At the end of 1931, it was, in addition, confronted by a formidable threat in Colonel Sánchez Cerro's victory at the presidential election. The Apristas protested loudly that the election had been fraudulent. Sánchez Cerro was installed, but a bitter struggle developed between his adherents and the Apristas, who possessed an important minority in the Constituent Assembly. They were expelled from this body (*desaforados*) and Víctor Raúl himself was arrested at Lima. A rising broke out at Trujillo in July 1932, involving the murder of several officers and the execution of some hundreds of Apristas in the Chanchán ruins outside the city. In 1933 Sánchez Cerro was assassinated, and the crime attributed to Apra. In 1935 José Antonio Miró Quesada, the editor of *El Comercio*, who had been conducting an implacable campaign against Apra, was shot by a youth named Carlos Steer, who claimed to have acted on his own initiative but was undoubtedly connected with the party. Except for a brief period in 1934, Apra continued to be outlawed until 1945, that is to say throughout the six-year presidency of General Benavides, whom the Assembly elected to fill Sánchez Cerro's place in 1933, and the first presidency of Manuel Prado (1939–45). This long period of under-ground existence, known to the party leaders as the 'catacombs', was of decisive importance for Apra's evolution, its cadres, organisation and psychology. The history of those years is still unwritten, and only a few sketchy details can be given in these pages. But to give the reader a notion of Apra mentality it is, I think, necessary to cite a few texts which afford a good description of the spirit of the 'cata-combs'.

Let us take first the 'Letters to Aprista prisoners' (*Cartas de Haya de la Torre a los prisioneros apristas*),[1] published in 1940 by Carlos Manuel Cox, since Víctor Raúl was either underground or himself in prison when he wrote them. The selection of letters is of course arbitrary but is certainly significant. This is the picture they give of Apra's values as expressed by the founder of the party.[2]

'We Apristas must persevere in our arduous task of setting Peru and Indo-America an example of virility, integrity and loyalty. This is the best and highest type of heroism: for greatness and valour are not displayed in short-lived bursts of enthusiasm. What is truly exceptional (*egregio*) in a fight like ours is to see things through, to

---

[1] Editorial Nuevo Día, Lima.
[2] The most typical passages will be found in chaps. V to VII (pp. 55–71).

shun fear and bitterness, to maintain oneself at the highest pitch by means of serene energy and unswerving endurance (*la serenidad enérgica y la persistencia indeclinable*).'

Thus Apra's cause is defined as a 'fight', justified by its political and moral objectives. The preoccupation with setting an example is one we have already noted several times. The struggle is to be waged in a 'manly' fashion (*varonil*). This is emphasised by the contrast between the example held up by Víctor Raúl and that presented, according to him, by his 'civilianist' adversaries. 'We have been told that Peru is a country without brave men; ... the civilianists ... have portrayed us ... as a race of eunuchs without firmness of character or steadfastness in rebellion. We Apristas, who have resisted without fear, without complaint and without asking favours, are the only ones whose courage gives the lie to these slanders.' Thus Apra's virility is contrasted with the softness, effeminacy and lack of staying power shown by other Peruvians.

Besides being heroic fighters and *men* in the full sense of the term, the Apristas are educators in will-power. 'Apra is a school in which will-power is taught, a place of correction for the unstable' (*un gran corector para los versátiles*).[1] 'Driven underground or thrust into prison, we can still give lessons in how to suffer for a cause, and set an example for its sake.' This teaching is developed further on: 'Apra's message to youth is that it was not born to eat and sleep, to live selfishly amid second-rate pleasures and to die leaving no great work behind.'

Fighting or teaching, the prize to be won in political life is the esteem or admiration of others. This striving after recognition appears in several passages.

'With every day that passes, Apra grows in importance. Many articles have been published in the United States, and more than one book speaks in praise of our movement. Living in Peru, you do not realise how strong we are in the eyes of foreigners ... The London Institute of Foreign Affairs has published a report by a group of experts under Mr. Hay ... In Colombia, J. Eliecer Gaitán[2] has extolled us as the only great party of Indo-America ... The eminent French poet André Breton has just said in Mexico City that Apra is the mainspring of Latin American emancipation ... From Buenos

---

[1] Haya de la Torre, *Cartas* ... , p. 15.
[2] The left-wing liberal leader whose murder in May 1948 touched off the fearful explosion of violence known as the *bogotazo*.

Aires we hear the same . . . In other countries too, such as Cuba and Venezuela, Apra's prestige is truly extraordinary.'[1]

I have quoted this passage at length for two reasons. Firstly, for the information it gives as to the effect produced in America and Europe by Apra in its early stages, and the Latin American network maintained by comrades in exile. Throughout the 1930s, Apra showed great skill in mobilising progressive opinion in Latin America and using the continent as a sounding-board. But Víctor Raúl's emphasis on the affection and admiration felt abroad for the Apra cause is not merely a psychological device to keep up the morale of his troops: it springs from a genuine desire for recognition and respect. 'It is our duty and our pride as Apristas to command respect wherever we are.'[2] To be recognised, taken seriously, acknowledged as a force (*ser algo muy serio y muy fuerte*)[3] is the party member's first duty. The advantage of this attitude is that it discounts others while exalting Apra itself. 'Creole communism' and the 'near-communists' who threw in their lot with reaction and civilianism are 'hysterical bawlers, sunk in Bohemian anarchy and opium-sodden dreams';[4] they are 'cowardly sensualists, devoid of principle'. We, the opponents of this hysteria, are true and complete men, 'sound in heart, brain and guts, as men should be and as the party needs us'.[5] This self-confidence is expressed in unbreakable resistance. 'For us, to resist is to conquer.'

The nature of this resistance is worth examining. To resist means not to yield, bend or capitulate. Those who give way, for instance those who joined Apra but abandoned it as soon as persecution began, are 'cowardly sensualists, devoid of principle' (*cobardes, sensuales e insinceros*).[6] But Víctor Raúl speaks not only of resistance, but of persistence: not only refusal to yield, but patience in the face of the delays and hindrances imposed by circumstances. 'Obstacles, failures and long periods of waiting must be borne with optimism.' I have already quoted a passage from the speech of 8 December 1931 in which he defines the attitude of active expectation, of not waiting for the fruit to fall of its own accord. Those words were spoken before the period of the 'catacombs', to which the utterances we are now examining belong. During long stretches of time when 'apparently nothing is happening', expectation may suddenly be rewarded by a 'God-given surprise'. In chapter VIII of the *Cartas*, under the

[1] Op. cit., pp. 56–8.   [2] Ibid., p. 62.   [3] Ibid., p. 27.
[4] Ibid., p. 24.   [5] Ibid., p. 15.   [6] Ibid.

date of 26 January 1939,[1] Víctor Raúl writes: 'I know that *very soon* we shall reap the reward of a complete, perhaps a surprising victory' (*tal vez insólita victoria*).

Even if the 'God-given surprise' is long in coming–be it the tyrant's death or the revolt of one military clique against another–the wisest course is still to wait. The party has laid down three rules for itself: 'to let the rival groups in power weaken one another by their quarrels; to maintain party unity and discipline; to demand electoral guarantees and be prepared for any eventuality'.[2] In this way, comrades will be saved from the demoralisation which a long wait may entail: they have been warned that it is precisely their weariness on which the enemy is counting. 'Our tyrants believe that a few lashes are enough to bring everyone to his knees.'[3] General Benavides ('*el Tirano*') is credited with the contemptuous remark that 'the Apristas have lost courage and faith in themselves'.[4] The 'tyrant's' object, as Víctor Raúl sees it, is to demonstrate that the comrades' long resistance is leading them nowhere, and thus to break their spirit. They must reply to this 'mental poison' with renewed affirmations of faith and discipline, and also by refusing to be forced into a position of static warfare. Waiting is not simply a matter of holding one's ground but of manoeuvring. This is reflected in the third precept,[5] in which the party signifies its readiness to negotiate with any and all opponents, provided only that sufficient electoral guarantees are forthcoming to enable it to carry on a campaign.

Such is the basis of the optimism and confidence that Víctor Raúl demands of his followers. 'In spite of everything, we are content and do not complain. We have suffered and still do so, but we have never given way to despair and dejection, which would be unworthy of our sacred cause.'[6] The quality of Apra morale depends on two sets of conditions. From the point of view of factual realism, the long period of trial involving resistance and persistence can be endured only if comrades are convinced that their hardships may be cut short at any moment by unforeseeable circumstances and favourable events, just as they are sure to be terminated in the long run by the unalterable course of history. But in addition, day-to-day revolutionary propaganda must offer members of the outlawed party a

---

[1] This was written shortly before *carnaval* (Shrovetide), when General Benavides' Minister of the Interior staged a coup against him which almost succeeded and of which Apra had prior knowledge.
[2] Op. cit., p. 46. [3] Ibid., p. 56. [4] Ibid., p. 78.
[5] Ibid., p. 46. [6] Ibid., p. 77.

minimum of satisfaction or compensation. The admiration of outsiders, self-assertion and the boast of one's own virility are strong
themes, to which Víctor Raúl adds another. In suffering, exile and
prison he cheers his followers with the assurance of their superiority:
'Aprista, be proud of your great party!' (*Aprista, ten orgullo de tu
gran partido*).[1]

What must the party be like in order to offer the faithful an image
commensurate with their fervour? In a 'Christmas message' issued
from Lima gaol in 1932, Víctor Raúl declared:

'I consider that the main task for our party is to train young people,
especially the youngest ... We Apristas number half a million in a
population of six or seven million; so the half-million must realise
that it constitutes an advance guard, the educative force (*docencia*) of
the party. In other words, we are half a million potential leaders and
we must prepare to win over, direct and organise the millions who
will one day join our ranks ... Here is an example you should use:
under the treaty of Versailles, the German army consists of only
100,000 men. But these 100,000 men of all ranks are in fact 100,000
officers, ready to lead an army of four or five millions. So it is with
our party ... every comrade must know that we have a like mission:
to constitute a body of half a million leaders which will be needed
when we have the four to six million new members who will one day
join us and whom it is our duty to enrol.'[2]

These figures are to be taken as expressing general estimates
rather than exact statistics. It is very unlikely that Apra members, in
any strict sense of the term, numbered half a million in 1932; and in
the latter part of the above quotation, this figure is represented more
as an objective to be aimed at than as an actual fact. As for the 'four
to six million new members', this seems highly unrealistic in a
country which, like Peru in 1932, was three-quarters agricultural. But
the message serves to reassure young people as to the party's future
and arouse their enthusiasm for its potential greatness. By exhorting
the 'youngest' to take seriously their task of recruitment, Víctor Raúl
is inviting them to form a sort of *corps d'élite*. The party is at once a
vanguard, an instrument of education and a secret army after the
fashion of the *Reichswehr*.

Proselytism was thus made an essential objective of the underground party, and rewards for success in this field were among its
chief means of strengthening the loyalty of young people by confer-

[1] Ibid., p. 61.　　　　　[2] Ibid., pp. 29–31.

ring on them the dignity of 'leaders'. The tasks of a leader are set out by Rómulo Meneses in *Por el Apra, en la cárcel, al servicio del P.A.P. (Partido Aprista Peruano)*.[1] In the party vocabulary of those days, recruitment was known as 'cell-forming' (*celulación*), a term which calls for two comments. Firstly, recruitment does not take place on a person-to-person basis, but under the control and on behalf of an organisation, and the token of its success is the addition of a new member to the organisation. Secondly, the term *celulación* shows a clear affinity with communist language. The method employed is that of 'agitation': 'to stimulate discontent . . . with the immorality and bankruptcy of the civilianist bourgeoisie'. This, of course, takes diverse forms: the leader's technique and objectives will vary according to whether he is addressing students or workers. The first stage of penetration leads to the establishment of *grupos de exploración* which act, so to speak, as feelers, and also as centres for the relaying of directives throughout the community in question. If the first stage is successful, the next consists of setting up *grupos de constructores y animadores*, who operate in an institutional framework, whereas the *exploradores* are isolated liaison officers, without initiative, whose role is to pass on directives from above and report reactions to them. Finally, at the highest level, the initiatives of the *animadores* are supervised and co-ordinated by *grupos de conexión*.[2]

Every party member has duties in the political, trade union and cultural fields. That is to say, he must belong to a union and be active in a cultural institution, for example the People's University. Throughout his career he will, as it were, be serving several masters concurrently: for example, he must distinguish between the objectives of the political cell and those of the trade union cell organised to defend the interests of a specific group. This situation demands exceptional self-control. To penetrate workers' and students' circles and to organise active yet disciplined cells which will transmit and amplify the instructions of the party's central committee without affording *provocateurs* a chance to take advantage of the hotheadedness of younger leaders—to achieve all this, four revolutionary virtues are necessary: caution, level-headedness, discretion and

---

[1] Atahualpa, Lima, 1933.

[2] The organisation is strictly hierarchical, in accordance with the needs of clandestine work. Each *célula de conexión* reports to the party's general secretariat. The individual units are kept as watertight as possible and, to ensure the safety of the top leaders, the basic cells 'must not know the location of command headquarters.'

perseverance. Caution is a precondition of survival for those who have accepted the risks of clandestine life (*existencia ilícita*); and the Aprista's level-headedness and discretion are contrasted with 'creole frivolity'. 'We must rid (*redimir*) ourselves of the low Peruvian tendency (*nuestra tendencia baja peruana*) to make fun of everything ... of the coast-dweller's vice of clowning around (*vicio costeño de charlatanería*).' The Apra leader who combines these outstanding traits is described as the 'true revolutionary intellectual'. Other sought-for qualities are those of will-power, responsibility, self-sacrifice and endurance. Finally comes the key formula: 'The leader is the personal embodiment of collective aspirations.' He is, in fact, a member of the organisation or apparatus, valuable in so far as he refrains from putting himself forward and expresses adequately and efficiently the will of a revolutionary collective.

As long as the period of trial continues, the party tends to constitute a close-knit fraternal body. Personal relationships, 'family ties and those between friends and colleagues must be systematically exploited'. Regular networks ensure communication between agitators who have moved to Lima and their relatives and friends in the provinces. Party fraternity consists above all of mutual aid among individuals united by ideology and a common discipline and exposed to the same risks of underground life. The symbol, one might almost say the sacrament, of this fraternity is the subscription system. 'The Aprista is a man who pays his dues,' Meneses writes, adding that he does so 'from conscience'. The sacrifice thus required of comrades is justified on the objective plane by the need to support the party machine, but its implicit function is perhaps even more important: it commits (*compromete*) members to the party and is a tangible sign of their allegiance. Not only does the system express the Aprista's dependence on the party, but it acts as a test of the honour and loyalty of subordinate leaders. The passage in which Meneses speaks of 'Aprista honour in the handling of funds' (*honradez aprista en el manejo de la cotización*) enlightens us on the way in which the hierarchy maintains control over the lower levels.

But the party, as a closed society, must as far as possible remain a 'democratic' one.[1] Meneses is at pains to warn comrades of the damage which may be done to the spirit of fellowship by the high-handed and provocative attitude of certain junior leaders. 'We prefer statement to discussion, and we have an unhealthy tendency to let a

[1] In the psycho-sociological sense.

discussion turn into a dispute and a dispute into a quarrel.'[1] Such bad habits tend to sour relations within cells and to discourage well-wishers. The life of the party militant is a school of will-power, and the most stalwart and zealous are those of whom most is required in the way of discipline. Thus, for example, resort to a hunger-strike, ennobling as it may seem to the most generous,[2] is not allowed as a matter of initiative but is subject to strict party control.[3] 'No individual or group may exercise an initiative in this respect without taking into account the responsibility which they thus incur *vis à vis* the organs of party discipline.'

As described by its leader, Apra in the 1930s appears as a dedicated *corps d'élite*, in which heroic youths are taught the grandeur of absolute devotion to a just cause. We are left asking, will this small but compact body stand the test of time? Will the party succeed in overcoming obstacles and allaying mistrust? Above all, will the young heroes learn how to negotiate, and how to wait?

'To him who waits . . .'

From the outset, Víctor Raúl's endeavours were thwarted by numerous obstacles. The passionate hostility of some traditionalists, whose chief organ was *El Comercio*, and rivalry with the small nucleus of communists, involved Apra in a war on two fronts. None the less the party survived, but without ever gaining the decisive victory for which its leader had hoped. In the '*frustración aprista*', the image is not so much that of a collision of wills as of a constant pressure from without, an anonymous, impersonal force opposing the individual's desires.

Hostility from the right was not long in declaring itself: it may be described as 'putting Apra into a sanbenito', from the Inquisition's practice, before burning its victims, of clothing them in a garment painted with flames and devils. As early as 1931, *El Comercio* depicted Apra as a communist front party, and never referred to it except as 'the sect' (*la secta*). In the original version, Apra and communism were one and the same thing, or at least Siamese twins,

---

[1] Ibid., p. 91.
[2] Víctor Raúl himself went on hunger-strike several times.
[3] Ibid., p. 97.

'sprung from the same source, with the same tendencies and aspirations'. Sometimes the net was cast wider, to include, along with Haya de la Torre, Zapata and Sun Yat-sen (30 September 1931). And, on 19 February 1932: 'A party which sets out to nationalise the country's sources of wealth differs from communism only in name.'[1] At other times the accusation is cast in the form of an 'irrefutable' syllogism: 'Marxism is communism; the Apristas are Marxists; therefore the Apristas are communists.'

It was all the easier to pillory Apra in this fashion since frequent acts of terrorism were attributable, if not to the party itself, to individuals belonging to or sympathising with it. When General Sánchez Cerro, the President of the Republic, was shot down in 1933, the crime was imputed to Apra although the assassin, who was put to death on the spot, had no chance to speak. On 15 May 1935 José Antonio Miró Quesada, the editor of *El Comercio*, and his wife were murdered in the centre of Lima, on their way from the Hotel Bolívar to lunch at the Club Nacional, by Carlos Steer, who had links with Apra. Speeches made at the funeral were published by *El Comercio* on 17 May, and included the following words by José de la Riva Agüero: 'I was able to appreciate yet again his fair-mindedness and moderation–qualities ignored and blasphemed against in the disgraceful propaganda ceaselessly carried on by the ferocious spokesmen of hatred and envy who have hypnotised this besotted, unwitting murderer' (*voceros de la invidia y del odio, hipnotizadores del torpe asesino inconsciente*). In a leading article next day, the newspaper developed this theme, describing the murderer as a 'base instrument (*vil instrumento*)' who had committed his crime at the instigation of others. 'This man is only of secondary importance . . . The main responsibility for the tragedy falls on the one who stood and still stands behind him, devoted to the criminal purpose of disturbing public order, preaching hatred and stirring up (*azuzar*) man's most primitive instincts.' Fair-mindedness and moderation must not degenerate into weakness towards the 'gang which is poisoning the minds of youth, perverting the country's institutions and even spreading its influence into the barracks'.

[1] On 28 February 1932, *El Comercio* published a letter which it regarded as conclusive proof of collusion between Apra and the communists. This was written by Víctor Raúl on 22 September 1929 to his friend Mendoza, and read: 'I think we should continue to work without the communist label (*sin nombre comunista*). In this way we can steer clear of the bogy (*el cuco*) and can do effective revolutionary work. Labels and affiliations do not matter: what matters is to be thorough-going revolutionaries.'

'Only Apra can Save Peru'

These extracts give a clear picture of how Apra appeared to conservatives at this time. It is not only a 'sect' but also, and perhaps more fundamentally, a 'gang' or 'horde'. The first term relates to its organised and regimented aspect; the second evokes images of mob-rule and the primitive instincts of a Caliban. In a country whose population consists for the most part of illiterate Indians, the spectre of elemental forces unleashed may well terrify those who feel threatened by them. But Apra is not a mere sorcerer's apprentice: its leader, with incurable perversity, incites, like so many savage beasts, the wretched, ignorant and feeble-minded individuals whom he hypnotises with his gospel of envy and hatred.

The Trujillo rising of July 1932 made it possible to present Apra as an anti-military organisation. Some members of the party, mostly peons from the sugar-cane plantation at Laredo, captured the prefecture and the town hall and installed as prefect a relative of Víctor Raúl, who was in prison at Lima at the time. The rioters occupied the O'Donovan barracks, and when the troops loyal to Sánchez Cerro's government recovered the city, they found the mutilated bodies of several dozen officers. This rising–likened by El Comercio to the Paris Commune–was not the first or last mutiny in which Apra was involved; the most recent took place in October 1948, when part of the fleet stationed at Callao rose against President Bustamante y Rivero. From 1932 to 1945, the army carried on a merciless fight against Apra: in 1945-8 it acquiesced in the first convivencia experiment, but immediately after the elections of 1962 it deposed Manuel Prado, who had been governing with Apra support since 1956. Even during the period of Apra's legality, the military remained distrustful.

Describing the situation in 1948 after the abortive Callao mutiny, an officer named Víctor Villanueva,[1] who was at that time connected with Apra, remarked that during the thirties and forties the party's penetration had taken different forms in different branches of the armed services and at different levels of the hierarchy. 'In the infantry, 95 per cent of the conscripts are serranos ... illiterate, unmarried, with no family responsibilities and no social or civic conscience ... In armoured units, on the other hand, the men are relatively skilled.' As regards the navy, 'the volunteers, who make up 50 per cent of the total force, are genuine professionals who mostly come from a life of

[1] Cf. Víctor Villanueva, La tragedia de un pueblo y de un partido, pp. 58-9; also Edwin Lieuwen, Arms and Politics in Latin America, Praeger, New York, 1960, pp. 131-2.

hardship on the coast . . . They have contacts with civilians and are interested in their affairs, so that they are accessible to political propaganda. A large number of Apra supporters are recruited from this class.' Having considered the rank and file's vulnerability to Apra influence, Villanueva turns to the officers. Naval officers, whom he describes as a regular 'caste', were 'not in the least likely to furnish revolutionary leaders.[1] But officers of the land forces, the police and the gendarmerie were generally of humble origin and susceptible to Apra appeals. Army discipline, however, had enabled the government to control the revolutionary leanings of these officers, who had not risen to high rank in the thirties and forties. To sum up, the 'sect' might be described as disruptive (*disociadora*): it set men against officers, senior officers against junior ones, and branches of the armed forces against one another. In so far as the army was identified with the state, Apra could be denounced as a permanent conspiracy aiming not only to subvert the social hierarchy but to destroy the very foundations of the Peruvian state.

On the left wing, Apra's position was no easier than on the right. Its relations with the communists were ticklish from the start, both at top level and among party workers. When Apra was founded at Mexico City in May 1924, it proclaimed itself an international body – if not world-wide, at least continental in scope. At that time there was no socialist or communist party in Peru, and the extreme left, being as yet undifferentiated, seems to have tended to join Apra groups. As early as 1928, complications arose over two issues. Firstly, that of relations with the communist International: Víctor Raúl seems to have sought contact with Moscow, but to have shrunk from committing himself.[2] Secondly, should Apra remain an 'alliance' or coalition of socialists, communists and bourgeois radicals, or should it set up as an independent party? The crisis came to a head in 1928 over the foundation of the Partido Nacional Libertador which put forward Víctor Raúl's candidature for the Presidency of the Republic. Mariátegui, who was then editing the review *Amauta*, refused to join it; and the Paris cell, whose secretary was Eudocio Ravines, broke up on 1 May 1929, following the establishment there under Ravines'

[1] Villanueva, op. cit., p. 60.
[2] For the correspondence between Víctor Raúl and Losovsky representing the International, cf. Eudocio Ravines, *La gran estafa* (The Great Swindle), p. 111; also Martínez de la Torre, *Apuntes para una interpretación marxista de la historia social del Perú*, vol. II, pp. 307–10, which quotes the International's polite but negative reply to Víctor Raúl's overtures.

direction of a Peruvian Socialist Party, with which Mariátegui was for a time associated. Meanwhile the first communist groups came into existence at Cuzco, and correspondence took place between them and Mariátegui on 1 January 1930.[1]

At this period, Apra was denounced by the left as 'disguised fascism' and by the right as 'crypto-communism'. What with this and the hostility of the army, which never wholly forgot the Trujillo affair, the party was in danger of being encircled from all sides–a situation known at Lima as *'carga montón'*.[1] Víctor Raúl did his best to prevent the circle from closing in, and as early as 1931 he endeavoured to dispel military suspicions by a sort of pact: Apra undertook not to use the army for political ends (*aprovechar el ejército políticamente*), and promised it on the state's behalf 'not only independence and progress, but dignity and honour as well'.

A single frustration may suffice as a lesson in prudence, and the theme of *no meterse* took the form of two precepts: not to fall into the traps set by provocateurs, and to maintain party unity at all costs. But the effect of a long series of frustrations–the defeat of 1931, the trials of the catacombs, a second proscription in 1948–was to teach Apra a specific brand of realism which became more distinctive as time went on. 'Realism' here signifies, first and foremost, paying close attention to the nature of obstacles. Adjustment to reality is not achieved either by submitting to constraint or by challenging superior forces. The Aprista does not surrender or give up his objectives, but if he is to triumph in the long run it will be because everyone else has come to think as he does–or at least to recognise that Apra was right and that the victims of persecution were forerunners of a better future. Víctor Raúl's realism springs from three sources: an admission that the adversary may be stronger, a belief that he can be influenced, and a certainty that time is on Apra's side.

This attitude is shown clearly in two major speeches–one delivered at the outset of the electoral campaign of 1931, and the other in 1961, when he stood a second time for the Presidency–in which he dealt with the question of the role of foreign capital in national development. In 1931 he made the point that young countries–the term 'under-developed' had not yet come into use–desperately needed foreign capital, but were in danger of being enslaved by it. On 23 February 1961, he reverted to this theme in the following words:

[1] From a game in which the object is to isolate a single player who is then set upon by the others.

169

'In 1931 I compared the effect of foreign investment to that of blood transfusion on a weak organism ... I emphasised that the transfusion must be on a moderate scale and carefully adjusted to needs, since otherwise it would lead to hemiplegia or general paralysis ... I said then and I repeat today that foreign capital is necessary to underdeveloped countries. I said, and I repeat, that it is as vital to us as water to the desert: but what we require is water for irrigation, not a devastating flood.'[1]

While both speeches refer to economic evolution as a 'predestined process', there are two important differences between the situation today and thirty years ago. In 1931 the only sources of export capital were the advanced countries, chiefly the U.S.A. and Britain, which were in the throes of an economic crisis. In 1961 the North Americans and Europeans, especially Germany, were investing in Peru a steady and increasing amount of capital, not only in mining but in a variety of profitable enterprises. Secondly, in the early sixties the abundant flow of 'water for irrigation' no longer came only from capitalist countries. Could the 'socialist camp' be relied on to furnish aid without strings attached?

In reply to this question, Víctor Raúl defines what he understands by 'socialism' and the conditions governing foreign aid. He begins with what he calls a 'semantic revolution ... We speak, for example, of Russian or Chinese communism ... but there is no communism in either China or Russia: what they have is state capitalism.' Thus the Russian solution is deprived of its universal value. Moreover, 'capitalism in which there are many owners and many different masters' (i.e. the American variety) is preferable to 'capitalism with a single, formidable totalitarian master' (as in the Soviet Union).

Víctor Raúl dwells on this theme to bring out its importance. 'Is there any fundamental difference between the money sent by Russia to aid an under-developed country and that sent by the west, say the United States or Britain?' Of course, 'capitalist countries ... do not make free gifts: they lend at interest and naturally expect to make a profit from the money they invest. Do the other side behave differently? Not at all. I have never heard of the Russians making a gift to anyone: they too charge interest and grant loans to countries that ask for them.'[2] In short, 'we can never hope to receive foreign investments as a Christmas present. If our people want to be rescued from

---

[1] Haya de la Torre, vol. IV, *El plan de Acción*, pp. 207–8.
[2] Ibid., pp. 210–11.

their under-developed state, they will need foreign aid, but they will have to repay it at interest.'[1]

There is, however, an essential difference between Soviet and American aid, in that the Soviet Union is a totalitarian country and the United States is a democracy. 'The former says to its nationals: "You must produce, and if you do not, you are committing a crime against the state." The latter says: "You must produce, but if your wages are not sufficient we will talk things over and see if we can avoid a strike." In a country under Soviet rule, no-one can say "Down with Soviet imperialism! . . . Under private capitalism, the workers can shake their fists and cry "Down with imperialism! Raise our wages, or we'll go on strike." '[2]

We can see why imperialism is 'in the nature of things', and we shall see wherein its political forms differ. Víctor Raúl's attitude towards U.S. imperialism is instructive in this context. In his early writings, he demanded the internationalisation of the Panama canal; but he changed his tune in the late 1930s, even before the outbreak of the second world war. In February 1938, in a paper headed *Incahuasi* (i.e. 'the Inca's abode', a mythical name given to his hiding-place during the time of the 'catacombs') he takes a fairly optimistic view of the first effects of the 'good neighbour' policy of President Roosevelt and his Secretary of State, Cordell Hull.[3]

Whatever his reservations as to U.S. policy, Víctor Raúl sees the difference between North American imperialism and that of fascist Europe.[4] An imperialism which 'turns racial differences into an ideal and declares that men are superior or inferior according to the blood that flows in their veins, or the colour of their skin' is essentially perverse, whereas 'economic imperialism' can always be checked and amended.

'A nation which dominates and exploits because it is rich may

---

[1] Ibid.

[2] Ibid., p. 212.

[3] 'Relations between the two Americas have vastly improved under Roosevelt's government.' (Vol. I, pp. 105–6). But the improvement is precarious. 'The present policy is a temporary one and there is no knowing how long it will last.' The President may be succeeded by a Republican 'of the type of the first Roosevelt, progressive and anti-monopolist at home but a complete imperialist in foreign policy'. (P. 108.) Moreover, the policy of the present U.S. government is far from perfect, since 'in the name of democracy it continues to uphold tyrants, both great and small, and so alienates the sympathies of the oppressed peoples of our continent'. (P. 108.)

[4] '*Hay un imperialismo democrático*', in *La defensa continental*, Buenos Aires, 1942, pp. 98–9.

easily lose its dominant position by becoming poor, just as a man who is a capitalist today may be a beggar tomorrow ... This, as I see it, is the fundamental difference between an imperialism which is not only economic but also racial, as with fascism and Nazism, and imperialism of the Anglo-Saxon type which does not judge men and nations by blood and colour but solely by their economic situation ... If European Jews, many of whom have fair hair and light skins, are persecuted and oppressed, what fate is in store for us Indians and half-castes of Indo-America?'

It was possible to get on with the North Americans nowadays (i.e. about 1940), not only because they were neither racialist nor totalitarian – whereas the fascists and Nazis were both, and the Russians at all events clearly totalitarian – but because their attitude had changed. When Víctor Raúl was accused of watering down his doctrine and allying himself with the Americans after denouncing them so fiercely, he replied to the editor of *El Diario de Costa Rica*: 'It is untrue to say that I have turned from an enemy into a friend of the United States. I was never an enemy of that country, but only of its economic imperialism ... It is not Apra but, thank Heaven, the U.S. government which has shifted its ground.'[1] He associates the change with the transformation of U.S. foreign policy by F. D. Roosevelt – 'the most remarkable step forward ... since the Monroe doctrine'.[2]

Apra has not changed, but its opponents have come closer to it, yielding to its influence. The right course therefore is to prepare patiently for the future, avoiding equally excessive haste and a purely negative attitude. As we saw, even during the catacomb period, Apra declared itself at all times willing to negotiate provided a minimum of guarantees were forthcoming. Similarly, in the economic field, it would be criminal to embark on radical policies which would bring about the destruction of wealth in the name of social justice or national independence. Thus Víctor Raúl, recalling in 1961 his attitude towards nationalisation thirty years earlier, emphasises the virtues of caution and patience: the bill for demagogy would have to be footed not by those who freely bestow their advice, but by the poorest in the land.

'There was in the Trujillo area a U.S. copper concern called the Northern, which was hard hit by the 1929 slump. The population were alarmed at this, since the company had brought about a real

[1] Ibid., p. 136.   [2] Ibid., p. 115.

social transformation in the whole region . . . So the workers came to me and asked . . . "Does Apra mean to pursue its anti-imperialism so far as to destroy this foreign firm's capacity to produce and to employ labour? You see, sir, when we worked on the land . . . we earned 20 cents a day, plus our food and a few coca leaves. Today we have clothes and shoes and a club of our own, and we make the equivalent of two or three dollars a day; so you can see how much better off we are. Shall we have to go back to our old bosses now and live as we used to?" And I replied to them: "No, my friends, Apra's anti-imperialism is of the constructive kind." '[1]

Apra's boast of constructiveness is expressed by the well-known saying: 'We do not wish to take wealth away from those who have it, but to create it for those who have none.' (*No queremos quitarle la riqueza al que la tiene, sino crearla para quien no la tiene.*) In the political field, it leads Víctor Raúl to play down the more radical aspects of his programme by distinguishing between 'maximum' and 'minimum' demands.[2] It also finds expression in the theme, emphasised in the 1962 campaign, that the party is right and that it perceived the truth sooner than others. For example:

'We declared that America must unite politically and economically, and also that the land must be given to those who work on it by means of a clear and straightforward (*limpia*) measure of agrarian reform in the national interest . . . We demanded free education at the primary, secondary and higher levels . . . and pointed out that co-operatives ought to be developed in a country which possessed a similar tradition in the Inca community (*comunidad incáica*) . . . *We were right too*[3] when we said that in countries like ours the economy moves at two

[1] Víctor Raúl gives a similar account of a conversation in 1931 with some miners employed by the Cerro de Pasco Corporation in the central region. 'We stand for nationalisation, but it must be progressive: we must never sacrifice the worker or add to his burden of suffering. The well-known formula "I'll improve your lot and bring you progress, but you must first wait forty-three years" may be all right in Russia, but not for us.' (Vol. IV, p. 223.)

[2] Apra's maximum programme laid down very general objectives of national, continental and, so to speak, world-wide application. '1. Action against U.S. imperialism. 2. Action for the political unity of Latin America. 3. Nationalisation of land and industry. 4. Internationalisation of the Panama Canal. 5. Solidarity with all oppressed peoples.' Its minimum programme was defined by Víctor Raúl in an article entitled 'What is Aprism?', published in the British *Labour Monthly* for December 1927. This includes the continental objectives, especially points 1, 2 and 5, and those which belong to the national context, especially point 3. Point 4 represents a specific demand *vis à vis* the United States; but the claim for internationalisation of the Canal, put forward in radical terms in 1927, was much toned down by the late 1930s and gradually disappeared from Apra literature.

[3] Italics added.–F.B.

173

different speeds, the slow native one and the rapid pace of the foreign imperialist world.'[1]

Inter-American unity, land and educational reform, the encouragement of co-operatives and the advancement of the Indian population –in short, the development and modernisation of the country: all this had been advocated by Apra for the past thirty years, and now figured in the programme of every party and candidate in the 1962 Presidential election. 'I believe that everyone is now agreed on the land reform question, . . . Latin American economic union, industrialisation and the nationalisation of the country's sources of wealth.' In other words, if a consensus was taking shape concerning national priorities, it was Apra which had fostered it.

Víctor Raúl's claim to constructiveness also leads him to retort to his opponents' charges: 'What you say is not true of me, but it is true of yourselves.' We have seen how in 1931 he struggled to throw off the Nessus shirt in which his enemies sought to destroy him. This is how he endeavours to clear Apra of the stigma of 'sectarianism': 'If the word "sect" refers to our deep-seated faith, then it applies perfectly to us Apristas, as it did in the last century to the liberals, to Mazzini and his Italian patriots, to the Freemasons and the Carbonari.'[2] To the charge of conspiracy, he replies: 'There can be no responsibility without freedom . . . If a party such as ours is not granted freedom, it cannot be held responsible for the actions of groups or individuals who may have belonged to or sympathised with it, but who embark on hazardous courses on their own account.'[3] Víctor Raúl thus disclaims responsibility for all acts of violence, from 'selective terrorism' to armed uprising, on the ground that a persecuted party has no means of controlling its members' initiatives. Violence is the fault of reaction: revolutionary violence is, strictly speaking, counter-violence, a necessary answer to repression. But–he goes on to claim–Apra's activity could be controlled and regulated 'like that of a boxer or footballer, judging coolly how best to use force',[4] if its leaders were not prevented by a foolish policy of repression from exercising their responsibilities.[5]

---

[1] Haya de la Torre, vol. IV, p. 233.
[2] *Páginas de divulgación aprista*, p. 36.
[3] Ibid., p. 39.   [4] Ibid., p. 25.
[5] Cf. the following statement made by Víctor Raúl in 1932 when he was in prison under the Sánchez Cerro government, and recalled by him in 1961. 'When I entered politics I was like a chess-player: I set out my pieces, and the others broke up the game by throwing the board at my head. Of course, I knew there were those too who hid under the table and did their best to

But he sticks his neck out even further: 'Today, men come forward and offer as their own the very solutions which we devised and advocated two or three decades ago.' Víctor Raúl is at pains to treat this plagiarism lightly. 'I find it a good joke: it reminds me of a story Madame Montessori once told me in London ... She said that the highest compliment was paid to her method of teaching children to read without their noticing it, when one of her small pupils asked her one day: "Can you read too?" ' But if Víctor Raúl thus accepts the role of a teacher–in the spirit of his distinction between commanding and governing[1]–is he prepared to pay the price involved in terms of calm, detachment and renunciation?

'The supreme leader'

Apra grew up around a single man, a hero. In his dedication to Víctor Raúl's letters to Aprista prisoners, Carlos Manuel Cox wrote: 'To you, our leader and master, we owe the scientific doctrine of Aprismo, its constructive ideals and its programme of action. In you, our guide and companion, we follow the standard-bearer (*abanderado*) of liberty, the paladin of justice and supreme representative of our people. From you, our brother and our friend, we learn the lessons of hope, steadfastness and faith in final victory.' In this invocation, hierarchical and egalitarian values are nicely balanced: the leader, master and guide on the one hand, the companion, brother and friend on the other. The picture is one of a virile band of brothers, led and inspired by Víctor Raúl. 'Haya de la Torre is a statesman of such eminence as our America has never before seen: not a mere governor or politician, not a theorist nor even simply a man of action, but a magnificent combination of all these in the strong personality of a leader' (*vigorosa personalidad directora*).[2]

The image which the 'supreme leader' (*jefe máximo*) seeks to give of himself is complex and changes, at least partially, with circumstances. One group of qualities centres around the theme of resolution and self-control. A good example of this stoic attitude may be found

interfere. .... Surely each of us ought to sit down to the game and move his pieces in a sensible and honest manner (*con responsabilidad*).' (Vol. IV, p. 215.) Politics are, or should be, an orderly game in which people behave honestly; but there are cheats who break the rules and force honest players like ourselves to adopt practices which we are the first to condemn but for which they hypocritically blame us.

[1] Cf. *infra*, p. 176.
[2] Antenor Orrego, in *La Tribuna* of 16 October 1945.

in his speech of 8 December 1931, the day on which his adversary Sánchez Cerro took over the Presidency. 'This day is not one of sadness for us: it is the beginning of a testing-time for the party.' This call to endurance is accompanied by a threat and a warning to any comrades, or rather 'companions' (*compañeros*), who may be tempted to lose heart. Let cowards and traitors do what they will: though Sánchez Cerro be President, 'nothing is lost'.[1] Víctor Raúl justifies his confidence by making two distinctions. Firstly:

'Governing does not mean the giving of orders and the perpetration of abuses; it does not mean using one's power as a stage for the exhibition of one's lower passions, an instrument of revenge or a gibbet for the mangled remains of liberty. Governing means leading and educating, setting an example, succouring the oppressed . . . Those who thought that Apra had no other object than to occupy the seat of power (*llegar a Palacio*) are mistaken. Anyone can seize power who chooses to buy it with gold or conquer it at gun-point. Our task is to reach people's hearts, not with gold or with guns, but as we ourselves were won over, by the light of a doctrine, by love of justice and the glorious example of self-sacrifice.'[2]

The distinction between 'governing' and 'giving orders' performs several functions. Explicitly, it confirms the Aprista antithesis between unprincipled, day-to-day politics *a la criolla*–a mixture of cunning and violence–and a policy based on the science of development and awareness of democratic values. The man now taking up his abode in the presidential palace, and those who are preparing to give orders at his behest, are swayed by 'lower passions'; their power is devoid of 'moral authority . . . They do not deserve the honour which belongs to men who follow their conscience: they have laid violent hands on the state and treated it as a source of pillage.' The misdeeds of these arbitrary rulers show up by contrast the virtues of the Apristas, devoted to the noble tasks of 'leading and educating, setting an example, . . . and making people free. They may give orders,' the speaker goes on, 'but it is we who continue to govern'.[3] This statement is, in the first place, a cry of defiance: 'If you thought you had done with us, you are mistaken: we are stronger than ever.' Secondly, it enabled Víctor Raúl, though vanquished in the elections (although the results of these and some succeeding ones were dis-

[1] Haya de la Torre, vol. IV, p. 72. [2] Ibid., pp. 72–3.
[3] Ibid., p. 72.

puted), to present himself as the real winner and disparage his rival by belittling the latter's victory.

'Nothing is lost': Víctor Raúl reassures himself and his followers by skilfully depreciating the trappings of power for which he professes not to care, and by exalting the importance of the influence and authority which he himself claims and which cannot be taken away from him. 'It is we who have come out best; the fruits of power are not yet ripe for us. In any case, the supposed winner is the loser, and the losers will win some day if they have not already done so.' Time will bring Apra the victory, but it will not do all its work for it. 'We must wait, but not in passive repose, or under the delusion that events happen of their own accord. Our expectation must be active . . . we must work ceaselessly, in absolute confidence that it is we who will give destiny its shape.'[1]

We may pause here to consider Víctor Raúl's conception of 'waiting'. Its primary purpose is to introduce a long-term perspective. By emphasising that what is lost today may be gained tomorrow, he is guarding against the 'creole' tendency to lose heart (*desanimarse*) if the object of desire (rather than of the will) is not attained at once. As for the 'long term', it is not a matter of time bringing forth its own offspring. Víctor Raúl holds forth a voluntaristic and Promethean image of the political leader, not least in the portrait which he gives of himself. 'I also waited–during eight long years of persecution, prison and exile . . . Eight years of solitude and unshakable resolution. I often felt the horror of being alone, forgotten or misunderstood, but I never lost courage (*no desmayé nunca*) . . . I vowed to myself that the party would rise victorious over fear, ignorance, disorganisation and oblivion–and it has in fact risen as an invincible force. My eight years' struggle was not wasted.'[2] This passage is not only remarkable for its insistence on the theme of will-power; 'I never lost courage . . . I gained eight years of unshakable resolution.' It does justice to the theme of suffering, whether this be due to the loneliness of imprisonment or exile. This loneliness is a formidable reality (*realidad tremenda*) because it cuts us off from others and makes us liable to be misunderstood or, more often still, forgotten. Just as the leader himself was forgotten during those eight years, so the party faces a similar trial: it will cease to be talked about, the public will forget it, while the machinery of terror will be used to decimate it.

[1] Ibid., p. 74.   [2] Ibid.

What is to be done?

But suffering has a redemptive value. We have noticed once or twice Víctor Raúl's use, in his definition of the party's tasks, of the word *redimir* (redeem, ransom, liberate). Suffering 'redeems' the Apristas too, not as a punishment for past offences but as a token that they are among the elect. 'Aprismo is a child of the will which has begotten a people in suffering and imbued it with a sense of organic strength, a vital instrument for the achievement of justice.'[1] We notice here the profusion of vital and emotive images: *engendrando ... fuerza orgánica y poderosa ... instrumento vital*. By this exaltation of suffering, not as something passively undergone but as a trial to be welcomed, the theme of willpower takes on a masochistic tinge. In the above passage, this element is still well under control and, as it were, subsumed in the dynamism of revolutionary zeal. But it has affinities with the 'optimistic sadness' which was repudiated in the previous quotation, where the temptation to wait passively on events was spurned in the name of heroic endeavour.

The speech of 8 December 1931 concludes with a description of the 'profound joy' (*alegría profunda*) with which the leader contemplates the magnitude of the task, the greatness of the cause and his own will to victory (*decisión de vencer*). In the face of the party's first major setback, Víctor Raúl's reaction takes the form of a double psychological readjustment: he cuts his losses in the short term and pins his faith on a rendezvous with History, the date of which it alone can reveal. In this way the stiffness of his character as a Herculean champion is tempered by the pathos of the wounded warrior. The future is his according to promise, and his certainty of it is in proportion to the severity of his trials; but he knows too that nothing will be granted him easily, and that he must achieve his reward at the price of an unceasing battle with himself and others.

Having seen Víctor Raúl in adversity, let us now turn to a period of good fortune, when he may reasonably consider that success is within his grasp. On 20 May 1945, in the Plaza San Martín at Lima, he made a fighting speech which ranks among the most brilliant pieces of Aprista rhetoric. The party has emerged from the catacombs; Víctor Raúl has come out of hiding, and has promised to support the Presidential candidate, José Luis Bustamante y Rivero. In return for this he hoped – and events proved him right – to secure the election of a large number of his followers to both Houses of Congress. To the

[1] Ibid.

vast crowd assembled in the great central square of Lima, he addressed a speech which by his standards was relatively brief, and which began by referring to the 'intimacy (*intimidad*) of this splendid gathering'. It was thus intended primarily for his own supporters, even though some of those present may have been moved by curiosity or hostility.

'We return to civic life, and we do so without ill-feeling' (*sin rencores*). Beginning on this note of serenity, Víctor Raúl gives a picture of the party, its leader and its tasks, with the emphasis on discipline, moderation and self-control. 'Who are we?' he asks. 'We are exemplary citizens belonging to an exemplary party (*los ciudadanos ejemplares de un partido ejemplar*).' The party is 'exemplary' because of the suffering it has gone through and the way in which it has borne it. 'We have suffered grievously (*hemos padecido*),' he goes on, and, after referring to the persecutions, adds: 'It is because we endured yesterday's trials that we deserve today's triumph.' The injustice of the sufferings inflicted on Apra would, no doubt, entitle it to take vengeance; but 'we have learnt how to meet the challenge and gain mastery over ourselves (*responder y superarnos*) . . . True grief, nobly borne, does not engender thoughts of revenge: at every Golgotha there is forgiveness for those who know not what they do.'

The theme of suffering as a badge of pre-eminence, which was touched on in the speech of December 1931, is now developed in all its implications. To begin with, it redounds to the honour of Apra and its leader: 'we are the party of the martyrs'. Next, it serves prudently to justify any reprisals which yesterday's victims may be tempted to exact; and finally, it emphasises the credit they deserve for remaining calm and fair-minded despite all too natural feelings. In this context, Víctor Raúl speaks of 'legitimate pride' (*orgullo legítimo*). We are 'exemplary citizens belonging to an exemplary party', victims who have forgiven their persecutors: above all, generous and responsible. Magnanimity is the keynote: 'When fascism triumphs, woe to its enemies; but when democracy wins the day, its adversaries are treated not as enemies but as brothers.'

The theme of self-control and responsibility is developed on two levels. 'I know that each of you is responsible to me and to our country.' But while each Aprista is responsible to the supreme leader, that leader himself is responsible to all his compatriots. 'I know that I answer for my party and all its members; I know that the fraternal discipline which unites us is equal for all.' And what is the promise which Apra's leaders and rank-and-file members, united as a single band of brothers, thus pledge themselves to observe? 'It is that we shall never commit any excess save in defending the principles of democracy, and will surpass all others in brotherly feelings (*sentirnos más hermanos que nadie*).'

This 'bond of brotherhood' is expressed in the final slogan of the speech: 'Brothers in battle, in suffering and in victory.' (*En la lucha hermanos! En el dolor hermanos! En la victoria hermanos!*) Does this brotherhood in fair and foul weather imply that all are perfectly equal? The speech draws a distinction between the people, the party and its leader. The 'exemplary party', the 'first party of the country', is a model of 'fraternal discipline'. As regards the leader's role, that is to say his own, Víctor Raúl is more explicit. Three features are emphasised: moral uprightness, intellectual eminence and, above all, the function of a mediator or guarantor between the party and the nation as a whole. From the very beginning, Víctor Raúl personalises the relationship between himself and his audience. He speaks first of the 'intimacy of this splendid gathering', and, shortly afterwards, recalls 'to each of you' the significance of the Apra programme. But after establishing contact he once more stands at a distance. 'You well know that I have never flattered you or anyone else (*nunca he adulado*).' He thus adopts the role of a guide (*rector*), leader and master; and this austerity permeates the content of his message. He has been able to eschew flattery, he explains, because his doctrine was truth pure and simple—*la verdad descarnada*. This intellectual and moral integrity entitles the leader to preach to his followers and recall to every single *compañero* the need to maintain fraternal discipline and behave in a worthy and responsible manner towards non-members of the party and the whole Peruvian people. In this way the leader can answer for 'his' followers and 'his' party, and his control over them gives him an eminent position on the national scene. His 'post', as he is well aware, is that of the highest honour (*de mayor honor*) but also the greatest danger (*de mayor peligro*). What is the danger to which he thus briefly refers? In the most obvious sense, it is the risk run by the leader of any great popular party, of offering a target for the forces of reaction. But there is another risk as well: can Víctor Raúl be as sure of his supporters as he is of himself? Will he always be able to answer for those who have followed his lead? and what if the masses, no longer charmed by the master's spell, were to run amuck? Of course 'we' are magnanimous, 'we' are masters of ourselves; but does this 'we' on Víctor Raúl's lips mean 'you', 'they' or 'I myself'? At all events, Víctor Raúl can for the present turn towards those outside the party and claim to be the sole mediator between it and the rest of the nation. In so doing, he ascribes to himself a novel type of office, a 'moral Presidency'. This implies not only a certain disrespect for the constitutionally elected President, but also a veiled threat against those who do not show fealty to the Apra leader as their only true protector.

Turning from the triumphant affirmations of 1945, the last speech of Víctor Raúl's which I propose to examine is a disillusioned, but serene and elegiac pronouncement, delivered at one of the most crucial moments of his career: on the night of 7/8 July 1962, during the period of crisis between the elections of 10 June and the military coup of 18 July. Víctor Raúl, who was born on 23 February 1895, was now sixty-seven years of age, so that little enough time remained to him in which to perfect his public image and achieve his destiny. The official results of the voting were not yet known, but two facts were clear. In the country as a whole, the 'people's party', the 'party of the majority', had obtained barely a third of the votes; and Víctor Raúl himself was soundly beaten at Lima, where he came in third place, not only after the architect Fernando Belaúnde but also after General Odría, who was well ahead of his two rivals in the capital. To make things worse, the army leaders, who had never looked kindly on Víctor Raúl's candidature, accused Apra of all manner of attempts to rig the elections. Would the results be annulled? After consulting his two chief rivals, Víctor Raúl appealed to his supporters to endorse a proposal suggested to him by the highest authorities of the Republic: namely that he should withdraw his candidature and allow Congress to choose whichever of the other candidates received the support of its Apra members.[1]

How could this withdrawal be justified without losing face and incurring the charge of cowardice? Víctor Raúl does not expressly meet this charge; but, having dwelt on the advantages of a negotiated withdrawal for himself and the party, he remarks that some may

[1] Under the Peruvian constitution, if no candidate secures a third of the votes, the President is elected by Congress, that is to say the Assembly and the Senate. In 1962, according to the results announced by the National Electoral Jury, none of the three candidates reached the required total, though Víctor Raúl – by a narrow margin – came nearest to doing so.

accuse him of over-subtlety and of seeking to get the best of both worlds, by taking credit for detachment while reaping the benefit of caution.[1] This accusation he rejects in the name of 'Aprista serenity': a virtue requiring a combination of aptitudes, any one of which is exceptional. As far as the leader is concerned, it involves readiness to negotiate; and Víctor Raúl here recalls the long series of compromises which Apra has had the wisdom to propose to its adversaries on various occasions since 1931.

'In 1936 we supported the candidature of Luis Antonio Eguiguren, a member of the opposite camp [he had been a follower of Sánchez Cerro] who nevertheless had the courage to protest when Apra deputies were proscribed by the armed forces . . . We enabled Dr Bustamante to achieve power, although we had nothing in common with him in the political sphere . . . except that he declared he would not accept the Presidency unless Apra was granted electoral freedom. In 1956, we helped towards the election of Manuel Prado, who had opposed and persecuted us during his first term of office . . . We even came to terms with General Benavides.'

But negotiation does not mean sacrificing one's principles. By supporting Eguiguren in 1936, the party shortened the military regime by nine years, and in return for voting for Bustamante in 1945, it obtained its own legalisation. Its support for Prado in 1956 opened the way to *convivencia* or 'coexistence'.[2]

Light is thrown on the value of negotiation by the distinction between two notions: *aprovechar* and *seguir adelante*. The former (literally 'taking advantage') may suggest either catching the ball on the rebound, or skilfully withdrawing to save one's face, or in any way turning one of history's trials into an opportunity. *Seguir adelante* means 'pressing onward': taking risks, plunging into the mêlée in order to advance the course of history, and exposing oneself to wrongs for the sake of righteousness.[3] The Apra leader's 'serenity' is based on the conviction that he has made the best of his opportunities and that history itself will pronounce in his favour because he is one of those who, even in the darkest hour, never doubted that it would do so.[4]

[1] Cf. Part III, chap. 3, p. 298.   [2] Cf. Part III, chap. 1.
[3] The distinction recalls that made by Víctor Raúl in 1931 between 'governing' and 'giving orders'.
[4] An example of 'optimistic sadness'.

'Only Apra can Save Peru'

'What avails it to have lived so long?'

Despite all his efforts, Víctor Raúl did not succeed in overcoming the mistrust of his adversaries. *El Comercio*–still in the hands of the Miró Quesada family in the 1960s–maintaining that 'Apra never changes', continued to write of the *secta* and the *sectarios* in the same way as in 1930. In July 1962 Víctor Raúl was excluded from the Presidential palace exactly as he had been thirty years earlier. But although Apra never achieved power, no persecution succeeded in breaking it. In 1945 it re-emerged after thirteen years of underground existence; and in 1956, after another eight years of outlawry under General Odría, Víctor Raúl's supporters returned in force in the so-called *convivencia* period under Manuel Prado. Deprived of influence in 1962 by a military coup, the party was once more firmly entrenched in Congress in 1963, and enjoyed a dominant position there thanks to an alliance with the followers of the same General Odría who had violently persecuted it from 1948 to 1956.[1]

Like Moses, Víctor Raúl did not enter the promised land. How is it that his quest of power, sedulous though it was, ended in failure? We are not concerned here with studying a man's destiny or writing the history of a party. I wish merely to examine how Víctor Raúl's long series of achievements and setbacks affected the way in which he and his party envisaged the aims, methods and resources of political action.

At the outset, Víctor Raúl defined as his task the modernisation of the country, and claimed that this task could only be achieved by a political party in which all the nation's energies were united under a single command. If he believed in 1931 that by winning the Presidential election he could attain his purpose without further ado, he was mistaken; the threatened oligarchy defended itself with remarkable tenacity. There is, indeed, no reason to suppose that at that time he imagined the oligarchy would collapse like the walls of Jericho. The extracts from his works which I have quoted envisage a short-term and a long-term hypothesis: the Aprista must be ready either for a long-drawn-out struggle or for sudden victory. But the two hypotheses do not rank equally: the former is clearly a second-best. Moreover, can a party which seeks to achieve a rapid break-through be organised in the same fashion as one which expects its task to be a

[1] Cf. Part III, chap. 3.

long-term one? Víctor Raúl sought to reconcile the two methods of approach–one heroic, the other stoical–by drawing on the absolute devotion and passionate adherence of his followers. He was also obliged to reinforce the authoritarian and, as it were, sacramental aspects of his party at the same time as he sought contact with others for the purpose of emerging from the catacombs and joining battle in the light of day.

Víctor Raúl did undoubtedly enjoy the devotion of enthusiastic, not to say fanatical followers; but he paid a high price for this exceptional popularity. Not only did he alienate many who might have been disposed to help, but he aroused stubborn mistrust and fierce hatred even in quarters where his message should by rights have won approval. By taking a tough line, Apra isolated itself; but it survived, and that was its leader's minimum objective. What were the reasons that enabled it to endure? Certainly the courage and determination of the underground leaders played their part. But we must also realise that the staying-power which Apra displayed in 1933–45 and 1948–56 was partly due to the fact that during those years there was no alternative centre to which its active members could have rallied. There seem to be two reasons for this. Firstly, there was no alternative on the left. The communist party was still too weak, and in any case the persistent and bitter opposition between Apristas and communists made it difficult, both objectively and psychologically, to switch allegiance from one camp to the other. Again, it is relatively easy for a party like Apra to exercise a monopoly of radical activity in a country such as Peru was in the '30s and '40s. It should be noted that at this period a revolutionary party could not be more than an ideological organisation. I have pointed out Víctor Raúl's insistence on his role as an educator: what other could he exercise at the time of the 'catacombs'? The party could not act as the advance guard of a working class which, according to its own doctrine, did not yet exist. At the same time, it was easier for Apra to lead an underground existence than it would have been for a party of the well-to-do, which can only attract followers by rewarding their services, or one linked with organised interests, as European socialist parties are linked with workers' or employees' trade unions.

After 1956, Apra's objective was relatively clear, namely to win the Presidential election of 1962. There was no question any longer of a *blitzkrieg* such as the party's leaders had dreamed of in 1930–1: if Víctor Raúl had become President in 1962, he would have had to make several compromises. But equally there was no question of siege tactics or a static war, as at the time of the 'catacombs'.

Up to now, we have distinguished two Apra 'styles' or methods of approach: the heroic, corresponding to the attempted break-through of 1930–3, and the stoic resistance which marked the two periods of outlawry. But the combined drawbacks of these two styles became a heavy liability when, from 1956 onwards, Víctor Raúl was obliged to resort to new tactics and what might be called a policy of manoeuvre. During this period, Apra enjoyed official recognition which was no longer to be withdrawn[1] or openly contested. Moreover, it was no longer associated with acts of violence: the Callao rising of 1948 was the last armed clash between Apra and the military. Would Víctor Raúl's opponents at last acquiesce in his election? To avoid yet another frustration, it was not sufficient for the Apristas to give and receive all kinds of guarantees: they had also to win at the polls. The party, which had taken for granted since 1931 that it represented the 'national majorities', does not seem at first to have paid overmuch attention to this point, though it took some steps to widen its influence and establish contacts which, it was hoped, would win it the support of uncommitted voters. It attempted, moreover, to include in its electoral lists 'independent' supporters of President Prado, or local notables; but this sometimes ran into difficulties. The party's departmental committees which had already drawn up their lists (a process known in Apra parlance as that of *preelecciones*) boggled at replacing the names of veteran militants by those of newcomers. As to the effect on public opinion of these attempts at liberalising the party's image, it was inevitably impaired by the 'black legend' (*leyenda negra*) which had been assiduously propagated for so long, the slanders and calumnies directed against Víctor Raúl himself and the charges of terrorism and totalitarianism which were levelled against the party.

To sum up, the reasons which account for Apra's early successes also explain its later difficulties. Formed as a fighting organisation to destroy the old society, Apra stood up stoutly to the counter-attacks which its youthful aggressiveness provoked. By a mixture of determination and flexibility, it succeeded in making itself felt and achieving recognition. But was it capable, after 1956, of attracting to its hard core of militant supporters the floating vote which was to be sharply contested by newcomers, in particular by Fernando Belaúnde?

[1] Even by the military junta of 1962–3.

2

Realists and Realities

One of the paradoxes of Peruvian politics is that although the Right is in power–in the sense that nothing is done against the oligarchy's will or at any rate without its consent–it has never succeeded in gaining acceptance for its ideology or in organising a strong conservative party.

In countries with which we are more familiar, the right wing represents, in varying proportions, one or more of certain basic ideologies. The first consists of rejecting modern values, condemning technical civilisation and advocating a 'back to the land' policy. There is also the fascist trend, obsessed with simple and violent solutions; but not all the Right is fascist and not all authoritarians are right-wing. A further ingredient is nationalism: the man of the Right is convinced that the motherland or *patrie* is still the only political unit within which the heirs of the Western tradition can fulfil their destiny as free men. While always ready to resist the designs of other nations, he is equally vigilant against plans of a regional, federalist or globalist character which, he believes, would transform living national realities into a soulless conglomeration. Finally, there is in today's right wing a managerial element. Those who belong to this type accept industrial society in the main and no longer advocate a return to old-style agricultural ways: they have come to see in economic development a source of national greatness and a possible means of reducing social tension. But they take the view that businessmen, or failing them officials of suitable calibre, are better qualified to lead industrial society into the realms of plenty than are those who specialise in agitation and bargaining. A right wing of this type is not reactionary but conservative: it accepts the basis of present-day society but is wary of radical changes, the risks and expense of which it tends to exaggerate, and it prefers injustice to disorder.

The Peruvian right does not fit into any of these main categories. To begin with, the right wing is no more inclined to violence than the left: the Apristas of the 1930s and today's pro-Castro elements are far more typical of authoritarianism[1] than Sr. Pedro Beltrán. As for the managerial school of thought, it certainly cannot manifest itself in a country like Peru in the same fashion as in the U.S.A., Britain or France–or even Brazil or Mexico, where the national bourgeoisie is conscious of its role. Again, the Peruvian right is not 'constitutionalist' like that of Chile, which proclaims its respect for tradition and the rule of law.

To clarify the issue as far as Peru is concerned, I propose to distinguish between what I shall call the 'paternalistic' and the 'practical' viewpoint. These are sometimes present simultaneously but are more often found in a mixed, rather than a co-ordinated relationship. The paternalistic element is more in evidence when the oligarch's power is not disputed. Once the process of social mobilisation sets in, the attitude of kindly condescension towards the submissive, unenlightened masses becomes liable to change. The second tendency, which I call 'practical',[2] accepts the challenge of mobilisation and endeavours to find sensible, prudent and efficient answers to the problems of development.

Paternalism

The most striking characteristic of conservative thought in Peru is its ambiguous attitude towards national tradition. This is not merely a feature of radical criticism, but is brought out clearly, for example, by José de la Riva Agüero, a man of wealth and good family who may be regarded as the most persuasive advocate of conservatism in the 1930s. I have already quoted his disdainful references to the 'silly colonial nobility',[3] the blend of pomposity and venality shown by the military *caudillos*, and the 'sordid Levantine [*fenicio*–Phoenician] egotism of a pseudo-bourgeoisie composed of speculators and

---

[1] As the term is used by Horkheimer and Adorno.
[2] With reference to José Pardo y Barreda, the founder of the 'civilianist' party, who set out in 1872 to create '*una república práctica*'–cf. Basadre, op. cit., vol. IV, p. 1917.
[3] Cf. p. 53 above.

exploiters who treat the country as if it were a lode of metal, a counting-house or a bazaar'. We see from this how completely the oligarchy lacks moral authority in the eyes of traditionalists who lose no opportunity of putting the upstart plutocrats in their place. Let us examine more closely the attitude towards the mother-country, or *nacionalidad*, of hidalgos of the type of Riva Agüero, very proud of his noble Spanish birth, or, in a later generation, Víctor Andrés Belaúnde, faithful to the traditions of Arequipa. I shall begin with some quotations from Riva Agüero in which his reflections on Peruvian history are most closely linked with genuinely conservative and traditionalist views.

The quest for symbols of identification is typical of cultures which are going through a crisis or a period of rapid change. We have seen how Víctor Raúl laid emphasis on the specific quality of Indo-America and the myth of a 'continental people'. Can Peruvian conservatives find a myth of equal potency in, for example, the state, the nation or its guardian institutions such as the armed forces? We may notice first of all the indifference, if not aversion, with which a conservative like Riva Agüero treats the epic of Peruvian independence. In *Paisajes peruanos*[1] he describes a visit to the battlefield of Ayacucho, where he meditates on his country's destiny with considerable disillusionment:

'My sense of patriotism, which had been exalted by the sight of Cuzco and the banks of the Apurímac, was clouded by sadness and perplexity as I beheld the field of Ayacucho . . . On that famous spot, a Royalist army whose rank and file consisted wholly of Indians, half-castes and creoles from Upper and Lower Peru, and of whose officers barely one-tenth belonged to Peninsular Spain, fought an insurgent army which was three-quarters Colombian and less than a quarter Peruvian, with a handful of Chileans and Argentines . . . Ayacucho means nothing more to our national consciousness than the memory of a civil struggle between two bands, each assisted by foreign mercenaries.'

One could scarcely go further in belittling the work of liberation which turned Peru into an independent republic. As a counterpart, Riva Agüero extols the colonial period, which he calls 'three centuries of civilisation *par excellence* . . . Colonial Peru is part of our history and of our moral inheritance.'[2]

The national consciousness expresses itself in terms of division and

[1] Op. cit., pp. 110–21.　　　　　　[2] Ibid., p. 113.

inner conflict. Riva Agüero, for his part, does not take sides in the conflict which decided his country's fate and in which one of his ancestors played an important and controversial role. His chosen symbol, the Spanish monarchy, represents the country's past as well as its divisions. In Peru as elsewhere, history is a civil war; nevertheless, this conservative thinker looks to the past as a basis for the sense of national unity. In his great work *La Historia en el Perú*–written in 1910, when he was far from being the diehard conservative that he became in later years–Riva Agüero seeks to clarify the main lines of Peruvian patriotism, and invokes the 'close relationship between patriotism and history'[1] as his justification for taking special pains to collect and analyse the reports of the first chroniclers of the Inca civilisation and the *Conquista*.

'The Peru which we have to study and love is not only that of today . . . Nor should our filial love embrace only those events which have taken place since the declaration of independence: our nationality has deeper and more ancient roots. We must go back to the colonial era to understand . . . how the race, the laws and the institutions of Spain brought European civilisation to our shores and created the essential elements of modern Peru. Nor is this all: we must look back at the barbarian empire which the Castilian conquerors found here, whose sons and daughters mingled with those of Spain and took part in the common defence and the common toil.'[2]

There are two main points here: firstly, that the national consciousness has an historical dimension. 'We do not have to *create* the national soul: it exists, although it is asleep.'[3] Secondly, this soul is a fusion of two elements: it owes much to Spain, but the blood of the conquerors has mingled with that of the vanquished. This physical and cultural *mestizaje* is glorified in the person of the Inca Garcilaso de la Vega, to whom Riva Agüero devotes a study of admirable insight and piety.

At first glance, then, it appears that conservative thought regards the mingling of races as the basic cultural fact of Peruvian history. But Riva Agüero immediately plays down this aspect by a more or less valid comparison between Peru and the nations of Europe. Unlike the Apristas, for whom *mestizaje* is the quintessence of Indo-America, Riva Agüero argues that a similar process is essential to the formation of any nationality. 'In the same way, medieval

---

[1] Riva Agüero, *La Historia en el Perú*, p. 522.   [2] Ibid., p. 523.
[3] Ibid., p. 524.

Spain did not take shape until the Goths and the Hispano-Romans merged into a single people, nor was England truly itself until the mingling of Normans and Saxons was complete.'[1] Moreover, the type of racial fusion in which Riva Agüero rejoices is a selective one, involving not the random mixture of cultural elements but a delicate process of sifting which retains only the best. 'The national soul represents the sum total of all that is best in us, our highest and most generous desires, together with those of the best of our forefathers . . . in this land whose outward form and climate have determined our characteristic interests and sensibility.'[2]

Thus, *mestizaje* is not promiscuity; but how is the selection achieved? In *Paisajes peruanos* we find an analysis, in fairly restrictive terms, of the causes and conditions which, in the author's opinion, made possible the Peruvian synthesis: the virtues of the conquerors and conquered produced an original civilisation not by the mere fact of racial mixture but by blending together various kinds of complementary excellences. We may note first of all that although Riva Agüero is a Liman of ancient family, he regards the sierra as the 'cradle of the nation . . . the real Peru'.[3] In fact, he treats the coastal synthesis with some disdain, as hybrid rather than *mestizo*: 'the coastal plebs is the result of a mixture between Spaniards, *yungas*[4] and negroes'.[5] This coastal mixture is colourful, gracious and sensual: it recalls 'the creole culture of . . . colonial Lima at its height . . . devout and sensual, the daughter of Seville and grand-daughter of a sultaness . . . But behind Lima and the coast–home of the siesta, black slaves and an easy life–there lay the sierra . . . the real Peru . . . an austere region of toil and sorrow, more enslaved and afflicted than Ireland, Palestine or Armenia.'[6]

The sierra is depicted as the rampart and 'sanctuary of the nation' . . . 'Peru's destiny is inseparable from that of the Indian: we shall be saved or destroyed with him, but we cannot abandon him without committing suicide'.[7] Riva Agüero develops his reasons for identifying the fate of Peru with that of the 'native race, our inseparable companion. Its temperament is docile, persevering and orderly. It is not basically unsuited–far from it–to the all-important common tasks of labour and defence: indeed, despite its present degradation,

[1] Ibid.   [2] Ibid.   [3] Riva Agüero, *Paisajes peruanos*, p. 186.
[4] A term used of the warm valleys and their inhabitants.
[5] I.e. the slaves imported in colonial times to work on the sugar plantations of the Lima and Chincha valleys.
[6] Riva Agüero, op. cit., p. 185.   [7] Ibid., p. 187.

we must acknowledge its two noble vocations of bearing arms and tilling the soil. Tireless labourers, clinging to the slopes of their steep hillsides, they cultivate fields so miserable that anyone else would abandon them; but their greatest joy is to till these little plots of ground . . . Nor should we despise their soldierly qualities: they are vigorous, hardy and full of fortitude.'[1] Whether as a peasant or a soldier, the Indian is patient and enduring. Riva Agüero completes the description by adding: 'They are devoid of initiative (*de iniciativa nula*) but are first-class in collective action and are obedient and disciplined in the highest degree.' Thus the virtues of the natives and their conquerors complement each other. The bulk of the nation consists of a patient, enduring, obedient mass; can it expect to find rulers of sufficient initiative, courage and public spirit to make the most of such valuable human capital?

The reason why the three centuries of colonial rule were an especially glorious period is that the Spanish crown, alive to its obligations towards the subject peoples, took steps to educate them to manage their own affairs. According to Riva Agüero, 'the colonial period . . . especially in Peru, was one of privileged infancy (*minoridad filial privilegiada*) thanks to which, while preserving our historical primacy in South America, the different races met and mingled, thus forging day by day the nationality of the future.'[2] Thus the colonial power was paternalistic and protective, treating the Indians with respect and consideration, as a father treats his young children. Thanks to this policy, Peru retained the supremacy which the Incas had gained for it over most of South America, while the Spanish administration continued the process of amalgamating different races and cultures which had already made strides under the old empire. To be a success, this required immense wisdom, prudence and devotion on the rulers' part and, among their Indian subjects, docility and confidence in their protectors.[3]

The reader will perceive from this account the special nature of the amalgam which Riva Agüero praises so highly. Our author is careful

---

[1] Ibid., p. 188.   [2] Ibid., p. 114.

[3] Praise of the mixed-race policy goes hand in hand with disparagement of the *mestizo*: this paradox is observable not only in Riva Agüero but in some indigenists such as Valcárcel. The portrait of the *mestizo* in Peruvian literature of the 1930s is not a flattering one. According to Valcárcel in *Tempestad en los Andes*, he is 'neither fish nor fowl' and is a potential traitor. 'Infected by European pride (*contagiado de soberbia europea*), he is prepared to deny his race and family to secure acceptance, if not recognition, by the governing class.'

not to suggest that equality has already been achieved as between the various racial elements: rather he is at pains to define the conditions for equality which may one day be accomplished.

Conservative thought accepts the *mestizo* on condition that he keeps his place and does not seek to upset the traditional order of society which, slowly but surely, is preparing him for the status he will enjoy after the long period of tutelage during which he must be led, educated and protected from himself and his own instincts. To Riva Agüero, the authority which thus takes an infant people under its protection is the Spanish colonial administration; to a Catholic such as Víctor Andrés Belaúnde, it is essentially the Roman church. In *La Realidad nacional*, Belaúnde quotes Riva Agüero's views on the mingling of races in opposition to Mariátegui's 'racist nationalism', and refers to Bartolomé de Las Casas in justification of the policy of gradual fusion between different races and cultures.

'By making the Indians free vassals of the monarchy, protecting their communities and opposing the *encomienda* and forced labour system, Las Casas and his followers imparted a moral element to Spanish policy which other colonists have lacked ... The Catholic view is not confined to the economic or political aspects of colonisation, but also takes account of its educative and technical side. Being neither dogmatic nor one-sided, but realistic and flexible, it does not destroy nationality, but preserves and strengthens it.'[1]

The conservative school of thought, whether inspired by Belaúnde's Catholicism or by the positivism of the young Riva Agüero, takes up a protective or, as its opponents would say, paternalistic attitude towards the Indian masses; but it envisages this condescension as the sign of its own special mission and its own realism. The conservative professes and feels an obligation towards the peasant, whose long tutelage is not yet at an end. Indeed, the Indian's submissiveness and deference towards a firm but kindly authority dates back to remote pre-Columbian times. On the strength of descriptions by Garcilaso de la Vega and the chroniclers of the conquest, Riva Agüero depicted the Inca empire as a closed society, and was struck by a resemblance between it and China. Invoking Prescott's authority, he writes: 'In Peru as in China – both essentially agricultural states – the emperor publicly honoured the land; he was the supreme head of the official religion and took the title Son of Heaven ... Inca Peru was a budding China, whose development was cut short by the Spanish conquest

[1] V. A. Belaúnde, *La Realidad nacional*, Paris, 1931, pp. 54–6.

192

while it was still at an early phase of evolution.'[1] The question arises, however, whether this agrarian and military Utopia had in fact any other value to Riva Agüero than to excite nostalgia for the past and enmity against the present.

In any case, does not Apra's militancy, of which Riva Agüero became a witness in his old age, render obsolete the attitude of paternalism which is appropriate to a closed, static, traditional society? In his speech at Miró Quesada's funeral, Riva Agüero spoke of the need for stern measures of repression. We should not, however, conclude from this that the conservatives' last word is to appeal to the sword or to a 'strong' government. Augusto Leguía's civilian dictatorship of 1919–30 met with deep disfavour in traditionalist circles.[2] Riva Agüero himself went into exile, as did some members of the great *civilista* families with whom Leguía had broken. As to military dictatorships, the attitude is less certain. A sword may at times be necessary; those of Sánchez Cerro and Benavides in the '30s, and Odría in 1948, all served their turn against the Apristas. But such allies are an embarrassment. For one thing, they tend to become a permanency, whereas they were only needed for a limited purpose. For another, they are unpredictable, and one never knows what their erratic initiatives may lead to.

Thoughts such as these have led some conservatives into a state of total pessimism which is reflected in the following remarks by Ventura García Calderón; they were probably written by him in Paris in the 1930s, and I came across them at the library of the Institut d'Amérique latine, in a copy of *El cesarismo democrático* by the Venezuelan author Laureano Vallenilla Lanz which had belonged to him. On page 188 the Peruvian had written in the margin: 'A terrible problem of social equilibrium, the same throughout Latin America: anarchy or tyranny, humiliating peace or savage war. No possibility of free government. Oligarchy or demagogy: García Moreno and Rosas.' This brief comment suggests two observations. Firstly, it expresses the decent man's hatred of violent solutions. Whether it leads to 'humiliating peace' or 'savage war', violence is an evil which confronts us with an impossible choice: anarchy and tyranny are equally reprehensible. In the last resort, there is no solution to the 'problem of social equilibrium'. The citizen of a Latin American

---

[1] Riva Agüero, *La Historia en el Perú*, p. 192.
[2] One of the most scathing denunciations of Leguía may be found in Part II of *La Realidad nacional*, where the President, who remained in power for eleven years, is branded as a tyrant, embezzler and agent of foreign interests.

republic, faced with the choice between two unacceptable extremes, is condemned to impotence. But this is not the worst. What is striking about García Calderón's note is that he writes first 'anarchy *or* tyranny' and, a little later, 'García Moreno *and* Rosas'. In other words, he is not only racked by an impossible choice, but feels threatened by the onslaught of both calamities: a bigoted tyranny such as García Moreno long imposed upon Ecuador in the nineteenth century, and the barbarous demagogy which Juan Manuel Rosas inflicted on the Argentine. A refusal to choose will not prevent his suffering all the woes attendant on extreme solutions.

The practical approach

Nevertheless, life must go on; and this fact is most present to the minds of those whom I shall call 'practical' conservatives. When considering the ideologies of the extreme left, we shall have occasion to note the contrast between the theme of 'humanism', or concern for individuals, stressed by a paper like *Libertad* in its appeal to a large public whose progressiveness is more warm-hearted than cerebral, and that of revolutionary violence which dominates the esoteric publications of tiny communist, Trotskyist, pro-Castro and Maoist groups. A similar contrast, expressed in different terms, appears in right-wing literature. Side by side with thinkers who ponder over the problems of coexistence between the Hispanic and Inca traditions and who dream of a kindly and protective élite presiding over a gradual and orderly mingling of civilisations, there is a right-wing school of thought which defends the legitimacy of plutocratic rule against sharp attack both from the radical left and from the champions of traditional values. This group, which some call realistic and others cynical, expresses itself most articulately, if not most frankly, in *La Prensa* and in utterances by friends of its editor, Sr. Pedro Beltrán. Sr. Beltrán is not an intellectual and does not waste time dreaming of the colonial and pre-Columbian era: he is no more moved by memories of Cuzco than of La Perricholi. Instead, he thinks in matter-of-fact terms: the balance of payments, a sound budget, foreign investments and the defence of the currency. The contents of *La Prensa*, stimulating as they are, may surprise the foreign observer by the seemingly paradoxical nature of its theses and the simple, vivid and often aggressive language in which they are expressed. The praise accorded to neo-liberal economists and to such men as Dr. Erhard, M. Pinay and Sr. Alsogaray give the paper a more cosmopolitan note than is common in the Lima press. But, besides supplying the plutocracy with the best possible rationalisation and justification of its position, *La Prensa*'s uncompromising neo-liberalism helps to reawaken in the conservative camp (using this term in its broadest sense) fears and defensive reactions which allow it to be alerted, mobilised and if necessary placed on a war footing.

La Prensa's economic doctrine is assiduously presented in its leading articles, which display maximum clarity and intransigence at times of crisis. On three important occasions in the recent past, economic events have led the paper to come forward with remedies. In and after 1953, when the prosperity due to the Korean war boom had spent itself and public expenditure remained at a high level, the country suffered from an excess of demand over supply which led to rising prices, a deteriorating balance of trade and a weakening in the rate of exchange. At that time General Odría was in power, and it was unwise to express views on public affairs which differed from his. *La Prensa*, while avoiding a direct attack on the President or his ministers, published a long series of warnings and criticisms, urging the authorities in outspoken terms to revert to a sound policy. In 1958–9 the country went through a further crisis which, in the view of big business circles, was of the same nature as the previous one, involving as it did problems of public finance, foreign trade and the exchange rate; and on this occasion Sr. Pedro Beltrán, the editor of *La Prensa*, was invited by the President, Dr. Manuel Prado, to head the government and apply his remedies. Finally, after the military coup of July 1962, an end came to the policy of 'economic growth combined with stability' which Sr. Beltrán, despite the sarcasms of his opponents, boasted of having maintained during his two and a half years at the helm, and *La Prensa* reverted to its Cassandra-like role.

The following quotations illustrate the second and third periods (June 1959; second half of 1962 and beginning of 1963). In its leading article of 10 June 1959, headed 'Speculation, prices and currency', the paper discussed the causes of the inflation and proposed remedies. The causes, it said, were not far to seek: they were not structural, as the ECLA[1] technocrats would have us believe, but were due to the

[1] The (United Nations) Economic Commission for Latin America (in Spanish C.E.P.A.L.), with headquarters at Santiago. Its secretary-general at the

bad economic policies of successive governments. *La Prensa* divides governments in general into two classes: the sound (*sensatos*) and the unsound (*insensatos*). The latter, which included those of Bolivia, the Popular Front in Chile and Perón's regime in the Argentine, were distinguished by 'spending more than their revenue, printing bank-notes by the million and so debasing their currency'; while sound governments 'spend according to their means and do not resort to the printing of notes ... If the cost of living continues to rise, it is because our government relies on the issuing bank to help it out of its difficulties.' To illustrate this simple theory, according to which price-levels depend solely on the amount of money in circulation, *La Prensa* popularised the symbol of the *maquinita* or engraving-machine. Its cartoons featured a character in shirtsleeves who, with malicious glee or morose indifference, kept turning the handle of a printing press out of which cascaded a flood of signs representing the currency. Next only to the evil effects of the *maquinita*, *La Prensa* inveighed against the inefficacy of government controls. The rise in the cost of living could not be checked for long by the official freezing of prices, and controls were bound to bring about three kinds of adverse effects. Firstly, rationing of any kind meant long queues, secondly it would create a black market, and thirdly a fall in production, since investors who could not get a return on their money would use it for specula-tion instead. This could only be put a stop to by 'fair prices' and a sound credit policy.

La Prensa's third bugbear is nationalisation: a fact all the more significant in that it is not Peruvian capital that is affected so much as foreign and especially U.S. investments. Thus in criticising the nationalisation policy *La Prensa* is indirectly advocating a certain attitude towards foreign capital. On 3 December 1962 it published an instructive leader entitled 'The fiasco of nationalisation'. The pretext for this was an agency report that the president of the Bolivian Mining Corporation (COMIBOL) had gone to Washington to nego-tiate a credit from the World Bank. The leader-writer emphasised that the credit, if obtained, would be used 'not to raise production or finance investment, but–such is the parlous state of COMIBOL– simply to pay the several months' arrears of wages which this nation-alised concern owes its workers'. And this in spite of the fact that:

'As everyone knows, when Bolivian tin was in the hands of private

time was Sr. Raúl Prebisch, an exponent of 'structuralist' theories concerning the inevitable deterioration of terms of trade from Latin America's point of view.

firms, they not only paid out wages promptly but supplied the state, through taxes, with enough revenue to finance practically the whole national budget. As a result, income tax in Bolivia was very low and import duties negligible, which was a very good thing for the consumer. Of course, the advocates of state control could not tolerate this: as they put it, "our generation must win independence in the economic field as our ancestors gained it in politics." ... In actual fact, instead of paving the way to a new Bolivia, they have opened the door to poverty; and the measures which they hoped would bring about economic independence have led to such chaos that even state officials cannot be paid without appealing to U.S. generosity ... Even the tin-mines cannot pay their own workers ... What was formerly a source of vast profits to the nation and government has become a liability.'

In this potted history we may note, firstly the description of a country which, under the show of protecting its economic independence, finds itself impoverished and enslaved to the very imperialism from which it strove to be free. 'Once again, state control has produced the opposite of the desired effect.' The idyllic picture of former times throws light on the writer's intentions, desires and fears: 'income tax was very low and import duties negligible'. This was certainly all to the good for taxpayers and consumers of imported products, but was not likely to be of great interest to the masses, or to any but the upper and middle-class city-dwellers at whom the lesson was presumably aimed.

As time went on, attacks on state control or dirigism were increasingly varied by attacks on planning.[1] The latter term became highly popular in left-wing circles from 1956 onwards. In its effort to stem the tide, *La Prensa* made more use of practical and utilitarian arguments than of moral or legal ones. 'Quite apart from jeopardising a long series of constitutional guarantees, it seems to us beyond question that authoritarian planning would do the country incalculable damage. It would inevitably lead to inflation, the collapse of the currency, a soaring cost of living, thousands out of work, the shrinkage of the national and per capita income, the flight of capital, universal poverty and the enslavement of the country to a corrupt *camarilla* which would batten on it behind the shelter of the laws.'[2]

[1] The terms 'planning' and 'dirigism' are frequently interchanged, probably for reasons of style rather than substance.
[2] Leading article of 21 July 1963.

What is to be done?

Two items in this formidable list of calamities may be specially noted. Firstly, the clear hint that property-owners would be fully justified in placing their money where it would be safe from the extravagances and follies of dirigism. Secondly, the spectre of a corrupt *camarilla* which would put import licences up for sale and devote itself to mutual enrichment at the state's expense. Thus the reader is expected to feel alarm on two grounds: firstly the just retaliation of the property-owning classes in the face of insane provocation, and secondly the wiles of cunning and corrupt politicians.

La Prensa has two main techniques for stirring up its readers. On the one hand it excites and keeps alive certain specific fears (as *El Comercio* plays on its readers' fear and hatred of Apra), and on the other it puts forward a simple doctrine by means of which the perils it conjures up can be averted. This doctrine, according to *La Prensa*, was vindicated by Sr. Beltrán's success as prime minister and by the country's economic progress under his wise regime. Once more, the appeal is to experience. Just as the planners' experiment in nationalisation was doomed to fail, so a sound policy of upholding the currency and attracting foreign capital is bound to succeed.

There are no economic miracles but only a few simple economic laws, as inexorable as those of physics. They have to do with the mechanism of investment, credit policy and the economic function of the state. 'When an individual or the head of a private concern makes a profit, he may either reinvest it in order to raise production and improve efficiency, or devote it to increasing salaries and wages or to his own enjoyment. If he is wise he will put it to all three uses, in proportions varying with needs and circumstances. But the main thing is that he is dividing up an actual profit and not a potential one.'[1] In other words, investment depends on previous saving and involves the use of profits which might otherwise be directly consumed by the capitalist or his employees. However, the strict view is modified to the following extent. 'It is legitimate to spend beyond one's actual resources and resort to credit, on condition that the revenue from the proposed investment is sufficient to cover the service of the debt ... The credit must therefore be devoted to investments which are sufficiently productive to enable the businessman to repay both capital and interest without difficulty.' These principles of private economy are equally valid in the political sphere. If the state has a budget surplus, it may 'devote the revenue

[1] Leading article of 17 April 1963.

to productive investments such as roads and irrigation works, which will eventually increase national production; or it may spend all or part of the surplus on social investments such as schools and hospitals, or increase the number of its officials and pay them more, or finally spend more on armaments'. But the state, like the private person, can only spend real resources and not imaginary future ones. Of course, it too may borrow (from its own nationals or from foreigners) 'in order temporarily to be able to spend more than it receives'. But a similar condition applies: as borrowed money must eventually be returned, it must be used to increase production and improve the nation's economy. The state must not run into debt in order to finance an increase in consumption which is not counterbalanced by goods already produced or in prospect (*ingresos producidos ni por producir*).

If these rules are observed, the *maquinita* holds no terrors: the currency remains stable, trade balances, and foreign capitalists are encouraged to invest or lend money for profitable purposes. All this is the result of a sound credit policy and strict attention to balancing the budget. As for the 'monetary discipline' which, according to a leader of 11 April 1963, is so hard to achieve, its purpose is to counteract the dangers of a too rapid expansion of means of payment (*medios de pago*) and especially of bank credit (*colocaciones bancarias*), above all when this is not the effect of previous saving. According to *La Prensa*, an 'over-liberal credit policy' leads to an upsurge in imports and the largely speculative purchase of foreign currency by banks and individuals. The relaxation of monetary discipline vitiates the balance of trade, by increasing imports and making export more difficult, and the balance of payments, by encouraging the flight of capital and speculation against the currency. To avert these dangers of credit inflation requires great wisdom and moderation on the part of bankers and capitalists–whose interests, as we have seen, are closely united. How are the monetary authorities to resist the pressure of the business world when favourable prospects of expansion increase the demand for short-term capital, or the protests which are raised when they restrict credit to avert or surmount a crisis? In one case they are accused of hindering economic growth, and in the other of causing or aggravating a recession.

Accordingly, the first principle is that rational economic development must be based on a 'sound' credit policy and constant vigilance against inflation. The article of 11 April 1963 emphasises that this is a 'preventive' policy and is one of the least expensive ways of ensuring steady expansion. Moreover, if the guardians of economic health discern untoward symptoms at any time, they can intervene to prevent disaster. 'If the state has taken some liberties with sound principles (*si ya se ha empezado en incurrir algunos excesos*), health may be restored by the use of minor restrictions, comparable to a diet or a slimming cure. But if, in spite of warnings, the patient persists in his excesses, the effect on the organism will be so ruinous that the doctor must give place to the surgeon. If measures in the field of credit are insufficient, the only remedy is to devalue the currency.'

If regular growth is to be achieved, not only the monetary authorities but the state itself must understand its proper function and abstain from causing inflation.

'The state is often tempted by the illusory hope that national consumption can be allowed to outrun production. It must be borne in mind that the state itself is essentially a consumer and not a producer. Virtually the whole of its revenue comes from taxing the vital forces (*fuerzas vivas*) of the nation ... But if the overhead expenses which it administers are allowed to become too great, the effect will be to hinder economic growth and dry up the productive resources on which its revenue depends ... The state should administer the sums which it levies on production with the same prudence and good sense as a wife managing the allowance she receives from her husband for housekeeping and personal expenses ... Certainly the housewife cannot always satisfy even her most legitimate wishes, and she may, alas, have to postpone the fulfilment of needs which, though essential, are less urgent than others. If she tried to do everything at once or to satisfy her wants irrespective of her husband's earning capacity, the household would soon be bankrupt ... In short, the state must base its revenue on a non-oppressive fiscal system and must strictly limit its expenditure to the level of its income.'[1]

This passage is significant both for the doctrine it conveys and for its choice of metaphor. Just as the husband supports the family of which he is the head, so the nation's 'vital forces' maintain the agency which controls expenditure and which, in return for its keep, presides over the general economy. Naturally, final authority rests with the partner who produces the wealth consumed by the household or the nation. As for the state, it is its nature to spend; but it must not squander or use up too much of the revenue. As between balancing

[1] Leading article of 14 April 1963.

the budget and observing a moderate fiscal policy, the latter precept is probably the more important. Even if the most legitimate grounds for expenditure present themselves in the shape, for example, of schools and hospitals, the state must not live beyond its 'husband's' income. The article of 17 April 1963, already quoted, distinguished between various objects on which the state could spend its resources: productive works such as roads and irrigation; social investment (schools and hospitals); a larger and better-paid civil service; or, finally, armaments and the apparatus of sovereignty. All these forms of expenditure are legitimate. The nation's 'social conscience' demands hospitals and schools; nationalists, and the military, insist on up-to-date equipment for the navy and air force; but, important as all these needs (*necesidades*) are, they differ in urgency. A good housewife will give priority to purchases which will save her time and work and reduce the overall housekeeping expenses. The state, for its part, should not only restrict to a minimum its share of the wealth accumulated by the 'vital forces', but should as far as possible return that share to productive uses, not indulging in over-elaborate displays of sovereignty or too rapidly increasing the remuneration of its servants and dependants.

All this constitutes a perfectly coherent doctrine, which I shall call 'creole liberalism'. Its keynote is the common-sense principle of not living beyond one's means and of managing state affairs with housewifely prudence. At the same time, sterner realities are evoked: if the government should be so misguided as to yield to the siren call of such high-sounding ideals as nationalisation and economic independence, the facts of life will soon have their revenge, and a moment's folly will be paid for by the horrors of inflation. *La Prensa* has less to say about the benefits which liberal methods will bring than the disasters which would come of forsaking them. The 'sound' policy may not promise much, but at least it will keep its promise; our progress may be slow and limited, but we shall be saved from calamities which would otherwise be certain and which are out of all proportion to the blessings promised by hasty and ill-advised reformers. The left wing is fond of accusing the oligarchy of frivolity–of being too selfish and unimaginative to foresee the disasters with which the country is threatened by its cunning but short-sighted policy. Although *La Prensa* seldom uses the term 'frivolity', it in fact levels a similar accusation against the left, but for different reasons. If the right wing is frivolous, it is out of egotism and callousness; the left, on the other hand, suffers from a lack of realism which leads it to confuse its own wishful fantasies with the objective order of things.

'By their fruits ...'

It is, of course, all the easier for the advocates of creole liberalism to take a 'realistic' view in that this bears a close correspondence to their own class-interest. A government which does not over-indulge in 'non-productive' social and cultural investments, which is at pains to defend the currency by limiting public expenditure and fiscal demands on the 'productive' sector, and which has a holy horror of the *maquinita*–all this suits exporters who need a 'realistic' exchange rate if they are to keep their position in the world market. It is equally understandable that this convenient doctrine is attacked from various quarters. To begin with, its proponents are accused of hypocrisy: creole liberalism is a mask for the nefarious interests of the export trade. On this score the extreme left, denouncing the plutocracy of the sugar and cotton magnates who form the Sociedad Agraria, finds common ground with those conservative circles which exploit the resentment of 'good families' at the ostentatious wealth of the oligarchy. This theme has been developed with great effect by *El Comercio*. But creole liberalism is perhaps more gravely threatened by the force of events than by any human volition. To be effective, the system presupposes several conditions, the combination of which will be more difficult to achieve as Peruvian society grows larger and more complicated.

To defend their position as realists, the upholders of creole liberalism must be able to claim not only that their system works efficiently –which, by and large, is the case–but to show that they are not insensible to the demands of justice and progress. As to the first point, a debate took place between an editor of the newspaper *Expreso* and an engineer named Jorge Grieve, formerly Peruvian Minister of Production and, at the time in question, one of the 'wise men' of the Alliance for Progress. Whether or not Sr. Grieve is to be regarded as an adherent of neo-liberal orthodoxy, he argued with great force and acumen, in the columns of *La Prensa*, that the Peruvian economy in the 1950s had developed at a very respectable rate; the system, therefore, need not fear criticism on grounds of inefficiency. To this the *Expreso* writer replied by distinguishing growth (*crecimiento*) from development (*desarrollo*). The argument continued on the following lines. Sr. Grieve contended[1] that there had been both growth and development, 'taking as indices the figures for the gross and *per capita* national product, gross capital accumulation and the gross rate of investment in the public sector'. In his view, while fully admitting the inequality of the distribution of wealth, 'there is no doubt that the Peruvian economy has achieved the necessary strength and is not far from take-off.'[2] Sr. Grieve's anonymous opponent replied as follows. 'We freely admit that there was growth under Sr. Prado's administration, but we deny that there was development.[3] . . . Growth is a purely numerical concept, signifying that the indices for a given year are greater than those for the preceding year or years . . . But for genuine development to take place, the net product must increase at a higher rate than the population . . . Moreover, the additional wealth must be applied to reduce inequalities of distribution, or at least the latter must not become more unequal as the product increases.'[4] Thus, for example, Kuwait and Qatar enjoy fabulous revenues, but the gap between the sheikhs' income and that of the masses does not tend to grow less–quite the contrary. The 'camel and Cadillac' societies are experiencing a rapid expansion of their gross product without any rectification of their economic structure or increase of productive capacity. Kuwait and Qatar are enclaves or transit points for the export of wealth produced by and for foreigners, and the import of luxury consumer goods for the governing class.

Thus *Expreso* raises the question whether the growth of which *La Prensa* and Sr. Grieve boast is not more like that of the oil sheikhdoms than true economic development. It is hard to answer, if only because of the uncertainty of demographic estimates. Naturally, *Expreso* chooses the highest rates of increase in order to show that the rise in the gross national product is swallowed up by the faster growth of population. Sr. Grieve, for his part, emphasises two points. He maintains that the country's productive capacity has not only developed but has become diversified, and that secondary activities have grown increasingly important as compared with mining, agriculture and stockbreeding. He also contends that the public sector has not been neglected and that while social investments have been

[1] *La Prensa*, 7 and 8 August 1962.   [2] Ibid., 30 July 1962.
[3] *Expreso*, 28 July 1962.   [4] Ibid., 1 September 1962.

kept within prudent limits, they have certainly increased. Thus, not only has the national product grown between 1960 and 1962, but the structure of the economy and of society has changed. Pessimists, however, object that the changes which have taken place in the nature of the apparatus of production are in many cases automatic effects of growth rather than evidence of development. The export of oil from Kuwait and Qatar has led to the construction of depots, workshops, harbour and dock facilities which statisticians class as 'secondary' activities, but does this mean that the sheikhdoms are in a state of development?

Some journalists rely on simpler arguments:

'The following figures are, in themselves, unanswerable . . . In 1941 the annual consumption of cement was under 175,000 tons, whereas in 1961 the consumption of Peruvian cement alone was 622,000 tons: an amazing increase of 360 per cent. In 1940, 19 million litres of beer were consumed, and in 1961, 139 million. Since no one supposes that the oligarchs increased their consumption to this extent, it would seem that the growth in purchasing power enabled a much larger number of workers and employees to drink beer . . . In 1940 Peru imported 140 refrigerators; in 1961 the figure was 16,420–an increase of 11,700 per cent. Who can say that refrigerators are today, as they were twenty years ago, a luxury article reserved for the élite? In 1941, bank deposits stood at a million soles per day; the figure for 1961 is over 18 million. This is out of all proportion to the depreciation of the currency, and can only be explained by increased consumption. Finally, the most spectacular figures relate to fishmeal . . . In short, the population is not growing as fast as was generally believed, nor is the national income growing as slowly as some maintain. In any case, it is quite untrue that *per capita* national income is declining. This did happen in 1957–8, but only as a consequence of the U.S. recession and the fall in the price and quantity of some of our exports . . . Peru has made and is making progress. It has not fallen back, like Bolivia, as a result of nationalist and revolutionary demagogy, or, like Cuba, owing to the communist whirlwind . . . The system of free enterprise is capable of surmounting even harder and more difficult trials than those it has already passed through.'[1]

The system, then, is efficient; is it also humane? Sr. Beltrán's enemies are given to accusing him of being cold, callous and cynical.

[1] Enrique Chirino Soto, 'Progresa el Perú?', *Revista mensual de la Cámara de Comercio de Lima*, April 1962.

Accordingly, *La Prensa* is at pains to show that modern liberalism is generous and does more to relieve the needy than demagogues with their empty promises. In 1953 it launched a campaign on the housing conditions of the thousands of provincials who were cramming the *barriadas*. In 1956 the Prado government set up a Housing and Land Reform Commission (*Comisión de Reforma Agraria y de la Vivienda*) in which Sr. Beltrán was to play a major role. On becoming Prime Minister in 1959 he adopted the slogan *techo y tierra*–'a roof and a plot of land'. The miserable conditions in which hundreds of thousands of Limas live huddled in shanty-towns around the capital may give food for many kinds of thought, but *La Prensa* rings the changes on two themes only. Firstly, that of pity: I have already discussed the stylised and distorted image of life in the *barriadas* which is current among 'the quality' (*la gente decente*), and which probably exaggerates the aspect of forsakenness and neglect. As I pointed out, the *barriada* is not an amorphous society but possesses a structure of its own, including an organisation which receives and protects new-comers. This organisation often throws up leaders who manage to gain the ear of the authorities and obtain varying degree of official help. But, while depicting the horrors of life in the *barriadas*, the journalists who 'study' the housing problem take occasion to warn their readers of the danger which it represents. With hundreds of thousands living in desperate conditions in hovels at the very gates of the capital, is there not a risk that some day they may go berserk? Such is *La Prensa*'s message for the well-to-do: the pitiable victims of fate may turn into ravening lions. Thus the newspaper appeals alternately to its readers' fear and pity: both charity and prudence demand that 'something should be done'. But what?

Acute though the danger may be, the remedies proposed by *La Prensa* are in strict accord with the well-tried maxims of creole liberalism. Certainly the scandal of the *barriadas* must be tackled, but in a practical and realistic manner. The government should help those who are worst off, but they must first help themselves. Government action has in fact taken the form of a National Housing Fund (*Instituto de la Vivienda*) which makes loans to co-operatives and itself receives grants, repayable or not, from the government and international organisations such as the Inter-American Development Bank and the Alliance for Progress. The Fund encourages the formation of housing co-operatives, provides them with land and the necessary equipment for preliminary works, and may even install such utilities as water and electricity points. On 18 August 1962 *La Prensa* reported the completion of the 'people's city' of Ventanilla, midway between Lima and the seaside resort of Ancón–a project to which Sr. Beltrán as Prime Minister had devoted much energy. A leading article entitled 'Low-cost Housing at Ventanilla' stated that 'Next Sunday, about a hundred members of co-operatives will be handed the keys of their own houses in the satellite town of Ventanilla, under the scheme whereby the Housing Fund receives loans from the Inter-American Development Bank for the benefit of housing co-operatives and their members.' This housing programme has two main features. In the first place, it is intended to promote ownership: the lucky inhabitants of Ventanilla will not pay rent but will be solemnly handed the keys of 'their own houses'. Secondly, they will have to repay a larger or smaller proportion of the loan made to them. The Fund's object, of course, is to 'help families of insufficient means', but this help is not available for the mere asking and is graded according to circumstances. Here again we find the principle of economy, based on a balanced budget and a sound currency, linked with a genuine concern for 'social progress without demagogy'.

Peruvian conservatism is not, of course, restricted to what I have called 'creole liberalism', but embraces many different tendencies. It is a far cry from *La Prensa*'s 'realism' to the paternalism of a Riva Agüero or a Víctor Andrés Belaúnde. None the less, the various types of conservatism have important features in common: not least the fact that none of them has succeeded in becoming a political, or rather electoral, force of any magnitude. Riva Agüero was Prime Minister, but only under the military regime of Benavides. Sr. Beltrán, the leader of the 'creole liberals', has been Minister of Finance and Prime Minister, but his attempt to stand for the Presidency at the end of 1961 was a complete failure.[1]

The fact seems to be that neither paternalism nor 'realism' is capable of making conservatism acceptable as a philosophy. I have used the term 'creole' to denote the somewhat cynical prudence of those liberals who profess to rely on foreign investment as a solution to development problems. Certainly the 'creolism' of a Riva Agüero has little in common with that of Sr. Beltrán, save in one important

[1] Similarly, in 1945 General Ureta, who was supported by *El Comercio* and the stoutest conservative adherents of the Benavides regime, was soundly beaten at the Presidential election.

respect. Conservatives of whatever school of thought start from the principle that the masses are, rightly or wrongly, on the margin of national life and can only be absorbed into it gradually and partially: otherwise, reason and civilisation will be swept away by a tidal wave of mendacious demagogy.

Apra, in its time, had the distinction of realising that the problems of social mobility called for a transformation of political methods. The conservatives have striven to preserve the essence of oligarchic control by a number of devices which they have engineered with some skill according to circumstances. It may well be that their chance of rallying depends on their ability to formulate political problems in terms other than those native to the oligarchic tradition.

Some such development has been visible since the late 1950s in the Catholic church. For a long time the church conformed to the usual Latin American pattern, with innumerable saints' days and time-consuming processions. To the masses, whether Indians or small-town *mestizos*, it offered the comfort of its rites and the baroque splendour of its ceremonies, while it influenced the educated middle class through its colleges, teachers and confessors. The Peruvian church of those days must be seen as an essentially conservative force, although, except in unusual circumstances–for example, the anti-Apra repressions of the 1930s–it studiously avoided involvement in political life, which nevertheless would have come easily to it, especially in the provinces.[1]

Things began to change with the arrival of more and more foreign priests, the training of Peruvian priests in Europe or North America, and the *aggiornamento* of the Latin American church in general. The church began to manifest its concern for social problems: from 1959 onwards, some priests took up their abode in the *barriadas* to which they ministered, and some burning questions were discussed which had hitherto been taboo.[2] The Catholic University of Lima played a part in spreading notions of 'social justice' which had long been regarded in Latin America as smacking of the left.

In Chile, it was the Christian Democrats who brought conservatism up to date. In Peru the situation is different for many reasons: there

---

[1] For an analysis of the church's position in various countries see Ivan Vallier, *Religious Élites in Latin America: Catholicism, Leadership and Social Change*.
[2] Cf. Part III, chap. 3, for the church's position on the land reform question.

is no conservative party, and the church in the late fifties was less progressive. Above all, in 1956, when the first Christian Democrats came on the scene, their potential following was diminished by a new star of the first magnitude, namely Fernando Belaúnde and his Popular Action Party (chapter 4 below).

3

Humanism and Terror: the Diehards of the Extreme Left

Beyond the bastion of Apra and the ranks of Fernando Belaúnde's Acción Popular, the political battlefield is dotted with minor left-wing forces: communists with allegiance to Moscow or Peking, Trotskyists and disciples of Fidel Castro. Their exact numbers are hard to estimate. According to the electoral statistics of 1962, if we add to the Communist Party (which, though theoretically banned, supports and controls such organisations as the Frente de Liberación Nacional) groups like the Movimiento Social Progresista and the Partido Socialista Peruano, the total of votes is still less than 60,000 out of a million and a half electors. (In 1963 the Movimiento Social Progresista put forward no candidates.) The figures, however, are differently interpreted. Both *La Prensa* and *El Comercio*, though from different points of view and for different purposes, have dwelt on the minute size of the extreme left vote; but *La Prensa*, which never misses a chance to scoff at the tiny numbers of communist, fellow-travelling and pro-Castro groups, is also swift to point out the dangers of communist infiltration, especially in the ranks of Sr. Belaúnde's party. *El Comercio*, on the other hand, which regards it as an eternal truth that communism and Apra are one and the same thing, plays up every sign which may point to collusion between Apra and the extreme left, as it did when President Dorticós of Cuba visited Lima in 1959. In any case, the importance of the extreme left in Peruvian politics cannot seriously be estimated on the basis of the last elections alone. We should in addition study its influence on trade unions and students, and also its chances of infiltrating and eventually controlling the large organised parties (Apra and the Belaúndists). Are these tiny groups, alternately derided for their weakness or held up as bogies by those in power, condemned to drag out a sterile existence, torn by internal rivalries, or is the dawn of the *revolución peruana* close at hand? The groups in question are united by their faith in a 'genuine' revolution which will sweep away the present governing class, though they quarrel as to the nature and meaning of this quasi-mythical event and the conditions necessary to bring it about.

Rather than analyse the relationships between these groups, I propose to discuss severally their preoccupations and views of the political scene. We may start with the theme of revolution as put forward by the Movimiento Social Progresista in its weekly *Libertad*, published until 1962. It is, of course, not enough to claim that the situation in Peru is revolutionary, or that revolution alone can bring about the triumph of humanistic values: we must also investigate the processes by which the revolution may be achieved.

The 'humanistic' revolution

I shall attempt in this section to analyse the principal themes developed by *Libertad* in 1961–2, immediately before the last Presidential election but one. The weekly describes itself as 'anti-imperialist, anti-Yankee, opposed to the oligarchy and *convivencia*, to Apra and the Prado regime'. Its positive values are socialism and 'planning', defined as a strategy for development (*estrategia para el desarrollo*); and the will towards revolution is symbolised by a fairly mythical image of Castro's Cuba. If we turn to consider the paper's style as opposed to its content, we notice three main tendencies.

A large part of each issue is devoted to questions of theory; but instead of the scholastic dissertations so frequent in Apra or communist literature, we are offered a great deal of information, whose accuracy I shall not try to assess. This consists partly of the sort of political gossip which is common in the Lima press, and is there known as *chismografía*, but also of lengthy accounts of the workings of the economy, the manoeuvres of private interests and the strategy of 'monopoly capitalism', with abundant references to the family headed by the President's nephew, Mariano Ignacio Prado. The tone of these accounts is 'objective' and indignant by turns. Then, on the back page, a regular column was contributed by 'Sofocleto', the pseudonym of a journalist who was for many years on the staff of *El*

Comercio before moving to Havana–a fact which enabled *La Prensa* to accuse its rival of harbouring disguised agents of communism and Castroism. Sofocleto is a bitter humorist whose style recalls, perhaps intentionally, that of the Paris *Canard Enchaîné*: its blend of vigour and venom is used to portray the authorities in a hateful and ridiculous light. Finally, *Libertad* possesses a third style which may be called 'lyrical', and which luxuriates in 'tropical' metaphors (as they are called in Peru) whenever Castro, Cuba or the revolution are its subject. This is the more remarkable in that the most dithyrambic passages are written by the same Sofocleto, who, when chanting paeans to Castro, signs his real name, Luis Felipe Angel.

Libertad takes it for granted that the entire Latin American economy is in a parlous state. In 1961 it devoted two full pages to reproducing an article published in the Mexico City *Gaceta* by Professor Samuel Shapiro of the University of Michigan.[1] 'Latin America is, geographically, not a rich area. Northern Mexico . . . is a huge desert. Large parts of the American west coast are completely arid and almost uninhabitable.' The Eldorado myth which, as we have seen, still fascinates Víctor Raúl from time to time is here abandoned. Moreover, 'economic growth is stultified by the lack of honest and stable governments . . . Batista and his henchmen in Cuba laid their hands on billions of dollars, and this was nothing to the amounts stolen by the dictators of Venezuela and the Argentine. What they did not steal, they squandered: Latin America is littered with marble relics of Odría, Perón, Pérez Jiménez and the rest of them . . . The democratic regimes are sometimes worse still . . . Kubitschek's Brasilia cost over five hundred million dollars to build.' To complete the picture, the author points out one of the most typical features of under-development: the hair-raising growth of population. 'Malthus's predictions have come true. In cities like La Paz, Lima, Mexico City and Buenos Aires, the young have no option but to join the vast army of unemployed. Lima, for instance, has doubled its population in the last twelve years, not as the result of normal economic growth, but because it offers shelter of a sort to the Indians who flock down from the Andean slopes.'

This description of South America in general is repeated with still more pessimistic variations when *Libertad* comes to depict the present situation in Peru. It begins by stating roundly that:

'We are an under-developed country . . . Some people, for

[1] Vol. IV, no. 5, 1961.

contemptible reasons of prestige, refuse to use this term and speak instead of an insufficiently developed or a developing country . . . Under-development is a precise concept denoting what is not only insufficient but abnormal, partial and lop-sided, the cause and effect of conflicts. It is due to a clash of cultures and an economic structure at war with itself–the result of introducing capitalist methods of production into a basically primitive country for the benefit of a big industrial power . . . which treats the natives in colonial fashion. This is true of Peru and most Latin American countries, as well as those of southern Asia, Africa and Oceania and, in former times, the Balkans and parts of central Europe.'

We recognise here the dualistic viewpoint developed in Víctor Raúl's speech of 23 August 1931, but presented now in sharper and more uncompromising terms. Peru is placed in the same category as the tribes of central Africa: no argument is spared in order to emphasise its backwardness and impending doom. According to the writer, its natural resources are not even fully exploited, while the population, which lies between 10 and 14 million, is growing at a rate of 3·5 per cent per annum, which means that it will double in less than twenty years. As far as cultivated land is concerned, the ratio of 1,440 square yards per man will then be halved, so that every acre will have to support six or seven men. The national income, which at present stands at 6 soles per head, will drop sharply if production cannot be increased at a faster rate. At present 12 per cent of the population receive 40 per cent of the national income, whereas 40 per cent receive only 12 per cent of it; 60 per cent of the population live by agriculture, which provides only 36 per cent of the national income. Economic power is in the hands of a small group of merchants, bankers and landowners; power production is monopolised by two or three foreign companies, and production in general is entirely geared to export.

We may note here the contrast between the argument of creole liberalism, as developed in *La Prensa*, and those of the extreme left. *Libertad* is assiduous in publishing and commenting on reports of all kinds, whether from international bodies such as ECLA, private bureaux of experts such as the Little organisation, or well-disposed visitors such as Fr. Lebret. In the issue in which Shapiro's essay is reproduced, an article entitled 'El paraíso se despinta' (paradise with the gilt off) denounces the government for attempting to throw dust in people's eyes and claims that its efforts are in any case vain, since the Little report, which the government preferred to Fr. Lebret's conclusions, 'could not escape telling the truth' (*no pudo evitar la verdad*): namely that, in the words of the report itself, 'The country's political stability and economic survival are threatened by the population explosion, the extremely low standard of living of half the inhabitants and the concentration of wealth in a very few hands.'

Clearly, this cumulative process of relative and absolute pauperisation can only end in revolution. Under the title 'Único camino, la revolución', one of *Libertad*'s editors, Abelardo Oquendo, writes as follows:

'According to various studies, our population, which at present numbers 12–14 million, will double itself in the next twenty years ... This would necessitate the investment of 1,000 soles per head per annum, that is to say nearly 500 million soles in 20 years ... With an inept government, a corrupt administration, an economy run by grasping bankers and exporters, and our wealth in the hands of foreign monopolies, there is clearly no hope except by a radical change which would restore that wealth to the community. Not only is this possible, but it is the only way of avoiding the crisis which threatens us.'

After rejecting any form of 'capitalist' solution ('All our history demonstrates that capitalism in Peru is a failure ... to entrust development to private enterprise would mean abandoning our future to avarice and usury'), the writer attempts to describe the coming revolution. 'Our national recovery must be based on labour-investment, which can only be efficiently organised by the people as a whole ... We must instil a new attitude and create a new organisation of labour, which is only possible in a new, revolutionary and socialist society.' This, however, is not dogmatic socialism. 'It is not a question of communism or anti-communism, humanistic socialism or Christian democracy, but simply of a struggle between two groups–those who are weary of suffering and starvation, and those who cling to their privileges, excessive wealth and odious power in order to stave off the necessary change.'

Revolution is inevitable, not only because the system is objectively incapable of satisfying the people's most elementary needs, but because all reform is blocked by an oligarchy as blind as its American masters. *Libertad* depicts this oligarchy with the features of finance capitalism. The banks suck the country dry, control the economy and

213

do business with the investors' money,[1] thanks to the credit system which they manipulate at will. . . .

'The banks mould the nation's economy to suit themselves and reduce it to dependence on the foreign trade cycle . . . They also control production . . . In 1959, 51·3 per cent of their deposits were used for commercial speculation or under a mysterious heading entitled "Various"; and 78·5 per cent of their total credit is invested in Lima although the capital of our centralised state only supplies 67·5 per cent of the country's total deposits . . . The banks control the whole of the nation's business: individual companies . . . foreign trade, the exchange, markets and price levels . . . the distribution of goods and profits . . . They are the absolute controllers of the Central Bank . . . Their power is reinforced by unfettered control in the political sphere: one of their chief representatives is the President himself, whose family is one of the most powerful in the banking world, and the Prime Minister too belongs to this group . . . The banks control public opinion through the press . . . radio and television, which are entirely in their hands.'

The above passage expresses forcefully, but without much subtlety, the theme of the domination of 'finance capitalism'. It presents the oligarchy as a homogeneous, vertically integrated group exercising iron control over the whole economic system. 'The banks' decide according to their own good pleasure where, how and what to invest, and in general prefer to use funds for speculation. They not only form a central, unitary power but are wholly autonomous *vis à vis* producers, who are completely subjected to the fluctuations of international trade. Thus, according to a headline of 21 June 1961, the government 'cheapens the sol to defend the dollar'.

So much for the anti-oligarchic theme; now for the anti-American. On 5 July 1961 *Libertad* published, in translation, a long article by Leo Huberman and Paul Sweezy, and alongside it a cartoon of President Kennedy with the caption 'Crisis in Sight'. The article argued that the U.S. economy was marked by a 'tendency to stagnation' due to the 'monopoly of big corporations . . . In an economy dominated by huge trusts, the price mechanism can no longer fulfil its function but serves to aggravate disequilibrium, as we see from the alarming figures of unemployment and excess productive capacity.' However, this picture of an America torn by internal contradictions and doomed to under-employment and stagnation is less frequently

[1] 21 August 1961.

met with than that of an imperialist power determined to enslave the peoples of the neighbouring continent to its own selfish interests. The murder of President Rafael Trujillo in 1961 afforded an opportunity to blame 'Yankee imperialism' for the 'horrors of tyranny in the Caribbean'.

On the occasion of Adlai Stevenson's visit in 1962, Sofocleto described his country's dependence on U.S. policy in the broad comedy vein of which he is a master:

'In a few days Mr. Adlai E. Stevenson will arrive at Lima . . . in the course of his tour of inspection of the Yankee colonies of Latin America. This *gringo*,[1] who is no stranger to the job, is whizzing through fifteen countries in the same number of days, after which he will certainly know all about our problems and will be able to report when he gets home that we love his compatriots and are fairly bursting with prosperity. He has allowed twenty-four hours for Peru, which should allow enough time to enact measures to raise production, refashion the social system, reform the economy, dish the communists, fight Castroism, promote education, protect democracy, and of course choose us a good President for 1962, because the last one they gave us was really a bit over the odds.'

In the next issue of *Libertad*, Sofocleto follows up this idea by describing a 'competition' in which would-be Presidents are summoned before Mr. Stevenson like so many beauty queens. 'After rejecting an anonymous suggestion that the competitors should pose in bathing drawers, and also the proposal emanating from a department store that they should wear the latest creations of creole fashion, the judges assembled at the residence of His Highness (just over 7 feet) the U.S. Ambassador and Viceroy of Peru.' The same number contains a letter from Stevenson to Kennedy. 'I'm writing from Lima, in Ecuador or Bolivia or wherever it is . . . anyway, what matters to us is the interest of these countries, we lend them the money and we keep the interest. They're important countries to us, important importers I mean . . . All the same, I can't see why we don't get rid of all these presidents and send them governors as we did to Puerto Rico.' And the letter ends with the salutation 'Cuba no, Yankee yes'.

The *gringo* is stupid, wicked and selfish: he is convinced of his own superiority, but the contempt he shows for others is only the

[1] A term used to denote foreigners, especially North Americans, with overtones varying from hostility to affection with a tinge of irony.

counterpart of their justified contempt for him. It is he, the puppet-master, who directs the petty stratagems of small-time Latin American governments. Any hope of improvement must come from outside the system. Revolution is inescapable (*incontenible*).[1]

What is the nature of the impending revolution which can no longer be averted? *Libertad* offers us no theory of revolutionary action, but defines the revolution by its objectives. In so doing it identifies or confuses revolutionary methods with revolution as an object of policy. 'The country's deepest longing is for revolution';[2] but this Peruvian 'revolution' is to consist of five basic 'reforms':[3] 'reform of the state, and of private enterprise, credit, education and land tenure'.[4] These reforms, all of which are designed to increase the pace of development, belong to the realm of progressive humanism; and the development in question is to be 'integral', that is to say, physical, economic and social. 'Integral development . . . is the co-ordination of every possible form of effort and intervention for the purpose of solving the manifold problems created by the rapid social and economic changes of modern life.'[5] Every task is present at one and the same time, and if there is to be a reasonable chance of success in each they must be tackled simultaneously. It follows that there must be a general plan (described also as 'integral'); but this 'does not mean regimentation from above. The ideal of democratic planning is not a perfect machine in which man is a cog deprived of liberty, but a free association of free beings, working together to perform a task which has been rationally prescribed and whose results are directly controlled by them.'[6]

Statements of this sort reflect the doctrine of 'humanist democracy': not only are objectives determined freely by the community, but the various stages of the plan are formulated, discussed, carried out, evaluated and checked 'freely, by free beings'. The note of concern for the individual had already been struck in the declaration of 1957 constituting the Movimiento Social Progresista, of which *Libertad* is the mouthpiece. 'The party recognises as its fundamental values the personal dignity and liberty of man, justice and solidarity in communal life, labour as the source of improvement and progress, and the autonomy and historic personality of peoples and nations.' The

[1] *Libertad*, 18 July 1961.   [2] Ibid., 7 July 1961.
[3] Note the shift here from radicalism to reformism.
[4] *Libertad*, 5 July 1961.
[5] Ibid., 21 July 1961: article by José Matos Mar.
[6] Ibid., 5 July 1961.

third paragraph states that 'The party rejects all forms of exploitation and slavery, all barriers set by private interests to the development of personal and communal life, all domination by groups, castes, sects or classes . . . all discrimination and segregation on the basis of race, birth or belief . . . all kinds of oppression and political dictatorship.'[1]

Humanist democracy also describes itself as socialistic; but in the definition of socialism given by *Libertad* on 10 May 1961, the humanist and pluralistic approach is clearly visible.

'Socialism is a form of government which recognises labour as the sole source of rights of all kinds, solidarity as the mainspring of social development, and human improvement as the keynote of ethics. It sets out to organise economic life on the basis, not of profit but of the harmonious satisfaction of social and individual needs . . . Such organisation is not compatible with the private ownership of capital goods (*bienes de capital*) . . . This conception of socialism must be distinguished from a collectivist, totalitarian form of state control. It involves, on the contrary, a hierarchy of communal institutions of an intermediate character (*instituciones intermedias*) . . . Within this system, in which power is decentralised, deconcentrated and democratically co-ordinated, each organised community . . . controls and regulates those below it in the hierarchy, without infringing their internal freedom.'

Thus the two main features of the doctrine are a vague 'humanism' which consists chiefly in resisting centralist and unitary pretensions, and a challenge to the right to private property–which, however, to judge from the above passage, is not to be abolished but to be re-examined and adapted to the needs of the new society.

Is the emphasis on 'humanism' more than a blind? Some clue to this is given by *Libertad*'s attitude towards Castro's Cuba. On 18 April 1961, at the time of the Bay of Pigs landing, the paper published a photograph of Castro with the caption 'Cuba's and America's leader', and an article by Sebastián Salazar Bondy drawing comparisons with events in Guatemala and depicting Wall Street as the power behind the anti-Castro operation. The same issue contained various telegrams expressing solidarity with Havana and a photograph of M. Jean-Paul Sartre in conversation with the Cuban leader. 'Cuba'–wrote José Martos–is a great lesson for us: it is a call to action and to awareness of the changes that are possible in Latin

[1] Ibid., 21 June 1961.

America when progressive groups take matters seriously in hand.'
Two foreign messages are placed side by side: one from Herbert
Matthews, whose reporting in the New York Times did so much to
bring Castro to the notice of world opinion, and the other from M.
Sartre, who said 'Cuba must triumph or all is lost for us, including
hope'. The Cuban revolution is not only presented as a feat of liberation: an article by A. Fernández Arce[1] argues at length that it is an
economic success:

'The lies put about by powerful international U.S. interests and
Cuban exploiters whom the revolution has swept away cannot shut
our eyes to the notable success which the new socialist order has
achieved in two short years ... In spite of all Washington can do,
this heroic and virile regime, full of joy and enthusiasm, has triumphed
and is forging prosperity for a nation six million strong ... The
peasant's purchasing power has gone up by 60 per cent and the Land
Reform Institute controls 80 per cent of agriculture; 12,500 farmers'
dwellings have been built and furnished free of charge. The output of
rice has doubled and there are 2,000 peasants' shops ... The sugar
production target of 9 million tons will soon be achieved ... Tenants
have become houseowners ... Rents have been reduced by 50 per
cent and the former owners are receiving fair compensation ... The
barracks have been turned into educational centres: Cuba will be the
first American country, not excluding the United States, to abolish
the scourge of illiteracy once and for all ... Industrialisation is
making great strides. There is a huge plan for the production of
700,000 tons of steel; the output of oil and electricity is to be doubled;
the shipyards will be able to build vessels of 6–10,000 tons, and
before long there will be an automobile industry. In three years from
now, every single Cuban's standard of living will have doubled.'

Land reform, a sensational increase in agricultural production, the
liquidation of illiteracy, more rapid industrialisation and a soaring
standard of life–such is the Cuban miracle. But Cuba is not only the
socialist revolution–it is also the country of Fidel Castro. In April-
May 1961 Sofocleto published under his real name a series of articles
describing a trip to Cuba and containing a long account of its leader.
The guests of the Cuban government–including a large Mexican
delegation led by General Lázaro Cárdenas–are waiting to meet
Castro at the Icap Hotel, which 'belonged before the revolution to a

[1] 5 July 1961.

218

shady character named Hornedo, who made millions as a speculator under the Batista regime'.

'At 9 p.m. the word went round . . . that Fidel would arrive at midnight for a round-table talk with his guests . . . The hour might seem strange, but in days of revolution – and Cuba's is a total revolution in every respect – men work round the clock to make up for lost time. Fidel, who, as we all know, possesses tireless physical energy, works eighteen or twenty hours a day, except on the occasions when he goes for two or three days without sleep. The excitement at the hotel is intense. In a few minutes we are to behold the leader of the incredible, heroic revolution which has opened a new era for the enslaved peoples of America and the whole world.'[1]

Fidel arrives at 1 a.m. 'He is 6′ 1″ in height, with broad shoulders and a massive chest, but his beard is less thick than one imagines. It is hard to guess his age because his voice, gestures and manner display a gravity beyond his years, though there is of course no trace of fatigue or softness . . . He is a good listener, and as he talks gently and calmly, with the mild expression that the beard lends to his face, one might suppose him to be a prophet and not the dauntless revolutionary who overthrew the Batista regime.'

Fidel, who misses nothing, recognises the Peruvian journalist although they had only briefly met the day before during a visit to a school. 'I was surprised . . . but he had recognised me by my height (two and a half inches more than his).' They get into conversation. 'How should one address Fidel Castro? Cubans generally use the second person singular to one another, and Fidel does so with most people, but those of us who are used to old-fashioned formality . . . are at first perplexed. In the end, we decide to follow his example and use the familiar form.' Fidel talks on every subject and has answers to everything. Towards five in the morning he launches into a 'complete exposé of the revolutionary process'. Sofocleto comments: 'We are clearly in the presence of an almost supernatural being (*un hombre casi sobrenatural*), the living legend of a revolution which is changing the face of the world . . . He already ranks with the great men of history, who will be remembered as long as the overthrow of Goliath by David's sling.'

Having thus made Fidel's acquaintance, we see him next amidst

[1] Here follows a Homeric list of Castro's titles: 'The hero of the Sierra Maestra, the Moncada barracks and the "Granma" exploit . . . the Cuban giant who, with twelve companions, set out to win freedom and sovereignty for his people.'

his people, as he accompanies his guests to show them his government's activities. 'We set off for Pinar del Río in a long convoy, headed by Fidel in his black car. The people recognise him as we sweep past, and hundreds of men, women and children shout his name rhythmically. These are not mere cries of admiration or loyalty but express a unique state of mind, overflowing with happiness and hope. Fidel, a modest man who has always rejected the "cult of personality", has become a living symbol of the Cuban revolution. He is not only the hero or the leader, but the embodiment of the whole Cuban people in its eagerness to do battle for freedom and progress.' Here Sofocleto quotes a U.S. journalist, Waldo Frank, according to whom

'The Cuban revolution is a revolution of love ... Only great love for an oppressed, starving people could have inspired the fabulous effort that began with twelve men in the Sierra Maestra ... The leaders of the Cuban revolution love the people deeply and have their happiness at heart; but the people in turn love their leaders because they have found in them justice, kindness, virtue, talent and energy ... That is why there is no cruelty in Cuba: cruelty makes no sense for a people whose one idea is to rebuild their country. But there *is* a refined, wretched and morbid cruelty among those who have sold themselves to imperialism or want to regain their former privileges.'

Sofocleto's portrait of Castro contains a number of features which may help us to understand the revolutionary intelligentsia. Fidel is tall, strong, handsome and energetic; but his strength is governed by conscience and innate political wisdom. He is at home with a tommy-gun, but can also instruct experts about the balance of payments or foreign exchange. He is a hero, a great general, a revolutionary leader, a man actuated by the noblest moral passions, and, above all, loved and admired by his people and by the whole of progressive humanity. He works for his people, and they know it. In a country which lived under the Batista regime, his honesty is above reproach. The word 'integrity', so often used in the political context, seems made for him. Fidel is the 'complete man' whose career is a real-life answer to the confused and frustrated ambitions of intellectuals who have experienced the baseness of oligarchies and felt the grandeur of the revolutionary task, but have so far been incapable of undertaking, much less achieving it.

Thus Fidel, as depicted by *Libertad*, is a very different being from the man of terror and of the firing squad, whom the conservatives of *La Prensa* depict. Clearly the romantic imagination may be fired by the picture of Cuba achieving the aims of the revolution of its own accord and at a single blow, under an inspired leader who, with a small band of followers, puts the enemy host to rout at the first encounter. But this hardly affords material wherewith to analyse the conditions of successful revolutionary action: can one be certain that the walls of other Jerichos will fall at the first blast of the trumpet? *Libertad* does indeed refer to the necessity of violence. In an article entitled 'An unanswered question', Francisco Moncloa is at pains to rebut the charge of totalitarianism and hostility to democracy which the conservative press levels against Fidel's admirers. 'We are accused of attacking democracy–we who are fighting for credit reform and the recovery of the country's oil resources, the liberation of our people and our economy. And they, the oligarchs, the parties and their paid leaders, with their democratic slogans and headlines . . . call us anti-Christian, anti-Western and communists because we uphold national sovereignty and our people's right of self-determination.' This argument, which we have already met with in the dispute between Apra and its opponents, can be interpreted in two ways. On the surface it means 'We, not you, are the true democrats'; but, looked at more closely, it may be seen as an attempt to foist on to the 'reactionaries' the blame for revolutionary violence. Perhaps its main function is to save the writer from having to concern himself with a pressing but awkward question. It is, in fact, easy enough to exculpate oneself in advance by blaming those who have made revolution inevitable; but it is less easy to foresee when and how the great day will dawn.

Action now?

Can immediate revolutionary action, such as urban terrorism or guerrilla warfare, be effective or not? This is the crux of the debate between orthodox Peruvian communists and the various 'activist' groups. These latter possess two newspapers, *Voz Obrera* and *Obrero y Campesino*, each of which styles itself the 'organ of the revolutionary workers' party (Trotskyist)'. During the middle of 1963 the *Obrero y Campesino* (Worker and Peasant) organisation published a collection of articles entitled *La revolución peruana* by one of their leaders, Ismael Frías.

What is to be done?

The 'Peruvian revolution' has of course a foreign model in Castro's, which all the fragmentary organisations of the extreme left take seriously. By and large, they believe with Fidel that the Cordillera of the Andes may become the Sierra Maestra of the South American continent. The orthodox communists, it is true, criticise the Castro movement for 'putschism' and adventurism, and warn against provocateurs and romantic illusions. But from 1962 onwards Castro's example has been reinforced by that of a young Peruvian, Hugo Blanco, who organised in the valley of La Convención – a province of the Cuzco department, tropical in climate and crops – certain 'underground' activities which caused a stir in the Lima press.

On what forces can the militant revolutionaries hope to base themselves? 'The peasantry is the essential strength of the Peruvian revolution, for Peru is a mainly agricultural country.' Such was Frías's first thesis,[1] which was accepted at the time by all the extreme-left groups. Peru would have either an agrarian revolution or none at all.

'The peasants are the motive force of the Peruvian revolution . . . As in Cuba and the rest of Latin America, the signal for revolution will take the form of a peasant rising aimed at seizing the land by means of guerrilla warfare . . . But the peasants are incapable of working out their own political programme and organising their scattered forces on a national basis. They must be helped by the urban population, which will paralyse and destroy the state by means of a general strike followed by an insurrection – that bourgeois state which has hitherto drowned peasant risings in blood . . . Without the peasants there can be no revolution; but the revolution cannot prevail without leadership.'[2]

Thus the revolutionary possibilities of the cities are not to be ignored: the trade unions, and above all the *barriadas*, may play an important part. Apart from Hugo Blanco's organisation, Frías cites two episodes: the 'capture of Cuzco by the people' in April 1958, and the 'march on Lima' by inhabitants of the shanty-towns in March 1959.

The first of these began with a taxi-drivers' strike at Cuzco following the announcement of a rise in the price of petrol. The Cuzco workers' federation ordered a general strike, and a demonstrator was killed by the police. The crowd marched to the prefecture, occupied

---

[1] Op. cit., p. 15.
[2] Ibid., pp. 36–8. Cf. the quotations from Hugo Blanco in Part I, chap. 3.

the parade-ground and took prisoner the garrison commander, General Vargas Dávila. 'Using the General as a hostage, they moved to the trade union headquarters and set up an assembly, a kind of rudimentary soviet, which exercised power for the next two days.' Frías draws five main lessons from these events.[1] Firstly, the march on the prefecture shows that the proletariat recognised its class-enemy in the local organs of the bourgeois state. Secondly, the organisation of a 'workers' militia' made up of 'self-defence groups'. Thirdly, the creation of a 'people's committee, the embryo of the new workers' state. This, we maintain, was already a soviet . . . a deliberating and executive organ of direct democracy.' Fourthly, 'the people closed down bourgeois newspaper offices – an act characteristic of the dictatorship of the proletariat'. Fifthly, 'the soldiers of the Cuzco garrison expressed their fellow-feeling with the workers'.

In this rigorous, not to say rigid analysis, the events at Cuzco in 1958 are equated with those of the Russian revolution of 1905 – the militia, the town soviet, the fraternisation of workers and soldiers. However, Frías admits that three factors were lacking. 'The soldiers and peasants' delegates should have been invited to join the people's committees; the peasants should have been urged to seize the land; and the newspapers, banks and radio should have been taken over and used to support the workers' cause.' These three omissions were all due to the fact that 'the Stalinist leadership of the local pseudo-communist party . . . sabotaged the revolutionary action and crowned its treason by allowing the captive General to escape and entering into negotiations with the Archbishop'.[2] The orthodox communists had thus hindered the movement instead of helping it; furthermore, they compounded their crime by publishing a communiqué ascribing the outbreak to 'camouflaged Trotskyists' and '*agents provocateurs* of the Yankee embassy and the F.B.I.'.

What is so far lacking, then, is a truly revolutionary leadership. But though it may be difficult to seize power today, an immediate task lies ahead which will enable potential leaders to be trained and tested while at the same time developing the masses' understanding of their situation and the means of remedying it. This task consists of political agitation, for which there are rich opportunities in greater Lima, thanks to the housing shortage and the development of *barriadas*. The inhabitants of the latter are to be given precise directives: 'First, to refuse to pay rent; second, to form self-defence

---

[1] Ibid., pp. 66–9.   [2] Ibid., p. 69.

groups to resist expulsion; third, to demand full freedom for the homeless to occupy and build on vacant lots in the suburban area; and fourth, to demand that a special tax be levied on the profits of banks, insurance companies, building societies and foreign corporations to finance water, electricity, drainage and refuse-collecting services in the *barriadas*.'[1]

The Peruvian Communist Party, for its part, shows great prudence as to the feasibility of agitation leading to a genuinely revolutionary situation.[2] It points to the Cuban example as 'disposing of the geopolitical lucubrations of traitors and defeatists such as Haya de la Torre and his ilk on the subject of historical space-time and 'continental peoples'. Cuba has shown that 'a radical revolution is possible in Latin America', and the Cubans have taken some praiseworthy measures: the nationalisation of imperialist enterprises, the uncompromising defence of national sovereignty, a radical land reform, industrialisation, and democratic participation by the masses in the government of the state. But the Cuban model should be regarded as an inspiration and not a pattern to be slavishly copied. 'The Cuban contribution and its influence on the revolutionary movement in Latin America is one thing; it is quite another to imitate it mechanically and seek to import it ready-made ['canned', *enlatada*] irrespective of the particular conditions of a given country.'[3]

What is dangerous in the Cuban example is the temptation to lyricism which assails some of Fidel's admirers, whereas revolution is a matter of scientific method. 'We must reject any tendency to adventurism, subjectivism, putschism or "spontaneism" ' which may be encouraged by the Cuban precedent. This warning against subjectivism is illustrated by a discussion of the two types of condition to which revolutionary action must conform if it is to be scientific. In the first place, care must be taken that the revolutionary situation is ripe (*madura*) and that the revolutionary forces are organised, united and well led. They must be directed 'not by a small band of adventurers, a fraction (*partidito*) or party of nondescript character, but by a genuine Marxist-Leninist party, a vanguard organisation based on dialectical materialism and scientific socialism–in other words, a communist party'. A revolution is more than a *coup d'état* or an

[1] Ibid., p. 75.
[2] Cf. the declaration issued after the Party's fourth congress in August 1962, in the form of a pamphlet entitled *Por la senda de Mariátegui*. Some passages of this are commented on below.
[3] Op. cit.

insurrection: it does not take place on a mere word of command. Frías admits that armed struggle was the chief factor in Batista's overthrow, but contends that the Cuban revolution nevertheless confirms the rule that 'even if the revolution takes the form of an insurrection, it can never dispense with other means of carrying on the struggle'. It is not quite clear what these 'other means' are, but he goes on to emphasise that the 'armed movement', even if it first breaks out in rural areas, can only succeed if it is based on the 'working class and the urban masses'.

Is Peru 'ripe' for revolution? Here again, the communist party is extremely cautious. 'Peruvian society in its present stage contains a fundamental contradiction. On the one hand, the forces of production grouped in industry show an independent and progressive tendency; while against these are ranged semi-feudal elements dependent on imperialism.'[1] The communists recognise the existence, due to imperialist enterprise, of a native capitalist sector which might, with some qualification, be described as a 'national bourgeoisie'; and to this extent they join issue with the radicalism of *Libertad*, which, as we have seen, insists that Peru is as 'under-developed' as the tribes of central Africa. In a country where a national bourgeoisie is already taking shape, can such methods as guerrilla warfare be effective by themselves? To this question the communists answer no, thus discounting the enthusiasm of those for whom the peasant masses represent an irresistible revolutionary force. 'The Cuban revolution shows that the peasantry played the most effective part in generating the revolutionary movement; but, while this signifies that in general the armed movement began in rural areas, we must not forget the decisive action of the working class and the urban masses.'[2]

The uncertainty of the situation demands caution. 'All that we are sure of' is that 'the ruling classes will only give way if they are forced to, and will always counter-attack'.[3] For the rest, 'we must be prepared for all eventualities and must, as Lenin taught us, control every method and form of combat'. Probably, Frías continues, 'armed action will begin in rural areas; but we cannot exclude the possibility of its taking the form of risings like those at Arequipa and Cuzco' (which were suppressed). 'Thus we must not commit ourselves in advance . . . but keep an open mind as regards all possibilities of mass action.'

The cause of revolution demands infinite patience. However, the

[1] Ibid.   [2] Ibid., p. 23.   [3] Ibid., p. 70.

225

most urgent task is perhaps not that of organising guerrillas, underground fighters and terrorist groups. The declaration of the Peruvian Communist Party begins by recalling that 'The struggle for peace is wider (*más amplio*) than the struggle for national liberation or socialism'. This does not necessarily mean that it is more urgent, but that it is of importance to all men, under whatever political and economic regime they live; national liberation, on the other hand, interests chiefly colonial or semi-colonial peoples. Besides laying down priorities in this sense, the declaration implicitly defines the nature and methods of the revolutionary struggle. If the principal task for communists is the 'struggle for peace', their chief aim will be to contribute effectively to the Moscow-directed strategy of the 'socialist camp'; whereas, if 'national liberation' is the first commandment, their most urgent task will be to initiate armed action in the most favourable circumstances. This choice of alternatives throws light on the Moscow-Peking conflict as it affects Peruvian revolutionary circles, although the Communist Party's declaration makes no mention of China. For the 'old guard' of leaders who have been running the party since the 1930s, revolution in Peru is one element in a world-wide strategy, and the overriding obligation now is to support the 'peace camp', as it was to support the democracies in the war against Nazism. The Party's adversaries, on the other hand, maintain that the 'appeasement policy' associated with Khrushchev tends to paralyse revolutionary action and to sacrifice the forces which are taking shape on the Latin American continent on the altar of a doubtful strategy. This was the basic theme of an article by J. Posadas in *Voz Obrera* of August 1963, which put forward certain Maoist views. Posadas begins, it is true, by telling the Chinese that 'We (i.e. the Trotskyists) have been saying for twenty-eight years all that you say today (about the ossification of the Soviet bureaucracy) . . . We have never ceased to repeat that the masses must be trusted and that it is they who will decide.' But Peking's contribution has been to realise that no East-West agreement 'can or should paralyse the permanent revolution'. Thanks to Peking's example, whatever mistakes its leaders may have made in the past, the radicalisation of the masses will continue, the revolutionary hope will not be betrayed, and the chances of revolution will be preserved in Peru as elsewhere.

One conviction is common to all the 'diehard' parties of the left:

'something' is bound to happen which will blow the old society sky-high. As to the time, manner and circumstances, there is no agreement. That being so, we should not be unduly surprised if we find, a little further on, some of these groups lending an ear to siren voices against which their revolutionary intransigence should have afforded them better protection.

If we wish to present the difficulties of the extreme left in a simple and systematic manner, the key lies in the concept of violence and the circumstances of its use. Castroists, *social-progresistas* and communists of all kinds are united in believing that Peru cannot be modernised without a revolution. The oligarchy and the *gamonales* will block every reform; and the penetration of foreign, especially U.S., capital, far from being of benefit to the country, will increase its dependence on external centres of decision which will more and more gravely distort its development. A clean sweep must therefore be made of the imperialists and the feudalists–those of the coast and sierra alike.

This revolution will in all probability be violent, since the U.S. capitalists and the oligarchy will only let go if compelled by main force. How is this force to be organised and made effective? Some lay stress on the fashioning of the instrument, i.e. a hard core of professional revolutionaries; others pay more attention to stirring up and maintaining a belligerent spirit among the masses, whom they seek to inform, guide and provide with leaders while respecting their 'spontaneity'. A second dispute concerns the point of application of the revolutionary force: will the landless peasants who, since the late 1950s, have been 'invading' the big estates of central and southern Peru turn out to be better instruments of history than the urban proletariat, the inmates of the *barriadas* and the employees' and workers' unions? Finally, there is the question of co-ordinating the revolutionary movement with other progressive forces: Moscow, Cuba and Maoist China.

All in all, the extreme left is exposed to a number of hazards, the effect of which may be cumulative. The danger of fossilisation is acute in the case of the original Communist Party, which strives to preserve its doctrinal purity and–without success–to assert its authority over the various workers' and peasants' movements, while adhering as closely as possible to the 'line' of the Third International. The Trotskyist and Castroist groups, who tend to favour 'action now' in contrast to the excessive caution of Stalinists and 'Khrushchevists', are liable to the opposite risk of subjectivism and 'putschism'. More-over, the Hugo Blanco episode has given rise to a further rift within this group. Should revolutionary action be geared to the rate at which the masses supposedly become conscious of their needs and resources, or should it be hastened and, if necessary, precipitated by a vanguard of professional agitators? This question remains un-decided on the theoretical plane: only events can answer it.

4

Acción Popular

The ideological situation in Peru as we have surveyed it so far is characterised by rigidity and violent antagonisms. Apra stands in opposition to both the extreme left and the conservatives, whom Haya de la Torre denounces respectively as 'creole communists' and 'cave-men' (*cavernarios*, i.e. in particular the Miró Quesada family who own *El Comercio*). In return, Apra is labelled by the left as a front for Yankee imperialism, and by the right as *extranjerizante*—a suspect brand of internationalism. The pejorative effect of these images explains the ease with which anti-Apra reactions are revived amongst the general public. We shall see later on how, in 1962, Víctor Raúl's road to the Presidency was blocked by a military veto—which, of course, did not declare itself as such but hid behind a profusion of legal arguments. The technique of damning an individual or party by an opprobrious label is known in Peru as *la tacha* (literally 'censure' or 'blemish'). While the various factions, sects and cliques are at daggers drawn and spend much of their time excommunicating one another, each of them is hard put to it to maintain any degree of cohesion within itself. This proliferation of rivalries reflects the hesitation and disarray of a left wing which is alternately tempted by violence and direct action and resigned to the delays of a long-term strategy. As for the conservatives, in fruitless search for a legitimising principle, they oscillate between a somewhat arid economic realism and appeals to a tradition which, for all its dignity, is at the same time both vague and artificial.

Until a few years ago, Apra visibly dominated the scene of party politics. It was the coiner of terms and slogans such as 'Indo-America' and continental solidarity against Yankee imperialism. Themes such as land reform and the advancement of the Indians,

229

while current in other groups of the left and extreme left, were for a long time marked with Apra's stamp. Apra was the standard by which others defined their positions: all loves and hates were concentrated on Víctor Raúl. In fact, the only political group which seems to have been immune from Apra's influence is the one which found itself obliged to seek contact and organise co-operation with it under the name of *convivencia* (Part III, chapter 1)–viz., the small nucleus of creole liberalism. Concepts such as 'Indo-America' and 'continental peoples' are, as one might suppose, foreign to Sr. Beltrán's way of thinking. To this man (who is equally at home in Spanish, French and English) such ideas are meaningless or, as they say at Lima, *pamplinas* or 'poppycock'. However, as a result of the central position which Víctor Raúl so long occupied as an initiator and instigator, introducing or popularising ideas to which others reacted in their several ways, he and his party have at times (e.g. in 1945–8) found themselves faced by a coalition of the left, right and centre, as in the game of *cargamontón* or 'all against one'. When perils thus strike a single individual from all points of the horizon, the Peruvians say with ironical pity: '*El pobrecito, todo le viene por encima*' ('Poor chap, everything happens to him at once').

The combination of a star central figure (or prima donna, as his enemies would say) and a swarm of lesser fry, whose only bond in common is hostility towards their successful rival, tends to produce a deadlock full of strains and inhibitions. The atmosphere may change with the arrival of a new actor, as it did in 1956 with the entry into political life of Sr. Fernando Belaúnde Terry. Belaundism stands for an ideological thaw; but is it itself an ideology? It embodies no doctrine such as dialectical materialism or historical space-time; but it puts forward a new way of defining national objectives and assessing the means of attaining them. It represents, in fact, a 'wind of change' in Peruvian politics.

To repeat: Sr. Belaúnde does not seek to erect a 'palace of ideas' as Víctor Raúl did in the 1930s–a philosophy providing answers to all problems of public and private life. What he offers is not a doctrine but a style, or rather a style plus an eclectic principle. Some of Apra's old themes reappear, but they have been re-interpreted and brought up to date. Víctor Raúl spoke, thirty years ago, of 'Peruvianising Peru'; Belaúnde proposes 'the conquest of Peru by the Peruvians' (the original title of his book which appeared in English as 'Peru's Own Conquest'). In the 1930s, indigenism had a revolutionary flavour which alarmed the orthodox; Belaúnde, however, presents a lyrical vision of Peru's destiny ranging from the socialism of the Incas to modern concepts of planning. For the left wing, his chapter entitled '*El Perú como doctrina*' recalls the achievements of the Cuzco emperors: roads driven across the Andes, efficient methods of cultivation, and the grandeur of an organisation based on human justice as well as national power. For the right, he emphasises the distinctive character of Inca planning and the inimitable originality of its methods, and thus protects himself from the stigma of Marxism. Similarly, when dealing with current affairs he keeps his distance from the Americans but is careful to give no colour to a charge of Castroism.

Belaúnde's courting of the left was prudent but effective: thanks to dazzling rhetoric and subtle empiricism, he achieved Presidential power after a campaign of only six or seven years. This in fact was from the outset his main, even his all-sufficient, answer to the question 'What is to be done?' Víctor Raúl, for his part, was in the last resort content with a 'moral presidency'; while to the *La Prensa* group it matters little in the end who is head of the state, provided that he does not tamper with sound principles and upholds the 'necessary freedoms'–i.e. chiefly, if not solely, the free circulation of goods and capital. Fernando Belaúnde is not a doctrinaire but a politician; but he realised from the very beginning that it would be no use confining himself to normal methods and conventional wiles. He therefore needed a doctrine and, more important still, a style and an image.

The architect's style

Fernando Belaúnde Terry made his début as a national figure in March 1956. In 1945–8 he was a member of parliament for Lima, elected on a list put forward by the Frente Nacional Democrático, which included several members of Apra (to which he himself did not, however, belong). His father, Rafael Belaúnde, the younger brother of Víctor Andrés, was the first prime minister appointed by Dr. Bustamante y Rivero in 1945. During the eight years of General Odría's government Fernando Belaúnde kept aloof from politics and, apart from some trips abroad, devoted himself to practising as an architect. In this he was so successful that he became Dean of the Faculty of Architecture at Lima. In March 1956, as Odría's term

231

approached its end, Belaúnde's candidature was put forward by a group of students, intellectuals and technicians (*profesionales*) who styled themselves the National Front of Democratic Youth (*Frente Nacional de Juventudes Democráticas*). His first electoral appeal began as follows:

'Youth is the battle-cry of the political campaign that I have been invited to lead. Disraeli said that "the youth of a nation are the trustees of posterity". I appeal now to those who wear the student's gown or the workman's overalls–those who display the glorious uniform of our country's defenders, and those who, in the lonely sierra, bear on their shoulders the multicoloured ponchos of their ancestors. I declare to them all, and through them to all my compatriots, that if they require my aid in this hour of battle they will find me at their side, sharing their ardour and their hopes.'

His programme was of no great originality: 'We must improve living standards, strengthen the national economy and be strict in the discharge of international obligations, thus keeping open our access to foreign credit which is the only means of rapidly developing our economy.' This last piece of orthodoxy was calculated fully to satisfy Sr. Beltrán and *La Prensa*, which at that time were supporting Belaúnde's candidature. But the event which made him a national figure and almost a hero overnight was the rally which took place on the Plaza San Martín on Thursday, 8 June 1956. Under Peruvian law, candidates for the Presidency require, in order to be officially registered, a minimum of 25,000 signatures. The National Electoral Jury (Jurado Nacional de Elecciones), which under the constitution is in charge of the whole electoral process, including adjudication in the case of disputed elections, made difficulties about Belaúnde's inscription, and as the deadline for this was 9 June, a rally was organised to put pressure on the Jury. Many were inclined to believe that General Odría's government would resort to any subterfuge to keep Belaúnde out of the running in favour of one or other of the 'official' candidates, Hernando de Lavalle and Manuel Prado. Belaúnde was skilful and lucky enough to avoid incidents between his supporters and the police, but also firm and threatening enough to persuade the Jury to give in at the last moment.

Thus Belaundism was born. It presented itself as a young people's movement, unfettered by any ties or promises, either to Apra, whose support was courted by Dr. Manuel Prado, the eventual winner, or to General Odría's government which was supposed, more or less correctly, to be backing Hernando de Lavalle. Such was the youthful and heroic note which the new leader struck in his speech of triumph and gratitude after the rally of 8 June: 'I thank the Peruvian people for my inscription as a candidate for the Presidency; I thank them for their courageous and fervent support in this hour of destiny.' And–as women were to vote in the election for the first time–'I thank, too, the women of Lima: those who joined in the demonstration, and those who, from their balconies, threw flowers which made us forget the bullets whistling about our heads.' The new candidate then described himself:

'I am not a man emerging from the "catacombs" to receive a martyr's crown, to which I have no title. I have come straight from the lecture-rooms of the University, to put into practice the lessons I have taught. Many are better qualified than I, by talent or experience; but few have enjoyed the confidence of public opinion as I have. It alone has raised me to those heights from which a democrat is privileged for a time to serve his people. Here, in the very centre of the capital, my workmates have erected this stand, this dais from which I address you, as it were from a scaffolding–the only elevation that I can occupy without a blush–in token of our readiness to set about building a new Peru. When I agreed to become a candidate, I knew well that I had no other claim to the honour than that of a man who, day and night, dreams of our country's future greatness.'

This self-portrait is a skilful blend of boasting and modesty. Firstly, Belaúnde draws a line between himself and the Apra leaders by disclaiming the martyr's role which, he hints, they deserve no more than he. The central theme of his self-praise is that of activity and dynamism. The allusion to the professor's dais and the architect's scaffolding, together with the 'elevation' of which, at least for the time being, he feels unworthy, and the reference to 'workmates' building a new Peru–all this suggests intense but orderly activity, since the architect busy on the site is also the professor putting into practice the lessons of the university. But this professor-technician, consecrated by popular acclaim, is not a technocrat: he is a modest, ardent young man who 'dreams day and night', who 'blushes' at his own future glory, and to whom women throw flowers.

In a speech of 15 June, immediately before the ballot, the candidate of youth, the self-styled 'architect of the new Peru' attacked the diehardism of his predecessors and denounced the 'immorality' of the electoral deal thanks to which Prado was in fact elected. He thus threw down the gauntlet to the 'establishment' and offered the people a choice between 'stagnation and renewal, the delusive strength of pacts and the power of popular spontaneity, the past with all its errors and the future with all its hopes'. David-like, the young hero challenged his elders: 'We entered the fight as independents, without the backing of any organisation, without signing any secret pacts, and in this way we built up the majority force that stands behind us today. We did not come obsequiously knocking at the palace gates, nor did we seek aid from the powerful. Our appeal is to the weak and humble, and it is to them that we owe our strength.' This youthful challenge implies an antithesis between strength and generosity on the one hand, weakness and subterfuge on the other: it is instinct with the speaker's confidence of success and sense of being born for great things.

But the attractive combination of high spirits and serious purpose is exposed to a grave risk: what if the hard hearts of politicians are proof against the hero's ardour? What if this eloquence fails to inspire the crowds of young people who are awaiting his lifegiving words, so that they lose heart (*desanimarse*) after the first lyric rapture? Although he does not say so openly, Fernando Belaúnde is haunted at this period, as was Haya de la Torre in the 1930s, by the fear that his comrades may desert him. The Apristas resorted to huge rallies as a demonstration of the strength of their party machine and its influence upon the masses. Belaúnde's method was to undertake a tour of Peru, village by village–*Pueblo por pueblo*, the title of a booklet which he published in 1959. This extreme mobility was already one of his assets in the 1956 campaign. 'There are three candidates, but only one has carried his message to every corner of the republic: the others have ignored most of the coastal area and have never even tried to visit the jungle, or ventured into the sierra where most of our population lives and where the drama of Peru is felt in all its keenness. I for my part have crossed the Cordilleras ten times during this campaign, in search not of cheering crowds, but of inspiration and ideas.'[1]

In spite of all this activity, Belaúnde lost the election to Manuel Prado; but, nothing daunted, he challenged the result, thus conforming to the Peruvian tradition which turns the aftermath of every Presidential election into a contest of accusation and counter-accusation. When Prado was nevertheless confirmed in the Presidency,

[1] Speech delivered on 15 June 1956.

Acción Popular

Belaúnde went into unremitting opposition, thus keeping up the morale of his supporters by convincing them that their hero, having suffered a first injustice in 1956, continued to be victimised by diehard politicians who were determined to exclude him from Presidential office. But how, during the six years which must elapse before the election of Don Manuel's successor, was he to maintain the enthusiasm of a body of followers who had been recruited, as it were, overnight, by the exercise of his personal charm and dash? Belaúnde's answer was to found a party named Acción Popular (Popular Action), the members of which distinguished themselves by strident opposition in both houses of Congress, while he himself embarked on a series of journeys throughout Peru.

In his speech of 15 June 1956, these peregrinations were already presented as a deliberate break with centralism and an endeavour to keep in touch with provincial demands. 'The provinces cannot be governed, like colonies, by remote control from the centre–a method which is not only inefficient but which offends the honour and sensibility of regions which my opponents have not deigned to visit.' Accordingly, the architect sets out on his travels, choosing the most arduous routes: party propaganda depicts him on muleback or perched on an old Ford lorry, being ceremonially welcomed by the notables of this or that remote village. 'We followed the road of the Incas from Huánuco to Ancash, and in the freezing mountain air I once again wrapped myself proudly in my Huarás poncho, as a priest puts on his sacred vestments, to recite a prayer to the past, present and future glory of Peru.' This piece of rhetoric combines a delicate allusion to the good people of Huarás (capital of the Ancash department, situated in the heart of the Santa valley and overshadowed by the 22,000-feet-high Mount Huascarán) for their generosity in presenting the architect with a poncho as a protection against the rigours of the *puna*,[1] with an adroit reminder of the traveller's hardiness in crossing by muleback the enormous and icy mountain chain which separates Ancash from its neighbouring department.

The journey, at once a crusade and a pilgrimage, enables the architect to make contact with forgotten provinces. 'I go out to meet the people, to give ear to their complaints and hopes. I do not wait idly at home for them to knock on my door: I seek them out wherever they live, on the coast, in the sierra or the jungle.' *Noblesse oblige*: but Belaúnde takes care that his solicitude should not appear condescend-

---

[1] The mountain plateau, rising to a height of over 13,000 feet.

ing. The needy have a claim on our interest, and we cannot refuse it to them. 'We are not speaking to fortune's favourites or to those who have enjoyed the benefits of culture: we are addressing the broad masses, with the certainty that they will understand us and that those who are better educated will not take offence at the homeliness of our language. Our words are meant for the people, our illiterate masters who have taught us to read the message of our national history.'

This patronising yet respectful, dignified yet familiar attitude towards the people is well expressed in the following episode:[1]

'We had just crossed the Cordillera by the Porculla[2] pass, on the way from Chiclayo to the Marañón valley . . . We stopped at a *fonda* to share the drivers' lunch of *encebollado*.[3] A countryman who had been looking hard at me and finally realised who I was, came up and greeted me . . . I invited him to sit down and share our meal. He turned out to be a muleteer, on his way with a drove of cattle from the Sierra de San Felipe to his native village of Olmos in the sandy desert of the coastal zone. I soon appreciated the liveliness, energy and patriotism of this man, whose constant trips across the Cordillera had hardened him in body and at the same time opened his mind.'

With this preamble, the architect relates how the muleteer's wisdom showed its superiority to that of foreign technicians. The conversation turned to an irrigation plan by a U.S. engineer named Sutton which the Peruvian government had rejected as too expensive, so that the region in question remained parched, as it had been for centuries. 'To my great surprise, this unassuming man suggested to me, with great respect, certain objections to the U.S. expert's plan.' The story continues, and the upshot is that the muleteer's view triumphs: the Lima technicians, when consulted, agree that his native good sense is nearer the mark than the foreign expert's calculations. The architect concludes by saying that 'This journey taught me once more to appreciate, in this rough muleteer of the Cordilleras, the innate qualities which our pseudo-democracy, in its conceit and ignorance, refuses to acknowledge in the common people, so that it may continue to deny them the ancient right to manage their own affairs.'[4]

---

[1] *Pueblo por pueblo*, pp. 80 et seq. [2] In the department of Piura.
[3] Beef stew with onions. [4] Op. cit., p. 86.

Acción Popular

'Peru as a doctrine'

From these visits to the remotest parts of the republic, Belaúnde returned as the advocate of a 'doctrine'. This term did not imply, as with Apra in the 1930s, a set of propositions comparable to Marxism or other great philosophical or pseudo-philosophical systems. The architect-president is not a doctrinaire but an inspired empiricist, who puts forward his ideas as if they had come to him during his wanderings about the sierra: and indeed they vividly express his experience of the up-country population and the problems of a Peru 'remote from the areas of progress and severed from our cosmopolitan capital'.[1]

This experience inspired the primary feature of his doctrine, namely nationalism:

'We have succeeded in imbuing the people with the conviction that the source of our inspiration and doctrine is to be found on our own soil, and that there is no need to import political ideas into a country which has produced them in abundance ever since the most distant past ... If we can take pride in anything, it is in having found a genuinely Peruvian solution to Peruvian problems ... Being original is not so much a matter of skill and imagination in devising new things as of returning to one's origins ... We are original because we have returned to our fount and origin, not in sterile and backward-looking complacency, but in order to find on our native soil a solid foundation for the Peru of the future. I recall with deep national pride that the great civilisations of Egypt, Mesopotamia and Rome were favoured in their development by kindly geographical conditions; whereas the ancient Peruvians, in their quest for the sun of culture and the light of justice, chose to inhabit ... the steep and rocky summits of the Cordillera, which the creators of western civilisation would not perhaps have succeeded in dominating as our ancestors did ... Let us then reject any accusation or attempt to deprive us of the merit which, for my part, I claim without blushing and which belongs to every member of Acción Popular–that of doing justice to the nation by heeding the age-old message which comes to us from its tombs.'[2]

This emphasis on the national past inspires, first and foremost, a plan on the national scale: that of reawakening the people and reviving its energies under the slogan 'Acción Popular'.

[1] Ibid., p. 87.   [2] Ibid., pp. 164–9.

237

What is to be done?

'Whenever I stand on a mountain-peak and see a village below, I ask the same question and receive the same stirring reply. Looking at the humble village with its picturesque spire, I ask my guide: "Who built the church?"; and he replies "The people built it." And when I ask "Who built the school?", he again replies "The people built it". And as we ride along the winding road from one peak to the next, I ask "Who made this road?"; and once more, as the expressive and eloquent answer rings in my ears like the burden of a triumphal march, I feel within me Peru's whole history, its today and yesterday and the promise of its tomorrow: "The people made it, the people made everything here." The people made the road, the church and the school; they made the terraces[1] where crops grow on our mountain-slopes, and the embankments which keep the torrents within bounds. They too, when the order comes, send their sons to the wars ... The people have been deprived of their ancient right to elect leaders, they have been humiliated by the rule of strangers, cheated of their property and their meagre income; but of one thing they could not be robbed, namely their traditions. They have gone on building roads, schools and churches; and if the villages of Peru have been forgotten, they themselves have not forgotten the history of Peru.'

The speech quoted above was made in April 1956 at the village of Chincheros in the Apurímac department, some sixty miles from Cuzco. Its theme was the reconciliation of conservative and indigenist traditions. The left-wing and Aprista writers of the 1930s had associated praise of the Indian with demands for social justice; while the conservatives envisaged the Peruvian tradition in terms of a synthesis of different races and cultures, achieved thanks to the wisdom of the Church and the colonial administration. The indigenist movement distrusted and even resented the Spanish contribution, whereas for the conservatives tradition required the Indians to show obedience, in return for which they would enjoy, in the fullness of time, complete integration in the national life. The point of the Chincheros speech was that the Indian need not be either a slave or a rebel, but possessed positive virtues of his own, embodying as he did the most genuine traditions of the nation. The men of the sierra had been forgotten, but they themselves had forgotten nothing and disowned nothing. The Indian, moreover, was the source of all wealth. Though robbed, exploited and humiliated, it was he who had

---

[1] *Andenes.*

238

made everything and continued to do so; bridges, schools and churches were all the work of the Indian communities.

Belaúnde, following Riva Agüero, contends that a political doctrine cannot be a product of pure intelligence or the work of an individual thinker, however great. It must spring, first and foremost, from contemplation of the national tradition; and in Peru the tradition is that of 'popular co-operation', embodied in two basic institutions: the Indian communities and the *cabildo* or municipal council. 'While Spain conferred on us the vigorous institution of the *cabildo*, ancient Peru bequeathed a philosophy no less respectful of the principles of local autonomy. The *ayllu* and the *marca* chose the most capable men as leaders, and the sum total of those thousands of separate but coherent forces was the glory of the ancient empire. If the Incas had tried to centralise the appointment of local authorities at Cuzco, it is likely that their power would never have extended much beyond the confines of that legendary city.'[1] Historians may express some surprise at this account: for, although it seems clear that many officials, especially those of middle and lower rank, were not appointed from Cuzco, there is no evidence that they derived their authority from election by the *ayllu* or the *marca*. But the passage serves to proclaim the vitality of local government and to recall that on this point the Inca and Spanish traditions of Peru converge.

Acción Popular glorifies the spirit of mutual aid and co-operation among fellow-villagers. 'To stimulate initiative, which shapes men and forms leaders; to fan the still burning flame of creative spirit':[2] such as its first precept, and this appeal to spontaneity echoes the themes of indigenist literature. In *Yawar Fiesta*, José María Arguedas relates in epic strain how the *comuneros* of Puquio, in the southern part of the Ayacucho department, built a road to Nazca on the coast. 'In January 1926 news reached Puquio that the *comuneros* had held an assembly at Coracora, the capital of the province of Parinacochas. The parish priest had spoken in Quechua and Spanish, and they had agreed to make a road which would serve the port of Chala, so that a man might travel to Lima in five days. The villagers of Coracora intended to show their mettle and let it be seen which were better,

[1] Op. cit., pp. 77–80.
[2] *La conquista del Perú por los Peruanos*, Lima, 1959, pp. 37–8; English version, *Peru's Own Conquest*, Lima, 1965, p. 103.
In subsequent footnotes, references are given to the English version where possible, but otherwise the Spanish, as the two do not coincide verbatim. (Translator's note.)

they or the men of Puquio.' Thus the project begins as a double challenge: to nature, which is to be tamed by a superhuman effort, and to the neighbouring communities, who are to be surpassed in courage and endurance. As soon as the news gets about, the men of Puquio take up the challenge. 'The *mistis*–the white folk–would never have dreamt of such a crazy plan. Two hundred miles from Puquio to Nazca, with the cordillera in between!' But the *varayoks*–the headmen of the four *barrios* or *ayllus*–take up the idea and vow to accomplish it. Here is the description of the collective exploit:

'From the bottom of the valley, where fields and houses were strung out along the river, people could see the dust raised by the ten thousand *comuneros* who were forcing a way through the mountain . . . From time to time they heard the sound of rocks being dynamited. The men set to work at dawn and did not cease till late at night. The sound of their singing could be heard everywhere–in the depths of the valleys, in the hamlets and lonely mountain dwellings. At night they played the flute and sang, assembling for the purpose in *ayllus* of a hundred, two hundred or five hundred men, according to the size of their villages. To keep warm at night they made campfires alongside the route, near the place where their tools were stored. They sang festive songs and drank the liquor which the *mistis* had given them at Puquio, but in moderation as the *varayoks* commanded.'

The community effort had several distinctive features. In the first place, it was a mass operation, employing thousands of pairs of hands which had until then been idle. Secondly, it was carried out by the Indians themselves, with encouragement from the *mistis* but without their active help. Finally, it was a joyful undertaking, accompanied by drink, dancing and song.

But 'popular action' is not conceived as an Indian monopoly: its object is to unite in a single glow of enthusiasm all members of the community, whether *mistis*, half-castes or Indians. This serves to allay conservative fears which might be excited by the notion of Indian crowds on the march: the suggestion, instead, is that of putting idle hands to work. But can the chronic surplus of labour (which Belaúnde contrasts with the equally chronic deficit of capital)[1] be overcome by a multitude of small undertakings? A school here, a bridge there–even if such enterprises, related as they are to the capacity of local leaders and limited local resources, help to awaken

---

[1] '*Déficit de soles y superávit de brazos*': *Pueblo por pueblo*, pp. 95–102.

the small towns of the sierra, can such sporadic, primitive and uncoordinated initiatives suffice to give the country the infrastructure it needs and provide employment for its growing population? As Belaúnde writes: at Chincheros, 'everything has been done by local effort . . . Only a few corrugated sheets had been sent from Lima to roof the boys' school, which had neither floors nor windows, locks nor sanitary equipment.' But, as he adds at once, 'If they could do everything with their own hands, the "Chincheros" would have no problems; but economic aid is an inevitable necessity in order to acquire the tools and materials that are only produced by large industries. Peru must cease being an archipelago of isolated villages. Regional interdependence is inevitable and necessary. Nobody can expect much from towns lacking resources; they must be given a hand.'[1]

'Popular action' is completed by planning. Belaúnde is fond of emphasising that Peru's 'tradition of planning'[2] goes back to the Incas, and is perhaps their most precious legacy. At all events, the reference to the Inca system throws most light on the importance of planning in Belaundist doctrine. The plan is thought of primarily in real terms and only secondarily in terms of money: it is an architect's and town-planner's concept rather than that of an economist or an auditor-general. However, it includes collecting statistics as well as making roads, and among its objects is to feed hungry mouths by means of redistributing land and increasing agricultural production. In general, its objectives are expressed in terms of physical and concrete operations which it is the government's task to co-ordinate without stifling popular initiative and spontaneity.

'The first lesson to be learnt from the past, then, is the need to study and to learn the innermost secrets of this realm. The early chroniclers speak of the detailed models of the different regions made before the Conquest, which presumes the existence of cartography.'[3] Let us pause here for a moment. For Belaúnde the architect, knowledge precedes action: we have seen him introducing himself as the professor setting out to put into practice the teachings of the lecture-hall. This knowledge, moreover, is interdisciplinary: its object is to draw up an inventory of the entire nation. The National Institute for Advanced Studies whose creation Belaúnde advocates[4] would bring together ethnographers, sociologists and geographers and send them

---

[1] *Peru's Own Conquest*, pp. 101–2. [2] Ibid., p. 87.
[3] Ibid., p. 89. [4] Ibid., p. 208.

into the field to prepare monographs—preferably with the help of teams of researchers under the direction of a professor who would lay down broad terms of reference and embody their results in as precise and striking terms as possible. This is a qualitative, descriptive and intuitive type of learning, wary of abstractions and believing only the evidence of its senses. Thus Belaúnde shows a marked affinity with the nineteenth-century naturalists and explorers who, like himself, travelled all over Peru on muleback, such as Humboldt and, even more perhaps, the Italian Raimondi.

This form of social science, which owes more to the naturalist than to the sociologist, finds typical expression in the importance given to roadmaking. Roads are a link:

'The road from Cuzco to Quito ensured the unity of the Andean region and was the backbone of the empire. Having a thorough knowledge of geographical conditions, the ancient Peruvians built their roads along mountain-tops, thus avoiding landslides and reducing the need for bridges. They climbed up to these roads by means of stone steps . . . sometimes over a thousand in number, but so devised that they could be negotiated by men and llamas . . . When horses came on the scene the roads were unusable by them, and the introduction of the wheel also necessitated other means of communication . . . Thus the old Inca highway fell into disuse. In any case, the conquerors were not interested in maintaining the unity of the sierra. Whereas the Incas' system of communication ran from north to south, the colonial administration built mule-tracks to provide access from the highlands to the coast. To the colonists, the unity of the sierra meant the threat of a native insurrection against the central power at Lima.'[1]

Belaúnde compares the ancient road system to a 'necklace on which the Inca cities and *tambos*[2] were strung'. The necklace has been broken, and the task now is to restore the link between the scattered townships and villages of the sierra. One of the main themes of the Acción Popular campaign is the large number of departmental and provincial capitals which, in mid-1959, were not joined by any roads. Four of the twenty-one departmental capitals—Iquitos, Moyobamba, Chachapoyas and Puerto Maldonado—had no connection with the outside world except by air and waterways.[3]

Thus the first task is to make roads; but it is important to decide

[1] *Pueblo por pueblo*, p. 89.   [2] Staging-posts and storehouses.
[3] *Peru's Own Conquest*, p. 94.

where and how. Besides bringing Lima closer to the provinces, the road programme must open up and develop new areas. 'In the past, road engineers have been primarily concerned with uniting two separate points. In the classical view of road building, this union is achieved by selecting the economically shortest route between the origin and the destination. But ... linking two cities is not the primary criterion in a colonisation road; what is important is to ... give access to the greatest extension of productive lands.'[1]

The Inca tradition is not only one of great engineers linking distant regions by a system of communications no less monumental than that of the Roman empire. Besides being architects and builders, the Incas were agriculturalists or rather agronomists. 'Prosperity and progress and social justice in ancient Peru originated from the basic premise that each consumer would have a plot of arable land to ensure sustenance.'[2] The 'man-to-land ratio' remained favourable throughout the period of the old empire because the Incas succeeded in 'bringing new lands under cultivation by irrigation, or by the creation of new areas by means of *andenerías*–artificial terraces built on the sides of the mountains. Because of their monumental proportions, the *andenes* of Peru have been compared with the pyramids of Egypt.'[3] Today, unfortunately, subsistence does not increase as fast as population: 'the Indian communities have fixed boundaries, and the population growth has overpopulated the land, reducing indigenous farmers to underfed paupers'.[4] In this way the author recalls the well-known troubles of Andean agriculture: erosion of the soil, dwarf holdings and the almost worn-out condition of cultivated areas. This situation is intolerable even today, since the peasant is underfed in terms of both quantity and quality, but a disastrous prospect threatens at the end of the century: the amount of land available per head of population is at present 1,700 square metres and is expected to fall to 533 square metres in 1994.[5] The solution, Belaúnde insists, is not to be found by means of importing foodstuffs. 'An under-developed and remote country should not depend on others for the supply of its basic foods, especially when the difficulties of its terrain and its geographical location burden foodstuffs with high freight rates.'[6]

We may already observe the two basic differences between Belaúnde's approach and that of creole liberalism. In the first place,

[1] Ibid., pp. 158–9.   [2] Ibid., p. 90.   [3] Ibid.   [4] Ibid., p. 92.
[5] Ibid., Spanish version, graph on p. 40.   [6] Ibid., English version, p. 91.

he regards the sierra's interests as primary, and in the second, he looks askance at solutions which would increase the country's dependence on foreign markets and capital. The only salvation lies in an autonomous effort of production, a 'popular action' inspired, guided and sustained by the government and devoted to meeting the real needs of suffering, toiling humanity. As we have seen, planning in Belaúnde's eyes is much less a matter of analysing functional relations between global economic factors, than a series of concrete operations and tasks in which the spontaneity of the population is enlisted and which finally take the tangible form of roads, bridges and schools. By thus adopting the engineer's approach rather than the economist's, Belaúnde draws a line between his own doctrine and that which he ascribes to the oligarchy, and especially the bankers.

One of the main aspects of the doctrine is what he calls the 'revolution of credit'.[1] Credit is expensive in Peru because the banks are 'institutions that lend the poor man's money to the wealthy'.[2] Not only this, but they are unprincipled enough to pay high interest, often more than 8 per cent, on money held in current account.[3] The argument is not necessarily watertight, but the middle-class inhabitants of Lima who is having a house built for himself cannot fail to lend a willing ear to a speaker who denounces the system of mortgage credits. 'We consider that the solution of the mortgage problem . . . is fairly simple. In order to increase the percentage of the loan based on the value of the property, we advocated some years ago a system of mortgage insurance,' to be financed by private savings which would thus be devoted to building instead of finding their way into the banks' coffers.[4] For these savings exist: 'the man in the street, poor though he is individually, constitutes in the mass an important client of the insurance companies, which should adopt without further delay a large-scale programme to improve his standard of living and especially housing'.[5] All that is needed is that the concerns with which private savings are deposited should, instead of using small savers' funds for the benefit of the oligarchy, furnish credit on liberal terms to those who need it most, and especially to the poor who are, unfortunately, the most numerous class.

Not only do the banks mobilise the resources of the poor for the benefit of the rich, but they swallow up provincial capital for the

---

[1] Ibid., pp. 181 ff.   [2] Ibid., p. 185.   [3] Ibid., Spanish version, p. 52.
[4] Ibid., p. 69; cf. English version, p. 185.
[5] Ibid., Spanish version, p. 66; cf. English version, p. 184.

benefit of Lima. 'In December 1957, the investments of commercial banks in the coastal region amounted to 4,892 million soles, whereas the sierra, in which a majority of Peruvians live, obtained only 317 million, and the *selva* (the topical and sub-tropical area), which urgently needs an economic stimulus, received the miserable sum of 34 million . . . Moreover, while 94 per cent of the sums deposited by clients in greater Lima were invested locally, this was the case with only 62·5 per cent of savings accumulated outside the area of the capital.'[1]

Some features of the Belaúnde system now begin to emerge. The oligarchy is its bogy: it is not hard to rally support among either the left or many of the right wing for an attack on the 'old-style financial clique'. By proposing concrete tasks in the field of building, settlement and colonisation, and by appealing to great national traditions, the architect-president is able to answer the call for renewal and satisfy the aspirations of youth or of its spokesmen. The 'humanistic socialism' extolled by *Libertad* might well, it would seem, be achieved by Acción Popular in strict accordance with Catholic and national traditions. A system of planning based on encouragement and exhortation rather than compulsion, and geared to concrete objectives which all can understand, is clearly in accord with the Inca tradition as Belaúnde expounds it. Thus an 'opening to the left' becomes visible, though the President has at no time called himself a socialist and was fiercely attacked by splinter-groups of the extreme left in the electoral campaign of 1962. The thaw, in fact, cannot be far off: the left, absorbed though it is by the interminable vendetta between Apristas and communists, Trotskyists and Stalinists, pro-Chinese and pro-Castro elements, must realise sooner or later that the country is on the move. And the conservatives for their part may emerge from the neo-liberalist fastness of caution and mistrust in which they now remain as the ghosts of a petrified tradition.

Indeed, Belaundism may have its attraction for some sections of the oligarchy, such as businessmen who welcome the prospect of expansion unclouded by fears of inflation. In two passages of his book, Belaúnde appears to be courting the national bourgeoisie. For example: 'We cannot achieve economic emancipation as long as our exports consist mainly of raw materials in an unworked state . . . To get the maximum benefit from our mineral resources and to make the

[1] Ibid., Spanish version, pp. 55–6.

operation of marginal mines worth while,[1] we must clearly set up foundries and refineries of our own ... Thus our ore would no longer be exported in the form of bulky and heavy concentrates, but in a refined condition, so that we should be offering to world industry products of a substantial economic content (*alta densidad económica*) and correspondingly wide range of use.'[2] In short, it is more profitable to export ingots than raw ore, not only from the country's point of view but from that of the industrialists concerned with working it, and particularly the owners of small 'marginal' mines who could thus stand up better to Cerro de Pasco. The second suggestion of this kind is for the creation of a motor industry or at least a plant for assembling lorries and small vans, which would save a good deal of foreign exchange.[3]

If one seeks to define Belaúnde's doctrine, various terms come to mind; none is exactly appropriate, but in combination they give us an idea of its originality. In the first place, his movement proclaims itself as a nationalist one, while the Apristas of the 1930s were anti-imperialist. There is a clear connection here, but the terms are far from being synonymous. Belaúnde is proud to be the heir to a civilisation 'admired throughout the world'. The twofold grandeur of the Inca and Hispanic tradition confers on Peruvians a national identity which not only distinguishes them from the peoples of Europe but entitles them to an advantageous position among their neighbours: Lima, as Belaúnde notes in passing, is the ideal site for the future inter-American bank. Whereas Víctor Raúl's nationalism was 'continental', Belaúnde's is more strictly Peruvian. Secondly, we may note the latter's skill in his treatment of relations with the great powers. His speeches contain no diatribes against the Yankees, but neither do they insist on the importance of foreign capital as do the spokesmen of creole liberalism or even the Apristas. While frankly recognising the need for foreign help, he is careful to emphasise that it is not the answer to every problem. Thirdly, his nationalism takes on a sharper tone when it comes to expressing mistrust of the big foreign corporations, especially the International Petroleum Company. *El Comercio*–which showed some sympathy for Belaúnde from the beginning of the Prado regime in 1956, and supported his candidature for the Presidency after the military coup of July 1962–

---

[1] The intention here is evidently to appeal to the *pequeña minería nacional*, which is more or less independent of the big foreign companies.
[2] Op. cit., p. 134.   [3] Ibid., p. 154.

carried on a fierce fight against foreign monopolies and never tired of denouncing the questionable circumstances under which Prado's government granted concessions to powerful international interests. Belaúnde associated himself with such criticisms, without going to extremes. His parliamentary followers took up a radical position in the debates over oil nationalisation; he for his part, while adhering firmly to the principle of a 'genuinely nationalist' oil policy, showed great caution as to the form which such a policy should take.

Besides being a nationalist, Belaúnde is concerned with social problems even if he is not actually a socialist. He makes free play with the notion of planning, which *La Prensa* has long treated as a bugbear.[1] It is true that we are struck by the vagueness of this concept, its *gaseosidad* as they say at Lima. But elasticity like this has its advantages, since it enables him to switch at will from the notion of an inventory to that of compulsory planning, from a straightforward reconciling of interests to the exercise of command by an all-powerful administration. For the same reason it is bound to excite apprehension, since on the one hand it offers a standing temptation to left-wing extremists who dream of using the planning system to smash the oligarchy, while on the other it provokes the neo-liberals of *La Prensa* to denounce the attempts of technocrats to subject the country to absurd but all-powerful controls. To avoid these quicksands, Belaúnde is obliged to give the term 'planning' as reassuring a content as possible; and indeed its real significance for him is to draw attention to the country's backwardness and potential resources, both physical and human, and the need to make better use of the human factor.

His intentions in the social field are the more completely reassuring in that they coincide with the teachings of the Catholic church, or at all events with the most recent pastoral letters of the Peruvian

[1] However, the words *plan*, *planeamento* and *planificación* were introduced discreetly into his programme. Their increasing prominence may be traced in successive editorials in *El Comercio*. Having denounced *La Prensa*'s liberalism as old-fashioned 'Manchesterdom', the rival newspaper presents planning as a legitimate device which should hold no terrors for those acquainted with the progress of economic science. 'Planning ... is a genuine remedy for the evils of backwardness, stagnation and underdevelopment. It stands for order and the integration of all sections of the economy: it means that the entire country, on the local, regional and national levels, must be prepared to advance by stages and to accept sacrifices, corrections and adjustments. For this purpose we must begin with a sound diagnosis of the nation's position ... a detailed inventory of what we are and what we have–our human, technical, social and economic resources.' (Leading article in *El Comercio*, 30 March 1963. Cf. also *El Comercio*, leading article of 13 August 1963.)

episcopate. For many years the church in Peru was content to pay strict observance to the picturesque and appealing cycle of *fiestas*, without unduly stressing the ascetic aspects of doctrine. Hence the pastoral issued on 1 May 1963 was of great originality, both for the anxieties it reflected and the remedies it proposed. The bishops declared that:

'A stop must be put to what is nothing less than a process of social decomposition, and the public must be awakened to the urgent necessity for profound changes ... There are still too many who persist in following the old ways. They should realise that their callousness is most likely to bring about a violent outcome: for when those who suffer perceive that their rulers (*los que tienen poder*) are determined to keep them in a state of misery, they see no remedy but force. Let it not be thought that we say this in order to justify in advance any who may take the law into their own hands ... Just as one side should not give way to fear, so the other should not give way to resentment; but all of us, being alike concerned to uphold human and Christian dignity, ... should regard ourselves as children of the same Father, as brothers to whom God has assigned our mother-country as a common spiritual home.'[1]

To appreciate the weight of this utterance, we should first note its clarity. The bishops do not hesitate to speak of 'decomposition', and this tone is maintained in their reference to the danger of a 'violent outcome' (*desenlace violento*). Moreover, while not excusing or justifying violence, they represent it as an inevitable consequence of the state of despair to which the poor have been reduced. The need for renewal and a breach with the 'old ways' is presented as a patriotic, moral and religious imperative, binding on all who are 'concerned to uphold human and Christian dignity'.

Belaúnde is thus fully in line with the bishops' teaching, and his appeal for change, justice and progress has aroused answering echoes in the conservative camp, where his alliance with the church has disarmed the resistance of many. This was seen in the Presidential election of 1963, when *La Prensa* strove in vain to identify him with the communists. To cover his rear still more thoroughly, he was at pains to win sympathies in the army. We have seen what care Víctor Raúl took in his speech of 1931 to conciliate the military leaders, and how in return for their neutrality he held out the prospect of an up-to-date army equipped with all modern techniques. Apra's

[1] Quoted from *El Comercio*, 2 May 1963.

manoeuvres failed, but Belaúnde, over twenty years later, had more success with similar blandishments, for various reasons which I shall consider more fully in Part III. Writing in 1959, he assigned a task to the armed forces which was admirably calculated to meet their current preoccupations. Recalling the article of the Constitution which conferred on them 'the noble mission of ensuring the rights of the Republic, compliance with the Constitution and laws, and maintenance of public order', he observed that 'the rights of the Republic are not solely restricted to the defence of frontiers'.[1] No-one, he argued, was going to attack Peru, because the country was strong enough to deter aggression and because there was no serious threat to peace among the sister-nations. The task of the armed forces was to help develop the national territory. In his own words: 'To economically develop a region has equal, or greater, military importance than the establishment of a frontier post whose effectiveness lies principally in the support it might give the country as a rearguard. If we must lament the loss of vast jungle regions, it is partly due to a neglect of communications and lack of opportune development postponed so long; for the dedicated guardians of our frontiers, the high jungle could have been a support point in men and supplies.'[2] This allusion to the unsuccessful quarrel with Colombia in 1933 over a piece of Amazonian territory shows a desire to reconcile two main preoccupations of the military. On the one hand, in accordance with traditional ideas, they tend to give priority to the problems of conventional warfare and to the acquisition of submarines, tanks and jet aircraft. On the other, the more active elements feel impelled to quit their barracks, take part in the nation's life and make an effective contribution to development. Animated by this desire and aware that old-style frontier wars are a thing of the past, they see as the first duty of national defence the exploitation of the immense wealth which lies dormant in the marginal areas of the republic.

A great design

But it is not sufficient to awaken enthusiasm: if you are going to harness men's wills, you must give them a realistic target. The ability to do both these things is what is properly called 'vision'. A man of vision is one who can see far into the future and is not blinded by

[1] *Peru's Own Conquest*, p. 198.   [2] Ibid., p. 199.

sordid calculations of immediate interest; but he is a practical man as well as a man of ideas. By associating his name with a great design, Belaúnde showed himself as both an inspired propagandist and an imaginative technician.

The object of any genuinely national policy is to maintain or re-establish an adequate relationship between men and the land. If this fails, catastrophe soon follows, since the country is unable to feed its population. This being the objective, how is it to be attained? 'The fastest and most economical solution . . . [is] the incorporation of new agricultural lands in the *ceja de montaña*, or high jungle, into the national economy by means of access roads.'[1] Peruvians have long been fascinated by the Amazon basin: Iquitos has never known the prosperity of Manaus in Brazil, but even since the fall in the rubber market, 'the east'–*el oriente*–retains its magic. Belaúnde's project, however, envisages the colonisation not of the distant and inhospitable Amazonia but of the *selva alta*, the eastern slopes of the Andes. Attempts have been made in this direction in the past. Without going as far back as colonial times, we may mention the settlement, towards the end of the last century, colonists in the Chanchamayo valley, which today produces excellent coffee, or, during Manuel Prado's first presidency (1939–45), the establishment of a centre of population in the Tingo María area on the upper waters of the Huallaga.

The creation of a 'Marginal Forest Highway' (*Marginal de la Selva*) is the great design to which the human and material resources mobilised by Acción Popular are to be devoted. The planner-in-chief cannot content himself with a few local or even regional projects: the dispersal of resources would be uneconomic, and the small scale of each individual plan might quench enthusiasm. This is how Belaúnde describes his project: 'Its planning would take the form of a geo-political study with the participation not only of road engineers but also of geographers, military experts, sociologists, agronomists, stockbreeders and, above all, economists. The basic idea would be to amortise the cost of building the road by bringing into cultivation lands extending, on an average, five kilometres to either side of it.'[2] The road would be planned in relation to the waterways system based on the Amazon tributaries: 'it would begin where the river ceases to be navigable, so as to supplement it without duplication.'

In this way, communication from north to south would be established between small communities isolated in inaccessible river-basins, whose only previous link with the rest of the country beyond the sierra consisted of the east-to-west routes leading to the coastal valleys. 'With the object of uniting the cultivable land in the north and south and providing each sub-region of the coast and sierra with its own colonisation area in the pioneering zone of the upper Amazon, the Marginal Forest Highway would provide communication between the valleys of the Mayo, Huallaga, Pozuzo, Perené, Ene, Apurímac and Urubamba ... It would meet the Ucayali river at the port of Atalaya and the Huallaga at the port of Yurimaguas, which it is proposed to link with the coast by the Olmos road.'[1]

Does this cascade of river- and place-names, of which most Limans have never heard, suffice to render the great design convincing? At all events, it enjoys the major advantage of all colonisation plans which offer the prospect of opening up virgin territory and do not raise delicate questions of ownership. Furthermore, it is distinguished from previous plans by its all-embracing character. Whereas the compact area of the Amazonian basin has so far only been broached by a series of disconnected east-west approaches, it is now conceived as an organic whole based on a north-south axis. Belaúnde scouts the suggestion that the scale of his plan is out of proportion to Peru's present resources. 'By taking a distance of five kilometres to either side of the road, the land brought under cultivation would double the country's tillable area at a cost which could be financed in the course of a single Presidential term' (6 years).[2] This claim is based on a few simple assumptions. Firstly, the new highway will make it possible to exploit the vast forest resources of the *selva alta*, for which there will be no difficulty in finding markets. Secondly, the area is highly suitable for growing citrus fruits and pineapple, as well as coffee and cocoa. 'More important than coffee, which suffers from worldwide over-production, is the cultivation of cocoa, which our country still imports and for which there is an unsatisfied world demand.'[3] Finally, stockbreeding yields excellent results, not to mention the cotton and tobacco crops which at present have to be transported to the coast by air.

The important thing is not to choose the wrong site for one's Eldorado. Hitherto, colonisation plans have suffered from two basic flaws. In the first place, they were sketchily planned from the technical point of view; state aid to colonists was parsimonious, and crops could not be got to market because of the lack or inadequacy of

[1] Ibid. [2] Ibid., p. 99. [3] Ibid., p. 100.

transport. Secondly, projects announced with great fanfare and dropped shortly afterwards were, above all, opportunities for speculators and politicians to make money. Once the cleverer ones (*vivos*) had made their pile in real-estate speculation and pulled out of the game, the duped settlers were left to their fate and no more was heard of the enterprise. Against this discouraging background, Belaúnde owed it to himself to vindicate the clear-sightedness of his project. It so happened that in the past decade a U.S. engineering firm named Letourneau had attempted with the aid of tractors, excavators and bulldozers to establish communication between Tingo María on the Huallaga and Pucallpa on the Ucayali; but their efforts, though expensive, were unsuccessful. This Belaúnde put down to their mistake in choosing the wrong route. 'If Letourneau had made their attempt in the *selva alta* and not in the much less valuable area of the *selva baja* (the Amazon basin properly so-called), the results would have been excellent and settlers would have come to take advantage of the new road system.'[1]

Thus Sr. Belaúnde is at pains to emphasise that the undertaking he proposes is certain to be profitable and would pay for itself in a very short time. Moreover, it is politically most attractive from the pan-American point of view, fitting readily as it does into the context of continental planning:

'The Marginal Forest Highway, if extended from end to end of the South American continent, . . . would link the mouths of the Amazon and Orinoco in the north with that of the Paraná in the south. This would mean the creation of a continuous system of land and water transport which would be a tangible contribution to the formation of a common market . . . The Forest Highway is a better solution, from the geo-economical point of view, than the Pan-American coastal highway, which merely duplicates the means of communication already offered by the Pacific Ocean. In view of the continental character of the Forest Highway and the wealth of the areas that it would open up for cultivation, it is to be expected that it would enjoy the support of international development banks.'[2]

Thus the 'conquest of Peru by the Peruvians' would be set in motion with the aid of all Americans and for their benefit. Regions hitherto isolated would be brought together, and those not yet exploited would be cultivated; waste lands would be settled and crowded areas relieved. Belaúnde, in short, invites his fellow-country-

[1] Ibid., p. 101.　　　　[2] Ibid., p. 113.

men to replenish and animate the land which nature has given them–
'to fully conquer our own territory'.[1] And this conquest, based on all
the resources of technology, will not only integrate and unite the
country from the economic and social point of view, but will endow it
with a myth upon which the whole of the nation's energy can be
centred. 'The solidarity and sense of co-operation which Indian
tradition has kept alive in the villages, and which is expressed in the
still living institution of the *minka*,[2] will be all the more intense when
the national effort can be concentrated on an ennobling object.'

Thus the argument comes full circle: the mobilisation of human
resources by Acción Popular will solve the economic, social and
political problem. The Belaúndist synthesis surmounts the obstacles
against which both right- and left-wing ideologies stumbled: it exalts
both planning and private enterprise, nationalism and international
co-operation. The plan is not an order handed down from above by
soulless technocrats: it is the recognition of needs and resources, the
galvanisation and mobilisation of energies; the determination of
concrete objectives and the facilitation of local and regional initiatives by the full application of the state's resources. The symbol of the
'Marginal Highway', leading towards dormant riches with which the
hungry can be satisfied, sums up the Balaúndist programme by
offering a goal to the imagination and the will, and a theme which
unites all Peruvians by promising well-being for all.

We may here note a few typical aspects of Belaúndist ideology.
First, a liking for dynamic images: the themes of 'action' and 'conquest', the symbols of the road and of wayfaring recur constantly in
its utterances. In the field of theory it is circumspect–or, as its
enemies would say, wretchedly impoverished. Belaundism is an
impulse rather than a dogma, and it is noteworthy that–unlike Haya
de la Torre, who is profuse in references and invokes Marx, Einstein
and Toynbee at every turn–Belaúnde is extremely frugal in this
respect. I do not recall meeting, in his speeches or writings, the names
of any of the foreign philosophers, economists or sociologists who
are the staple of Aprista literature. Belaúnde is content to evoke the
past glories of his own country and the vitality of the Inca tradition,
and to assure his compatriots that the secret of that glory is not lost.
But his skill in avoiding options and his consummate art in the
handling of stirring images exposes him to a double charge of

[1] Ibid., English version, p. 197.
[2] The system of collective labour on a community basis.

syncretism and inconsistency. If the sleight of hand is too unfailing and spectacular, it may in the end alienate and disquiet those who clearly perceive the artist's hand and the magician's tricks.

The effectiveness of the grand gesture

Belaúnde's object, then, is to awaken and combine all available energies. From this point of view his speeches of 1956 recall those delivered by Víctor Raúl in 1931. Both display the same youthful, ardent and heroic tone. Belaúnde, like Víctor Raúl in his time, is a newcomer on the political scene and is at pains to distinguish himself from the 'old gang'. But the two leaders differ in their hierarchy of values. For Víctor Raúl, the first task is to do away with the oligarchy. Belaúnde speaks of popular co-operation and grandiose designs in the 'high jungle' area, in a tone which combines audacity and reassurance. His opponents may jeer at the emptiness of his programme, but they cannot accuse him of hatred and a mania for destruction, as *El Comercio* did in its attacks on Víctor Raúl and Apra in the 1930s.

Indeed, we have already seen how careful Belaúnde is to avoid provoking hostile reactions. True, he attacks the oligarchy; but who has not done so since 1956? Even General Odría, as we shall see, described himself as a socialist. Belaúnde is on the right side of the Catholic church, which is itself displaying concern with social problems. The reforms he advocates are prudent as well as generous. He evolves high-sounding plans, but is ready to discuss and amend them in detail. Even within the oligarchy, some groups are attracted by his programme of major public works. It may be contrary to strict financial principles, but why should the risk not be taken, provided inflation can be kept within bounds?

While skilfully disarming prejudice, Belaúnde sought in the late 1950s to capitalise on the vague aspirations towards change which were present throughout the country. His first problem was to centre existing hopes and goodwill on his own person. For this purpose, in 1956, he created an Acción Popular group in each chamber of Congress; but this party was very different from Haya de la Torre's of thirty years earlier. Apra was formed in secrecy, while Acción Popular was a machine for winning elections, more particularly the Presidential election of 1962. To win this election, Belaúnde had to put his case across to the public, or rather the many different publics to whom his appeal was addressed. The method he chose was not that of strict party discipline, of a precise formula or catechism. But he had one highly effective means at his disposal: his ability to dramatise political debates and strike effective attitudes. Three examples may be quoted of his tactics of turning a challenge to his own advantage by means of heroic gestures or attitudes.

The first was the famous rally of June 1956, thanks to which Belaúnde secured the legalisation of his candidature for the Presidency. This episode–in which he played a personal role comparable to Napoleon's at the bridge of Arcole–illustrates the effect of skilful pressure against an irresolute enemy, vanquished by a threat of street riots which may have been a bluff.

Sometimes, however, his bluff was called, as in the affair of the barricades of Arequipa. On 9 July 1962, almost a month after the elections (cf. Part III, chapter 21), Belaúnde made a speech on radio and television in which he gave the returning officers three days in which to complete the count of votes and investigate protests put forward by the military in certain departments in which Apra candidates had been declared elected. As in 1956, he sought to overcome the authorities' hesitation and gain his ends by a show of force. 'Circumstances oblige us to utter a formal warning, a month after the election–a month filled with dilatory manoeuvres which we regard with the utmost suspicion. We, whose duty it is to defend universal suffrage, hereby proclaim to the whole country our demand that the election results should be made known within a space of at most two or three days, and that they should be in accordance with justice.' This stirring declaration combines various aspects of Belaúndism. Firstly, its leader is the champion (*abanderado*) of democracy: his cause is that of righteousness, and all who oppose or hinder it place themselves outside the pale; the tactics and delays of the returning officers are 'highly suspect'. Nevertheless, the speaker moderates his indignation: though well aware of the adversary's underhand procedures, he is wise enough to wait and hold his fire. 'In my last speech I urged the people to display the utmost calm, and I expressed the hope and desire that this election, falsified though it was at the outset, might be concluded in accordance with justice.' Confident in his cause, having displayed patience and forbearance, the speaker now issues his challenge: he allows the authorities 'two or three days' in which to do their duty, annul the results favourable to Apra and acknowledge his victory.

What is to be done?

What was the effect? Next morning, Belaúnde's party announced that he had left the capital, and during the 12th he arrived at Arequipa. 'The atmosphere here'–*La Prensa* reported–'is one of great excitement: a Belaundist deputy has stated that when the three-day time-limit expires, the party will seize the prefecture and install a revolutionary government. The candidate's father, Sr. Rafael Belaúnde, declares that active measures will be resorted to without delay ... At Lima, the secretary-general of the movement states that its leader has left the capital to keep his appointment with history.'[1] But the appointment was a fiasco. True, the leader emphasised on arrival at Arequipa that his only purpose was to prevent a 'fearsome conflict' between the army and the Electoral Jury, which had refused to entertain charges brought by the military against irregularities in the departments of La Libertad (Trujillo) and Amazonas. (By specifying in this way, Belaúnde offered the authorities a chance to bargain.) After declaring that the time-limit of three days was wholly reasonable, he insisted on the inflexibility of his determination. 'Acción Popular demands that an honorary electoral tribunal be set up ... and it is my duty to state that I shall remain here, on the public highway, ... until that obligation is fulfilled.' In conclusion, he invoked the threat of intervention by the military. But, whereas in 1956 the authorities had given way, on this occasion the walls of Jericho failed to collapse. The Electoral Jury ignored his threats, and the army bided its time. Driven into a corner, Belaúnde was forced to take action. His followers tore up the paving-stones in a few streets, and young men mounted guard on hastily-erected barricades; but the insurgents were dispersed by the rigours of a winter's night, and withdrew to their homes after the leader had spoken a few rousing words. The current jest at Lima was that this was not a *barricada* but a *borricada* (drove of asses).

It may be doubted whether Sr. Belaúnde really expected the electoral authorities to give way to pressure: it is more likely that his speech of 9 July was intended to trigger off military intervention. If so, his chief mistake was not to underestimate his civilian adversaries but to misjudge the intentions of his military allies. His 'gesture' came dangerously close to a piece of braggadocio or even clowning. But note that this was not the end of the story. Arequipa, the scene of the *borricada* of July 1962, presented Belaúnde with a huge majority at the election of June 1963. How was it that, for so

[1] *La Prensa*, 12 July 1962.

many electors, the fiasco passed into oblivion so soon? Perhaps what the public really wants is not that the champion should win or escape discomfiture, but that he should enter the arena and, as it were, give them their money's worth. It is not for nothing that the term for the bullfighter's art—*faena*—has passed into Peruvian political language. Belaúnde's followers would not have allowed him to submit tamely without showing his mettle: he had to do something to show that he was not taken in by his adversaries and would not yield without a fight. In this way he saved his face (*salió con la suya*). The more risky the bravado by which the discomfited leader seeks to regain his equilibrium (*compostura*), the more successful his gesture will be; but all is lost if it appears as a mere prank (*mataperrada*) or graceless clowning (*payasada*). None the less, it is not entirely clear how Belaúnde's feat of 1962 succeeded in escaping both these classifications.

Even if a gesture has no practical effect, it may leave its author's image intact, at all events in the eyes of his supporters. This is shown by another episode in Belaúnde's career. In May 1959 he attempted to organise a rally at Arequipa: this was forbidden by the government, which, in difficult political circumstances, had suspended constitutional guarantees, including that of free assembly, as the President is entitled to do for a period of thirty days. Belaúnde defiantly announced that the rally would be held nevertheless. He left Lima unobtrusively, but was arrested by the police some thirty miles from Arequipa (wearing, according to *La Prensa*,[1] a poncho, a *chullo*[2] and dark spectacles) and was interned on the Isla San Lorenzo off Callao. *La Prensa* further relates[3] how, on the occasion of a visit from his friend Senator Dammert Muelle, he jumped into the sea and boarded the cutter on which the Senator was approaching the island, to which he thus voluntarily returned. This exploit divides into two parts, of which the first is a fiasco and the second more creditable. To be caught thirty miles from his goal in such incongruous attire as a poncho, a *chullo* and dark spectacles—*qué desgracia*! But to show that one could have escaped and then return, simply and nobly, to one's prison—that is the act of a *caballero*, a sportsman and a man with a sense of humour.[4]

---

[1] 29 May 1959.   [2] A sort of Balaclava helmet worn by the *serrano* Indians.
[3] 31 May 1959.
[4] However, a different account of this incident is given in the Introduction by David A. Robinson to *Peru's Own Conquest* (op. cit., p. 17). According to this, Belaúnde was in fact attempting to escape. (Translator's note.)

What is to be done?

Whatever is the immediate effect of a 'gesture' in Peruvian politics, it is all the more appreciated in proportion to how much magnanimity it demonstrates. During a visit to Cuzco in May 1962, a few weeks before the presidential election, Belaúnde was hit in the face by stones thrown by a group of demonstrators of the extreme left. According to *La Prensa* of 21 May, 'he had concluded his speech and was walking towards a group who were booing him and shouting for the F.L.N. (the communist-supported Frente de Liberación Nacional) when this group threw stones of which one hit him in the forehead. With blood streaming down his face, he once more mounted the rostrum and said: 'It is of no importance that a drop of my blood should be shed here in the market-place of Cuzco, where Túpac Amaru, the forerunner of our independence, was put to death. But let each and everyone know that I am not only prepared to shed a few drops of blood from a trifling wound, but to give my very life to confound the lies of the Apristas and communists of Cuzco.' After these triumphant words his supporters bore him back, shoulder-high, to his hotel. Here again we note his ability to turn every moment of his life into an historic event or, if one prefers, into melodrama. General Odría, who was similarly attacked at Huancayo, was struck speechless, whereas Belaúnde promptly recalls Túpac Amaru. Note also the tendency to hyperbole: 'I would give my very life, not only a few drops of blood'; and the swiftly following challenge in which the Apristas and communists are denounced as liars. At Cuzco, this challenge was successful; Belaúnde's enemies were routed by the dignity of his gesture. But is symbolism of this kind sufficient to ensure the victory of a party?

PART THREE

THE RULES OF THE GAME

The Presidential elections of 10 June 1962

Key to Departments

HAYA DE LA TORRE

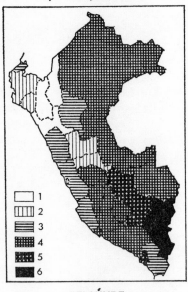

BELAÚNDE

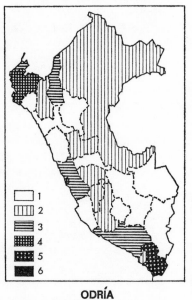

ODRÍA

1. Under 20%
2. 20–29·9%
3. 30–39·9%

4. 40–49·9%
5. 50–59·9%
6. 60% and over

The expression 'the rules of the game', which is much used nowadays by political observers, calls attention to two main points. Firstly, it emphasises that political action posseses at least a certain degree of autonomy, and secondly it suggests that such action has a structure peculiar to itself: that it is subject to conditions which oblige the statesman, according to circumstances, to compromise and postpone or to take the initiative and force the hand of his associates or rivals.

If, in Peru, we attempt to draw up a list of the groups which offer answers to the question 'What is to be done'?, we find parties (Apra, Acción Popular), institutions (such as the armed forces) and interests which are more or less organised and conscious of the implications and consequences of their 'demands' for the community at large. Let us consider for the moment the two principal reformist parties. The differences of style between Apra and Acción Popular are remarkable, the more so as their programmes have much in common. The reason is that Apra was originally conceived as a crusading force which would storm the battlements of the old order, whereas Acción Popular appeals without distinction to all national forces in search of a 'new deal'. Apra, accepting more or less explicitly the dualistic view of society, tended to prefer an aggressive strategy aimed at destroying the oligarchy, even though it was obliged in the course of time to fall back on *convivencia* as a second best. Belaúnde's party, on the other hand, basing itself on the concept of a rapidly changing society with a range of collective priorities that brook no delay, professes to represent a spontaneous consensus of opinion, though it too has to achieve its ends by bargaining. For both parties, negotiation and compromise were a regrettable but necessary concession to realism;

261

but for Apra they were a means of securing recognition and a more broadly based legitimacy, whereas for Acción Popular their purpose was to involve others in the execution of the party's plans and infect them with its own dynamism.

Since the protagonists thus differ in strategy, in motive and in their concept of their own interests, can one speak of a single 'game' whose rules are to be analysed? There are, in fact, several games going on at once and according to different rules. For example, during the crisis of June-July 1962, negotiations took place between Apra and the army which were partly implicit and even unspoken, partly public but still cryptic and obscure: their upshot, as we shall see, was a tacit compromise whereby the elections were annulled but Apra, on condition that fundamental freedoms were preserved, agreed to confine itself to legal methods and not boycott the elections which the junta promised to hold within a year. Similar negotiations were carried on by Apra in 1945 and 1956, though their position in 1962 was considerably weaker. Belaundism, it is true, rejects such bargaining on principle, just as Apra in 1931 set its face against *componendas* and costly short-term expedients. From the beginning of his campaign in 1956, Belaúnde acted as if his task was merely to put into practice a consensus that already existed, and for this purpose to enlist the co-operation of all men of good will. But his efforts to project an image of boldness and generosity duly tempered by good sense did not save him from having to negotiate on a 'power to power' basis with the army or the big landowners.

Thus it is not sufficient to analyse Peruvian politics as a contest between competing strategies: there is a plurality of games which cannot at present be reduced to a common denominator.[1] From the slogan '*Apristas a luchar*' (Apra into the fight) to the practice of *convivencia* (see next chapter), Apra's evolution denotes not only a change of style but a new concept of the political battle and the nature of power. It is possible that we may some day witness the acceptance in Peru of a single set of rules for all players; but for the present, it is the multiplicity of styles and strategies that must engage our attention.

---

[1] We must distinguish between a 'strategy', in the sense of a combination of methods of varying efficacy, and a 'game', i.e. a set of rules and procedures within which different strategies can be applied against each other. Thus, the 'game' of the extreme-left activists is incompatible with that of Apra or Acción Popular, whereas, for example, the British Conservative and Labour parties are divided only by their differing strategies.

1

'Convivencia'

For thirty years, the recurrent question for Peruvian politicians was what to do with Apra or how to get rid of it. The support it commanded was such that even skilful and prolonged repression did not succeed in destroying its influence. The party was outlawed throughout the period 1931–45–the 'long years underground'–except for a short *détente* during the first months of General Benavides' government. General Odría again outlawed it from 1948 to 1956, and forced Víctor Raúl to take refuge in the Colombian embassy till 1954. Each period of proscription ended with an arrangement which allowed Apra to put up candidates for Congress: in 1945–8 a majority of deputies and rather more than 40 per cent of the senators were Apristas, and in 1956–62, while not equalling this record, Apra had considerable support in both Houses. But, in 1945 as in 1956, it failed to secure the Presidency despite its parliamentary strength. In the former year, Víctor Raúl threw the weight of his support behind José Luis Bustamante y Rivero, and in 1956 Manuel Prado was elected thanks to the Apra vote; but neither Bustamente, the austere Catholic from Arequipa, nor Manuel Prado the cosmopolitan man of the world, citizen alike of Lima and Paris, were themselves members of Apra.

In his skilful apologia entitled *Tres años de lucha por la democracia en el Perú*, Sr. Bustamante justified the agreement of 1945 by recalling that the rights of assembly, free speech and the franchise, which are expressly guaranteed by the Constitution, belong to all citizens, whether Apristas or not. The state, it is true, can and must defend itself against the threat of subversion, especially by an 'international sect'; but the suspension for an indefinite time of such fundamental guarantees is equivalent to a confession of failure on its part and a disavowal of its own principles.

263

The Rules of the Game

The task before Bustamante was, then, to bring back Apra and its leader into normal political life; but his attempts to do this led him into an impasse which was only resolved by his deposition at the hands of the military. He endeavoured, as President, to hold the ring between Apra's relative majority in parliament and its opponents of the right and left which, determined to force the issue, refused to take their seats and thus paralysed the work of both Houses for want of a quorum. But he found himself both suspect to Apra and unable to influence the motley coalition whose sole object was to bar its way: the would-be arbiter had no means of enforcing his arbitration.

Apra's second attempt at a come-back, in 1956, took place in more favourable conditions. The question at this time was whether General Odría, who had seized power in 1948 and was elected President in 1950, would attempt to prolong his tenure of office beyond the six years laid down by the Constitution. From July 1955 onwards, it was clear that if he did so he would be courting a very serious crisis. On 20 July *La Prensa* published a manifesto in which a large number of personalities, especially from the business world, demanded 'the necessary guarantees and freedoms' in view of the forthcoming elections. Could the President ignore these and appeal to the army? He was far from enjoying the support of all his brother officers. In July 1954 he had thought it prudent to send into exile General Noriega,[1] who had been his chief associate in the coup of October 1948; while in February 1956, a few months before the elections, the general commanding the Iquitos division proclaimed a revolt and issued a long communiqué demanding free elections in similar terms to those of the July manifesto.

Two obstacles stood in the way of a prolongation of the military regime: the oligarchy's mistrust and the officers' own fears that the 'armed institutions'—*los Institutos Armados*—might become identified, for good or ill, with the success or failure of General Odría. The latter, faced with the constitutional ban[2] on immediate re-election to the Presidency, and lacking the unconditional support of the armed forces, was forced to allow the elections to take place. This meant that Apra, though still outlawed, became the arbiter between the two main candidates, Hernando de Lavalle and Manuel Prado—neither of

[1] Cf. Michel Martin du Bois, 'Les élections péruviennes de 1956', *Revue française de science politique*, Jan. 1957.
[2] Under Article 143 of the Constitution the outgoing President may not be immediately re-elected.

whom could be considered a valid national choice if Apra abstained
from voting.

In the end, these two candidates were joined by a third: the
architect Fernando Belaúnde Terry, aged only forty-four. Hernando
de Lavalle was a well-to-do member of the best society and a consulting barrister of high repute. Manuel Prado, a President's son and
himself President from 1939 to 1945, belonged to one of the richest
families in the country. Nevertheless, both of them well knew that
they could not succeed without the Apra vote. While Hernando de
Lavalle was embarrassed from this point of view by his ties to General
Odría and the fiercer conservative opponents of Apra, Don Manuel
had taken care to keep his hands as free as possible. While engaging
in conversations with Apra, he had observed two counsels of
prudence: not to commit himself so far as to run the risk of appearing
to have sold out to them, and not to make any promises as regards
the legalisation of Apra except in return for pledges, if not guarantees, as regards the orders to be given to its rank and file for election
day.

Apra's objectives and methods at this time were set out in a
'Manifesto to the Peruvian Nation' dated 21 May 1956. 'We have
never believed that fidelity to our ruling principles as an independent
nationalistic movement precluded us from striving to bring about an
atmosphere of democratic coexistence (*convivencia democrática*) in
which all parties and political groups could live together har-
moniously, without fear or subordination to one another.' To
achieve this, it was necessary to 'banish violence from external and
internal political relations'. Political parties should be large, 'stable
and well organised, with a programme and doctrine in which various
interests and trends of political thought could find expression'. On
the eve of the Presidential election, this 'democratic coexistence',
which the manifesto also defined as 'national', called for 'the rallying
of all political forces behind a leader whom all branches of democratic opinion can accept'. The document went on to make clear that
the party had taken a decisive part in the conversations leading to
Hernando de Lavalle's candidature.

Did this mean that he enjoyed full Apra support? The document
stressed the 'disinterestedness' (*desprendimiento*) of a party which,
owing to the 'proscription under which it has suffered since 1948 . . .
is unable to put forward candidates' for either House of Congress or
for the Presidency. However, Apra did not intend to boycott the

elections. 'It has done everything in its power to facilitate . . . coexistence and national unity . . . It comes before the country with clean hands, proving that it is actuated neither by the desire to dominate nor by any unworthy motive.' Three of Apra's characteristic themes are discernible here. Firstly, the policy of making an appearance: although not legally recognised, the party intends to play a role in the preparations for the Presidential election. Secondly, the note of self-justification: it is not Apra's fault if agreement has not been reached – or rather not yet been reached, for the last lines of the manifesto express 'the hope that the present difficulties will be finally overcome'. Apra, indeed, has made the greatest sacrifice by waiving questions of personality for the sake of unity (*en aras de la unidad*), to the point of not objecting to one of the Vice-Presidencies being offered to 'a signatory of the decree which outlawed the great party of the Peruvian people'. Finally, the document illustrates the pertinacity of Apra's desire to make use of its full rights and emerge from the 'catacombs'.

In the event, the contest between Manuel Prado and Hernando de Lavalle was won by the former, who offered the Apra leaders and particularly Ramiro Prialé, the secretary-general who negotiated on Víctor Raúl's behalf, everything the party could desire, at a time when it was too late for Lavalle to raise the bidding. At a rally held on 12 May in the Plaza San Martín, at which the Apristas seem to have been present in force, Lavalle had made promises which declined into ambiguous formulae. 'The functioning of organised, representative political parties . . . is without doubt essential to a democratic regime . . . All parties without exception have the right to take up positions in accordance with their ideologies. But this right is subject to the essential condition that they recognise and respect the national Constitution, which forbids them to subordinate the country's interests to foreign interests and ideologies.' This appears at first sight an eminently fair statement: all parties are placed on an equal footing, and Apra members of Lavalle's audience might have taken note with pleasure that he intended to put an end to discrimination against them. But, by referring to the prohibition against 'subordinating the country's interests to foreign interests and ideologies', Lavalle drew attention, without expressly quoting it, to the famous Article 53 of the 1933 constitution which bans 'political parties dependent on international organisations' and debars their members from 'all public functions'.

This reference to Article 53, which was bound to be taken as a veiled threat to Apra, may have been a necessary sop to certain of Lavalle's allies. At all events, from then on the Apra leaders, who had been hedging their bets, began to swing towards the Pradist camp. In a speech on 15 June, on the very eve of the poll, Lavalle sought to rectify matters. 'If I am elected . . . I shall strictly observe the Constitution, and laws in conflict with it will no longer prevail . . . There will be an end of political discrimination, . . . a political amnesty and a statute governing the existence of parties which will make possible full democratic coexistence among all citizens.' But these words again seemed to blow hot and cold. The Apristas would be gratified by the promise of an amnesty and the suggestion, imprecise though it was, of the repeal of repressive laws, particularly the internal security law on which Odría had leant heavily; but the renewed mention of the constitution and of a statute concerning parties was calculated to confirm Apra's misgivings.

As for Manuel Prado, his first speeches were an assortment of generalities, vaunting the achievements of his previous administration and promising, if he were elected this time, to do better still. On 21 April he made a speech which appeared to have two objectives: to present himself and his record in a favourable light, but to avoid carefully any firm commitment, thus preserving full liberty of action at this early stage of the campaign. Once Don Hernando had spoilt his own chances of coming to terms with Apra, the way was clear for his wily opponent; but the latter did not show his hand till the very last day, thus preventing any danger of Lavalle's overtrumping him. Of the three candidates who addressed the electorate on the eve of polling day, Manuel Prado did so at the greatest length. Amid the interminable list of promises aimed at different sections of the community (the army, housewives, trade unions, provincials, the teaching and judicial professions), a single vital declaration stood out. 'My government's first act will be to grant a far-reaching political amnesty, to abrogate exceptional measures and those which conflict in any way with the precepts of democracy.' Then comes the thrust at Lavalle: '*Nor will it be necessary, in order to restore to Peruvians the fullness of their rights as citizens, to resort to the futile and time-consuming process of drawing up a statute on the position of political parties.*'[1] And, to dispel Apra's last suspicions: 'I consider it right and necessary to recognise the full independence of any political party on

[1] Author's italics – F.B.

the sole condition that it makes a public announcement of its plan of action, its programme and ideology.' The threat of Article 53 was thus finally lifted.

'Convivencia' or 'conivencia'?

The pact between Apra and Prado, sealed by the latter's victory, remained in force for six years, although at the outset it had appeared to be a mere expedient. The chief explanation of this lies in the advantages which it brought to both parties. In a speech of 14 June 1956, Ramiro Prialé declared that *convivencia* had turned the Apristas from second-class citizens (*semi-ciudadanos*) into men and women enjoying full civic rights. On 15 June 1957 he returned to this theme: '*Convivencia*, as we have said a hundred times, stands for a joint effort to create a new climate in Peruvian politics: it is like the air we breathe . . . in a country where we are at last allowed to assemble in broad daylight, without strife or hatred . . . where citizens may disagree while continuing to respect one another and to practise the widest tolerance.' As radicalism is a 'state of mind', so *convivencia*, according to Ramiro Prialé, was 'a climate, an attitude, a new way in which the country expresses itself'. After this series of metaphors describing the 'style' of *convivencia*, Ramiro expounded its methods and techniques. 'Pacts, understandings and mutual relationships (*pactos, entendimientos, relaciones entre los unos y los otros*) all find their natural place within it.' To those who preferred to remain outside the field of *convivencia*, the members of the governing coalition offered 'respect and tolerance'; amongst themselves, negotiation and compromise were the keynote.

Was there not a risk, however, that Apra would forfeit its freedom of action through alliance with the Pradists, who were so close to the oligarchy, and that *convivencia* might degenerate into *conivencia*? Prialé replied: 'We have made no pact with the Prado party: the only promise we made before the election was to fight together for the restoration of civil liberties and the abolition of distinctions among Peruvians. President Prado has kept his word and we have kept ours – that is all: but it is natural that this should give rise to a confident and cordial relationship.' It was right and indeed necessary to make contacts with intelligent, frank and honest conservatives; but these must not be allowed to compromise Apra's principles or degenerate into promiscuity. Therefore, Prialé declared, 'Apra has no post in the government and no pact with the Pradists'. In terms of France between the wars, the situation is like that of Léon Blum *vis à vis* Edouard Herriot: 'support, but not partnership'. It might appear that Prialé contradicts himself, in that having listed 'pacts' as a feature of *convivencia*, he at once adds 'We have no pact with the Pradists.'[1] But in fact the word seems to be used in two senses. The Apristas and Pradists do not consider themselves bound to one another by any specific obligations: they have merely found themselves united at a given moment in the pursuit of a general objective, namely to abolish anti-Apra discrimination and restore the fullness of republican liberty. This was an aim in which all men of good will could join, whatever their party; and, having achieved it, they were free to go their several ways (*allí terminó la cosa*, in Prialé's words). But the confidence which grew up between honest associates led to easier and more frequent contacts; so that, while there was no pact between Apra and Prado in the strict sense of the term, relations between the two parties which had each kept their word (*cumplieron ellos y cumplimos nosotros*) had become close and natural.

Let us now turn to Víctor Raúl's summing up of the experiment after six years, at the beginning of the 1962 election campaign. He defines *convivencia* in different ways: firstly as a 'convalescence, a period which enabled the party to recover and gather strength . . . before embarking on a fresh journey'. The need for such recuperation lay mainly in the trails undergone by the party during the Odría dictatorship of 1948–56. The definition of *convivencia* as the pause preceding a leap forward is calculated to satisfy the most impatient of Víctor Raúl's followers; but may it not by the same token alarm conservatives, to whom Apra's moderation may seem to be a feint and a trap? Consequently we are offered a second interpretation: *convivencia* represents the introduction of a genuinely constitutional regime. It is, in fact, a resumption of the experiment of 1945–8, which was interrupted by the *coup d'état*, and in which Apra 'sought to bring about a working democracy by voting even for those who had opposed it, in the hope of inaugurating a civilized dialogue in which all ideas

---

[1] In a speech of 14 June 1956 Prialé stated: 'As regards the Presidential election, we shall conscientiously consider (*consultaremos con nuestra conciencia*) which candidate appears most likely to make a reality of democracy in our country.'

would be respected and agreement and disagreement would alike be the subject of honest judgments.'[1]

Convivencia is thus a dialogue in which the most diverse interests and opinions can be freely expressed provided that the game remains 'civilized': it is, in fact, a matter of peaceful coexistence. 'This great experiment in civilized living together (*convivir civilizadamente*) is called in other latitudes "coexistence" . . . And if the most antagonistic empires with their differing ideologies have tried it, why should not we Peruvians do so, who are brothers even if we differ in our opinions?'[2]

But *convivencia* is not merely an expedient: it has an educative value as well. 'The strongest party, which in the 1956 elections came forward as an elector without the power to be elected, made known in this way its readiness to sacrifice itself for democracy in Peru, and decided to support a *regime* without necessarily supporting a particular *government*.'[3] *Convivencia*, in fact, was not just an Apra trick but a fresh proof that this great party, the strongest in Peru, was prepared to make a present of its strength to a candidate from whom it required nothing in return except the promise of liberty for all. The only winner by the 1956 pact was democracy – the 'civic liberties' which were finally secured, not only for Apra but for all parties. *Convivencia* thus appears as an important educational exercise, a 'lesson in dialectic (*enseñanza dialéctica*), bringing home to our fellow-countrymen the distinction between supporting a regime and preserving one's freedom of judgment in regard to a government'.[4]

This distinction may be looked at in two ways. In the first place, the Peruvian constitution separates the President's functions from those of the head of the government. The President 'represents the nation' but is not responsible to Congress: the cabinet and the prime minister whom he appoints are not only the executants of his policy but must also enjoy Congress's confidence. Thus, in voting for Prado as President, the Apristas were not committing themselves to support all the actions of the prime ministers whom he might appoint, especially as there were enough of the President's friends in Congress between 1956 and 1962 to provide a majority even without Apra's help. But the distinction between regime and government also has a deeper sense. A regime possesses a legitimacy of its own which entitles it to expect loyalty from its citizens, even if they disapprove of

[1] Haya de la Torre, vol. IV, p. 202.
[2] Ibid.
[3] Italics added. – F.B.
[4] Op. cit., p. 204.

the government's policies. The opposition must observe this rule even if it is fighting the government's policy tooth and nail, always provided that the regime allows it every chance to criticize the government and eventually replace it. This safeguards the possibility of effective yet peaceful competition for power. If Víctor Raúl has succeeded, as he claims, in bringing home these facts to the Peruvian electorate, he may boast with some reason of having carried out 'the most effective experiment in the history of our political education.'[1]

Furthermore, *convivencia* makes possible 'the appearance of new parties, doctrines and ideologies, and fresh types of organization.' Víctor Raúl continues: 'Many of you will remember that in 1956, when I set out for Venezuela, Colombia and Central America, I declared: "We need other parties–we do not wish to be the only one, just because the others do not know how to organize. They must organise." And I suggested, with a touch of humour but without mockery, that we might send them Apra instructors to show them how to do it.'[2] Thus the party of the 'national majorities' desires that there should be other parties with which it can engage in debate or cross swords. How seriously should such wishes be taken? They are prompted by fear on the part of the Apra leaders lest their adversaries should accuse them of aiming at a dictatorship. This fear was particularly noticeable in 1945–8, when Apra's dominant position provoked the right and the left to join forces and denounce it as fascist and totalitarian. But the wish expressed by Víctor Raúl is hedged about with qualifications and precautions. To begin with, his emphasis on the other parties' inability to organise suggests that he does not take them very seriously; and this impression is confirmed by the long paragraph that follows, which is aimed at Belaúnde's Acción Popular though he does not expressly say so. In this passage he is at pains to make clear that the size of the latter's vote at the elections of 14 June 1956 was due to the freedom which Apra's secretary-general, Ramiro Prialé, allowed to members of the party, who in some areas probably voted for the young architect and his newly-founded group. But Víctor Raúl stresses that 'it would be a delusion to expect these votes to be cast the same way in 1962'; and he makes light of the 'cheerful statistics' (*alegres estadísticas*) according to which Apra is alleged to represent only 30 per cent of the electorate.[3]

Apra, therefore, claims the role of a dominant party. It has no objection to others entering the lists, and it accepts their equality of

[1] Ibid. [2] Ibid. [3] Ibid., p. 205.

rights under *convivencia*; but it has no doubt that the newcomers are very young and that it has the advantage of them in authority as well as in age. Apra has not only succeeded in being recognized as a force to be reckoned with, but also in imposing what it regards as the supreme rule of democracy–the distinction between regime and government, whereby the latter is free to govern and the opposition to criticise–while maintaining intact its claim to represent the 'national majorities'.

For a coalition such as the *convivencia* to survive, it must satisfy various conditions. In the first place, its leaders, even if they do not attempt or do not manage to formulate and carry out a long-term policy, must be successful in solving current problems as they arise. In Peru, for example, inflation is tolerable only in relatively small doses, owing to the oligarchy's insistence on a liberal economy; while, if those in power are not to lose out to the military, they must limit the extent and duration of any repressive measures to which they might be inclined to resort in order to damp down the claims of workers', employees' and peasants' organizations, or to stifle revolts in the sierra. Secondly, a coalition must be able to maintain a minimum of cohesion among its supporters: and here appears the risk of jealousy between Apristas and supporters of Manuel Prado over the distribution of spoils–embassies, ministries, prefectures and subprefectures. Moreover, it must be expected that the 'outs' will do all in their power to split the coalition.

In 1956, the opposition to the Apra-Prado coalition was a motley one, including such of General Odría's followers as had not climbed on to the Pradist bandwagon in time, and diehard opponents of Apra on both the right and the left wing. All these elements, as we shall see, rallied to the standard of Fernando Belaúnde, who, as soon as the election had taken place, challenged its validity and embarked on preparations for his campaign in 1962. But despite his tenacity and the determination of the various opposition groups, Prado's regime survived the ups and downs of the next six years. Apart from the President's skill, this was because two of the conditions we have mentioned operated in his favour. In 1956–62, although long-term prospects continued to be sombre, the day-to-day situation did not get any worse, and the government's friends stoutly maintained that it was getting better. Their optimism seemed justified after 1959 on the basis of indices which, though of limited value in themselves, are of significance to large sections of the urban middle class: trade surpluses and a favourable balance of payments guaranteed the stability of the exchange and thus made possible a rapid rise in imports of semi-durable goods. Moreover, from 1960 until 1963 consumer prices at Lima scarcely rose at all, while salaries in the public and private sector improved steadily; and the budget, which balanced in 1960, showed a surplus in 1961. True, *barriadas* multiplied around the main cities, and the situation in the sierra was bad, especially in the south: a dry year sufficed to bring tragic consequences, as in Puno. At the end of 1958 and in the first half of 1959, the country went through a crisis owing to the fall in quantity and value of ore exports and to a budgetary imbalance which was partly inherited from General Odría and partly due to the open-handedness of Manuel Prado's administration in its early months. But apart from this period, Prado never encountered any of the difficulties of President Bustamante, under whose rule basic foods such as meat, rice, tea and sugar had had to be taxed and rationed.

The regime was helped to weather its difficulties – though, according to its enemies, at the cost of mortgaging the future – by the fact that the associated parties succeeded in preserving a minimum of cohesion and solidarity. The situation appeared most perilous in the first half of 1959, when Prado's prime minister was under persistent attack from the sector represented by Sr. Pedro Beltrán and *La Prensa*; but the President had the shrewd idea of challenging Sr. Beltrán to apply himself, as prime minister, the financial remedies he had been vaunting in his newspaper. If Beltrán refused, he would lose face and be obliged to moderate his campaign for a time; and if his methods failed, at least the President would be rid of one of his critics. In fact, after a difficult start, Beltrán managed to put the economy in order and – despite furious attacks by the parliamentary minority, with *El Comercio* as their mouthpiece – remained in power till December 1961, when the Presidential election was six months off, leaving behind him a businessmen's government in which the chief posts were held by his nominees. This achievement was the more notable in that co-operation between Beltrán and the Apristas had seemed likely to be especially difficult, both because of past events[1] and because of Beltrán's uncompromising championship of creole liberalism, which Apra was not expected to find palatable.

---

[1] In 1945–8 *La Prensa* had pursued Apra with such virulence that when its editor was murdered at the end of 1947, many suspected Apra of having a hand in the crime.

Why, after enduring for six years, did *convivencia* not survive Manuel Prado's term of office? Many reasons may be suggested. Firstly, the opposition groups seem to have succeeded by degrees in discrediting the coalition and destroying its basis of legitimacy, so that in the end it had no defenders outside Apra. In order to win the election of 1962, it needed an accretion of conservative or uncommitted votes which was not forthcoming, partly as a result of the denigration of which it was the object. The coalition suffered, moreover, from a numerical imbalance between the mass of Apristas and the comparatively few conservatives who supported it. This made itself felt when the time came to designate a Presidential candidate. How could Victor Raúl not stand for election? Yet, if he did stand, could he appease the hatred and mistrust which had gathered during his long career; and if he withdrew, could Apra mobilise support for a conservative candidate?

The violence and continuity of the opposition's attacks on the coalition are noteworthy. For six years, without respite, every opposition group assailed the President and his prime ministers, especially Pedro Beltrán. *El Comercio*, in particular, kept up an incessant guerrilla warfare: the word *fastidiar* denotes a series of actions of this type which, while they do not suffice to capture the enemy citadel, nevertheless demoralise its defenders. One of the rules is in no cirstances to acknowledge that the adversary is right or has been successful. From 1960 onwards the foreign exchange reserves began to grow once again, the budget was in balance and retail prices were almost stable: nevertheless, when Sr. Beltrán resigned at the end of 1961, *El Comercio* criticised his record on a note of doom:[1]

'Sr. Beltrán's term of office has been a succession of mistakes and failures . . . His financial policy has not achieved what it was designed to: a balanced budget, fiscal austerity, a stable cost of living and a limit to note-issuing by the Central Bank . . . The boasted budgetary equilibrium is more apparent than real, since it has been achieved by laying heavier burdens on the country . . . There is no fiscal austerity, since the increase in the budget is out of proportion to the development of the economy. Inflation still continues, for the amount of currency in circulation has increased during the period in question by a record figure of six thousand million soles . . . Nor do we enjoy monetary stability, for the dollar remains at a high parity which signifies the continued abasement of our national currency.'

[1] 4 November 1961.

To this, *La Prensa* retorted that no-one had ever succeeded in restoring budgetary equilibrium except by increasing taxes, and that the six thousand million soles did not represent an 'inorganic' issue of currency designed solely to balance the budget (which was now in surplus), but were the counterpart of dollars which had flowed in to swell the Central Bank's reserves. But the best summing up of *El Comercio*'s line of attack was perhaps that given by a humorous writer in the rival paper: 'The government is a disaster on account of what it does and what it does not do; what it tries to do and what should be done; what it has not done, any more than anyone else; and what it has done that others would like to have done, but haven't.'[1]

Not content with incessant sniping, the opposition did its best to convict the government of malversation. Contracts between it and foreign capitalists were denounced as betrayals of national sovereignty on the part of self-seeking politicians. For instance, when President Prado visited Europe in 1960 he tried to negotiate a contract with Dutch interests to finance the construction of naval dockyards at Callao. Peru's ambassador at The Hague at this time was the Apra leader Manuel Seoane. *El Comercio*[2] repeatedly demanded the revision of the Verolme contract (the name of the firm in question) and denounced the method of adjudication and the favourable terms which the Dutch had secured: it hinted, moreover, that the Admiralty had not been properly consulted but had been rushed into the deal, and that the navy itself was in danger.

The coalition was attacked on a personal basis also. Apart from the crimes imputed, as we have seen, to Apra, the opposition's attacks were mainly directed against Manuel Prado's 'frivolity' and Pedro Beltrán's 'cynicism'. The term *frivolidad* has several connotations, beginning with irresponsibility: a 'frivolous' or 'futile' government is one which takes no thought for the morrow–or, in Lima, the year 1980, when the population will have doubled and there will not be enough jobs for newcomers to the labour market. Another connotation is that of vanity, of excessive concern for forms and courtly ceremonies. A 'frivolous' man is by no means necessarily a fool: he is likely to be an egotist, and may well show great skill in the defence of his interests. Such were in fact the qualities which the extreme left ascribed to Manuel Prado, in unison with *El Comercio* or even a

[1] *La Prensa*, 9 March 1961.
[2] Cf. especially the issue of 19 February 1961.

paper like *Caretas* ('Masks'): so that, by the end of his second term in 1962, the President had become a living symbol of *frivolidad limeña*.

On 10 May 1961 *Libertad* published a caricature of the President 'without head or feet' (*sin pies ni cabeza*), wearing full uniform with the sash of the chief national decoration, the grand cross of the Legion of Honour and an impressive display of other crosses, medals and stars: across his white waistcoat was looped a gold chain from which hung the heavy insignia of the Peruvian order of the Sun. In a similar vein, *Caretas* published at the end of 1956 a photograph of Prado in a tail coat covered with decorations, sticking out his chest and waving a top hat with an engaging smile on his face: the caption read '*Ya volvió el circo*' ('the circus is here again'). An expression often used to characterise the regime was that of Manuel Prado's 'court' and the 'Versaillesque' atmosphere that prevailed there. The President travelled a great deal; on 10 May 1961 *Libertad* carried a large headline 'President's tour continues', and, in smaller type, 'In search of decorations':

'We are used to the President packing his bags and going on tour to show off his decorations and pick up a few more of them (*hacer lucir e incrementar sus condecoraciones*). But while this goes on . . . the country gets poorer and poorer. When he comes back, the President will unpack his bags, proudly display another medal or two (probably the same ones that our foreign friends used to dish out to Batista) and announce that while on his travels he has solved all our problems by a few talks with industrialists and financial groups, and that any day now a saving avalanche of millions of soles will descend on the country. The medals will take their place on the President's manly chest, and as for the plans, they will be put to sleep at the bottom of a drawer somewhere.'

This passage summarises all but one of the features which opposition folklore attributed to Manuel Prado. Apart from the decorations, the taste for travel and the desire to be fêted and acclaimed in Washington, Paris or London, the President's 'frivolity' appears chiefly in his alleged conviction that the nation's economic problems can be solved by a few personal contacts with eminent Western financiers. Even if sincere, this conviction is ludicrous, since the investment plans of which the President is so proud will merely go to swell dusty archives. No doubt his vanity is tickled by the performance; but are the medals really all he gets out of it? The reference to Batista suggests a less innocent interpretation. However, *Libertad*'s frequent attacks against the 'Prado empire' are directed as a rule not against the President himself but against his great-nephew, Don Mariano Ignacio.

The additional feature above referred to is that Don Manuel, besides being 'frivolous', is a bringer of bad luck (*es salado*). Sofocleto in *Libertad* thus described 'A trip with Him to Japan': 'In view of the imposing list of fatalities with which this eminent demographer has been associated, we made our will before leaving Lima. The aircraft, which had been sprinkled with holy water and decorated with pictures of the most efficient patron saints, is an old Flying Fortress equipped for safety's sake with additional armour-plating, auxiliary engines, a first-aid room, oxygen containers, a priest for the last sacraments and a collapsible morgue.'[1] The character of a Jonah is combined with that of the 'frivolous' man: not only do the latter's plans misfire with disastrous effects for those in his company, but, by an ironical paradox, he himself passes unscathed through the calamities caused by his presence. Thus the extreme left was able to depict the Prado regime as a series of disasters while acknowledging the grace and good humour of the adroit politician, skirting one precipice after another but keeping his own equilibrium at least until the eleventh hour.

While the President was 'frivolous', his prime minister was 'cynical'. 'Corruption in the cabinet', cried *Libertad* on 28 June 1961. Three ministers were accused: the prime minister, Pedro Beltrán, whose name was linked with 'petroleum scandals', the Minister of Public Works in connection with a cement factory, and the Minister of Foreign Affairs with reference to the Gloria dairy plant at Arequipa. The most constant and violent attacks were directed against Pedro Beltrán. 'The prime minister governs by decree, has all the cars and foreign exchange that he wants and, which is much more serious, puts up the price of petrol whenever he feels inclined–thus ensuring fat profits for the oil companies of which his family and friends are shareholders and directors.' In a four-column article on 15 June 1961, *Libertad* took up this theme and added: 'Beltrán and his family own the oil companies, but merely as puppets of the I.P.C.'[2]

'Sheltered by the law of 1952 on the oil companies, and using the power and influence of its members, an oligarchic petroleum clan has

[1] *Libertad*, 10 May 1961.   [2] International Petroleum Company.

come into being: its chief figures are the prime minister, Beltrán Espantoso, his nephew Felipe Thorndike, and the lawyer Carlos Rizo Patrón, acting editor of *La Prensa* . . . All the shares in the companies set up by these individuals are held by members of their families. These family partners (*socios familiares*) engage in complicated transactions through five puppet companies, buying and selling one another's shares with the object of masking their true ownership and the fact that they control the market . . . These so-called national companies claim the privileges which the law grants to Peruvian citizens and naturally secure the best concessions. Prospecting then takes place either directly or, more usually, through foreign companies. In any case, when oil is first struck the foreigners appear on the scene and the Peruvian concerns are turned into mixed companies or, in some cases, made over lock, stock and barrel to powerful foreign monopolies. Our shareholders have no interest in extracting, refining or exporting a single drop of oil–they never so much as see it, but are sniffers-out of oil only (*son olfateadores de petróleo*).'

These accusations are mild compared with those which *Libertad* brought against Beltrán's plan for colonising the valley of the upper Apurímac,[1] in an article of 9 August 1962 entitled 'Bogus land reform will create new latifundia'. 'After spending a few hours in a helicopter above the area in question, the prime minister produced what he is pleased to call a thorough survey . . . No doubt this visit stirred up official interest in the forgotten part of the jungle on the right bank of the Apurímac.' Then came the charge that 'The Minister of the Interior and his brother have, we are informed,[2] bought two 1,000-hectare lots at a cost of 10,000 soles each.' The writer goes on to contrast the enrichment of oligarchs and politicians who acquire these holdings for ready money, with the wretched fate of the 'small native colonist' who, tempted by a loan, leaves his village in the sierra and, if he can pay off the debt, becomes the owner of a miserable plot of land fifteen years later.

The disputed election

A 'frivolous, cynical and corrupt' government will obviously endeavour to cling to power by fair means or foul: so, as the 1962

---

[1] The eastern part of the department of Ayacucho.
[2] Note the prudent qualification.

elections approached, the opposition hastened to accuse the coalition of planning to falsify the results. Fraud is indeed the major theme of the Peruvian electoral tradition. In a well-known article,[1] Manuel Vicente Villarán described nineteenth-century practices:

'Whether all literate citizens had the vote or whether it was a two-degree process, the essential preliminary which decided the result was the *toma de las mesas* or occupation of the polling stations. On the eve of the election, the respective candidates assembled mercenary bands, well supplied with arms and liquor, on premises close to the public squares: they remained there all night, and at dawn broke forth to do battle for the polling stations and ballot-boxes. This system was based on an ultra-democratic law which provided that the people would elect a provisional team of returning officers who would themselves elect a definitive one . . . All that was necessary was to expel the members of the rival party, after which the returning officers could proceed peacefully to conduct a sham election. This naturally meant a few hours of tumult, gunfire and bloodshed, during which the population shut themselves up in their homes and listened to the din of battle; by eight or nine o'clock all was over, the stronghold was captured and the community returned to its usual calm.'

This 'original' system, as the writer calls it, was completed by a procedure for the adjudication of disputes in which Congress had the last word. The adversaries who had fought out their dispute at the polling centre appeared at Lima before a special Congressional committee, which began to deliberate as soon as the election of a sufficient number of deputies was confirmed.

The practice as described by Villarán was first modified in 1895, when President Nicolás de Piérola decreed that the returning officers should no longer be elected by the voters but that the local authorities (the prefect and subprefect) should choose them by lot amongst the richer taxpayers. (This of course afforded the officials in question opportunities that they were not slow to use.) In addition, voting became public: each voter had to declare his choice aloud and then sign the register, with the object, according to Villarán, of putting a stop to 'our inveterate practice of falsifying votes'.[2] Finally, under Piérola's reform, part of the responsibility for adjudicating disputes was transferred to a complicated system of commissions and juries, the forerunner of the 'electoral authority' which must now be briefly described.

[1] 'Costumbres electorales', *Mercurio peruano*, July 1918, pp. 11–19.   [2] Ibid.

In 1931 two basic provisions were adopted. Firstly, the secret ballot was reintroduced: the advantages of publicity had turned out to be slight, and opinion was increasingly conscious of the drawbacks of obliging the voter to state his choice in front of the local authorities. Secondly, the whole adjudicating machinery was removed from the competence of the administration and judiciary and placed under that of a separate organ of the state known as the 'electoral authority'. Article 88 of the new Constitution set up an autonomous National Electoral Jury (Jurado Nacional de Elecciones) with the duty of supervising the regularity of elections; but it did not regulate the functioning of the new institution, which was to be governed by the ordinary laws.

Various abuses threatened the integrity of the electoral process: to begin with, the violence which a partisan group might exert upon its rivals and the numerous means of pressure open to the administration in favour of its own candidates. The *toma de mesas* is a good illustration of the anarchy which prevailed in the provinces during a large part of the nineteenth century, when Lima had not enough soldiers and police to send to out-of-the-way regions. Another form of fraud was carried on not by local *caciques* but by the central administration: here the *toma de mesas* was replaced by *anforazo* or the switching of ballot-boxes. This was the easier in that, up to and including 1956, the votes were not counted locally in the candidates' presence or that of their representatives (*personeros*), but at the chief town of each department. 'In the last few years . . . elections have been falsified by the substitution of ballot-boxes, which were brought from the various polling stations to each departmental capital . . . When the votes came to be solemnly counted two or three days after being cast, the boxes were no longer the same ones; and every precaution had been taken to prevent disagreeable surprises [for the government candidate].'[1] Hence one of the reforms most urgently demanded was the *escrutinio en mesa*, i.e. that votes should be counted on the spot. Moreover, it was necessary to ensure that this count was not 'revised' at the departmental capital, with results which of course usually favoured the *oficialistas*. General Odría did not disdain these small artifices in 1950, and it was only on Hernando de Lavalle's insistence that the practice was altered at the last moment in 1956. Juggling with ballot-boxes, while effective, is a trifle blatant, and the authorities had other strings to their bow. The registration of voters is a

[1] *La Prensa*, leading article of 23 June 1961.

sensitive point, since suffrage is not universal but is reserved by Article 86 of the Constitution to those who can read and write. According to the strictness with which this is interpreted, an individual may figure on the electoral roll or be excluded from it. Thus the local jury, whose functions cover the preparation of electoral rolls, the organisation of the election, the counting of votes and the declaration of results, is the object of widespread suspicion. As we saw, the Constitution proclaims the electoral authority to be 'autonomous'; but the national jury's independence of the executive is not clearly established. Some of its members are chosen by lot, but three are nominated respectively by the President, Congress and the judiciary. The departmental juries are more or less closely controlled by the national body. Does not this elaborate machinery open the door to fraud and enable the outgoing majority to secure the election of a President and Congress after their own wishes?

A debate on the electoral law took place in Congress in May-June 1961. Certain principles were accepted on all sides: the votes should be counted at local stations, and the departmental juries should not be competent to revise the count: their importance was thus greatly reduced. The debate concentrated on the composition of the national jury. Three of its seven members were nominated, as already mentioned, by the President, Congress and the judiciary, and its *ex officio* chairman was to be the senior judge of the Supreme Court. The remaining three members were to be chosen by lot amongst the members of departmental juries when these were set up. The opposition were not slow to point out that in this way four out of seven members of the national jury would be directly or indirectly representatives of the government and the majority in power. They proposed instead that the three non-nominated members should be 'qualified persons' who, in theory at least, would be politically neutral or independent: viz. the president of the Bar and the rectors of San Marcos and the Technical and Agrarian Universities.

The opposition also pressed their attack on another ground. The 1933 Constitution speaks in vague terms of 'the representation of minorities with due regard to proportionalism': a prudent formula which, while not imposing proportional representation, indirectly censures the system under which some politicians were sure of easy election in rotten boroughs. In the name of proportionalism, the single-member system which had been invariable in the past was replaced by list voting. In addition, it was decided that in the more populous departments a certain number of seats would be reserved for the minority party, whatever its size. Thus, for the department of Lima in 1956, there were six deputies *por mayoría* and two *por minoría*. Did 'proportionalism' affect only the number of seats allotted to the majority and minority respectively, or did it apply to the ratio between the number of electors and the number of inhabitants? Which of these latter should be taken as a basis for calculating the number of deputies and senators to be returned by each department? If the number of electors were the basis, it would be to the disadvantage of the sierra, where illiteracy is sometimes as high as 70 per cent. A compromise was reached whereby the up-country departments received considerably more seats than their number of electors would have entitled them to, but fewer than they would have got on a population basis. The voters of the sierra, particularly the landowners, were thus 'over-represented'. The Belaundists, for their part, stood out for the furthest possible application of 'proportionalism' by the *cifra repartidora*, the electoral quotient obtained by dividing the number of electors by the number of seats to be filled. This apparently egalitarian proposal does not seem to have attracted much support in the debate. The main battle was fought over the question of the *cédula única* or single list: were voters to be allowed to select individuals regardless of party, and also indicate their order of preference, as a race-goer may indicate his first, second and third choices? If not, was the voter's freedom not being circumscribed? The advocates of the *cédula única* based their argument on the fact that it would diminish the chances of fraud. Up to and including 1956, one of the administration's most effective tricks had been to prevent the voting papers, which it was the candidates' business to distribute, from reaching the local offices in time. The *polla*, or system of splitting up one's vote among parties, increased the risk of papers being spoilt or declared invalid because of marks from which the voter's identity could be deduced, etc. With the *cédula única*, he merely tore out the list of his choice from a sort of booklet provided by the authorities, and was not allowed to alter the order in which the candidates were enumerated. Under the compromise finally adopted, the Jurado Nacional was made responsible for distributing voting papers, and one possibility of fraud was thus eliminated. The opposition did not succeed in securing the adoption of a fixed-order list: the majority agreed in rejecting the *polla*, but upheld the principle of the preferential vote.

The majority made a further concession of decisive importance, when the Senate declared that the army would be associated with the electoral process as a guarantee of fair dealing. The statesmen of the coalition seem to have regarded this as an adroit measure from their own point of view; but, as we shall see, the lightning-conductor drew the storm down upon the house it was supposed to protect. Article 213 of the Constitution defines the role of the armed forces as, *inter alia*, to 'protect the rights of the Republic, and to ensure respect for the Constitution and laws and the maintenance of public order'. Under this provision, the legislature is clearly entitled to entrust to the army the task of keeping order at elections and ensuring that they are properly conducted. But the Senate went further by proposing that at every polling station a record of the votes cast should be handed to the representative of the armed forces–who might be expected to discern evidence of fraud in cases where the national jury would, at worst, have seen certain 'irregularities' which, however regrettable, could not be allowed to affect the result of the poll.

Although the opposition failed to secure the *cifra repartidora*, the number of seats allotted to the minority was considerably increased. The most blatant abuses associated with the departmental juries, particularly as regards the distribution of voting papers and the right to revise local results, were put a stop to or at least much reduced. The opposition, however, were not satisfied. In the last few weeks before the election of June 1962, while not challenging the electoral law itself, they made a point of calling attention to every irregularity connected with the election preparations. Were registrations being carried out properly under the authority of the national jury, and was not Apra causing minors and illiterates to be inscribed on the electoral roll? 'It is common knowledge' wrote *El Comercio* on 1 May 1962 'that two dangerous foreign lawbreakers have succeeded in obtaining identity documents. Apart from these scandalous facts . . . it is known that many inscriptions on the electoral rolls are completely illegal. Young people under voting age have received polling cards from the offices of parties belonging to the coalition, and it is reported from all over the country that many illiterates have been registered as voters.' Returning to the attack in a leader on 20 May intitled 'The army and electoral fraud', *El Comercio* called openly for army intervention. 'There is no doubt that the electoral process has already been vitiated and that corrupt practices have taken place; nevertheless, we hope that the electoral authority will purge the rolls of unauthorised names as far as lies in its power.' Then comes the threat: 'If the national jury should unhappily fail to perform this task which the country demands of it, it would be assuming the gravest responsibilities. It would not, however, in so doing, affect the political future of the country; for our people are determined, come what may, that on 10 June next their profound desire for a beneficial change shall triumph over obscure machinations of every kind.'

On 22 May the national jury stated that 'we have not found any confirmation of reports concerning the mass registration of minors or other large-scale irregularities, or the issue of several polling cards to a single voter'. The jury added that it had made the dossiers of a number of electors available to the army for inspection. Would these assurances have the desired effect? At the end of May, a fortnight before the election, rumours of a military coup were rife. However, *El Comercio* stated on 29 May: 'There is no objection to the election taking place on 10 June, since General Odría or Sr. Belaúnde will certainly be at the head of the poll, and this will mean that the unquestioned majority which supports these two candidates will have asserted itself in spite of everything. However, if Haya de la Torre should appear to have gained a majority, it would manifestly be necessary–since Apra's fraudulent practices are already known–to complete the purge of the electoral rolls before announcing the results of the election.' In other words, Víctor Raúl could not be elected; if he should appear to be, it would be a proof of fraud, and the rolls would have to be 'purged' until the general or the architect could be adjudged the victor.

A few days before the election a fresh storm broke over the question of indelible ink. Apart from registering minors and illiterates, dishonest persons might cause electors to vote twice over, despite the safeguards afforded by identity documents and certificates of registration. On 26 May the army issued a communiqué demanding that voters be also required to produce their military papers. Referring indirectly to the national jury's reassuring communiqué of 22 May, the army also indicated that they had checked 3,696 service records out of the 30,291 which the jury had forwarded to them, and had found 2,105 to be in order, while 1,591 were doubtful. On 28 May the Jurado published a six-column statement which began by accepting the military demand for the production of service records and then expatiated on the problem of indelible ink–the military having raised the question whether the ink into which every voter's hand was dipped to prevent his voting twice was as indelible as the authorities supposed.

'As regards ink, the Jury has gone beyond what the electoral statute requires, for, instead of a single finger being dabbed on an inked pad, they have recommended the immersion of the first joint of the left forefinger. They have duly sent a sample of the ink to the chemical laboratory of San Marcos university. [Here followed an analysis of the ink.] However, they have no objection to the use of any other ink which the Ministry of War might wish to provide, to be bottled (*envasada*) under the armed forces' supervision and distributed by them.'

On 2 June the national jury addressed circular instructions to the chief returning officers. 'The officer shall pour on to the pad furnished by the representative of the armed forces a suitable quantity of the ink also furnished by him, and shall then spread it with a brush until it is properly absorbed . . . He shall also ensure that the voter inserts his second finger into the ink provided by the national jury.' Rather than dwell on the comic aspect of these minute prescriptions, I would point out that the whole electoral process, from start to finish, is regarded as open to challenge. No doubt the national jury took a malicious pleasure in embarrassing the army by multiplying precautions to the point of absurdity. (It was praiseworthy to have the ink analysed at the university laboratory, but how do we know the bottles were not switched between there and the jury's headquarters?) The military, in any case, made clear in their statement of 26 May that, whatever guarantees the jury might agree to, they would never regard the operation as having been properly conducted unless the outcome was to their liking.

Thus the coalition's legitimacy was contested to the very end. Denounced at the outset as a shady expedient, it was accused in its last days of seeking to perpetuate itself by fraud. Whether the individuals and groups who were excluded from it could prevent its survival depended on various circumstances. In the first place, who would be its spokesman? If it appeared that the success of *convivencia* meant that of Apra, and that this in turn meant that of Víctor Raúl, then anti-Aprism was likely to revive in all its virulence. Secondly, the opposition were more likely to succeed in winning the election – or having it annulled if Víctor Raúl should win it – if they could find a popular candidate around whom to group themselves. They would also score a decided advantage if they could persuade the army that it was bound in honour to challenge the election results in view of suspicions that Apra had engaged in fraudulent practices. Of course, if the coalition should head the poll by a large majority, the opposition would have to accept the situation, at least for the time being. The Americans, and especially their ambassador at Lima, who made no secret of his friendship for Víctor Raúl and his party, would not understand and would probably not tolerate the ostracism of a group which professed good will towards them and enjoyed an unquestioned majority at the polls. But what would happen if the race was so close that no candidate gained a third of the votes cast and that consequently, under the Constitution, it fell to Congress to designate the new President?

2

'*Dictablanda*'

*C*onvivencia was based on an agreement between Apra and certain
conservative elements–the 'Pradists' and a small group of Pedro
Beltrán's friends–who had gradually come to believe that the stability
of power depended on reaching an understanding with a large
popular party, reformist but not revolutionary, idealistic in its
objectives but prudent in action, which would agree to share the
conduct of affairs with them. Members of Apra joined the government and received ministries and embassies; trade union leaders
affiliated to the party were treated with respect, and there was a
prospect of large democratic reforms, particularly in the sphere of
land tenure. In the main, however, it was intended that the basic
rules of creole liberalism should continue to be observed. In this way
the country would develop at a reasonable pace without falling into
inflation; necessary changes would take place without the need for
violent shocks; and Peru would go through its destined evolution
without having to suffer the effects of a tragic conflict. Moreover, the
position of the governing class would be strengthened by its having
helped the country, quietly but efficiently, to turn this awkward
corner in its history.

The Gordian knot

In 1962, this hopeful design encountered two obstacles. Firstly, in
order to consolidate the understanding between Apra and the conservatives of the Prado or Beltrán school, who regarded themselves
as 'enlightened' and whom their opponents dismissed as 'frivolous'
or 'cynical', it was necessary for all the parties and interests involved

in *convivencia* to agree on a single candidate for the Presidency. The problem was to find, once again, a man connected with the 'establishment' but sufficiently popular and impressive to capture a certain number of floating voters, and who was at the same time acceptable to Apra. In 1956 the choice had fallen on Manuel Prado, and this had not worked out badly from Apra's point of view; but the position now was different. At that time, with its leader in exile and several of his lieutenants in prison, Apra had had no choice but to forgo a candidate of its own. The compromise by which the party regained its freedom in exchange for its votes was certainly to its advantage and in no way dishonourable: no-one could accuse an outlawed party of cowardice. But how could its leaders in 1962 explain to the rank and file, without risk of demoralisation, that Víctor Raúl would again not be standing for President, although there was nothing this time to prevent him from campaigning? This was all the more difficult in that throughout Prado's term of office they had reassured their followers with the prospect of the magic year in which Víctor Raúl would at last take over the Presidency.

A further difficulty stood in the way of the coalition's putting forward a single candidate. If Víctor Raúl had once again held back, to whom would the party's votes have been switched? It would not, in theory, have been difficult for him to support a technician of Aprista leanings such as the then Minister of Public Works. But such a person would certainly have been denounced as a man of straw, and his prestige would have been quite insufficient to outweigh the disappointment that the mass of Apra voters would have felt at their leader's withdrawal. The latter could only be politically advantageous if it opened the way for an 'independent' candidate of sufficient standing to attract some conservative and floating votes; and the chances of finding such a one were not good. Pedro Beltrán would probably have liked to play this role, but his attempt to launch a campaign did not even get off the ground. To be a Presidential candidate one needs, in the first place, 25,000 signatures. This in itself is not too difficult, and in December 1961 a *Movimiento de los Independientes* was set up for the purpose: Sr. Beltrán himself took no public initiative, but its founders belonged mainly to the circle of his friends, relatives and clients. The Prime Minister confined himself to restating his economic and social doctrines to an unresponsive public, and desisted when his failure seemed likely to be embarrassingly complete.

The multiplicity of candidates, and the weakness of each one, is a consequence of the Peruvian right's lack of political strength–using 'political' in its narrowest sense. On the one hand, the 'establishment' has no need to govern directly in order to ensure that the economic principles to which it attaches importance are observed by the men in power; and on the other, ideological developments in recent times have pursued directions foreign to conservative thought. As a result, since the demise of the 'civilista' party the right wing has not succeeded in creating a strong conservative party after the Chilean pattern. Since 1914 no President except Manuel Prado has come from an oligarchical family, and he himself owed his election for a second term in 1956 to the decisive support of Apra. Candidates supported by the right were beaten in 1931, 1936 and 1945, and the same happened to Hernando de Lavalle in 1956. In 1962, the difficulty of rallying conservative votes was enhanced by the fact that *convivencia* had profoundly divided right-wing opinion. The anti-Apra faction which regarded Manuel Prado and Pedro Beltrán as traitors would certainly not vote for a coalition which *El Comercio* never ceased to denounce as immoral and unpatriotic.

To add to the confusion, General Odría announced early in 1961 that he intended to stand. The General had been abroad since 26 July 1956, the day on which Manuel Prado assumed the Presidency: he was living in the United States and had spent some months in a military hospital for the treatment of a hip wound by which he had been immobilised during his last months of office. From time to time he had been visited by friends at Washington, but he had abstained from sharp criticism of his successor. However, on 21 March 1961 he made it known that he was returning to Peru, and at the end of the month he was greeted at the airport by a large assembly of his friends and supporters: former ministers, advisers and clients, but also a crowd of humble men and women from the *barriadas* who had been mobilised to acclaim the dictator of 1948–56. Before leaving the airport, the General made a speech announcing all the themes of his proposed campaign. Firstly, he declared, under his rule there had been work for all–and indeed the employment rate had in general been fairly high, at all events in Lima and up to 1954, owing to the building of various large administrative offices, a Ministry of Education, great modern hospitals etc. Secondly, food prices had shot up since he left the Presidency–in actual fact, Lima retail prices rose by about 35 per cent between 1956 and 1961. Taking his stand on realism, with the slogan '*hechos y no palabras*' (deeds, not words), the General used the lapidary phrase '*La democracia no se come*' (You can't eat democracy) in order to blacken the *convivencia* as a gang of lawyers and windbags who let the poor rot in shanty-towns while the cost of living soared sky-high. *Convivencia* was not only misgovernment, bungling and incompetence: it also stood for intrigue and jobbery (*chanchullo*). The General also inveighed against the oligarchy, or at least the Prado-Beltrán section of it which had joined forces with Apra. There was, of course, nothing surprising about his attack on Apra, which he had proscribed throughout the eight years of his rule; but he was careful to appeal to his audience by concentrating on its inefficiency and shameful association (*contubernio*) with the powerful interests which it professed to oppose.

In this fashion the Unión Nacional Odriista (U.N.O.) was launched, and it was at once clear that it was a force to be reckoned with, particularly by those who sought to capture conservative or floating votes. From the very start it displayed three features. First, the General had behind him a group of rich and powerful men who were prepared to give him strong financial backing. Secondly, he enjoyed a measure of support in the provinces. His own home town was Tarma, and he had not forgotten its interests while he was President. He had also shown favour to the departments of Tacna on the Chilean frontier and Piura in the extreme north, where an expensive irrigation programme in the Quiros valley had been launched during his term of office. Thirdly, he could expect a large slice of the shanty-town vote. I have already discussed the conservatism of the *barriadas* and their susceptibility to authoritarian pleas, provided these are couched in down-to-earth language and are more concerned with potato prices than with national glory.[1] The slogan 'deeds, not words' offered this section of the public more or less what it wanted. Odriista committees began to spring up throughout lower-class areas, setting up food distribution centres and promising their 'forgotten' inhabitants that if the General was elected, such amenities as water, gas, electricity and sewerage would be provided in the shortest possible time. In addition, the General was clever enough to use his wife's homely, reassuring charm in support of his campaign. Doña María Delgado de Odría was a woman of humble origin in whom the public could recognise the virtues of a good housewife, accustomed to making ends meet on a slender and uncertain income.

[1] Cf. Part I, chap. 3.

'Dictablanda'

She had shown great dignity as First Lady, engaging in charitable works effectively but without ostentation, and was as popular with humble folk as with the ladies of high society, whom she made no attempt to dazzle by her position. Víctor Raúl was a bachelor ('for well-kown reasons', according to the ever-malicious *El Comercio*), while Fernando Belaúnde was separated from his wife; the General, by contrast, appeared in photographs in the company of his good lady, at their respectable home in the calle Vargas Machuco.

The General and his wife thus presented a reassuring picture. To the very poor he offered work; to those of the rich who sided with him, alluring profits, and to all citizens, peace and a quiet life. Nevertheless he was fiercely attacked, in particular by the small group of Christian Democrats who, in 1956, had secured the return of some deputies and senators for the departments of Arequipa and Lima. In 1962 this party had adopted a doctrinaire and moralising style, under the leadership of Héctor Cornejo Chávez. As a fellow citizen of Arequipa, Enrique Chirino Soto, put it,[1] 'Héctor is a man from Arequipa–one might almost say, *the* man from Arequipa. An ardent Catholic . . . living on his earnings, with little or no money to spare, . . . he is at once a lawyer and a passionate local patriot, imbued with the poetry of his native region.'[2] Among the spiritual fathers of Christian Democracy was the ex-President José Luis Bustamante y Rivero, whom Odría had deposed in October 1948; and it was therefore no surprise that the leaders of this party harried the General without respite, in particular demanding information as to the sources of his wealth. This campaign began on the very day of his return to Peru (28 March 1961), and on 10 April the party issued a volley of questions: 'Is it true that some public works were farmed out without tenders being called for? Did the contractors in whose favour these irregularities were committed present the General with a plot of land near the Monterico racecourse, on which he subsequently erected a mansion? And is it true that in 1954 the General had on deposit, in American banks alone, the equivalent of two hundred million soles?'[3] Further controversy extended into the realm of internal and domestic accountancy: a Christian Democratic member of parliament claimed that the General's son had drawn on

[1] *La Prensa*, 14 May 1961.
[2] Cf. Víctor Andrés Belaúnde's description quoted in Part I, chap. 1.
[3] Equivalent at the time to about 10 million dollars.

291

the Treasury for the greater part of his wedding and honeymoon expenses.

The powerful competition of General Odría's faction threatened to rob the Apra-Prado coalition of part of its right-wing support and of some floating voters; but Belaúnde, who stood as the coalition's main adversary, also had serious difficulty in uniting the forces opposed to it. The Christian Democrats were bent on putting forward a candidate of their own, which meant another few thousand votes likely to be wasted. As for the tiny groups of the extreme left–communists of various hues, Castroists etc.–while they were unlikely to command many votes, these might be decisive in view of the constitutional provision requiring the successful candidate to secure at least a third of the total. Not only did Belaúnde fail to reach agreement with the *social-progresistas*,[1] but the Communist Party, alarmed by the latter's independence and fighting spirit, decided to lend its support to a Frente de Liberación Nacional (F.L.N.), headed by a retired general and a priest on bad terms with the hierarchy. Finally, the Socialist Party, whose influence was confined to the oil-bearing area in the northern department of Piura, decided to launch a candidate of its own, Luciano Castillo.

By the beginning of June 1962 one point seemed clear: the election would not be prevented by a political coup. But which candidate would come out on top, and by how big a majority? Neither politicians nor observers seem to have paid much heed to the risk that no candidate would obtain the necessary third of the votes cast. Each of them in turn held rallies, and on the following day it was duly announced by the adherents of the party in question that their rally far surpassed in size any that had previously been held. On the 10th the election took place without incident, but three facts appeared as soon as the provisional results were made known. Firstly, the collapse of the extreme left (Movimiento Social Progresista and Frente de Liberación Nacional) and the marginal parties (Christian Democrats and Socialists) was more complete than had been expected: the electorate had voted 'realistically'. Secondly, the 'big three' were very closely matched, and it was a question whether any one of them had secured the requisite majority. Finally, at Lima General Odría was ahead with 30 per cent of the votes; Belaúnde was runner-up with 25 per cent, and Víctor Raúl well behind with 21 per cent.[2]

---

[1] The Movimiento Social Progresista, whose organ was *Libertad*.
[2] A breakdown by polling-stations (*mesas*) is not available: the Electoral

'Dictablanda'

The results at Lima depart from the pattern familiar to students of electoral geography in that there seems at first glance to be little difference between fashionable districts and outlying or plebeian ones: for example, while Odría scored his chief victories in the *barriadas* of Fray Martín de Porres, he also did very well in the elegant southern part of the city, although the well-to-do inhabitants of this area showed a slight preference for Belaúnde. Víctor Raúl, on the other hand, achieved his greatest success in the old lower-class districts such as La Victoria. In London terms, it is as though the same candidate had topped the poll at Hackney and at Kensington. At all events, General Odría had secured a very large percentage of the shanty-town vote – in some cases between 40 and 50 per cent.

The provincial results were less surprising. The extreme left and the marginals, who had wasted 17 per cent of the Lima vote, played no part here except in the Piura department, where the oilfield workers owed allegiance to the socialist Castillo, and at Arequipa, the home of Christian Democracy. Apart from Piura and from Tacna, where Odría was victorious, the country seemed to be divided into two large zones, supporting Belaúnde and Apra respectively. The former triumphed in most departments of the south and east, gaining 64 per cent of the votes in Puno, 53 per cent in Cuzco and 55 per cent in Moquega; also 44 per cent in Loreto, 42 per cent in Arequipa, 41 per cent in Junín, 40 per cent in Huancavelica and 37 per cent in Ayacucho. Víctor Raúl carried eleven departments including the Apra strongholds of the north-west: La Libertad with 75 per cent of the votes (here Manuel Prado scored 64 per cent in 1956), Cajamarca with 57 per cent, Cerro de Pasco (56 per cent), San Martín (49 per cent), Apurímac (49 per cent), Ica (47 per cent), Amazonas (47 per cent), Ancash (44 per cent), Huánuco (40 per cent) and Tumbes (29 per cent).

While the contrast between Apra's 'solid north' and the Belaundist south is immediately obvious, other equally instructive facts emerge. The north, which voted for Apra in 1962, had already done so in 1931; while in 1956 Prado had conquered Lambayeque and La Libertad with majorities quite comparable to those now scored by Víctor Raúl. Again, while Apra possessed a faithful regional base in

Jury seems to have been disinclined to provide it. No abstentions are recorded, as voting is compulsory. In some departments there is an appreciable discrepancy between the number of votes gained by a candidate for the Presidency and the lists of candidates for parliamentary seats put forward by his party; this phenomenon is not examined here.

the north, other areas once more showed themselves unresponsive to its appeal. Further, in the two departments which showed the biggest majority for either leader (Puno for Belaúnde and La Libertad for Víctor Raúl), the figure was still not above 75 per cent: in other words, even where one of them was clearly ahead, the other was not eliminated. We may also notice that in eleven of the provincial departments, the successful candidate's majority was less than 50 per cent. The party organisations or 'machines' of at least two of the three main candidates–General Odría scored under 25 per cent in most departments–were active throughout the country, and no party seemed completely to dominate any given area: the Apristas perhaps came closest to this in La Libertad, where Víctor Raúl gained 75 per cent of the votes, leaving Belaúnde with 14 per cent and Odría with 9 per cent.

How far did Apra reappraise its position after the relative failure of June 1962? There is little indication of this in *La Tribuna* before Víctor Raúl's important speech at the beginning of July. The outside observer can only base his conclusions on the results of the 1962 election as compared with those of 1956, 1945 and 1931; but some inferences can also be drawn from what we know of the party's organisation. In 1962, Apra boasted of possessing half a million followers:[1] this is not an official figure–as far as I know, none were ever published–but is based on the estimates of party leaders when they were questioned. If this number, which is doubtless not a very exact one, is compared with the total of votes cast for Apra, it will be seen that the ratio between party workers and voters must be extremely high, from which it would follow that Apra has little power to attract those outside its fold. Failing a nation-wide poll, there is no way of confirming this conclusion, but many arguments point towards it. In the first place, the violence and persistence of anti-Apra stereotypes–the right-wing nicknames of 'sect' and 'horde', the left's charges of totalitarianism and subservience to U.S. imperialism–must operate to prevent the party's making headway in circles thus prejudiced against it and its leader. An indication of the stubborn resistance with which it was confronted may be found in the history of the trade union movement after 1956, when Apra was re-legalised by President Prado. By and large, at this time it recovered its position in its former strongholds, and the unions of the 'solid north', i.e. particularly the sugar-cane workers, came to the fore again; but the

[1] Not all of these had the vote.

party was less successful in the new organisations of bank employees, building workers etc. which had come into being in the Lima area during its period of eclipse in the 1950s.[1]

Up to June 1962 the Peruvian problem had been how to govern against the majority, in so far as it was conceded that Apra was the majority party but could not be admitted to power. After the election, Apra's claim to predominance and to represent the masses was destroyed; but the difficulty which now arose was that no-one had a sufficient majority at all. For the first week, *La Tribuna* put a bold face on things and proclaimed that Víctor Raúl's election was assured. *La Prensa* was more cautious: on Tuesday 12 June its headline ran: 'Belaúnde ahead but with uncertain majority', and underneath, 'Congress will have the last word'. On Friday the 15th it stated that, 'according to estimates based on semi-official information', Víctor Raúl, whose score was improving as the provincial results came in, would gain 32·71 per cent, Belaúnde 32·32 per cent and Odría 27·95 per cent, the rest going to the socialists, extreme left and Christian Democrats.

Despite the General's success at Lima, Belaúnde and his party had found the preliminary results encouraging. On the evening of 10 June he already regarded himself as 'virtually elected' and declared: 'I am in a position to announce our final victory, by such a margin that no Congressional vote will be necessary to designate the next President of the Republic'. In his own rhetorical style, he paid tribute somewhat over-hastily to the scrupulous conduct of an election which he believed he had already won. 'I lay down the sword and bestow on the outgoing government the laurels which it has earned itself by the freedom of this electoral process.' But, as results favourable to Víctor Raúl continued to flow in, voices were heard again raising the charge of fraud which had been forgotten in the enthusiasm of the first evening. On 15 June *El Comercio* published an article entitled 'Corrupt practices again?', followed on the 17th by 'Electoral fraud and the army'. The former article referred to a number of petitions for annulment (*impugnaciones*) submitted by Apra and affecting not the Presidential but the legislative elections (deputies and senators are

[1] Some Peruvian observers speak of Apra as an 'ageing' party; but there is no study which bears out that its supporters at the polls or party workers are older than, for example, their Belaúndist opposite numbers. What is clear is that the party consists of a 'hard core' without much penumbra, representing in fact a sort of political ghetto.

elected on the same day as the President). The writer at this date took the view that 'thanks to the efficiency and vigilance of the armed forces, the election has been fairly conducted', but went on in the same breath: 'Clearly there has been open attempt at fraud'. Thanks to Providence and the armed forces, these attempts by the coalition and its supporters had been foiled, and the results as now known should be accepted on all hands. By way of confirming his view, the writer points to the 'desperate attempts of the Apristas and their allies who, now that the election is over, resort to spurious petitions by which they hope to invalidate its results, with the help of departmental juries and perhaps the national jury itself'.

In the second article, on 17 June, *El Comercio* discussed a report which had been drawn up and published by the army's liaison officer attached to the Cerro de Pasco departmental jury. This stated that a number of unregistered persons had voted and that many more had been improperly registered at the last moment; others again had received duplicate polling cards which employees of the national jury had issued in return for bribes. The article concluded with a far-reaching interpretation of the powers of the armed forces. 'By publishing this report, the officer in question has fulfilled the duty which rests upon the armed forces according to law. Their role of guardians is more than a mere police function . . . Their task is much wider than that of ensuring public order and the intactness of ballot-boxes . . . The will of the majority may be falsified at other times than that of the vote itself: fraud has subtler and more effective ways of operating.' Thus it was no longer a question, as on the 15th, of showing up and frustrating the coalition's post-electoral manoeuvres: it was stated in so many words that corrupt practices had occurred in at least one department, and the army was assigned the function of a court of appeal from the national jury, whose own good faith was called in question.

The army waited till 28 June to issue a communiqué, which contained a threat and perhaps an invitation to negotiate. It began with a terse restatement of the position. 'It is being alleged in various quarters that the proper conduct of the elections has been guaranteed and supervised by the armed forces. Since such allegations involve an incorrect view of the army's responsibility and functions, the following points are brought to public attention . . .' The first point embodied a much narrower view of the army's responsibilities in regard to the election which had just taken place: it had been responsible for maintaining public order on election day, 'which does not mean in any sense that it was invested with control over the whole electoral process'. Thus the military were at pains to restrict the definition of their role, which *El Comercio* on 17 June had sought to extend so as to cover the prevention of even the most subtle and secret types of intended fraud. At the same time, however, they justified their position by invoking article 224 of the Electoral Statute. Having safeguarded themselves against a charge of exceeding their powers, they proceeded to take the offensive in points 2 and 3 of their statement – in fact, reversing Lenin's dictum, they took 'one step back and two steps forward'. Point 2 recalled that the armed forces had proposed and secured the adoption of measures (in the matter of the ink and the obligation on voters to present their service record) which should have 'at least partly prevented illegalities which, unfortunately, nevertheless occurred to some extent'. Then came specific accusations. 'Grave irregularities took place in the departments of Lambayeque, Cajamarca, Amazonas, La Libertad, Huánuco, Pasco and San Martín.' Point 4 stated that the army possessed 'proofs' of these 'irregularities'–which, it will be noticed, relate exclusively to departments with an Apra majority–and reserved the right to make these known after forwarding the relevant documents to the national jury.

On 30 June, *La Prensa* pointed out in a front-page headline that 'if the elections in the seven departments in question were declared invalid, Belaúnde would have his one-third majority: for Haya de la Torre would lose 204,672 votes and Odría 57,925, while the first-named would lose only 64,428.' The percentages for Belaúnde, Odría and Víctor Raúl would in that case be respectively 35·41, 31·28 and 26·12. It is a matter for speculation whether the newspaper's object in publishing these figures was merely to throw light on the nature of the outcome which the military were suggesting to the political parties, or to discredit it by pointing out that a single candidate would bear the brunt of the proposed invalidations. The latter hypothesis seems the more probable. In any case, the military's pressure gave Víctor Raúl the opportunity for a skilful riposte.

On the night of 4 July the Apra leader, in a speech to senior members of his party,[1] informed them that he had just had a conversation with

---

[1] Apra's chief governing organ, the Comité Ejecutivo Nacional (C.E.N.), is composed of three parts. The *buró central* consists of the party leader (*el jefe*),

297

Manuel Prado in which the outgoing President had told him that the army vetoed his election. Relations between Apra and the military–Víctor Raúl went on–had always been difficult. Some believed that the 'sect' had from the outset been at daggers drawn with the *Institutos Armados*. In reality Apra respected the army; unfortunately some members of the latter, ruled by ambition or blinded by passion, had persecuted the party without mercy. Within the party, too, some hotheads or provocateurs had played with the idea of a rising. The two views of who was to blame had been most clearly in evidence over the Trujillo disturbances of 7 July 1932.[1]

Would Víctor Raúl now give in to the military *Diktat*, or would he fight? His plan, he declared, was to negotiate over the question of withdrawal and endeavour to turn the situation to his own advantage. He hoped to postpone or prevent army intervention by dealing directly with the other two candidates. He seems to have had in mind two alternative plans which were, however, connected inasmuch as one could only be achieved by means of the other. We may call A the more ambitious strategy, aimed at breaking the veto, and B the prudent course of cutting his losses. The position was apparently

the secretary-general and assistant secretaries, and the chairmen of the special committees. These deal with trade union affairs, political affairs, and internal party (disciplinary) affairs, plus a 'planning committee' which is responsible for the party's political doctrine and plan of action. The *buró ampliado* consists of the same members together with the committee secretaries. The *plenario* contains, besides all these, the secretaries of departmental federations and such trade union leaders as are party members.

Two points should be noticed here: the special position of Víctor Raúl as founder and life chairman of the party, and the question of the extent to which the party leadership controls its subordinate bodies. Until such time as Apra provides us with a monograph on the subject, this remains obscure; but I would tentatively contribute the following suggestions. (1) As regards the control exercised by the party apparatus over its active workers, use has been made more than once (most recently in 1959) of the process of *reinscripción* or renewal of membership, by which backsliders can be unobtrusively got rid of. (2) As regards the control of the *jerarcas* or party officials over departmental federations, the difficulties over *preelecciones* in 1962, referred to on p. 185 above, are relevant. (3) As regards relations between Apra and the C.T.P., the attitude of some union leaders towards the party's call for a general strike after the coup of 18 July 1962 would also repay close study.

[1] This tragic episode, which *El Comercio* never ceased to denounce, was thus commented on by Ramiro Prialé on 7 July 1958:
'There was no disturbance of public order on our part. Lives and property were respected. . . . No bloodshed was committed by the Apristas in retaliation for the persecution we had suffered under Sánchez Cerro's government. . . . It was only when the troops were mobilised to crush the movement of revolt that a conflict took place and fellow-countrymen of ours on both sides lost their lives. . . . These were victims of civil war: but it cannot be said that our dead were victims of the army or that the army's dead were victims of ours. Each and every Peruvian who fell was a victim of the oligarchy.'

such that in order to achieve B (a retreat in good order to prepared positions) it was necessary to go through the motions of pursuing A.

What cards did Víctor Raúl hold? By publishing his conversation with the President and divulging the army veto, he could place the debate on a new footing. Instead of being in the dock on suspicion of fraud, he could force his opponents on to the defensive for imposing a wilful and arbitrary veto. But, at this point in his address, he was at pains to present matters in a dispassionate, realistic and almost cynical light. According to Víctor Raúl's account of his conversation with Manuel Prado, Apra was being offered a bargain whereby, if its leader withdrew, it would receive assurances that 'everything which has been gained by the people's will and the free vote at the recent elections . . . will be respected, that the elected parliament[1] will not be called in question, that the party will receive fuller guarantees than before . . . In short, the consolidation of democracy in its essentials.' Víctor Raúl did not intend to bring this surprising offer to public notice without assuring himself of the President's endorsement, since the army could not then go back on it without denying the President's word also. But meanwhile, he was able to present himself to his hearers in an advantageous light. 'My reply could not have been other than that which any responsible Peruvian would give if he were asked to sacrifice ambition, rights or even life itself in return for a firm promise that constitutional order would be maintained . . . Since I myself was the stumbling-block, I could only reply: "For myself, I am willing." But I was entitled to ask in turn why I was being subjected to this strange procedure and why sentence had been passed before I was heard in my own cause.'

So that, the hearer supposes, is the end of the matter: Víctor Raúl is going to withdraw. But–the leader goes on to say–if I give up the Presidency, shall I not be making improper use of a favourable situation? Then follows a long debate between considerations of personal reputation ('the great aim of my life has been to achieve a record which shall survive intact when I am no longer able to feel the caresses of vanity') and those of political wisdom. Does this mean– the puzzled hearer says to himself–that Víctor Raúl is, after all, accepting the challenge to fight and maintaining his candidature? It does not; but he is concerned to present his withdrawal as the result of a stoical decision and not a shirking of responsibility. The magic

[1] In which Apra commanded a relative majority.

formula by which he does so is that of 'Aprista serenity'. This is how it works to justify the policy of coming to terms with General Odría:

'I wish to erase from memory the wrongs which have been committed against us ... The most fearful hates and rivalries have divided our country and drenched it in blood. I have often remembered Darwin's account of how, when he was once at Lima on the 28th of July, the rival bands in one of our innumerable civil wars fought, not under the national flag but under the skull and crossbones ... Peruvian history is full of such tragedies ... but we must not go on living in an atmosphere of hatred and revenge and the memory of all these horrors.'

Víctor Raúl's position is by now sufficiently clear. His offer to withdraw is coupled with a warning: his opponents are forced to reckon with him, they cannot rule him out of the game, and the humiliation that he is being asked to swallow is itself a recognition of the party's impregnability. Aprista serenity requires, it is true, that 'we have the courage ... to admit that as of today we do not command more than one-third of the total number of votes, though it would be more if the illiterate were counted[1] ... and that means that, like the other parties, we have two-thirds against us.' But, while recognising that Apra is in a minority, Víctor Raúl once more puts a good face on the situation. 'None of the parties is in a position to govern by itself, and our doctrines and behaviour must be adapted to this new state of things': in short, there must be a coalition government. 'No party is Fortune's darling, no one has a divine right to govern: what counts is the distribution of votes, leading, as it has done, to small majorities with little room for manoeuvre.' The conclusion drawn from this is that 'Peru must be de-presidentialised'. Since the President's party, whichever it may be, represents only a third of the electorate, the opposition will have a majority in Congress and the President will have to come to terms with it. The proper working of democratic institutions will depend on co-operation between President and Congress and a spirit of toleration–*convivencia*–among the three main parties.

Was there a possibility, at this stage, of negotiation over the choice of a President and the distribution of seats in Congress? The chances appeared slight. Meanwhile the National Jury held its ground and declared the validity of the departmental elections which

---

[1] Under the Constitution, the vote is denied to illiterates. It was extended to women in 1956.

had been impugned by the military: the latter's 'proofs' were, in the Jury's view, merely data which it reserved the right to assess for itself. Apra hit back at its rivals by maintaining that the abuses of which Belaúnde complained had taken place not only in the seven pro-Apra departments but in those where Acción Popular had topped the poll. The latter party drew up a list of charges against the authorities which were thus reported by *El Comercio* on 28 June: 'issuing forged polling cards, tampering with electoral registers, allowing votes to be cast in the name of deceased persons, passing over electors who held anti-government views, falsifying returns from polling-stations, exerting pressure and intimidation through the agency of Aprista officials appointed for the purpose, and influencing public opinion by a systematic campaign of defamation and slander directed against Acción Popular by the same authorities.' Leaving aside the vaguer charges as regards e.g. the appointment and transfer of specially designated officials on the eve of the elections–practices which are not confined to Peru–we may consider for a moment the irregularities in the drawing up of electoral rolls, the issue of polling-cards and the compilation of returns. On 9 July *La Prensa* published an Aprista announcement which, in parallel columns, cited Acción Popular's complaints of corrupt practices in Cajamarca and gave its own account of what had happened in the department of Puno. 'Were there illegalities at Puno city, where Belaúnde headed the poll with 32,685 votes and Haya got 5,660? We print below a photocopy of two electoral returns: No. 65 shows more votes than the number of registered electors, and No. 37 shows fewer. If we were to follow the slanderous technique of Acción Popular, we should say that this points to fraud. Actually, it is a mere matter of miscounting due to the inclusion or non-inclusion of blank, invalid or doubtful votes in the respective columns.' And, the Apra statement goes on, 'these are not isolated cases: samples from elsewhere in Puno show a huge number of similar errors.'[1]

By the beginning of July, as the impasse continued, it seemed inevitable

[1] Was the election as a whole fraudulent? Certainly, as the Apristas themselves recognised, there were local irregularities; but it is less certain that these were all committed for the benefit of the *convivencia*. If it had happened, as it did in 1963, that one of the candidates out-distanced his nearest rival by more than 5 per cent of the votes, it is unlikely that the election would have been declared invalid; but Víctor Raúl's margin in 1962 was so slender that there was a strong temptation to accuse Apra of having won by fraudulent means. According to the parties concerned, the elections were the cleanest that had

that Congress would be called on to designate the new President and that the parties would have to accept the election results as they stood: these latter were due to be proclaimed by the Jury not later than the 28th, on which day the law required that the new administration should be installed. As it became clearer day by day that Congress would have to choose the President, the parties began to take soundings and to explore the possibilities of coalition. General Odría seems to have taken the initiative, being the candidate furthest from having obtained the necessary one-third of the votes. His first attempt was to reach an understanding with Belaúnde:[1] this, if it had succeeded, would have imposed on Apra the role of an opposition minority. Such an arrangement appeared at first to be on the cards and may even have been envisaged during the campaign itself, at any rate in the form of co-operation between the Belaundist executive and the parliamentary group of Odría's supporters. At all events, the two leaders were at pains to spare each other and concentrate their attacks upon Apra.

Feeling himself threatened, Víctor Raúl sought to break out of his encirclement by approaching Belaúnde, who was thus courted by each of his opponents in turn and then by both at the same time. As affairs stood in 1962, it was natural enough that Víctor Raúl should turn first to Belaúnde, since, despite the hostile treatment he had received from the latter and especially from the Belaundist party, the two groups had in common the profession of a populist ideology. Besides, during the election campaign Apra had levelled against General Odría in person the old charges of corruption and nepotism with which the Christian Democrats had sought to overthrow the ex-dictator. *La Tribuna*, punning on the General's initials (his full name being Manuel Apolinario Odría), had nicknamed him Mao and, among other civilities, compared him to General Batista of Cuba. The echoes of the campaign were of course already fading into the past; but in the delicate negotiations now beginning, the combination of Odría and Haya seemed much less likely to emerge than that of either of these with Belaúnde.

Apart from these three possibilities, a fourth seemed to present

ever taken place in Peru, and this is certainly true compared with those of 1956, 1936 or 1931. None the less, it is open to doubt whether Víctor Raúl's lead of a mere 30,000 votes over Belaúnde was in fact genuine.

[1] Cf. *Presente*, No. 86, August 1962, p. 9. This pro-Apra review provides a fairly reliable and detailed account of events during the weeks preceding the military coup.

itself: namely that before Congress met, the three candidates should reach agreement for the unanimous election of one of them to the Presidency. Various 'outsiders' sought to promote this course, and meetings were held in the early part of July, though none were attended by the protagonists: the General preferred to play a waiting game, or was kept at arm's length by the other two, but emissaries of these met on Sunday 8 July at the house of the Minister of Public Works of the outgoing government. Next day, Apra published the text of the draft memorandum which its representatives had submitted for Belaúnde's consideration. In the preamble, the two parties – one might almost say, high contracting parties – agreed to recognise each other; the draft went on to stipulate that Acción Popular should acknowledge the legitimacy of Víctor Raúl's candidature and his victory at the polls, but suggested that 'in view of the similarity of their respective programmes and the comparable volume of their electoral support', the two parties should consider themselves equally qualified to exercise power. On this basis, it proposed a series of specific undertakings. The parties would agree to abide by the final results of the poll as announced by the National Jury, i.e. each would waive its demands for the unseating of the other's members. The two leaders would agree on a candidate for the Presidency, whose name would be submitted to Congress for approval; if they failed to do so, recourse would be had to a committee of 'wise men' (*comité cívico*), whose numbers and identity were not stated in the first draft. Ministerial portfolios were to be divided on an equal basis, and the chairmanships of the Chamber and Senate were to alternate between the two parties. The latter were to endeavour to extend the agreement thus reached to embrace other parties also. A rider, added subsequently, dealt with the composition of the proposed *comité cívico*: it was to consist of the Cardinal Archbishop of Lima and a representative of the armed forces, plus three individuals to be selected on personal grounds, among whom Víctor Raúl proposed Hernando de Lavalle.

The draft agreement was politely rejected by Belaúnde, who approved its general intention but refused to agree that the National Jury should have the last word as regards the electoral results. In his view the composition of parliament should conform to the 'spirit of the agreement' – in other words, the two parties should divide up the seats between them without paying too much attention to the exact proportion of votes cast or their geographical distribution. As regards the preamble with its mutual recognition clause, Belaúnde declared this to be quite unacceptable: he maintained 'his ideological postulates in all their originality'.

The attempt at a deal between Haya and Belaúnde having thus failed, the latter began to force the issue. On 9 July he called upon the National Jury to decide within three days on the petitions put forward by his supporters for the annulment of specific election results. In so doing he attacked the Jury and opposed it to the armed forces. 'We are witnesses to the scandalous spectacle of an electoral authority which turns a deaf ear to the authoritative spokesmen of the armed forces. The latter did not intervene in this process arbitrarily: they did so in pursuance of a constitutional and legal obligation, and the reports assembled by them are essential documents for the purpose of judging the issues now submitted to the electoral authority.' Having uttered these words, Belaúnde left Lima for Arequipa, where his supporters erected barricades to give force to his ultimatum. (Cf. Part II, chapter 4.) How is this romantic episode to be interpreted? Was the speech of 9 July a signal made in concert with the army leaders, and did the latter dupe Belaúnde by using him as a tool and then, for some reason, leaving him high and dry? In any case he seems to have acted precipitately, and his barricades were a laughing-stock to the Limans during the week which elapsed between his speech and the military *coup d'état*.

Belaúnde's dominating principle appears to have been his claim to legitimacy and his refusal to regard the Presidency as negotiable. His rivals accused him of claiming it by divine right, and on several occasions during the campaign he indicated that he could not fail to be elected. Two reasons may be discerned for his attitude. Firstly, he had inveighed with such violence against the illegitimacy of *convivencia* that he could not but avoid at all costs the elaborate and underhand dealings, the bartering and compromise which would be necessary if he were to owe the Presidency to a vote of Congress. Secondly, he might well see an advantage in presenting an image of integrity to public opinion, shocked as it was by the sight of candidates falling into each other's arms so soon after bandying the most infamous accusations.

On the afternoon of Monday 16 July, a piece of news spread which seemed to indicate that the crisis was over: an agreement had been reached between the General and Víctor Raúl. The Apra leader withdrew his candidature, and his followers undertook to vote for the General in Congress. According to the Apra journal *Presente*, many of the party's officials, including Manuel Seoane, found the deal distasteful. Víctor Raúl may have played with the hope that it would be possible to keep a free hand as regards the Congressional vote; but in the event he solemnly announced his withdrawal and undertook to support Odría for the Presidency, the latter promising in return to include Apra in a government of national unity.

At first sight the wheel seemed to have come full circle: *convivencia* had been extended into *superconvivencia*, and the Apra leader was allied to the military dictator who had outlawed him in 1948 and made him a prisoner in the Colombian embassy for the following six years. But the union, which was a marriage of convenience rather than a love match, was never consummated. In the small hours of the 18th, a military group occupied the Palace, deposed President Prado (who was allowed to fly to Paris after remaining under guard for some days), and installed a Junta de Gobierno.

Radicalisation or creolisation?

Who were the soldiers who seized power? What were their aims and abilities, and how did they intend to govern? The coup was not the deed of a single *caudillo* like Colonel Sánchez Cerro, who overthrew Leguía in 1931, or even General Odría, who put an end to the constitutional rule of President Bustamante with the help of some business circles. This time, the intervention was that of the army as a whole.

As a glance at Peruvian history will show, *pronunciamientos* are particularly common at election times; but the operation of 18 July 1962 was of a new type, as we can see by comparing it with an episode of the 1956 campaign. On 17 February 1956, *La Prensa* published a manifesto in which General Merino, the commander of the Amazonian division stationed at Iquitos, protested against the Odría regime for 'seeking to use the army as an instrument of terror in order to impose on citizens an electoral process which would mean the continuation of the present regime'. The attempted coup misfired owing to poor leadership and the failure of General Merino's allies to support him; but during the week which elapsed before it was finally put down on 25 February, various discussions took place behind the scenes as a result of which the General and his team were able to save face. In a telephone conversation which was recorded and widely distributed 'in order that the officers of the Division may be directly informed of the course of events', General Merino and the Commander-in-Chief of the army defined their respective responsibilities and exchanged appropriate guarantees. General Merino said *inter alia*:

'I hope that you, General, will agree to two conditions which I now state with the frankness with which I have always addressed you. Firstly, it must be understood that no officer of the Division, of whatever rank, will be prosecuted or suffer in his professional career by reason of having taken part in the Iquitos *pronunciamiento*. . . My request is that you should personally inform the officers concerned that you accept this condition. Secondly, I am at present at Iquitos with my family: I wish to be allowed to arrange for their departure without hindrance, after which I shall be at the disposal of my superior officers.'[1]

This long-forgotten episode is typical of the old-style *pronunciamiento*, in which a local commander 'pronounces' against the government and resorts to political action on behalf of a particular group of interests or section of the community. The coup is an individual affair, and if it fails the army can wash its hands of the matter. The officer corps may, at worst, throw their comrade to the wolves, or they may protect him from retribution; but in either case the reputation of the Institutos Armados is unscathed. It is true that if the coup were to succeed, the credit and benefits would accrue to the officer caste as a whole. But when a military leader who has gained the Presidency in this way eventually lays down his office (e.g. General Odría in 1956), those who succeed him are wise enough not to identify the army with the late regime. By a fiction which no civilian leader would have the temerity to challenge, it is understood that the army is above party strife and neither defends nor combats any particular group, except of course those 'sects' which conspire against the nation's integrity and safety.

The army, in fact, is no-one's instrument but belongs to the nation as a whole. Its claim to act as arbiter and ultimate judge of the nation's interest is opposed by no-one, at all events openly – neither by Apra nor by the communist, Trotskyist or Castroist groups of the extreme left. I have shown the care taken by Apra, in the person of

[1] Quoted by Ramírez y Berrios in *Grandeza y miserias de un proceso electoral.*

306

its leader and its secretary-general, to keep on the right side of the army, and by Congress to associate it with the electoral process.[1] The sphinx impassively receives the homage of politicians, some of whom fear its reactions while others hope to turn them to account; but all without exception show it the greatest deference.

In 1962 the army performed its appropriate role as a watchdog, but this time it acted as a body and not in the person of a single *caudillo*. What took place on 18 July was not a *pronunciamiento* of the classic type but a '*golpe institucional*'. The proclamation issued at Lima that morning bore not one signature but four: the commanders-in-chief of the three arms and the chairman of the joint command (*Mando Conjunto*), General Pérez Godoy. The junta published three decrees: one annulled the elections of 10 June 1962 and another provided that fresh ones would be held on the second Sunday of June 1963, thus setting a term to the junta's own authority. Finally the army commanders assumed the Presidential prerogative of suspending constitutional guarantees and freedoms in regard to meetings, the press and publications generally.

In a speech delivered the same morning on behalf of the junta, General Pérez Godoy made three points. Firstly, 'we have been witnesses of a dishonest election in which the plainest and most elementary rights have been disregarded'. Secondly, the junta 'solemnly promises to hold the clear, straightforward, honest elections that the whole country wants as soon as possible, and within a year at latest'. Thirdly, the army is the champion of the people's interests. 'The armed forces are the people, they exist for the people; their one patriotic desire is . . . to serve the people and the nation's inalienable interests.' In the course of this first day, the army used two arguments to justify its action. In the first place, it presented itself as a guardian whose duty it was, in the last resort, to guarantee to its fellow-citizens the exercise of fundamental rights of which a civilian government had unworthily sought to deprive them. By annulling corrupt elections, the army had simply been defending the constitution and the law of the land. But the army was not merely a state institution with power and authority to intervene whenever it should see fit to do so: it was also–and this was a new note in Peruvian history–a direct expression of the people's will.

The army leaders were the paladins of the constitution. The coup, as we have already observed, was a *golpe institucional*, and the junta

[1] Cf. Part III, chap. 1.

claimed to be acting from the highest moral motives. Their skill and tact were indeed such that the new regime came to be known as the *dictablanda*.[1] The military no longer rode roughshod as they had in 1948 and during the bloodstained rule of Sánchez Cerro. None of the coalition leaders were arrested: Víctor Raúl went into hiding for a few days, but no search was made for him. The newspapers were not interfered with: *El Comercio*, it is true, greeted the coup with jubilation, but *La Prensa* was reserved to the point of hostility. *La Tribuna* was shut down on the 18th but reappeared on the 20th. The Apra-controlled C.T.P. (the main trade union organisation) called for a general strike, but this collapsed after a few hours at Lima and had little effect even on the sugar cane plantations of the northern coast. The junta's Minister of the Interior, General Bossio, maintained order without imprisoning anyone, and paid no attention to Apra's fulminations. Some students, or rather schoolboys, paraded after nightfall in the main streets of Lima, but were soon dispersed with truncheons. Some Apra ladies, in token of mourning for the cause of liberty, laid a black-ribboned wreath before the San Martín memorial.

The consolidation of the junta's authority took place in several stages. Firstly Apra's conservative allies, while condemning the coup, did so with such qualifications as virtually to recognise it *de facto*. It had, in fact, not come as a great surprise to anyone: for more than a year past the newspapers and parties had predicted army action, either as the last safeguard against fraud or as a manoeuvre of Apra's opponents to snatch victory from the coalition's grasp. Now that the coup had taken place, observers were struck by its unusual features, which they may have exaggerated a little. On Sunday 2 September *La Prensa* published an article analysing recent events under the title 'What the coup has put an end to', in which the anonymous author enquired: 'Does the 18th of July mean that the age of *caudillos* is over? Can we be certain that one of the four leaders of the junta, or some other person as yet unknown, will not come forward as a dictator?' The question was not answered; but the apparent demise of the *caudillo* was associated with a number of changes in the style of Peruvian political life. Two photographs accompanied the article. The first was a romantic picture of a vociferous crowd grouped about a flag in the main square; the

[1] A play on words: *dictadura* means 'dictatorship', *dura* 'hard' and *blanda* 'soft'.

second, a bleak scene of a tank standing in front of the railings of the President's palace and guarded by two parachutists in camouflage uniform. The *coup d'état* had moved into the technical era.

The coup of 18 July exploded another popular idea: that of the efficacy of mass rallies. On 10 June, the success of the respective candidates at Lima was in inverse proportion to that of their public meetings. Fine speeches are no more a recipe for winning an election than for preventing a coup or ensuring its success. 'In former times', wrote *La Prensa*, 'a would-be dictator knew that he stood no chance unless he issued a more or less high-flown (*rimbombante*) proclamation. Today'–it went on with some surprise–'the literary style which still flourished when Sánchez Cerro was overthrown in 1931 or when Odría ousted Bustamante in 1948 has given place to dry, terse military announcements which come over the radio in telegraphic form.' Formerly what was needed was a gesture to impress the 'masses', who were in fact limited in number because virtually the only Peruvians who had the vote and counted politically were the townsfolk of Lima, Arequipa and Trujillo. Today, 'what counts is to gain the voter's allegiance within the framework of his new social life. In consequence ... the old familiar devices, from switching ballot-boxes to holding street processions, are no longer of much importance. The education of public opinion has progressed so far that the military themselves have to justify their intervention on grounds of electoral integrity. Does not this signify that a new democratic custom is taking root among us?'

In other words, the best proof that democracy is thriving is the style of the latest military coup. The summary optimism of this judgment may cause raised eyebrows; but *La Prensa*'s 'realism' is a token of the conditional and rationalised support accorded to the coup by the conservative branch of the former coalition–practical men who decided from the outset to come to terms with a set-up which might be distasteful but which there was no sense in dramatising. Their position was defined and defended in an article by Enrique Chirinos Soto, published in *La Prensa* on 28 July and entitled 'Neither *naïveté* nor cynicism'. It was useless, the writer argued, to adopt the attitude either of Don Quixote or of Sancho Panza. On the one hand, he condemned the intervention of the armed forces. 'They have, in my judgment, committed a profound historical error ... by ignoring elections which, though full of imperfections and illegalities, are still the freest and least tainted in

309

our national history.' But the writer, while denouncing sin, was merciful towards the sinner. 'The error committed by the armed forces may not, after all, be irreparable. There is no reason to think that harmony can never be achieved between them and the rest of the nation.' The note of prudence is then struck. 'We must choose the lesser of two evils and make the best of every situation, especially if, like this one, it is unalterable and admits of no remedy.' And again: 'We cannot spend the rest of our lives blaming the military for the coup of 18 July.' What is done is done, and it is better to pick up the pieces than to cry over spilt milk. It must also be admitted that 'up to the present, there has been no such climate of oppression as was formerly the result of a military coup', and the soldiers' record so far did not justify unconditional opposition. 'We shall not judge the junta by what it says or professes to do, but strictly by its acts.' If the four generals respect public liberties and promptly restore constitutional guarantees, and above all if they do not cling to power but show themselves prepared to keep their promise and hand over to a new regime, then we conservatives for our part will not make heavy weather over the unfortunate events of 18 July.

The Apristas, of course, were not in a position to adopt so serene an attitude. Nevertheless, as early as 28 July they published a manifesto calling for a firm policy of *constitutional* opposition to the junta:[1] the adjective limits the sphere of resistance and circumscribes its means. In essence, this policy accepted the *fait accompli*: for it announced Apra's intention of taking part in the forthcoming electoral campaign, of interesting itself in the 'formation of a national civic centre',[2] and of closely following the elaboration, as promised by the junta, of a new electoral statute. These points were confirmed in a long statement published by *La Tribuna* on 2 August. 'The party is certain of the legitimacy of its victories of 10 June, and, in reply to the accusations of interested persons who seek to despoil it, to limit its influence or thrust it aside (*arrinconarlo*), it hereby declares to the people that it accepts the challenge of the elections fixed for 9 June 1963. It hopes, moreover, that those elections will be held in an above-board fashion, without vetoes of any kind and with undisputed results, including the return of those deputies and senators who were elected this year in the departments where our lists were victorious.' On the same date, a leading article proclaimed that the

---

[1] Author's italics. F.B.
[2] Section II, paragraph 3 of the manifesto.

party, 'confronted by the *de facto* government of the junta, is resolved to maintain an attitude of legal opposition.'

Thus, in less than a fortnight, the generals had secured recognition for their seizure of power, provided it remained temporary and limited: the *dictadura* was accepted on condition that it remained a *dictablanda*. The next hurdle was that of recognition by the United States. This was tricky for several reasons. In the first place, the U.S. government is inclined by custom to keep newcomers waiting, and this traditional practice had been accentuated by the Kennedy regime. The Americans had indicated more than once that they would not recognise any government resulting from a *coup d'état*, and their ambassador at Lima made no secret of his predilection for Apra. As is well known, the U.S. government has effective means of pressure on its allies, especially those in Latin America: if it had cut off the aid programme, the junta would have been in serious difficulties. The Apristas, as was to be expected, appealed to continental solidarity and applauded the Venezuelan move (President Betancourt's Acción Democrática was on close terms with Apra) to bring the Peruvian question before the Organisation of American States. But before this body had met, twenty-odd states, including the Argentine, Mexico, Chile and Uruguay, had announced that they maintained normal relations with the Peruvian junta. On 17 August –less than a month after the coup–the U.S. government followed suit. As the note in which it did so was couched in qualified terms, the junta's Minister of Foreign Affairs was able, in a stiffly-worded statement issued next day, to indicate that, while he took note of Washington's decision, he took exception to its being accompanied by observations on the internal situation of Peru: these, it is true, were favourable and took the form of a 'clean bill of health', but were nevertheless improper in the eyes of the Peruvian government.

This defiant attitude on the part of the junta was greeted in *El Comercio*'s leader of 19 August as a 'manifestation of dignity and independence . . . an affirmation of national sovereignty . . . in the face of U.S. violation of the rule of non-intervention and the sacred principle of the self-determination of peoples and states.' The junta had not in fact taken any great risk: the Venezuelan approach to the O.A.S. was doomed to failure from the beginning, and before the end of July the representatives of the chief U.S. interests in Peru had urged Washington to relax the 'unprecedented pressure' which was being exercised against that country. The President of the Peruvian-

American Association, advocating the 'early recognition of the present government', declared that 'the present policy may have disastrous consequences for U.S. interests established in Peru or having dealings with it.' As for the American president of the Cerro de Pasco Corporation, he had sent a telegram of congratulation to the leader of the junta. 'Cerro de Pasco sends its best wishes to you and to the government over which you preside. You may be sure that we shall continue our co-operation for the country's welfare.'

By the end of August, the junta was firmly in the saddle. The military were in power but had promised not to remain there; and the ample liberty granted to the opposition seemed to confirm that they would keep their solemn pledge to hold elections in June 1963. Not only were fundamental freedoms respected, but business continued to prosper. The outflow of foreign exchange which had followed the coup had been more than reversed by the first half of August. *El Comercio*, which had never ceased to rail against Sr. Beltrán's policy, suddenly discovered that the economy was flourishing and published statements by representatives of the International Monetary Fund on the healthy condition of public finance and foreign trade. None the less, some ground for anxiety remained. Would the army be content to hold the ring for the politicians, or would it be tempted to sit tight? Excuses could be found for doing so: the junta could argue that a year was not a long time in which to prepare free elections, and above all it might, as some of its supporters desired, set itself the task of 'renovating' the country by transforming and modernising it.

Some of the military in fact toyed with the idea of an 'opening to the left'; and the leaders of the tiny extreme-left groups which had been mauled at the election began to look hopefully towards the junta, which had not only taken Apra off their backs but seemed to be espousing some aspects of nationalism and populism, opposition to the oligarchy and anti-imperialism. In August, the Communist Party issued a carefully-worded statement concerning the junta, and on 26 July *Unidad* discussed the coup as follows. 'The army has inflicted a severe reverse on imperialism, on the oligarchy and its henchmen, the followers of Haya and Odría... Up to now it has taken useful measures and has foiled the imperialist plotters who sought, contrary to the people's will, to impose first Haya and then Odría as President. It annulled fraudulent elections ... and has respected the liberty of the press and other information media.' True, the junta had also declared itself in favour of the Alliance for Progress and against communism; but 'there is a clear difference between the recent change of government and the traditional type of coup. The events of 18 July have perhaps not yet advanced the people's cause, but they have certainly not retarded it.' The communist newspaper summed up its analysis in the form of a dilemma. 'Either the junta will align itself with the people, for freedom and social progress, or it will turn back towards oligarchy, dictatorship, exploitation and oppression.' The Communist Party's mission was to put pressure on the junta to break with the forces of conservatism, thus opening the way for more radical tendencies of which the progressives should take full advantage.

'A foreign observer'[1] – wrote Hugo Neira in *Expreso* on 28 July – 'has remarked that the junta will have to choose between creolisation and radicalisation.' The former course was that advocated by the conservatives: the army leaders should prepare the way for 'fair' elections, they should not, on the pretext of major reform, jeopardise the economic achievements due to the good husbandry of the coalition, and above all they should bow out at the first convenient opportunity. As for radicalisation – which was clearly Neira's own preference – it would be achieved, if at all, by a group of progressive officers whom political observers at that time had christened 'Nasserites'. The limits and composition of this group were somewhat difficult to define. In general, they were neither at the top nor at the bottom of the military hierarchy: they were not junior officers on the make, dreaming of a career like Batista's, nor elderly generals who had passed their best days, but were to be found at about the rank of colonel. How strong was this group among the junta's adherents? Of its four leaders, none appeared especially 'progressive': the only member of the team who showed clearly radical inclinations was General Bossio, the Minister of the Interior, who in the first few days after the coup had shown skill in keeping Apra under control while interfering very little with fundamental liberties. Apart from him the levers of command were in the hands of officers who, for the most part, had reached their military ceiling and showed no particular yearning for adventure.

Using the term 'Nasserism' to denote a populist and nationalistic trend within the armed forces, we may say that its centre of diffusion

[1] Whom the present author has every reason to know well.

313

was an institution founded in 1958, the Advanced War Studies Centre (Centro de Altos Estudios Militares–C.A.E.M.), where, according to a laudatory article in *El Comercio* of 10 August 1962, 'civilians and military men foregather to discuss national problems'. One of the main features of the Centre was that its syllabus paid more attention to history, international relations, social sciences, geography and economic planning than to the subjects traditionally taught in war colleges. The C.A.E.M. had influenced the officer corps in a variety of ways: it had interested them in the 'state of the nation', and had at the same time given them grounds for belief in their own mission.

What are the functions of the armed forces in a country like Peru? Firstly, of course, to guard the nation's frontiers: Ecuador, after all, still claimed part of the departments of Loreto and San Martín, and no Peruvian could quarrel with the defence of Iquitos against what were regarded as mad pretensions. But national frontiers are better guarded by the *pax Americana* than by the forces which two such adversaries as Peru and Ecuador can deploy against each other. The second traditional function of armed forces is to defend public order. In the name of this principle it fell to the army under Benavides' rule to repress or persecute Apra, and the same situation recurred during the eight years during which General Odría held power. But by maintaining order, was not the army helping willy-nilly to maintain privilege? Many officers, disquieted by this suspicion, declared that they no longer wished to be the oligarchy's watchdog (*el perro guardián de la oligarquía*). Any members of the armed forces who felt doubts of the social value of the institution they represented and the legitimacy of the power they were called upon to exercise – not only in the barracks but *vis à vis* the mass of the population, since the Constitution conferred on them extensive powers which their leaders used to depose Presidents and annul elections – any such officers found a congenial answer to their self-questionings in the ideology of national development, a variant of the *desarrollismo* of which we have spoken earlier. If the country is to be developed and backward regions opened up, what is better fitted to perform this task than the army, which can drive roads and build bridges with the cheap labour furnished by its recruits? And who knows the needs of provinces forgotten by the capital, better than officers whom the accidents of their career have brought into contact with every part of the country?

Desarrollismo is not in itself a radical movement, but it can easily

314

become one if the officer class comes to believe that development is being frustrated by a selfish oligarchy and shallow politicians. In such circumstances, the army is the only group which, by its independence of private interests, its technical training, patriotism and habit of command, is qualified to direct the development process. This is why terms like 'planning' and 'structural change' have a strong appeal to many of the ablest and best-trained officers. In 1962 the army was in power but not, for once, as an instrument of the oligarchy; nor was it, this time, involved in a baleful task of repression or in the ludicrous ambitions of a self-seeking *caudillo*. Its hands were free and it felt that the people stood behind it. Was it to let slip its chance, or would it succeed in imposing, in an orderly fashion, the far-reaching reforms that the country longed for?

As far as the senior military officers were concerned, we may doubt whether many of them in fact saw their mission in this light. The most thoroughgoing and radical forms of Nasserism were probably confined to rather small groups. Everyone in the army, of course, was in favour of development and against oligarchy, and was convinced that a military government was better fitted to step up progress than a civilian one; but prudence set in again when the risks attendant on 'radicalisation' became clearer. The honeymoon was a short one, and by the last quarter of 1962 the junta was committed to the path of 'creolisation', as foreseen by the foreign observer whom Neira quoted.

How were the radical tendencies of certain military circles curbed, and how was the junta prevented from drifting leftwards? In the first place, the communist danger was invoked as a check on those who wished to involve the junta in a crusade against Apra. As early as 25 July, *El Comercio* spoke of the necessity of 'reorganising' the C.T.P., in a leader which began by rejoicing at the failure of the general strike thanks to the workers' patriotism. 'How could the Apra leaders have supposed that the working class would follow them in their anti-patriotic action at the very time when a campaign was being launched in favour of foreign intervention in our affairs?' An example must be made of the C.T.P., 'whose immediate reorganisation is being demanded by the most powerful trade unions in the country'. The term 'reorganisation' appears deliberately ambiguous: the writer suggests the summoning of a grand convention of anti-Apra unions and the spectacular launching of a rival confederation in opposition to the C.T.P. On 10 August the paper wrote:

315

'Many delegations from all parts of the country are meeting on Thursday in a national conference which will open up new prospects for the C.T.P. This body, which is at present controlled by Apra and whose leaders have enjoyed rich emoluments from government sources, must be reorganised from top to bottom.' This plan gained some momentum during August, but the 'orthodox' leaders of the Peruvian Communist Party did not seem much attracted by it. They may have feared that a split would reveal how little support the Party enjoyed in trade union circles, or that Trotskyists and Castroists might capture positions in the new confederation and launch it on dangerous courses.

In any case, the term 'reorganisation' as used by *El Comercio* may well have been used in the sense of 'government intervention': the Ministry of Labour, it was thought, might assert the right to suspend the secretaries of the pro-Apra unions and appoint others in their place. Pretexts would not have been hard to find: it could have been alleged that some leaders, like Arturo Sabroso, the secretary of the textile workers' federation and a long-standing target of *El Comercio*'s, were 'not real workers', and that those who had been prevailed on to stand as Apra candidates were not genuine trade unionists but politicians in disguise; moreover, with a bit of luck one could have discovered irregularities in some of the unions' accounts.

However, to halt the offensive against the C.T.P. it sufficed to point out that the main beneficiary was likely to be *la subversión*-a favourite theme of *La Prensa*'s. On 26 July, in a leader replying to *El Comercio*'s call for the reorganisation of the C.T.P., the rival paper declared that 'the failure of the strike called by the C.T.P. may be used by the communists, who have infiltrated into the trade union movement and who hope by this means to gain control of it. . . No doubt the ideal would be for the unions to remain entirely independent of party politics. . . But, failing this, it is better that their leaders should be . . . men of democratic views . . . and not totalitarian agents, as with Peronism in the Argentine, or, worse still, communists.' Once more recommending the policy of the lesser evil, *La Prensa* held that in default of a non-political trade union movement, Apra should be left in control of the unions lest they fall into the hands of communists or 'totalitarians'

La Prensa emphasised the risk of communist 'infiltration' in connection with disturbances which took place in December 1962 at La Oroya, on the occasion of a strike of the Cerro de Pasco miners.

'Dictablanda'

Under the heading 'Conflagration in the Andes', the paper reported on Sunday 23 December that:

'On the pretext of a wage claim, the communists have provoked the bloodiest incidents in living memory in the central mining zone. . . This violence and arson, this thirst for death and destruction, are part of a communist plan to plunge the country into chaos and bring the Reds to power. . . The Cerro de Pasco Corporation was careful to warn the government of what was likely to happen at La Oroya . . . and the plan for a coup was reported to the General Staff . . . but the junta paid no attention to either of these reports. . . If the government remains supine in this way, there is every reason to fear that such events will repeat themselves . . . and the blame will fall on the armed forces which have arrogated to themselves full powers to govern the country.'

Reverting to this theme on Sunday the 30th, *La Prensa* published a long sarcastic article entitled 'Good and bad communists'. The first category comprised 'wide-awake, resolute young people, zealous in the fight against oligarchy and reaction'. These 'good communists', disguised as anti-imperialists, progressives etc. and taking advantage of the credulity of 'useful numskulls' (*tontos útiles*), were of course only a front for arsonists and murderers. The junta was guilty of blindness and frivolity; were some of the 'useful numskulls' to be found among the generals? In any case, the latter should cease to listen to the 'pernicious advice of those who use their influence to protect the Reds, excuse their crimes and give them control of the trade union and student movements, when the only use they make of all this power is to incite to violent attacks on the police, the destruction of private property and murder.'[1] The article concludes with an admonition: 'The junta, which assumed power on the army's behalf, undertook to govern not in favour of one section against another, but for the good of all Peruvians.'

In plain terms, anti-Apraism must not be allowed to justify the toleration of communists: by giving the latter a free run, the junta were exposing soldiers and policemen to the risk of being murdered by agitators whom they had foolishly imagined that they could make use of without risk to themselves. The junta took this advice, suspended constitutional guarantees and, at the beginning of January 1963, proceeded to carry out wholesale arrests of communist, Trotskyist and Castroist leaders and, for good measure, a few Apra trade

[1] *La Prensa*, 22 December 1962.

unionists. On 10 February *La Prensa* commented on the effects of this action: 'As soon as a few communist leaders were arrested, the country became quiet again. This clearly demonstrates the causal link between arrests of communists and social peace.'

Thus the conservative elements of the former coalition had succeeded in preventing an alliance between progressive supporters of the junta and the anti-Apra wing of the trade unions. This success was due to the strength of conservative inhibitions and the weakness of the extreme left. The proliferation of violent strikes in the latter part of 1962 reawakened fears of reckless policies: it was all very well to oppose Apra, but not to the point of opening the way to communism. *La Prensa*'s advice had fallen on receptive ears; and the outbreaks of workers' violence, by obliging the junta to take drastic action, had put a stop to the flirtation between the military progressives and the extreme left. During the (southern hemisphere) winter a series of skirmishes took place between *La Prensa* and the Minister of the Interior, General Bossio, who resigned on health grounds in the latter part of October. His crime was to make light of the movement which had been going on for some months past in the province of La Convención in the Cuzco department, and whose leader, Hugo Blanco, had acquired a certain notoriety. *La Prensa*, discerning the hand of Fidel Castro, had spoken of *guerrilleros*; the General laughed at these 'paper guerrillas', waxed ironical over 'journalistic visions' and suggested that *La Prensa* was making a mountain out of a mole-hill in order to sow panic (*espantar el gallinero*) and discredit the junta in the eyes of conservative opinion.

After General Bossio's resignation and especially the episode at La Oroya, the chances of a radicalisation of the junta's policy declined rapidly. There were now only six months to go before the June elections. The economy continued to flourish: as in Pedro Beltrán's time, foreign trade was in favourable balance and the exchange reserves grew steadily. Nevertheless, on the occasion of the junta's budget for 1963 *La Prensa* was at pains to recall the immortal principles of creole liberalism, complaining that the estimates were excessive. No doubt there were many urgent objects of social expenditure; but, the paper argued,[1] 'a state budget is no different from that of an individual. . . The fundamental task of the Minister of Finance and the members of the junta is to take their shears and pruning-knives and retrench wherever possible. It is essential that the

[1] Leading article of 5 December 1962.

budget should be strictly balanced and that estimates should be honest and reliable.' Despite this stern call to order, the proposed budget was not in balance; but Cassandra had two points to her credit. Firstly, she had the satisfaction of reading a lecture to the junta, and secondly, by warning the military against the prohibitive cost of certain reforms, she had done her best to discourage them from undue initiative and induce them to confine themselves to the prudent handling of current affairs. During April 1963, a series of leaders on inflation, its causes, forms and cure, served to recall that disaster was ever-present and might at any moment engulf those who were so foolish as not to heed the voice of experience.

The final proof of the 'creolisation' of the junta came on Sunday 3 March when President Pérez Godoy was deposed by his three colleagues. We do not know whether he intended to prolong the military regime beyond 10 June 1963 or to get rid of one or more of his associates, or whether he had sought to come to terms with one of the three main candidates of 1962 (Víctor Raúl, Odría and Belaúnde), all of whom had announced their intention of standing again in June. The communiqué published after Pérez Godoy's fall accused him of having 'governed in too personal a fashion'. According to *La Prensa*,[1] he was apparently working hand in hand with General Odría and had favoured the latter's interests against Belaúnde's in the matter of some appointments 'on which he had not consulted his colleagues'. Whatever the case, the unity of the armed forces was threatened. If factions came into being within it, siding respectively with one or other of the Presidential candidates, the army might pay dearly for its initiative in June 1962, by losing the right to present itself as an aloof, impartial arbiter and, what was more, exposing its leaders to a succession of vendettas. During the latter part of 1962 the example of the Argentine, where *gorilas* and *legalistas* were engaged in a confused battle, had been hinted at by *La Prensa* as a warning of things to come. Was this baneful prophecy to come true for the Peruvian army in 1963?

But why, in any case, should the military cling to power when one of the Presidential candidates, Fernando Belaúnde, was fully acceptable to them and had, this time, a good chance of being elected? Belaúnde's speech of 12 July 1962 had paved the way for the coup of the 18th. The barricade adventure had not done him much good at the time; but he alone among the candidates had refrained from

[1] 10 March 1963.

condemning the coup, in return for which the Apristas had christened him the generals' bootblack (*lustrabotas*). Moreover, his rhetorical themes–Peru as a doctrine, Peru's own conquest, the eulogy of Inca planning traditions–had an appeal for many officers who dreamt of 'development', mistrusted capitalism and responded to the combination of warm-hearted populism and vibrant nationalism. Of the three candidates, Belaúnde had the fewest declared enemies among the officer corps. Víctor Raúl had never succeeded in disarming its anti-Apra prejudices, and Odría was widely regarded as a symbol of intrigue (*componendas*). Those who were determined not to act as the 'oligarchy's watchdogs' were, by the same token, loath to see in power a man who had been Pedro Beltrán's ally in 1948; and those who were still dominated by hatred of Apra looked askance at the General who, after outlawing the party and its leader, had, on the eve of the coup in 1962, done a deal with his former enemies to secure their votes. For other reasons too, Belaúnde was in a better electoral position in 1963 than in 1962. He had succeeded this time in forming an alliance with the Christian Democrats; the extreme left had been scattered and its key cadres imprisoned since the disturbances at La Oroya, so that no candidates were put forward by the socialists, the communists, the Progressive Socialists or the Frente de Liberación Nacional.[1] If Belaúnde could succeed in capturing all the votes which had been wasted on these splinter parties in 1962, he had a very good chance of success.

Sure enough, by the evening of election day (9 June) it was clear that Belaúnde had won: he outdistanced General Odría at Lima, and was supported by about 40 per cent of the total electorate. On 28 July the military junta transferred to him the powers they had been exercising for the past year. During that time they had governed without undue violence and had, moreover, taken more than a few major decisions of the type which, the 'Nasserites' hoped, would launch the country on a course of reform from which there would be no turning back.

One cannot fail, however, to wonder what would have happened if, by some accident, Víctor Raúl had won the 1963 election. His chances were not good from the beginning: Belaúnde's pact with the Christian Democrats and his gains at the expense of the extreme left could only have been outweighed if a considerable number of those

[1] A single 'independent' candidate, Mario Samame Boggio, tried his luck but secured only 5,000 votes.

who had vòted for him or Odría in 1962 had swung over to Apra. But if Víctor Raúl had won, would the military again have declared the Presidential election invalid on some pretext, or would they have accepted the verdict of the polls? . . . Few people, in fact, seem to have wanted, or at any rate expected, Víctor Raúl to become President on this occasion. A last-minute attempt on his part to capture conservative sympathies on the ground that the communists were voting for Belaúnde was a failure: the implied smear was rebutted by the patriarch of the Belaúnde family, the illustrious Víctor Andrés, in an impressive television appearance. The architect-President had reached his goal, albeit without a majority in Congress. Would he now launch the policy of 'renewal' in every domain which he had been announcing without a break since 1956? Could he succeed in accomplishing without upheaval the great national and popular reforms which his followers expected of him?

3

An Opening to the Left?

On 9 June 1963, Fernando Belaúnde was elected 'constitutional' President of the Republic. What was the significance of this epithet? First and foremost, it meant that the President was elected in accordance with constitutional forms and did not achieve power by force. But the contrast between a government which owes its authority to proper elections and one imposed at bayonet-point must not be taken too strictly. As we saw, the armed forces not only claimed that they had acted legitimately on 18 July 1962, but maintained that they had done no more than their duty by deposing President Prado and invalidating corrupt elections. Apra, of course, had denounced the military coup as an act of violence covered by a flimsy veil of legality. For President Belaúnde to deserve the epithet 'constitutional', it was necessary for his opponents to concede the legitimacy of his rule and refrain from challenging its foundations.

In fact, Apra resigned themselves to Belaúnde's success from the outset. They could not do less than contest the validity of the results in some departments, and they made an outcry over certain incidents which took place in Ancash; but they were careful to concede Belaúnde's overall victory. This was all the easier for them as they had won a large number of parliamentary seats and could expect to control Congress if they succeeded in coming to terms with Odría's supporters. Would Belaúnde have to compromise with the survivors of the coalition, or would he disregard parliament's wishes? If a majority of both Houses stood out against him, would he appeal to the people over their heads? Since the Constitution provides neither for the dissolution of Congress by the President nor for a referendum (although one was held by General Benavides in 1936), the only way for Belaúnde to try conclusions with parliament would have been by calling in the military. This possibility was talked of at an early stage, but appeared unlikely. The army leaders had been disillusioned by their year in the saddle and were scarcely ready for new adventures; nor would it have been an act of wisdom on the President's part to sell out to them at the beginning of his term of office. In any case, there was no need for him to resort to drastic measures: he was still popular, and the opposition would have put itself in the wrong if it had set out to thwart his policies from the word go.

At this stage, then, Belaúnde's regime enjoyed what may be called quasi-legitimacy. The President's adversaries objected that he owed his power to the invalidation of the 1962 elections by the junta and to the *redada* or round-up of left-wing extremists in January 1963. But, while the Apristas regarded Belaúnde as little better than a usurper and complained that once again their leader had been robbed of his electoral success, and while many conservatives were uneasy at the President's policies, he was not confronted by an inexorable opposition. No-one in 1963 said, or appeared to think, 'Anything but Belaúnde', in the way that many on the right and left in 1945–8 had said 'Anything but Apra.'

The question therefore was whether Belaúnde enjoyed a sufficient degree of legitimacy to carry out the major policies he had been advocating for the past six years. One of his assets was that he claimed to believe in moderate methods. (So indeed did Apra: Víctor Raúl's slogan of 'bread with freedom' stood for thorough-going reform together with respect for liberty and the bases of the traditional order.) As *El Comercio*[1] urged, moderation was the attitude of all true men, and those who abandoned it were self-condemned. 'Sr. Beltrán's supporters frequently argue that ... we are faced with a choice between peaceful evolution and radical change on the Castro model; but in fact there are three possibilities. Besides the communists who desire social revolution, there are disinterested and public-spirited men who want to see this country change in an orderly and peaceful way.' The patriots who desired change but abhorred subversion were equally opposed to two types of extremists: those who lusted to destroy, and those who clung blindly and selfishly to the tenets of creole liberalism. Among the advocates of peaceful change for whom *El Comercio* claimed to speak were in fact some of Belaúnde's warmest supporters.

In his speech to Congress on 28 July the President announced three

[1] 4 August 1963.

important moves. First, a change in the method of collecting taxes, which had hitherto been farmed out by the state to the Caja de Depósitos or public trustee office–an unpopular privilege enjoyed by the oligarchy, for this institution was in fact controlled by private banking interests. Secondly, Belaúnde undertook to settle within three months the forty-year-old dispute between the state and the International Petroleum Company (I.P.C.), a subsidiary of Standard Oil. Peru produces just under 5 million tons of petroleum a year–almost all of it near Talara on the desert northern coast, between Piura and the Ecuadorean frontier–and the circumstances of its exploitation by the I.P.C. had long been the occasion of a rich variety of complaints by the opposition of both right and left. Some prospecting and research is also carried on by Peruvian interests, which makes it all the easier to denounce the 'imperialist' exploitation of the Talara fields. Moreover, the I.P.C.'s title-deeds have a long and obscure history, in the course of which Peruvian jurists have exercised a wealth of subtle dialectic at the expense of 'traitors within the gates' who have handed over the nation's wealth to foreigners.

El Comercio at this period led the attack on both legal and national-istic grounds. The I.P.C.'s title-deeds were invalid, it was defrauding the exchequer and exporting fuel for the war-planes of Peru's hostile neighbour. It was therefore an objective of the first urgency to get the Brea-Pariñas oilfields back into government hands. This was a cause for which it was not difficult to rally the progressives. The extreme left–communists and Castroists–demanded nationalisation without indemnity. When, in 1959, Beltrán as Prime Minister acceded to the I.P.C.'s request for a wholesale increase in the prices of petroleum products, which had been frozen for many years, there was an outburst of protest led by *El Comercio*. The parliamentary opposition at that time had harried the Prime Minister, the Minister of Public Works and the Minister of Foreign Affairs, who was pressed for an opinion on the validity of an arbitral award (the famous *laudo*) which the I.P.C. cited as a proof that it was not only a concessionary but the owner of the deposits in question. Under *El Comercio*'s auspices a 'Petroleum Defence Front' was set up, headed by a retired officer, General Pando. Any parties, trade unions and politicians, especially those belonging to Apra, who did not come out for immediate and unconditional nationalisation were branded as *entreguistas* (from *entregar*, to surrender) and servants of imperialism. Beltrán had been the principal target of this campaign, and when Belaúnde stood for

President he could do no less than proclaim himself a 'nationaliser'; but the electoral programme of Acción Popular was singularly moderate compared with a bill introduced in September 1959 by one of Belaúnde's extreme-left followers, Senator Montesinos. In the 1963 elections, the joint programme of Acción Popular and the Christian Democrats made no explicit reference to the petroleum question but concentrated on land reform, to which some twenty pages of the booklet were devoted.

By promising on 28 July to settle the vexed question of the oilfields within three months, the President was not only giving proof of his nationalistic and progressive views, but might hope to derive a double advantage from the difficult task he had set himself. There was always a chance that the I.P.C. might agree to some concession in order to clear its accounts and restore good relations; and if the President succeeded in asserting the claims of national sovereignty against this great foreign concern without provoking retaliation, he could boast that his career as a statesman had got off to a brilliant start.

Land reform

The third main announcement of 28 July was a surprise to no-one: the President undertook to introduce a land reform bill at the earliest possible date. The fortunes of this project are instructive in more ways than one. By tracing in detail the steps as a result of which, after many alterations and amendments, the new measure was endorsed by Congress and finally enacted by the President, we shall obtain valuable insight into the processes of Peruvian government. In addition, by comparing the programmes of the various parties with the parliamentary formulation of their proposals, we shall be able to judge whether Belaúnde's watchword of 'renewal' is any more than an empty phrase, and whether the 'opening to the left' which was demanded with such insistence by opponents of the *convivencia* represents a workable policy.

Land reform had been a subject of widespread agreement for some years: not precisely a consensus, but what might be called (cf. p. 342 below) a quasi- or pseudo-consensus. Before 1956, talk of land reform was a badge of radicalism. José Carlos Mariátegui[1] had

[1] In *Siete ensayos de interpretación de la realidad peruana.*

declared that the redistribution of property was a prior condition of solving the Indian problem, and Apra in its early stages had taken up a very similar position. The fact that Manuel Prado, immediately after his election in 1956, set up a 'land reform and housing commission' under Pedro Beltrán signified that the taboo on the land question had been lifted. There are a number of reasons why it should have become respectable about this date. Firstly, the conventional picture of Indian society had changed. For a long time, the fashion among conservatives and radicals alike was to imagine it as an historical relic, preserving its ancient virtues in a kind of petrified state.[1] But the time had come to recognise that, on the contrary, the Indian communities were on the point of disruption. The proliferation of tiny holdings, soil erosion and antiquated methods of cultivation put the Indians at the mercy of drought and famine and drove them to abandon their lands. The results could be seen at Lima: from the early 1950s onwards, the capital was surrounded by a zone of *barriadas*. The newcomers had to be given lodging, jobs and food. The rise in prices and drop in the output of foodstuffs was reflected in growing imports of meat and cereals.

Once the need for reform was admitted, the question was how to compensate expropriated landowners. In the conservative view, all compensation should take the form of a cash indemnity (*pago en efectivo*). Issuing bonds in profusion, as the bolder reformers suggested, would merely cause inflation, and the landowner would thus be robbed and defrauded. However, the bill introduced by Pedro Beltrán as Prime Minister contained an important concession to the radicals: if the expropriated land was valued by experts, after due consultation with the owners, at over 200,000 soles, 80 per cent of the excess amount would be reimbursed in five-year bonds, each annual instalment being not less than 20,000 soles. Thus, the principle of payment in bonds was admitted, although only to a limited extent, and that under the bourgeois auspices of Sr. Beltrán. The commission which reported under his premiership on 21 September 1960 took care to explain that:

'The reform will involve a considerable financial effort... A practical programme would require annual payments at the rate of not less than 3 per cent of the state budget... In 1961 this would involve spending 300 million soles on land reform ... making possible the annual expropriation of 5,000 hectares of tillable land on

[1] For example, in *Broad and Alien is the World*.

the coast and 30,000 in the sierra, plus 300,000 hectares of pasture-land in the latter region, at a total cost of 190 million soles. In addition, 30 million soles must be allowed for the improvement of the soil and habitation, another 30 million for technical aid to the peasants, and 50 million for increased finance and credit facilities for medium and small holders.'[1]

In August 1963, when President Belaúnde laid his own plan before Congress, *La Prensa*, which had featured the warnings and criticisms of the Sociedad Nacional Agraria in its columns, devoted a series of ten leading articles to the proposed reform.[2] 'The success of the plan in no way depends on the government's intentions, good though they may be. In this case, as in many others, hell is paved with good intentions. What we must do is to consider coolly and without panic what solutions are best from the technical point of view and what methods are most likely to bring about the desired advantages.'[3]

The operative word here is 'technical'. Social objectives must, of course, not be lost sight of, 'but the reform would not help to achieve these if the peasant, although he owned his land, went on living in the same type of hovel, raising the same miserable crops and using the same wooden plough as his forefathers did centuries ago'. But this self-defeating result was inevitable if the reform was carried out in a spirit of improvisation and demagogy. No serious reform was possible without a cadastral survey and the 'apportionment to settlers of lots appropriate in size and quality to the situation of each family'. The farmer must also have a decent house to live in, and how was this possible without government aid? Moreover, he should receive

---

[1] Pp. 111–12 of the Commission's report.
[2] Cf. also *La Prensa*'s leading article of 15 July 1962 entitled 'A genuine land reform'. 'We are confronted by three main problems: the maldistribution of land, low output and a scarcity of tillable soil. As a result, a large part of our population lives at subsistence level and the market for manufactured products is small, which makes industrialisation very difficult.' No-one denies these facts; but unfortunately 'many of those, including educated persons, who rightly proclaim the need for land reform indulge in extravagant ideas based on those of "reformers" who have led their countries to the brink of disaster'. The worst 'extravagance' is to think only in terms of expropriation and partition. Experiments in this direction are doomed to failure unless they are 'preceded by the establishment of a system for providing credit at low interest – an enormous and costly enterprise; they also require an advanced level of technical aid, and the adoption of fair and reasonable criteria for parcellation'. Land reform is necessary, but its first objective must be 'to increase production and improve efficiency': it must not 'destroy the climate of confidence and thus drive away the capital which we need in order to transform the country'.
[3] *La Prensa*, 13 August 1963.

327

technical training and concentrate on the raising of crops judged by agronomists to be most suitable for the area in which his land was situated. For this purpose inexperienced farmers should be settled where they could receive advice from those more highly trained; and they would need advances until such time as the new crops could be harvested.[1] All this meant a heavy outlay in terms of skilled personnel, credits and materials; but it was necessary lest, in the pursuit of justice, the wider aim of improving the peasants' welfare should be lost sight of. Such a costly reform could not be improvised. 'Surely we are not going to proceed in a slapdash manner (*a la criolla*)? We have seen fearful examples of heedlessness, squandering and time-wasting. . . If it is dangerous to improvise when planning the course of a road or carrying out some small public works (*obra*), how much more dangerous would it be . . . in the case of land reform.' Most of those who were clamouring for reform were impatient and ignorant; after all that had been written and spoken on the subject of the need for planning and co-ordination, was the country to jettison these wise principles at the first opportunity of putting them into practice?[2]

As for the extreme left, dreaming of wholesale expropriations and looking forward hopefully to the confiscation of the coastal haciendas, its policy was to deny the ex-landowners any compensation save in the form of long-term, low-interest bonds which should be strictly non-transferable. These views were expressed in emphatic terms by *Obrero y campesino* in November 1960,[3] in an article on the Beltrán proposals. These were a farce, a conjuring trick (*escamoteo*) and a put-up job by the *latifundistas*. To be genuine, a reform should satisfy four principles. The latifundia should be confiscated, the coastal haciendas being put under state management (*estatización*) and the big estates of the interior divided up among the peasants. Thirdly, the Indian communities should be turned into co-operatives. (Thus the large unproductive estates of the interior would be turned over to the Indians until such time, no doubt, as the revolutionary government was ready to take them over, whereas the cotton and sugarcane plantations would be brought under state control.)[4] The fourth principle laid down that all land belonged to the state.

Belaúnde sought to occupy a central position between these two extremes, neither disappointing his progressive followers nor alarm-

[1] Ibid., 18 August 1963. [2] Ibid., 23 August 1963.
[3] Reprinted in *La Revolución peruana*, pp. 76–90.
[4] Note the different treatment envisaged for the inland latifundia and the coastal plantations.

ing the conservatives whom he had brought on to his side. The First Vice-President of the Republic in June 1963 was an engineer named Edgardo Seoane Corrales, who had been a member of the Beltrán commission: he was the brother of the Aprista leader Manuel Seoane and had joined Belaúnde at an early stage. At the time of the commission's report he had expressed certain reservations, less of a technical than of a social character. In his own words, he objected that his colleagues had not taken sufficient account of the position of workers on the land, that they 'had not given legal force to the principle of a fair wage based on family needs, the labourers' right to form unions and to share in the capital and management of agricultural enterprises – all of which rights are in full accord with the social doctrine of the Catholic church'. Thus Edgardo Seoane opposed the sacred and indefeasible rights of the worker and his family to the 'productivist' viewpoint of Pedro Beltrán, concerned for his part to avoid infringing the landowner's rights and to limit the inflationary effects of the transfer of property. The representative of Belaundism gave priority to social over economic arguments,[1] whereas in Beltrán's view it was only common-sense to produce wealth before considering how to distribute it. Seoane's concern for social justice also led him to support a church-sponsored plan for 'management reform' which later figured in the Christian Democratic programme.

Seoane's views were indeed some way ahead of those of his party as a whole. Belaúnde was careful to keep his distance from the conservatives, but he did not intend to be classed with the left wing either. The paragraph on land reform in his 1962 election manifesto was very cautiously worded. 'We intend to work out a scheme of land reform embodying technical and regional criteria so as to give priority to areas in which feudal forms of tenure, cultivation and production are still prevalent. The essential features of this reform, which should raise production and improve the peasants' standard of

---

[1] In *Surcos de Paz*, published in 1963, Seoane begins by acknowledging that 'the big sugar, cotton and rice plantations and stockbreeding estates have reached a high degree of efficiency thanks to good organisation, reinvestment and constant modernisation. . . . They have made a contribution to our material progress.' (Pp. 97–8.) But after this praise comes criticism. 'Their bad points are . . . their excessive size; the unduly low level of wages . . .; their excessive influence on the life of the surrounding areas . . .; the obstacles they place in the way of the trade union movement . . . and above all the fact that these great enterprises occupy a large part of the best lands and keep whole sections of the population in a state of dependence' (p. 99). The best remedy would be for wage-earners to share in the profits (20 per cent of the latter being reserved for the owners) and also in management (pp. 99–100).

living, will be the transfer of land ownership, the resettlement of the peasantry and the introduction of legal regulations governing the use of water and irrigation.' The document went on to emphasise the need for 'technical' reform and to indicate that expropriation might take place on a gradual and 'regional' basis–this to reassure the powerful landowners of the coastal area. The manifesto thus combined two objects: the economic need to increase production and the social and humanitarian one of raising the peasants' standard of living. It was cautious as regards methods of expropriation, and indeed avoided this term altogether, replacing it by the more soothing one of 'redistribution'. In 1963, Acción Popular and the Christian Democrats issued a joint manifesto which spoke of 'structural changes', . . . a thorough, democratic and constructive reform *which will not reduce output*[1] but will reintroduce a system of freedom and guarantees'.[2] This reform is to proceed '*in stages, area by area* . . . starting with those where the problem is most acute, or tackling simultaneously two areas of different character'. The implication appears to be that the sierra will receive priority but that the coastal area will not necessarily be exempt, though the measures adopted there may be different.

Apra's programme showed the same judicious flexibility. In a pamphlet published in 1960 by the party's department for rural and Indian affairs, Rómulo Meneses stated that:

'Peru needs not one, but a whole variety of land reforms for different regions and according to differences of social structure . . . We cannot apply the same rules to workers on the great industrialised coastal plantations and to the nomadic Amazonian tribes. Land reform means one thing on the coast, another in the sierra and another still in the Amazon region. . . Of course, in all three cases what we are aiming at is the transformation of basic economic and social factors: land, labour, capital and agricultural methods. But each region needs a different plan, different measures and a different timetable.'

The suggested regionalisation of land reform points the way to an eventual compromise. The Lima oligarchy draws the bulk of its wealth from coastal agriculture, and does not much care what happens on the remote haciendas of Abancay, Ayacucho or even Cuzco and Puno. Apart from a few cattle-breeding ranches, these estates of huge size but low output belong to families whose local

[1] Author's italics. F.B.   [2] Manifesto, p. 28.

330

position is more or less assured but who have little influence at Lima, where the gentry are not disposed to take up the cudgels for the up-country *gamonales*. Apart from stockbreeding. the sierra is of interest to the oligarchy only for its mines. No doubt it is a pity that the latifundia should be broken up–'but, after all, between you and me, it is no more than the backward *hacendados* deserve.'[1]

However, while accepting the Beltrán commission's concept of a 'technical' and 'regionalised' reform with emphasis on maintaining productivity, Apra took a strong line over the problem of *yanaconaje*, the form of sharecropping discussed in an earlier chapter. The party denounced this as a system of servitude (*servidumbre*) and demanded that it should either be abolished or that the tenant should be protected by strong guarantees. The Apra programme of 1962 spoke of 'regulating the contracts between landowners and *yanaconas* and making the state a party to them'. The defence of the *yanaconas* played the same part in the Apra programme as management reform and profit-sharing did in Belaúnde's: viz. to make a show of radicalism which satisfied their more advanced supporters.

A basis for agreement between the government and opposition parties, and between them and the landowners, might be said to exist, at all events in theory. Land must be found for the sierra Indians who were suffocating in their communities, but the export agriculture of the coast must on no account be ruined. The latifundia must be broken up, but without spoliation and without issuing bonds on a scale which would bring about inflation. The Apristas and Belaundists could agree on such principles, and Pedro Beltrán himself, while not letting slip the opportunity to recall the eternal truths of creole liberalism–before we can distribute we must produce, and in our zeal for justice, however praiseworthy, we must not forget the inescapable laws of economy–had made up his mind not to oppose a reform which he had long seen to be inevitable and which did not endanger the coastal oligarchy.

But, when it came to putting the quasi-consensus into practice, various difficulties arose. The Apristas and Belaundists, whose agreement was a precondition, were rivals on this question as on others: each of them sought to present the promised law as the fruit of its own initiative and energy, and saw no reason to share the credit

[1] When I mentioned to a former prime minister the likelihood that reform would be carried out primarily at the expense of the up-country landowners, this astute man replied drily: 'It often happens that the innocent pay for the guilty, and it is not always a bad thing.'

with its adversary. Secondly, adherents of the status quo would be certain to raise the cry of communism and the rights of property. Finally, the extent of the common ground on which agreement might be reached was such that a 'reasonable' measure based on it was not likely to afford much kudos to the sponsoring party. The Belaundist left wing, some Christian Democrats and of course the extreme left parties would cry out that the cause had been betrayed. For all these reasons, land reform might have remained a pious hope for some time if a new factor had not supervened. At the beginning of August 1963 an outburst of 'invasions' by squatters took place in the central departments, whence they spread to Cuzco. By the end of the year the whole southern part of the country was affected, though apart from a few incidents the coastal haciendas remained immune.

The 'spontaneous anarchy' which had gained ground in the south was brought under control with fair success by the police, the army playing a quite minor role. Conditions became gradually steadier during the early months of 1964, as the landowners organised to meet the threat. The authorities were helped by the fact that the movement was almost purely a rural one. True, the textile workers of Cuzco had long since developed a radical political consciousness; but the traders and shopkeepers of *mestizo* communities looked askance at the organised peasants who demanded that they should put up their shutters in protest against some grievance or other and should make common cause with those whose slogan was 'land or death'. On 18 January 1964, the leaders of peasant unions who had called for a general strike at Quillabamba, capital of the province of La Convención, met with the passive resistance of the townsfolk. 'The small-scale traders of Quillabamba distrusted the peasant unions and were not disposed to join in their quarrels with the landowners or with the authorities.'[1] As Hugo Neira relates, a scuffle took place between the inhabitants of the township and demonstrators from the surrounding countryside, and as a result of this clash, the first of its kind, the peasants withdrew to their homes, leaving some wounded.

Differences in local conditions also prevented the movement from assuming a uniform character. Even at Puno, 'the home of absentee landlordism . . . where a mass invasion of half-abandoned estates appears to be in the offing',[2] it disintegrated into a series of small-scale, uncoordinated operations. The leaders themselves were often divided in their affiliations and loyalties. What appeared to *La Prensa*

[1] Hugo Neira, *Cuzco: tierra y muerte*, p. 31. [2] Ibid., p. 61.

as a rebellion fomented by international communism was in reality much more complex. The orthodox communists did not have the field to themselves, and in any case they displayed moderation. When Huamantica, the leader of the Cuzco communists, was killed in an accident in February 1963, the head of the textile firm where he had been employed told Neira that he had always thought him a 'very decent fellow' and a 'sensible leader'. Neira, in reporting this, adds that 'when the masses took over at Cuzco in 1955, it was Huamantica who saved the commanding general from being lynched. He was clever enough to steer a course between order and disorder, the state and the revolution... He may have saved the Indians armed with slings from being mown down by the army's machine-guns. What his secret was, he has not told us, but perhaps it was simply the patience of the good Indian.'[1] Huamantica has many heirs, but though they are all revolutionaries they are also rivals: Trotskyists, Castroists and radicals of all kinds invoke his name but act as they each see fit. This, however, does not lead to an all-out struggle but to a sharing of zones of interest. 'Who has reaped the harvest sown by Huamantica: in other words, who is the leader of the Cuzco revolt? No one person can be so described. Those who made speeches at the dead man's funeral did their best to smooth over the differences between Trotskyists and Castroists, orthodox communists and those outside the party...'

How did President Belaúnde deal with the crisis provoked by the squatters? The Prime Minister and Minister of the Interior, Dr. Oscar Trelles, tried to belittle the affair at first: in August and September 1963 he crossed swords several times with *La Prensa* as to the reality of the invasions to which the paper was giving front-page prominence. The Minister of Agriculture, for his part, described the situation as 'fluid' and predicted that the wave of invasions would recede. But could the government afford to wait for this? The landowners were demanding that their rights be defended; but if the government answered their appeal, matters might end in slaughter. Nothing would be more disastrous for the President than to begin his term of office 'with blood on his hands'.

In November and December, at the height of the agitation, Dr. Trelles continued untiringly to reply to the opposition's taunts of weakness: 'Do you want me to order the troops to open fire?' This

[1] Ibid., p. 16.

argument lost its force by dint of repetition, and at the end of December a hard-fought debate resulted in a vote of no confidence in the Prime Minister. The President appointed a successor to Trelles as Prime Minister and another as Minister of the Interior, who soon established himself as a strong man. By April 1964, order was more or less restored.

It remained to be seen whether the squatters' crisis and the way, or rather ways, in which the President and his successive ministers had handled it would hasten or retard the adoption of the land reform measures which had been promised on 28 July 1963. The incidents at Cuzco, Quillabamba and Sicuani were cited by the opposition as proof that the government's indulgence towards 'agitators' was exposing the country to the risk of an upheaval. But, while some accused the President and his party of having provoked agrarian unrest by their light-hearted promises, no-one dared to go back on the principle of land reform. As to the means of coping with the disorders, there was a difference of opinion among the governing class. Those who held that the agitation was a product of international communist subversion were dubious of the possibility of containing it by a few, albeit violent, police actions. Strong measures were advocated by some, especially victims of the 'invasions'. Other landowners in the south assured Neira that all that was needed was to clap a few hotheads into gaol.[1] One, of European origin ('perhaps a Yugoslav or Rumanian'), believed in 'powder and shot' (*meter bala*) and declared that 'the peasants' claims are all nonsense, something they've been put up to by the communists. All the talk of famine is so much eyewash – stories made up to bamboozle soft-hearted people by the Indians and their backers, the little half-caste intellectuals who pick up silly ideas at the university.'[2]

This type of argument was not far from *La Prensa*'s position. But neither Sr. Beltrán's paper, nor the Sicuani rancher who has just been quoted, nor his colleagues in Puno could make headway against the conviction which *Expreso*, then close to the Belaundist camp, voiced in a leading article on 6 March 1962[3]: 'Let the killing stop! . . . We believe that with Christian charity, a cool head and the use of modern techniques it must be possible to solve these problems, with difficulty no doubt, but without bloodshed.' The writer of this article contended that no policy could be justified if it involved violent action by

---

[1] Ibid., p. 78.　　　　　　　　　[2] Ibid., pp. 78–9.
[3] On the occasion of an *invasión* in the central region.

the government. 'The *comuneros* may be in the wrong, their methods may be culpable and illegal; it may also be that their understandable desire to possess the land ... is perverted by hidden mischief-makers. But even if this were so, we have no right to punish them for resorting to force in return for centuries of neglect. Property must be respected, but so, above all, must life.' And the article repeated in conclusion: 'Let the killing stop!'

The government's July proposals had a bad reception from the conservatives. All holdings without exception were subject to *afectación*, i.e. to expropriation for land reform purposes. However, the practical application of this principle varied from one type of holding to another. In the case of land cultivated by renters and share-croppers, including *yanaconas*, the law was to be applied in a radical fashion, by total expropriation. Owners who cultivated their lands might be allowed to keep part of them, the area differing according to the locality and to whether the lands were irrigated. Finally, large estates might be exempted from *afectación*, not as of right but by a decision of the projected Land Reform Institute: this privilege could not be enjoyed by any agricultural enterprise, however efficient, which did not agree to adopt profit-sharing on the lines advocated by Edgardo Seoane. Compensation was to take the form of bonds, not cash. A Land Reform Institute was to be set up under the President's direct control–thus escaping parliamentary supervision, as the President's acts can only be debated in Congress if they are countersigned by a Minister–for the purpose of designating the holdings to be expropriated in whole or in part, and the beneficiaries of such expropriation.

The proposed measures were attacked by the Sociedad Nacional Agraria, which, while admitting the necessity for reform, subjected the government's plan to stringent criticism. The S.N.A. had as its mouthpiece a first-class review, *La Vida agrícola*, and its senior officials had ample means of knowing what was going on in political and administrative circles. During Manuel Prado's presidency it had skilfully defended the interests of coastal agriculture and had been the means whereby the cotton and sugarcane magnates drew attention to their export difficulties. In 1959 the Sociedad protested at the subsidies paid to U.S. cotton exporters, and at the time of the Cuban crisis it used its influence with Sr. Hernando Berckemeyer, the Peruvian ambassador at Washington and a representative of big business interests, to persuade the U.S. Congress to increase Peru's sugar quota. In the fiscal domain, it devoted its efforts to combating the regulation which required exporters to pay tax in anticipation of profits. When Pedro Beltrán put up the price of guano in 1959 the S.N.A., always ready to claim due credit for its members, argued that the subsidy which had till then kept the price at a very low level was a meagre compensation for the services rendered to the national economy by the exporters of agricultural primary products.

It remained to be seen whether, in 1963, the S.N.A. would defend its members' interests as skilfully, not just over a precise and limited issue but in regard to far-reaching measures whose consequences were difficult to foresee. It began by directing its fire against certain well-chosen objectives, in particular the principle of universal liability to expropriation. In a statement issued on 1 September, the Sociedad emphasised that the threat of confiscation applied to all estates without exception:

'even if the land is well cultivated with modern machinery and yields an excellent crop; even if the employees are well paid, the unions flourish and stand up for their rights, and the workers enjoy social benefits such as housing, schools and hospitals. . . Where is the sense in applying the same yardstick to every hacienda in the country, whether it be big, medium or small, well or badly managed, on the coast, in the sierra or the Amazon area? The threat of whole-sale expropriation will produce the worst possible consequences: agricultural investment will be paralysed, food and export production will drop, the cost of living will soar and dollar reserves will dwindle.'

The S.N.A. also denounced the 'excessive powers' which, under the government's plan, would be enjoyed by

'the bureaucratic organs charged with carrying out the reform. It will be within their power to increase the public debt indefinitely by issuing bonds to conceal the fact of confiscation; to control sources of irrigation . . . and all forms of agricultural credit; to decide which parts of any given estate shall be expropriated, without the owner having any right of appeal to the courts except in regard to the assessed value; to designate at their own pleasure the persons to whom expropriated land shall be assigned . . . to decide in what way estates shall be divided and what area shall be allocated to the new owners' families . . . to regroup expropriated lands, even against the wishes of smallholders and of the new owners.'

All these rights, the statement emphasised, 'are to be exercised by bodies which are not subject to the political control of Congress'. However, as regards the method of compensation, the Society was careful not to attack the principle of a bond issue: unlike their counterparts in Chile or Brazil, the Peruvian landowners did not stand out for prior indemnification or contest the legality of deferred payment. The S.N.A. confined itself to arguing that the redemption period was too long, that the rate of interest was not high enough to compensate for monetary depreciation and that by leaving the Institute free to issue as many bonds as it thought fit, the government was rashly entrusting to it the future of the national debt.

Was there room for compromise between the Society's position and that of the government? Reading the replies put out by the Ministry of Agriculture, particularly on 1 September, one has the impression of a deadlock. The S.N.A. was concerned that the conditions of expropriation should be as narrowly defined as possible, and above all not left to the Institute's discretion. The government, for its part, wished to keep a free hand and insisted that the liability to expropriation should be universal. Even if such powers were placed in its hands, the Institute would of course not expropriate every estate in the country; but the Ministry was determined not to let its style be cramped by vested interests, for example in the matter of irrigation.

How could negotiations be got under way between the S.N.A., which was prepared to compromise but not to suggest terms, and the government, which would have given much to be rid, without bloodshed, of the 'invasion' nightmare, but which, while hankering after a radical reform, knew that the wholesale expropriation of the great coastal estates was likely to spell economic and political disaster? The two parties needed a mediator, or at least a go-between; and, paradoxically, this role was performed by the opposition. The Apristas, who together with their new allies of General Odría's party formed a majority in Congress, put forward a plan whose basic structure was easy to grasp. The position of the Aprista group in the Senate, led by Luis Heysen, was expounded in the review *Presente* for May 1964, which discussed whether the sugarcane estates of La Libertad and Lambayeque should be expropriated in whole or in part. The article declared strongly against what it called 'pulverisation'. In Apra's view, it would be a calamity to break up these production centres, which were 'noted for their output and technical efficiency', and the proposal to do so was a communist plot. If it succeeded, the communists would kill two birds with one stone. Politically, as the estates in question were 'in the north, where the Apra vote is strong, their disintegration would break the back of the trade unions which, in that part of the country, are largely Apra-controlled'. From the economic point of view, 'the break-up of these highly industrialised concerns would lead to mass dismissals and the labourers would have to seek work elsewhere, while their families would suffer the consequences of increasing unemployment. Instead of being an area where people worked hard and strove for a chance to work harder, the north would become a hotbed of political and social agitation.'

Whatever the precise scope of Apra's objections, it was clear that the party was resolved to save the sugarcane industry. The argument adopted for this purpose, and reflected in Article 38 of the proposals adopted by Congress, was that the sugar estates were not exclusively or even primarily agricultural, but belonged to the category of 'enterprises for the *industrial processing*[1] of products of the soil'. These enterprises were granted 'exceptional treatment involving the exemption from expropriation of such lands as they required for the efficient working of their industrial processing equipment'. The sugar-cane estates having thus been afforded a loophole of escape from expropriation, the next step was to protect them from the hazards of management reform, whereby, according to Vice-President Seoane's views, wage-earners were to be given a share in running the estates. The Apristas maintained that it would be arbitrary to apply this principle to agricultural industries alone, and that problems of management reform should be the subject of separate and general proposals to be introduced later.

Meanwhile, Apra put forward two other interesting compromises or modifications of the government's plan. The proposed Land Reform Institute, it will be recalled, had been denounced as a sort of bureaucratic Leviathan; in the law as passed by Congress, the monster was tamed. Firstly, it was not placed directly under the President's control but under that of the Minister of Agriculture, who was constitutionally responsible to Congress. Secondly, it was to be assisted (Article 195) by a National Agrarian Council (Consejo Nacional Agrario) of which the Minister of Agriculture was chairman but on which the executive power was heavily outnumbered by

[1] Author's italics. F.B.

representatives of agricultural interests and trade unions. Each House of Congress contributed a non-voting member to this body, which, in addition to long-term planning and research functions of a general kind, was responsible for drafting the decrees and regulations whereby the land reform was applied in particular cases. It was also empowered (Article 197, paragraph 5) to decide in which parts of the country the reform should be put into effect, and to 'study and approve suitable plans and measures, and the ways and means of financing them'.

The National Council was in turn flanked by two other bodies. The first, which was purely technical and advisory, was the Technical Council of Land Reform and Development (Consejo Técnico de Reforma y Promoción Agraria), which seems to have been intended as a compensation to those bodies (twenty-six of which are enumerated in Article 209) which were not represented on the National Council. The other body, the Land Reform Finance Corporation (Corporación Financiera de la Reforma Agraria, Article 215), possessed very wide powers. Its chairman was the Minister of Finance and its members included one representative each of the Ministry of Agriculture, the National Council, the Planning Commission and the two semi-public banks, the Banco Industrial and the Banco de Fomento Agropecuario, plus three representatives of bond-holders of the agrarian debt. The Corporation's assets consisted of such public property or funds as the state might place at its disposal (Article 207, paragraph 1), together with 'lands expropriated under the present law and the annual instalments, with interest thereon, paid to it by the purchasers of expropriated land and beneficiaries of the land reform'. Over a period of twenty years, 3 per cent of the state budget was allocated to the Corporation, which was expressly authorised (Article 207, sub-paragraphs (a) et seq.) to carry out all internal and external credit operations necessary for the performance of its functions. The Corporation, and not the government as provided in the bill of July 1963, was empowered to fix the total value of agrarian debt bonds and thus control the rate of expropriation. These bonds could, moreover, be presented to a Special Industrial Investments Fund (Fondo Especial de Inversiones Industriales), which would grant credit to the holders for projects approved by the Banco Industrial (Article 224). This provision served both to ensure that capital invested in agriculture was re-employed in industry, and to enable the Banco Industrial indirectly to limit the issue of agrarian debt bonds.

The Rules of the Game

As we have seen, the Apristas insisted throughout on the need for reform to be carried out on a regional basis, and on this point they were in accord with the Sociedad Nacional Agraria. Nevertheless, Article 7 of the law as voted by Congress on 15 May 1964 embodied the principle of universal *afectibilidad* in emphatic terms.[1] However, an order of priority was laid down in Articles 48, 49 and 50; and the Institute, acting with the approval of the National Council, was instructed (Article 50, paragraphs (a) to (d)) to devote its attention first to 'areas where demographic pressure is especially strong, landownership is in too few hands and labour relations are of the feudal type; or where wage levels are notoriously too low for the elementary needs of sustenance, housing and education'.

The terms of redemption provided for by the law were also such as to render the expropriation of valuable lands more difficult. Landowners were to be indemnified by means of three classes of transferable and negotiable bonds, A, B and C.[2] Class A bonds were redeemable in 18 years and bore interest at 6 per cent; for class B, the figures were 20 years and 5 per cent, and for class C, 22 years and 4 per cent.[3] Moreover, according to differences of location, types of crop and efficiency of cultivation, a certain number of estates were *inafectable* (Articles 22–37). Compared with the government's initial proposal, the law as approved by Congress raised the ceiling of such exemptions and widened the grounds on which they could be claimed.

In other respects also, the law showed a cautious approach. On particularly sensitive points such as irrigation, it sought to achieve a compromise acceptable to all parties (Articles 109–26). As regards rent and hiring agreements it took up a more radical position, aimed

[1] 'All real estate, by whomever owned and *wherever situated on the national territory*, is subject to the land reform law.' Article 8 defines *afectación* as a 'limitation of property rights applying, for purposes of land reform, to the whole or part of a domain and entailing its expropriation by the state and subsequent assignment to peasants who satisfy the conditions and qualifications specified in this law'. The grounds for *afectación* are defined in Article 15: 'Improper use of land; antisocial or feudal conditions of employment; the concentration of land in a few hands, stifling the development of medium and small holdings, or alternatively excessive fragmentation, involving the destruction of natural resources and the inefficient use of factors of production.' (Author's italics. – F.B.)

[2] A very small number of landowners were to be immediately compensated in cash. However, livestock and fixed equipment were to be fully paid for in cash.

[3] The interest is tax-free, which, as prices have hitherto risen only slightly, signifies a real though limited return on capital. The same sums invested in mortgage bonds would, however, fetch about 15 per cent. The measure proposed by Apra in August 1963 had envisaged a faster rate for the three categories of 10, 15 and 20 years respectively.

at doing away with 'antisocial methods of employing labour and of renting land on condition that the tenant performs personal services, even if these are remunerated on a cash basis' (Article 237). But the general effect of the law was to safeguard modern, industrialised agriculture and bring reform to bear principally on backward areas. The Sociedad Nacional Agraria was broadly satisfied, and on the day after the law was passed by Congress *La Prensa* emphasised that it was 'not the plan of a single party, group or sector, but an efficient and well-adjusted instrument, in which we may have confidence since it results from an all-round attempt at mutual understanding.'

It remained to be seen what view the executive would take of Congress's proposals. Vice-President Seoane had made no secret of his suspicion and hostility: like many Christian Democrats, he regarded the present scheme as a pseudo-reform, a dodge to enable the coastal oligarchy to hold on to its own. But the President took a kindlier view. On the occasion of the appointment of a new Minister of Public Works (his predecessor having been the object of a vote of censure), Sr. Belaúnde made a point of stating that the executive 'desired to show respect towards Congress even when it was not in agreement with it'. On 21 May he approved the bill as voted by Congress, and in a speech at Cuzco shortly afterwards he declared that 'with all its limitations, the law marks a definite step towards reform'.

Sceptics might wonder whether the law would be seriously applied; realists were more preoccupied by the conditions on which its success depended, and which may be reduced to three heads. Firstly, was the Institute's share of the state budget adequate, and how would the agrarian debt be administered? Two risks were discernible here. Over-caution might reduce expropriations to zero, with the Institute confining itself to intervening after the event in cases of 'invasion'. From this point of view, cynics saw the law as a system of insurance for estate owners whose lands were, or looked like being, invaded. But if the Institute only stepped in after the squatters had taken over, was it not putting a premium on violence? If, at the opposite extreme, the Institute launched into a full-scale expropriation programme, neither the budget nor public credit nor the currency would stand it. Nor were the limitations on reform purely financial and economic. Besides money, the Institute needed agronomists, agricultural instructors and experts to assess the value of expropriated lands. Were

341

all these specialists available in sufficient numbers? Last but not least, would the peasants, for whose sake the reform was enacted, have the patience to endure delays, and the skill to extract a less wretched living from their new lands? Here again there were two difficulties. Firstly, the recipients of land had to repay its value to the Institute. Article 100 laid down easy terms for this: repayment was to take place in twenty annual instalments, and the Institute had power to remit up to five of these and to fix the rate of interest on each. Nevertheless, repayment was bound to present difficulty; and what would be the effect of transfers of ownership on agrarian production? Sugar and even cotton exports would probably not suffer greatly, since the coast was unlikely to be much affected by the reform; but what of food production with its effect on urban standards of living?

Such difficulties are evident, but cannot be called insurmountable: as of late 1964, the catastrophe so often predicted did not appear inevitable. I shall not attempt here to prophesy the outcome of the reform; but a word or two may be in order to explain the sense in which I have used such terms as 'quasi-' and 'pseudo-consensus'. During the long pre-history of the measure which was finally adopted in 1964, there was a point of time at which land reform became, in the narrower sense, a political question. For decades previously, and indeed throughout the nineteenth century, men had deplored the wretched condition of the Indians and the low productivity of up-country agriculture. But reform did not become a political issue, as opposed to a question of philanthropy or a problem for agronomists, until José Carlos Mariátegui made it the war-cry of the left wing and the indigenists. In his day, it was a shibboleth dividing radicals from conservatives. Then it ceased to be a symbol of division and became common ground. 'Something must be done'; but what? The consensus was a broad one, embracing indeed almost everybody, but it was also weak and confused. The sincerest advocates of reform held violently opposed views as to its methods and scope, and, as they all suspected one another's intentions, none of them was willing to commit himself whole-heartedly to any specific plan.

Nevertheless, as we have seen, a law was finally passed which will, in all probability, take effect in some degree and will, for good or evil, accelerate the process of social mobilisation. For this to happen, several conditions had to be fulfilled. Objective pressure took the form of squatters' invasions, and a policy of all-out repression was from the start unlikely in view of the current of liberal opinion in parliament, in the press and in bishops' pastorals, as well as the reluctance of the military to use their strength to put down the peasants. As a result, an ingenious compromise was finally worked out and was wisely accepted by the President after his government's proposals had been rejected by Congress as well as by the Sociedad Nacional Agraria. The law of 1964 has not solved the agrarian problem, but it has cleared the way for a change to which even conservatives are becoming resigned, though they seek to limit its scope and shift the main burden of its cost on to the shoulders of others.

CONCLUSION

'Eppur si muove'

The Peruvian regime may be seen in terms of a highly abstract opposition between the oligarchy and the masses: on the one hand a few families who decide everything in their own interests, on the other a destitute people. Any such dualistic theory is *ex hypothesi* an extreme one, postulating as it does two poles which are at once positive and negative. The oligarchy is apparently all-powerful but in reality impotent, and the converse is true of the people. As the process of social mobilisation develops, the initial dualism gradually breaks down. The masses become differentiated and, above all, organised. They cease to be content with a passive role in society, and assert themselves either by fits and starts or in a more sustained fashion, e.g. as a result of education.

This, it may be said, is all the more reason to expect an early collision between the masses and the selfish, oppressive élite. But the difficulty with this view is that Peruvian society is no longer dualistic in any strict sense. The oligarchy is undergoing a process of change. As we have seen, it can be subdivided into several groups: the up-country *gamonal* is a very different person from the coastal estate-owner, who puts his money to work in land or financial speculations. The traditional oligarchy, whose wealth comes from sugar, cotton or the sale of metals in New York, London or Hamburg, regards with suspicion the newly-rich with their hazardous plans for rapid industrialisation. It may be answered that these groups, however disparate, are linked by a common interest in maintaining the status quo; but the debates on land reform have shown us that the coastal oligarchy is prepared to compromise, especially if the up-country latifundia are to be the first targets for expropriation.

Those who judge politics in terms of the interplay of conflicting

344

interests are committed to the risky assumption that those interests are politically organised. No doubt the Peruvian oligarchy, to judge by the statements of such bodies as the Lima Chamber of Commerce or the Sociedad Nacional Agraria, or of journalists and politicians more or less closely connected with these circles, appears irrevocably attached to the dogmas of free trade. Their narrow but coherent doctrine involves hostility to controls–i.e. any restriction on the movement of goods and capital, a horror of inflation and insistence on a sound currency and a balanced budget. One may of course wonder from time to time how sincerely these principles are really held: the sanctity of the budget receives varying emphasis according to whether those who stand to benefit from its infringement are or are not deemed to belong to the category of '*fuerzas vivas*'. Nevertheless, I am inclined to believe that until recent years the oligarchy took seriously the precepts of creole liberalism, which were admirably suited to its interests. But for how much longer will these interests be interpreted so simply? President Belaúnde's attempt at a 'thaw' is not only of political consequence but may well bring about a change in the oligarchy's notion of economic development. The aim of Belaundism, as I have tried to show, is to restore hope and confidence to the depressed classes and shake the rulers out of their scepticism and cynicism. If the government's programme of building roads and schools and developing the national territory should succeed, thanks to its own merits and to favourable circumstances, in providing work for the outcast without leading to violent inflation and obliging the President to lay impious hands on basic economic freedoms–then it may reasonably be hoped that the oligarchy's view of its interests might be modified and that it might take a more flexible view of the sacred principles of creole liberalism, since it would have been shown that a less orthodox policy could be embarked upon without disaster.

Without regarding such conjectures as of vital importance, I think it is clear that the oligarchy can no longer be looked on as a solid front, since its members differ in their views and attitudes on most questions of the day. Some of them supported *convivencia*, others rallied to Belaúnde's banner and some stood by General Odría. On land reform, very few took up a publicly hostile position: the majority sought to negotiate and manoeuvre. No doubt these differences might be quickly forgotten if the oligarchy ever felt itself directly and violently threatened as a group. But the tendency which seems to stand out in the last few years is the differentiation of the ruling group, which reflects the difficulties of its integration into the national life. Divisions among the oligarchy are indeed no new thing: clan rivalries, which were so prominent during Manuel Prado's second administration, can be paralleled with ease in the backstairs stories of nineteenth-century Peruvian history. But there are two new features. Firstly, the conflicts of rival groups within the oligarchy are no longer a purely private affair but have some significance for the community as a whole: the quarrels of family X and family Y are to some extent 'national' in their scope and content. Secondly, they can no longer be settled, in the old way, between the protagonists alone, with only occasional interference from the mob or the military. The oligarchy is no longer left to its own devices: the 'outsiders' can no longer be kept at arm's length or manipulated like puppets, but have become partners or adversaries in the game.

As the oligarchy has become differentiated, so it has developed a community sense: it has become more dependent on other social groups, and more conscious of that dependence. This process corresponds to the politicisation of the former outsiders, the *olvidados*, who are becoming confusedly aware of their own power and ability to make their voice heard. As a result of this double and symmetrical process. Peruvian society is moving towards a new political 'style'.

The oligarchy's power still rests on extremely strong foundations. The sugar and cotton magnates control a large part of the export trade, and are well entrenched in the prosperous fishing industry. It would be a great mistake to think of them as mere passive drawers of revenue, like the nobles and great landowners of the early nineteenth century of whom Saint-Simon remarked that if they were all to die overnight, no-one would notice the difference. But although the basis of their power remains firm, the conditions of its exercise are increasingly difficult.

It should indeed be noted that even at the height of its power, the oligarchy never succeeded in forming itself into a stable institution. It was, in fact, a collection of oligarchs rather than an oligarchy, still less an aristocracy. But its most striking demonstration of strength was when its preponderance was attacked directly by Apra in the 1930s. On that occasion the ruling group stood their ground and forced their enemy on to the defensive.[1] After keeping him in the 'catacombs' for many years, they finally consented to negotiate, but

---

[1] At that time, of course, agrarian agitation was not such a threat as it has come to be in recent years.

did not give way on any essential point. Among the oligarchy's virtues, as appeared over the question of land reform, is that of knowing when to cut its losses.

But the weakness of the oligarchs is that they have never captured the loyalty of the middle class or the *olvidados*, but are exposed to stubborn resentment on the former's part and uncontrolled violence on the latter's. There is no protective magic which legitimises their power, and the middle class of *mestizos* has found its own identity in opposition to them and to their authority. I am inclined to think that the newcomers in the shanty-towns are less radical than their predecessors, the half-caste graduates, who became prominent in the schoolrooms and campuses of the 1930s. But even though, as in 1962, the inmates of the *barriadas* can be got to vote for a General Odría, their increasing demands for more and more expensive public services (housing, education, health etc.) may in the end present a greater danger to the oligarchy than did the impassioned radicals of earlier decades.

In any case, the appearance on the scene of these masses on which Apra was never able to gain a hold constitutes a new element which may be decisive. In the first place, it does away with the dualistic theory which governed Apra strategy in the 1930s and which still feeds the hopes of Castroist or Maoist revolutionaries. If, as a result of popular action or co-operation, it is possible to awaken, enlist and strengthen energies which are still dormant, and if the more oppressive shackles can be gradually loosened, then a head-on clash with the oligarchy will cease to be the revolutionaries' dream and their opponents' nightmare. Secondly, and in the same line of thought, the centre of gravity of political life has been displaced by the appearance of this host of potential clients, whose presence is an ever more urgent reminder that 'something must be done before it is too late'. Instead of being simply a dialogue between organised interests, politics becomes the art of mobilising scattered and confused energies and turning them to one's own advantage.

This means a radical transformation of the political leader's role. It is no longer merely a question of negotiating as between one power and another or bringing sufficient strength to bear to overcome one's rival–though these abilities still have their use. It is also, and perhaps principally, a matter of recognising aspirations and giving them tangible form, convincing the public that things are moving and that times have changed. The legitimacy of the leader's power resides in

Conclusion

his ability to make things new—whether it be to right ancient wrongs by giving back the land to those who have been robbed of it, or, like the inspired technician in the forests beyond the Andes, to see in his mind's eye the 'marginal highway' which will carry the wealth of an entire continent.

What are the prospects of success in this effort to bypass old enmities and achieve a fresh community of purpose? In my opinion, it is scarcely possible to offer a prediction, since unfortunately the evolution of Peruvian society depends on several sets of data which are both unknown and refractory to human influence. The movement of import and export prices and the international flow of capital are not matters that can be exactly forecast; and there is little point in conjecturing what changes might result for Peruvian politics from the appearance of a new leader of the Castro type in one or another of the Latin American countries. The observer is equally powerless to assess a further point of no less importance: what effect is demographic pressure likely to have on subsistence levels and employment, average productivity and per capita income? Even if we were able to answer all these questions, what could we foretell as regards Peruvian institutions in ten years' time? There is no evidence that I am aware of that would enable us to choose between the views of the pessimists and optimists, including in the second category those who do not believe in the inevitability of an 'explosion'. It has not been the purpose of this work to decide between the prophets of disaster and their adversaries, but rather to discover how competing schemes and plans of action may be tentatively and partially reconciled in the light of their advocates' hopes and fears, memories and disappointments. What the study suggests, at least to my mind, is the need for an apparatus of information and regulation which would help Peruvian society to form a better idea of its own problems, if not actually to solve them.

Index

Acción Popular, 141, 229–58; and land reform, 330
Advanced War Studies Centre (C.A.E.M.), 314
Agricultural dualism (sugar and cotton of coastal valleys, sierra agriculture), 38–9
Alba, Senator Octavio, 49, 51
Alegría, Ciro, *El mundo es ancho y ajeno*, 21–2, 29–31, 34, 37, 78, 89, 90, 148
Allyus, 67
Alsogaray, Sr., 195
Altacongo, 'city of God', 115
Amaru, Túpac, early Peruvian leader, 258
Amauta (journal), 148, 168
Angel, Luis Felipe ('Sofocleto'), 210, 211, 218, 277
Antay, Don Joaquín López, a modern *cholo*, 66
Apra, Apristas, *see also* Haya de la Torre; analysis, by leader, of Peru's problems, 142–7; appeal to: heroism, stoicism, 184–5; scientific data, 147; basic intention 'to Peruvianise Peru', 145; birth of, 140; after 1931, 142 seqq.; main themes of ideology, 142–85; hostility from right and from left, 165–9; attitudes to communism, 168; maximum programme of 173 n.; morale of, 161–2; realism of H. de la Torre, sources of, 169; in 1930s, 160–9; 'catacombs' period of, 158–65, 183–4, 263; and army, 167–9, 262, 297–8; and the conservatives, 165–7, 169; and universities, 63; as intermediaries in industry, 104; objectives after 1956, 184–5; 'Manifesto to the Peruvian Nation', 21 May 1956,
265; claims to be dominant party, 271; 'pact' with Prado, 1956, 268 seqq.; and Acción Popular, 261–2; and the 1962 electoral irregularities, 283; attitudes to Belaúnde, 322, 331; relative failure in June 1962, 294–5; and land reform, 330, 337; and sugar cane industry, 338; calls for constitutional opposition to Junta, 310; membership, organisation, 160–9
Arce, A. Fernandez, on Castro's Cuba, 218
Arequipa, Belaúnde's actions at, 255–7
Arguedas, José María (on *la cultura mestiza*), *Yawar Fiesta*, 31–7, 66 seqq., 239
Army: and Constitution, 283, 314; as judge of nation's interest, 306–7; 1962 *golpe institucional* of, 305 seqq; and Apra, 167, 262, 267–9; and Odria's career, 264; association of, with the electoral process, 283, 296–299; and *desarrollismo* and Nasserism, 313–15; recruitment for, 167
Arrendires defined, 127
Atusparia, Pedro Pablo, rising led by, 90, 132, 157
Ayacucho, 15, 31, 65, 66, 239, 278

Banking: boards of directors, 40–1; and land reform, 239; employees' unions, 104–8
Barriadas, 15, 91–2, 114–23; Andes comuneros settling in, 137; population of not equated with proletariat, 116–17; vote of, important after 1956, 120
Basadre, Jorge, *Historia de la República de Perú*, 138, 139, 140

349

Index

Belaúnde (Fernando Belaúnde Terry):
career of, 231; as Dr. Bustamante
y Rivero's first Prime Minister, 231;
as architect, 231; March 1956 programme of, 232; as leader of forces
opposing Apra-Prado 'pact', 272;
distrusts ideology, 230-1; appeals to
tradition, 54, 239, 241; appeals to
people, 232-3, 238; dash, innovation and caution, 253-4, 255; elements of bluff, 254-5; oligarchy as
bogy of, 245; Presidency of, 56,
141, 181, 186; the 1962 election,
260, 271, 292 seqq.; refuses to regard Presidency as negotiable, 303-
304; 28 July 1963 speech to Congress, 323-4; founds Acción Popular, 235; attitude to some of its
projects, 250-1; attitude to Prado,
235, 272; 'Peru as a doctrine', 231,
237-49; *Pueblo por Pueblo*, 234,
240, 242; attitude to the army, 249,
319-20; in alliance with Christian
Democrats, 320-1; elected to Presidency, 321
Belaúnde, Victor Andrés, 61, 63, 192,
206, 321; as paternalist, 206;
Arequipa de mi infancia, 54-7; *La
Realidad nacional*, 192
Beltrán, Pedro, editor of *La Prensa*,
20, 105, 187, 194; heads government under Manuel Prado, 195;
desposes Apra ideologies, 230; puts
economy in order, 273; critics of,
204, 277-8; and land reform, 326;
and the I.P.C., 1959, 324
Benavides, President, 51-2, 158, 263,
322; coup against Apra by, 161
Berckemeyer, Hernando, Peruvian
ambassador to Washington, 335
Betancourt, President (Venezuela),
Acción Democrática of, 311
Blanco, Hugo, unionises *peones* and
arrendires (Cuzco), 127-30, 228,
318
Boggio, M. Samame, 40, 320n.
Bogotazo defined, 112
Bondy, S. Salazar, *Lima la horrible*,
83; pro-Castro article by, 217
Bossoio, Gen., of the Junta, 308, 313;
resigns, 318
Bourricaud, F., *Changements à Puno*,
60; and Dollfus, Olivier, 'La popu-

lation péruvienne en 1961', 16 n.,
39 n.
Breton, André, on Apra, 159
Bustamente y Rivero, José Luis,
President; Apra support for, 178,
182, 263; his attitude to Apra, 264;
on the Peruvian middle class, 59; as
'spiritual father of Christian Democracy', 291; and Callao incident,
167; economy during office of, 273;
overthrown by Odría, 305; *Tres
años de lucha*, 263; *Mensaje al
Perú*, 115

Calderón, Ventura García, quoted,
193-4
Callao mutiny, 167
Caravedo, Rotondo and Javier Mariá-
tegui, *Estudios de psiquiatría social
en el Perú*, 118
Cárdenas, Gen. Lázaro, 218
Caretas, attack on Prado in, 276
Casa Grande sugar strike, 124-5
Castillo, Luciano, Socialist candidate
for Presidency, 1962, 292
Castro, Castroism, 209; Castro des-
cribed, 219-20; Cuba and the
'revolution of love', 220; *La Pren-
sa*'s attitude to, 220-1; orthodox
communists' attitude to, 224
Cédula única voting device, 282
Cerro, Col. Sanchez, 176; overthrows
Leguía, 142, 158, 305; assassination
of, 158
Cerro de Pasco Corporation (lead and
zinc mining), 15, 40, 85 n., 93, 94
seqq., 126, 172 n., 312; the La
Oroya strike of 1962, 316-18, 320
Chanchán, ruins of, 151 n.
Chávez, Héctor, Christian Democrat,
291
Chimbote episode, June 1960, 108-14
Cholo: defined, 22, 65; aggression of,
22-3; ambiguous position of, 67,
71, 76; distinguished from *mestizo*,
66; livelihood of, 68; mobility of,
84; as student, 63-4; attitudes of:
towards force, 77-80; *cundería*
associated with, 83; and Indians,
76; *vivo* as stock epithet for, 77;
types of, 67-8
Christian Democrats: oppose Odría's

350

Index

Index

40; the sierra, *patrones* and *gamonales*, 28–37; coastal oligarchy, 38–9; 'specialisation' and 'exclusiveness' of coastal oligarchy, 38–39; four political types, 51; oligarchy and industry, 45–8; managerial class and technicians, 85; oligarchy as network of families, 42–3

El Tiempo, 151

Erhard, Dr., 195

Escrutinio en mesa, electoral reform, 280

Expreso, 20, 202, 313

F.E.B. (bank employees' federation), 107, 108

Ferrero, Rómulo, quoted, 39

Fishmeal export, as new industry, 15, 46–7

Fondo Especial de Inversiones Industriales, and other land-reform bodies, 338

Frank, Waldo, on the Cuban revolution, 220

Frente de Liberación Nacional, 209, 258: at time of 1962 election, 292

Frente Nacional de Juventudes Democráticas, 232

Frente Unido de Trabajadores, 107

Frías, Ismael, *La revolución peruana*, 221, 225

Gaitán, Eliecer, assassination of, 112 n.

Gálvez, José, *una Lima que se va*, 83

Gamonal ('accumulator of land'), 30, 31

Gens as basic unit of Peruvian oligarchy, 41–5

Germani, Gino, analysis of Peronism by, 92

Gesto bien criollo, 83

Gide, André, quoted, 141

Godoy, Gen. Pérez, chairman of Junta (1962) Joint Command, 207; deposed by colleagues, 319

Grieve, Sr. Jorge, on Peruvian economy in 1950s, 202–3

Guano prices, 336

Haciendas, sizes of (Cuzco and Puno), 38

Haya de la Torre, Víctor Raúl, 13, 52; background and family, 56–8; at 1917 Cuzco students' conference, 63; in the 1930s, 140 seqq.; founds Apra, 142, 168; arrest and imprisonment of, 13, 158; Indo-American theory of, 147–57; letters to Apristas from prison, 158–61; source of objections of, to communism, 152–6; El Plan de Acción, of, 142 seqq.; speeches (and philosophy) of: Aug. 23, 1931, 142–7; 'Christmas message' of 1932, 162; before electoral campaign of 1931, 169 seqq.; Feb. 23, 1961, 169–70; on U.S. policy, 170–2; in *British Labour Weekly*, 173 n.; his conception of 'waiting', 177; speech of May 20, 1945, 178–181; fails in Presidential elections, 181; sums up *convivencia*, 269–70; and the 1962 election, 293 seqq.; road to Presidency blocked by military veto, 229; 'nationalism' of, cf. Belaúnde's, 246; voting for, at the 1962 elections, 260

Hegel, *Philosophy of History*, 152

Heysen, Luis (Apra), 337

Huamantica, leader of Cuzco communists, 333

Huancayo, and other provincial universities, 65

Huaron, mines, unions, 94

'Humanist democracy', 209 seqq.

Identification, symbols of, 147–57, 188; creolism, *criollismo*, 82–3; *see also* Indo-Americanism, Apra (philosophy), Creolism

Indians, 13; excluded from political life, 14; exploitation of, 31; conservatives' view of, 90; indigenists' views of, 91, 147; of the shantytowns, 91–2, 114–21, *see Barriadas*; *sublevaciones* and peasant revolts, 130–3; as unionised farm labourers, 128–30; the *invasiones*, 130–2, 332–335, 342

'Indo-Americanism', Haya de la Torre's, 149, 230; symbols of identification of, 147–57

Instituto de la Vivienda (National Housing Fund), 205

Index

Inter-American Development Bank, 205, 206

International Petroleum Company, 20, 264, 277, 324

Junta de Gobierno of 18 July 1962, 305 seqq.; three decrees of, 307; the *dictablanda*, 308 seqq.

Juntas de Pobladores, 119

Keyserling, *South American Meditations*, 150-1

La Convención, province of Cuzco, peasant organisation in, 127

La Crónica, 106, 107

Land reform: early, not blindly opposed by oligarchy, 17, 20; in Cuba, 218; in Peru, 124 seqq.; Belaúnde's announcements and their sequel, 28 July 1963, 325, 327-43

Land Reform Finance Corporation, 339

Land Reform Institute, 335, 338

Lanz, Laureano V., *El cesarismo democrático*, 193

La Prensa, 20, 21, 39, 86, 100, 101, 105, 107, 110, 111, 112, 113, 114, 120, 24, 125, 126, 130, 132, 194-206 *passim*, 209, 211, 212, 221, 247, 264, 273, 278, 280, 294, 316-18; attacks on Apra, on Junta, 273, 273 n., 308-9, 319; on the 1962 election irregularities, 300; attitudes of, to Belaúnde, 248,256, 257, 258

Las Casas, Bartolomé de, 192

Latifundios, 38; government by military favouring, 48

La Tribuna, Aprista newspaper, 96, 97, 98, 99, 100, 102, 106, 108, 109, 110, 125, 175 n. 294; after the 1962 Junta, 308, 310

Lavalle, Hernando de, Presidential candidate in 1956, 232-3, 246-7, 289; Apra's attitude to, 265-7; proposed as member of *comité cívico* by Haya de la Torre, in 1962, 303

Left wing's minor forces, 209

Leguía, President, 50, 52, 142, 193; denunciation of, 192 n

Letourneau firm, U.S.A., work of in Amazon basin, 252

Lewis, Oscar, 116

Libertad, organ of Movimiento Social Progresista, 292; main themes of, 210-17, 245; attitudes of, to Manuel and Mariano Prado, 277-8; as anti-American, 214-17

Lieuwen, Edwin, *Arms and Politics in Latin America*, 167 n.

Lima newspapers, commitment of, 20-1

Losovsky correspondence, with Haya de la Torre, 168 n

Macedo, C.F., and the Chimbote episode, 113

Mancheco Muñoz, Senator, 49

Mar, José Matos, 216

Marcona iron deposits, 40

Mariátegui, J. Carlos (*Siete ensayos de interpretación de la realidad peruana*), 48, 61, 62, 63, 83, 147-8; edits *Amauta*, 168; and land reform, 325-6, 342; 'racist nationalism' of, 192

Martin, Enrique, *barriada* story by, 121-3

Martos, José, on Castro and Cuba, 217-18

Marxism, Apra's attitude to, 154

Matos, José, enquiry by into Lima *barriadas*, 116

Matos de Turner, Matilda, *Aves sin nido*, 147

Matthews, Herbert (*New York Times*), 218

Meneses, Rómulo (Apra), *Por el Apra . . .*, 163, 164; on land reform, 330

Mercurio peruano quoted, 279

Merino, Gen., 1956 manifesto of, against Odría, 305-6

Mestizo 'realism' (*no meterse* and other elements), 79 seqq.; disparagement of *mestizo*, 191 n., 192; *see* Arguedas

Middle classes: discontent of, 15; attitudes to élite and *criollo* tradition, 22; migration and urbanisation in 1950s, 15-16; numerical increase of, 59-61; definitions of, 59-61; as dependent, 92 seqq.;

Index

oligarchy never wins over, 347; and university, 63–5; the *mestizos* and (*see Cholo*), 65–77; *see also* Realism

Mills, Wright, on the élite, 27, 28

Minka (collective labour), 253

Miró Quesada family, owners of *El Comercio*, 20; *see* Quesada

Mistis, see Patrón

Mobilisation, social, 93 seqq.; second wave of (*las barriadas*), 114 seqq.; ideology as single common denominator of newly mobile classes, 140–1; university reform accelerating, 64

Moncloa, Francisco, on Cuban revolution, 221

Montesinos, Senator, Sept. 1959 bill introduced by, 325

Montessori, Madame, quoted, 175

Moreno, Garcia, 194

Morin, Edgar, 83

Movimiento Social Progresista, 105, 209, 210, 216; in 1962, 292

Muelle, Senator Dammert, 257

Nasserism, 313–15, 320

National Electoral Jury, establishment of, 280

Neira, Hugo (*Cuzco, tierra y muerte*), 52–3, 130–2, 332, 333, 334; on defects of oligarchy, 52; on Junta's choice between radicalisation and creolisation, 313, 315

Noriega, Gen., Odría exiles, 264

Obrero y Campesino (review), 128, 221; and Beltrán's land-reform proposals, 328

Odría, Gen. & President, main references to, 13, 14, 48, 51, 94, 124, 181, 183, 195, 231–2, 258, 290–1, 345, 347; outlaws Apra, 1948–56, 263; position of, in 1956, 264–5; and the 1962 elections, 260, 289, 292; condemns *convivencia*, 290; and *barriadas* vote, 293; Gen. Merino on, 305; *La Tribuna* on, 302; as symbol of intrigue, 320; Godoy accused of collusion with, 319; Belaúnde outstrips, 1965, 320

Oligarchy, 17 seqq.; as *gens* grouping, 29; dynamic and mechanical theories of break-up of, 17–19

'Optimistic sadness', 150–1, 178

Oquendo, Abelardo, an editor of *Libertad*, 213

Organisation of American States, 311

Orrego, Antenor, on Haya de la Torre, 175

Palma, Ricardo, *Tradiciones*, 83

Paramonga (sugar plantation) strike, 125–7

Pardo Herren, Sr. Juan, 44

Pardo, José, President, 52; and civilianists, 187 n.

Parsons, Talcott, *Structure and Process in Modern Society*, 27, 28, 35

Partido Nacional Libertador, 168

Patrón, misti, cholo and *varayok* types), 32–3; in political scene, 49–50; *patrones* and *gamonales*, 28 seqq.

Perón régime, Argentina, 196

Perricholismo defined, 83

Peruvian-American Association, 311–312

Petroleum Defence Front, 324

Piérola, Nicolas de, 56; electoral reform in presidency of, 279

Pinay, M., 195

Politicians, four classes of Peruvian, 51

Por la senda de Mariátegui, Peruvian Communist Party declaration, 224 n,

Posadas, J., on Maoist communism. 226

Prado, Manuel (President), main references to, 20, 44, 49, 50, 63, 94, 99, 101, 107, 120, 139, 158; reasons for 1962 deposition of, 167, 183, 185; reasons for Apra support of, 263–6, 289; elected, 233–4, 266; second term, 273 seqq.; and land reform, 326; Tingo Maria project of, 250

Prado, Mariano Ignacio, *Libertad* attacks, 210, 277

Prebisch, Sr. Raul, 196 n.

Presente (pro-Apra review), 302 n., 305

Prialé, Ramiro (Apra), and *convivencia*, 266, 268, 271; on the Trujillo rising, 298 n.

Pronunciamentos, 305–6

Index

Proportionalism in electoral procedure, 281-2

Quechuas, 91, 147, 148; see Indians
Quesada, José A. Miró, assassination of, 158, 166, 193
Quillamba, and peasant unions, 332, 334
Quiros valley irrigation project, 290

Ramirez y Berrios, Guillermo: *Grandezas y miserias de un proces electoral en el Peru*, 120, 306
Ravines, Eudocio, and Peruvian Socialist Party in Paris, 168-9; *La gran estafa* (Great Swindle), 168 n.
Realism, voluntarism, as two points of Apra philosophy, 147
Realists of Peruvian politics, 186 seqq; paternalistic viewpoint, 187-94; practical elements, 194-202
Riva Agüero, José de la (*La Historia en el Perú* and *Paisajes peruanos*), 52, 53, 166, 187-94; as most persuasive advocate of conservatism in 1930s, 187; type of 'creolism' represented by, 206; as Prime Minister, 206
Rosas, Juan Manuel, 194
Rostow, Walt, 129

Sabroso, Arturo, 316
San Cosme *barriada*, 120
San Marcos university, 65
Sartre, Jean-Paul, quoted on Cuba, 217, 218
Seoane (Corrales), Edgardo (*Surcos de Paz*), 329 & n., 335; in office, 338, 341
Seoane, Manuel, 275
Shapiro, Professor Samuel, quoted, 211
Sociedad Nacional Agraria: as pressure group, *La Prensa* as organ, 327; admits need for land reform, 326; on necessity for 'technical' approach to reform, 327-8; *La Vida Agrícola*, 335; activities before acceptance of Congress compromise, 335-41
'Sofocleto', see Angel
SOGESA (union), 113-14
Soto, Enrique C., on Chávez, 291; on the Junta, 309-10

Sparadra defined, 49
Spengler, O., Haya de la Torre's reading of, 152
Steer, Carlos, assassin of Quesada, 158, 166
Sugar exports, 13, 15; industry, see Apra

Tacha (smear) weapon, 63, 64, 229
Talara oil deposits, 20, 324
Technical Council of Land Reform, see Consejo
Temoche, Richard, 108
Tinterillos, 34, 60, 66
Toquepala copper mines, 15
Torre, see Haya de la Torre
Torre, Martínez de la, on correspondence between Apra and Communist International, 168 n.
Trelles, Dr. Oscar, Belaúnde's Minister of the Interior, 333-4
Tristan, Flora, *Mémoires d'une paria*, 54 n.
Trujillo rising of July 1932, 56-7, 167, 169, 173, 298

Uhle, Max, quoted, 151 n.
Unidad (communist newspaper), 312-313
Unions: bank employees', 104-8; miners', 93-104: sugarcane workers', peasants, 39, 332-4; see also SOGESA
Union Nacional Odriista, founded 1962, 290
United States of America, 15, 40; International Petroleum Company; and the military coup of 1962, 286, 311-12; see *Libertad*, Haya de la Torre
University: reform movement, 63; enquiry (San Marcos) into students' social origins, 65; relationships between teachers and students, 63-4
Ureta, Gen., 206

Valcárcel, Luis E., *Tempestad en los Andes*, 91, 147-8, 191 n.
Values, system of: creolism, 82-4; *señorio*, *noblesse oblige*, 54-5; 'optimistic sadness', 150-1, 178; virility (*machismo*), 159
Vega, Garcilaso de la, 192

Index

Ventanilla, people's city, 206
Verolme contract, *El Comercio* on, 275
Villarán, Manuel Vicente (*Páginas escogidas*): on education, 62, 64, 66; on fraud in Peruvian electoral tradition, 279
Violence, 89–133; in rural areas, 16; *see* Atusparia, Casa Grande, Paramonga; revolutionary, 127, 227–8; subterfuge replacing, 77; *see also* Chimbote episode, Trujillo rising

Voluntarism (appeal to nation's energy) in Aprista philosophy, 147
Voz Obrera, 221, 226

Yanaconaje: defined, 124; total expropriation proposal, 335

Zarak, Alex, quoted, 39